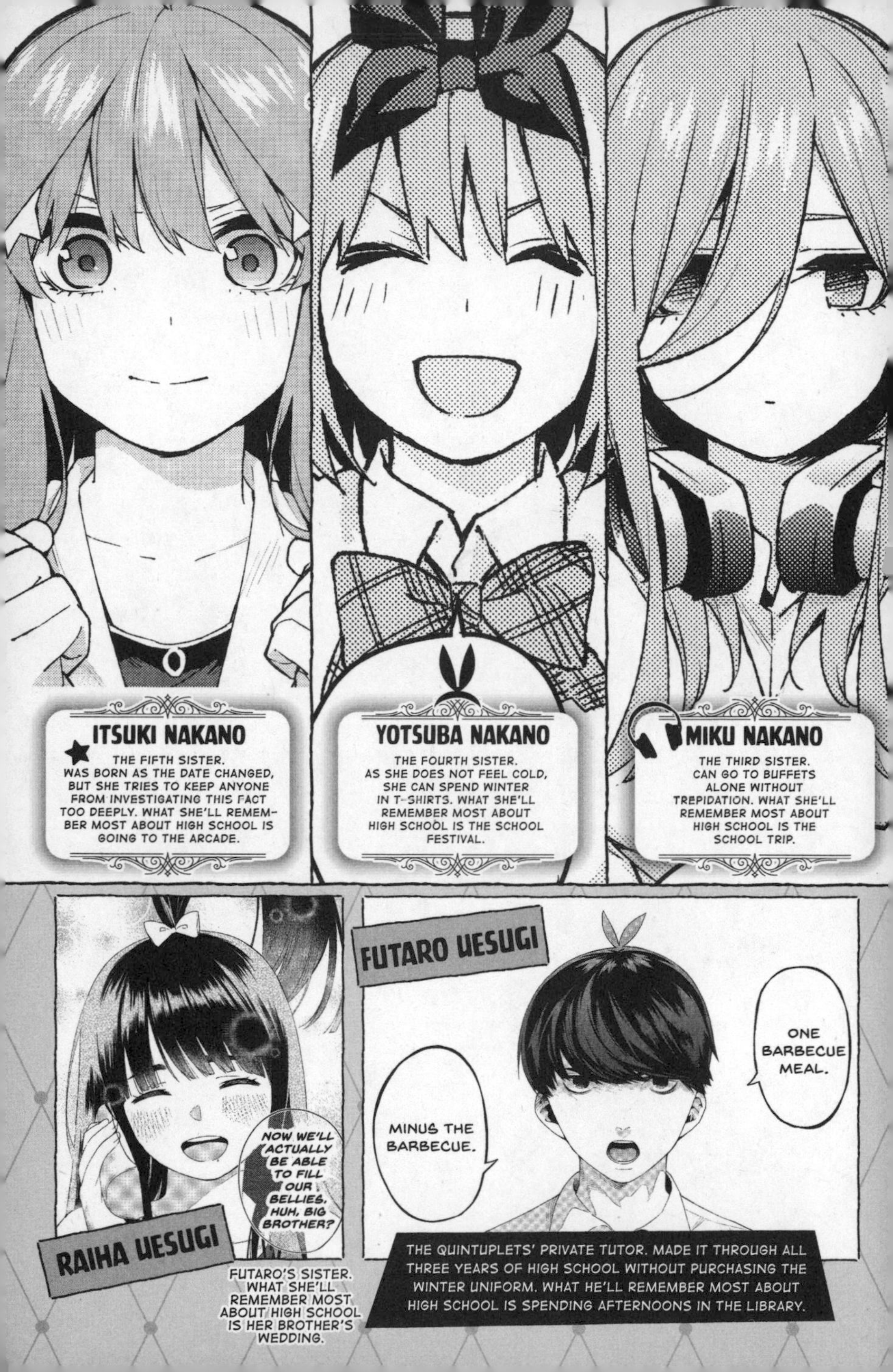
MIKU NAKANO
THE THIRD SISTER. CAN GO TO BUFFETS ALONE WITHOUT TREPIDATION. WHAT SHE'LL REMEMBER MOST ABOUT HIGH SCHOOL IS THE SCHOOL TRIP.
YOTSUBA NAKANO
THE FOURTH SISTER. AS SHE DOES NOT FEEL COLD, SHE CAN SPEND WINTER IN T-SHIRTS. WHAT SHE'LL REMEMBER MOST ABOUT HIGH SCHOOL IS THE SCHOOL FESTIVAL.
ITSUKI NAKANO
THE FIFTH SISTER. WAS BORN AS THE DATE CHANGED, BUT SHE TRIES TO KEEP ANYONE FROM INVESTIGATING THIS FACT TOO DEEPLY. WHAT SHE'LL REMEMBER MOST ABOUT HIGH SCHOOL IS GOING TO THE ARCADE.
FUTARO UESUGI
ONE BARBECUE MEAL.
MINUS THE BARBECUE.
THE QUINTUPLETS' PRIVATE TUTOR. MADE IT THROUGH ALL THREE YEARS OF HIGH SCHOOL WITHOUT PURCHASING THE WINTER UNIFORM. WHAT HE'LL REMEMBER MOST ABOUT HIGH SCHOOL IS SPENDING AFTERNOONS IN THE LIBRARY.
NOW WE'LL ACTUALLY BE ABLE TO FILL OUR BELLIES, HUH, BIG BROTHER?
RAIHA UESUGI
FUTARO'S SISTER. WHAT SHE'LL REMEMBER MOST ABOUT HIGH SCHOOL IS HER BROTHER'S WEDDING.

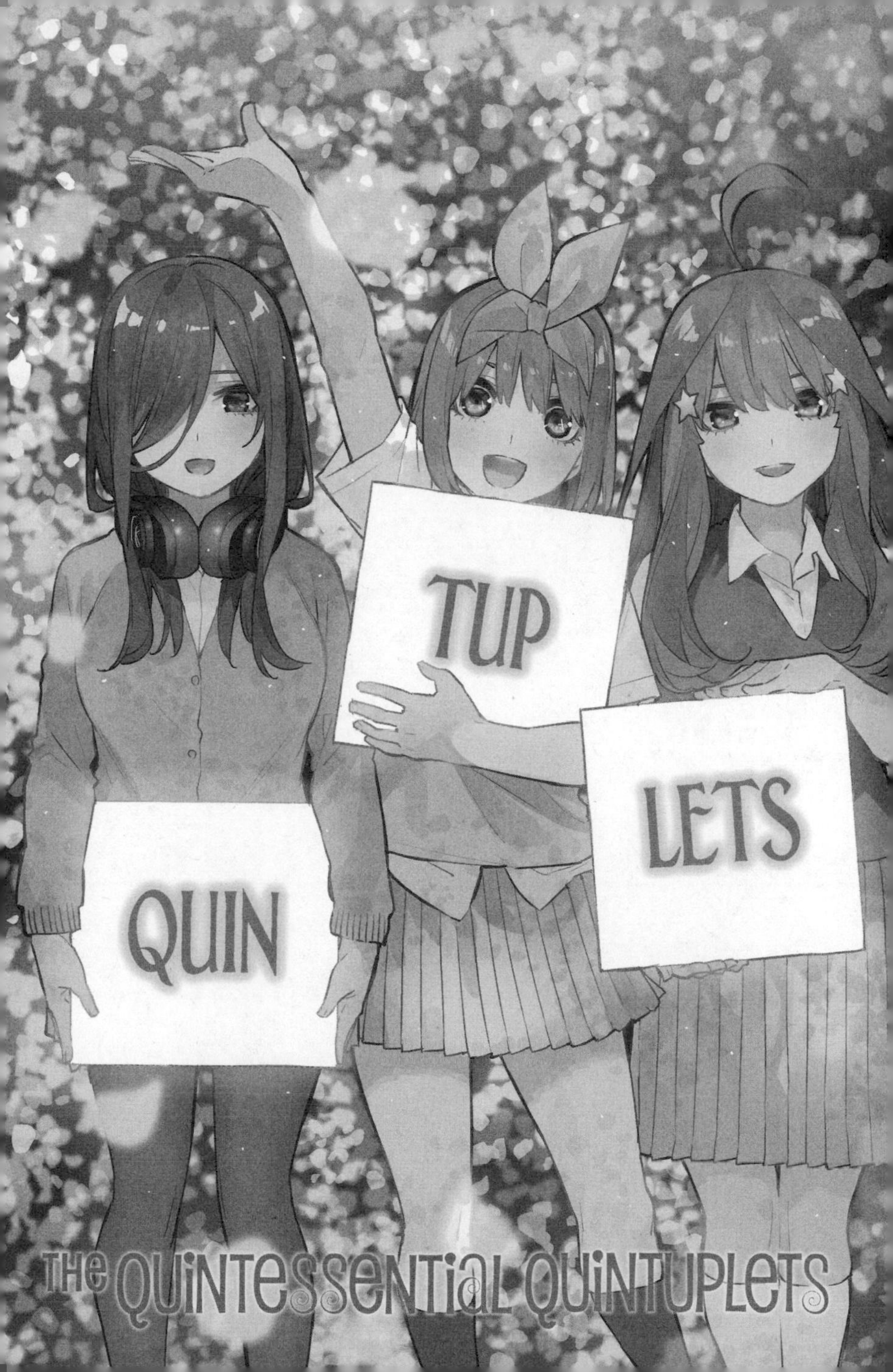

TUP
LETS
QUIN
THE QUINTESSENTIAL QUINTUPLETS

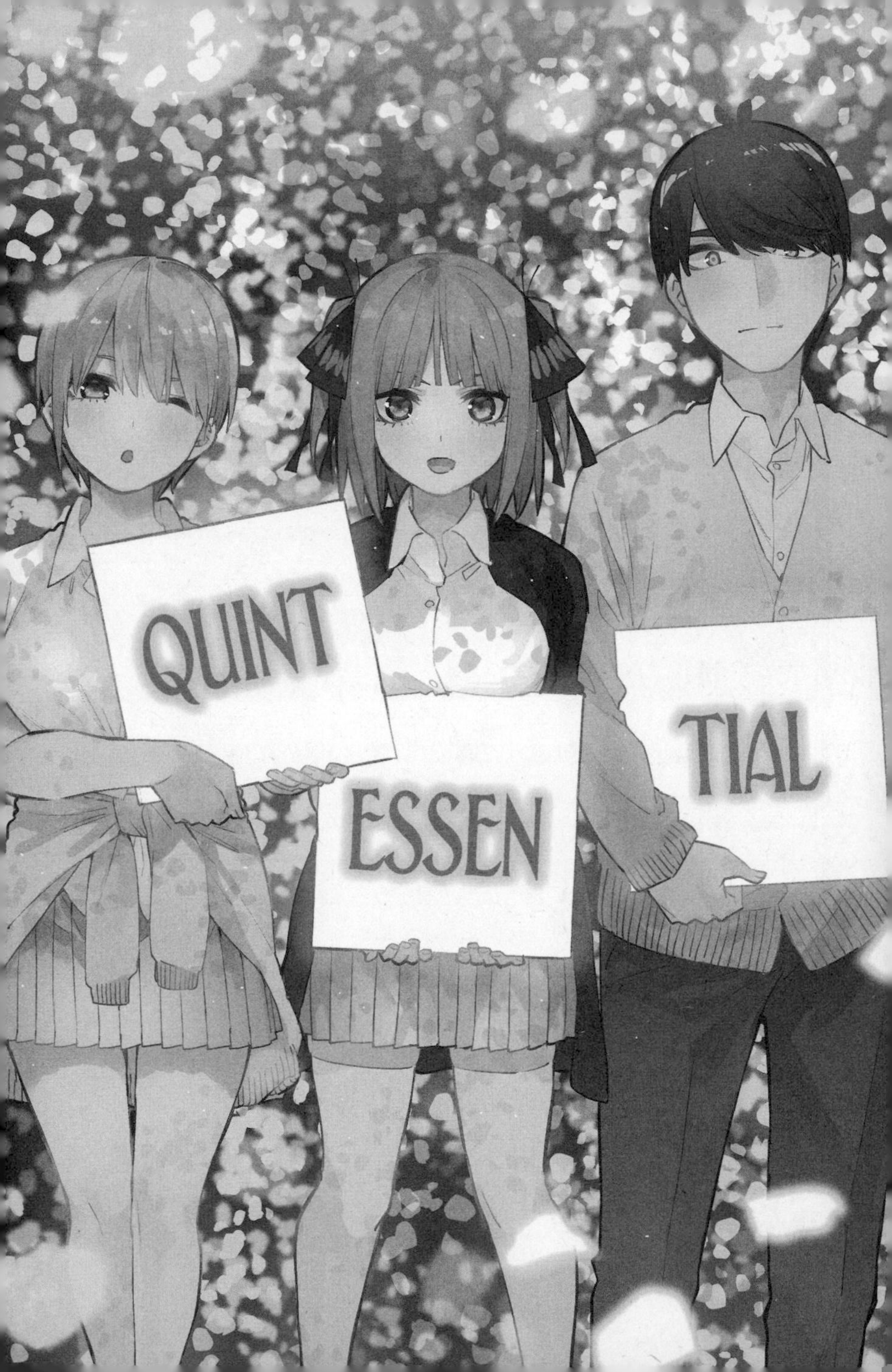
QUINT
ESSEN
TIAL

CONTENTS

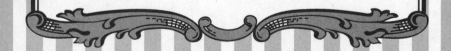

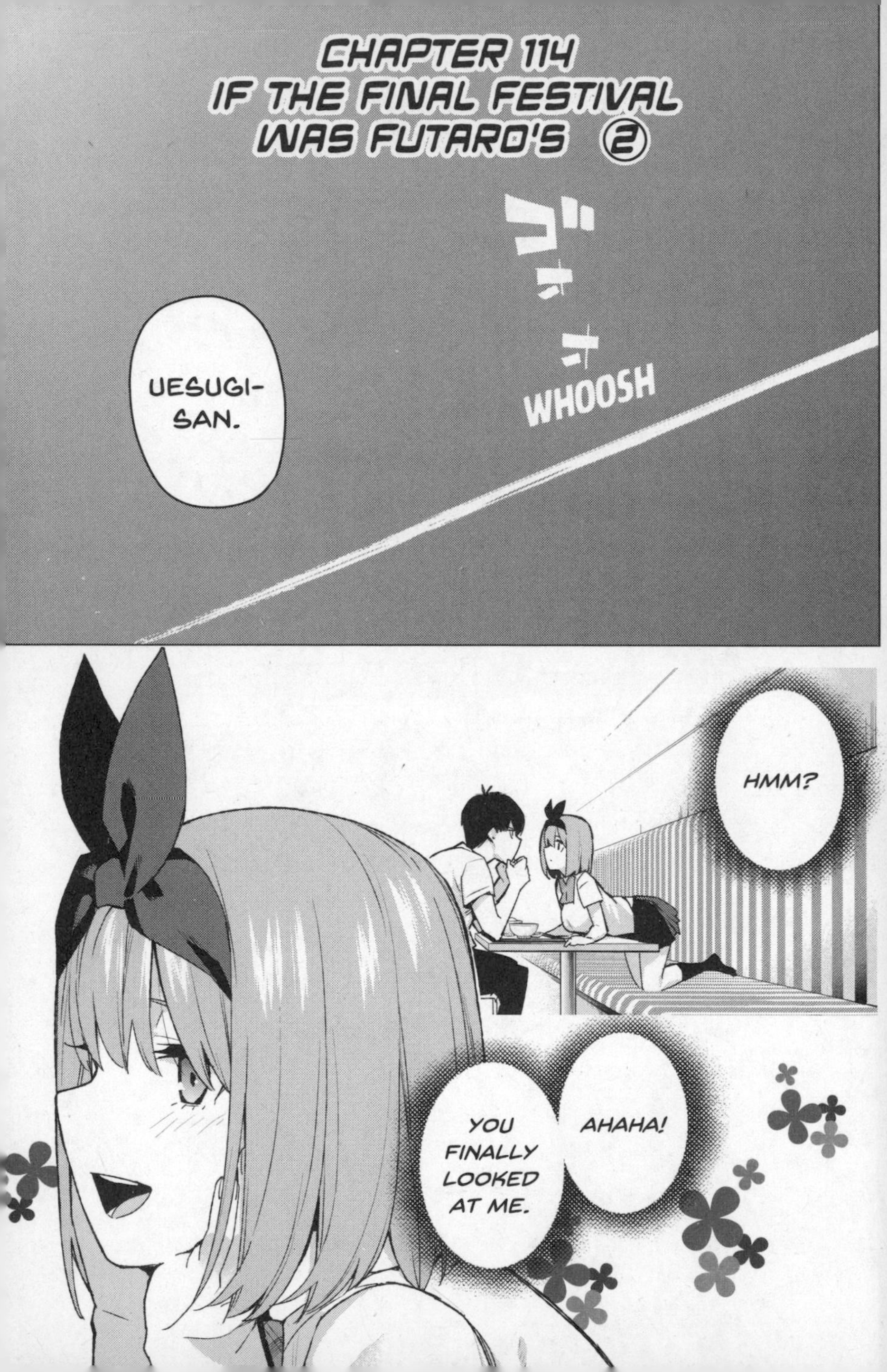
CHAPTER 114
IF THE FINAL FESTIVAL
WAS FUTARO'S ②
WHOOSH
UESUGI-SAN.
HMM?
AHAHA!
YOU FINALLY LOOKED AT ME.

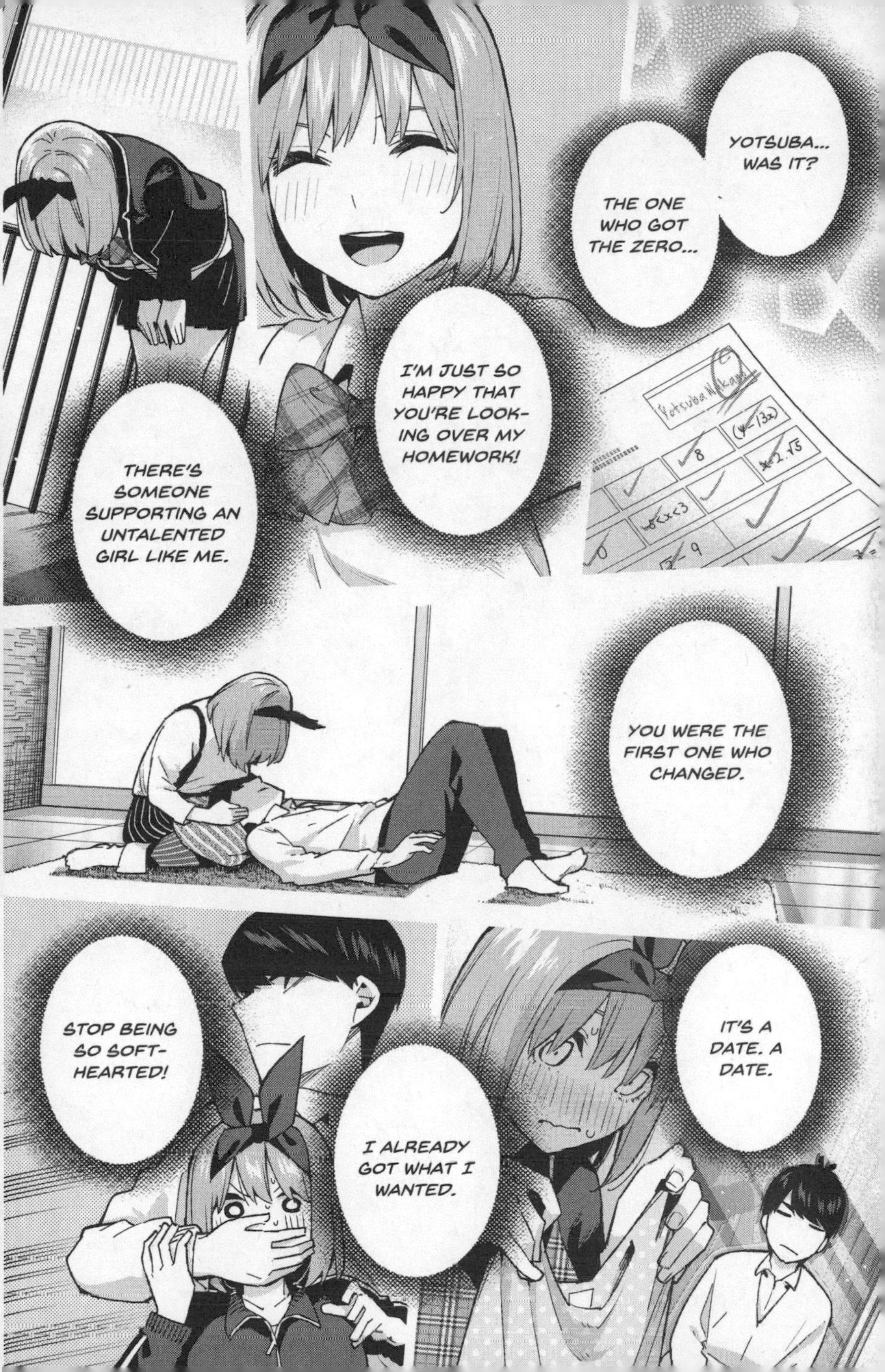
YOTSUBA... WAS IT?
THE ONE WHO GOT THE ZERO...
I'M JUST SO HAPPY THAT YOU'RE LOOK-ING OVER MY HOMEWORK!
THERE'S SOMEONE SUPPORTING AN UNTALENTED GIRL LIKE ME.
YOU WERE THE FIRST ONE WHO CHANGED.
IT'S A DATE. A DATE.
I ALREADY GOT WHAT I WANTED.
STOP BEING SO SOFT-HEARTED!

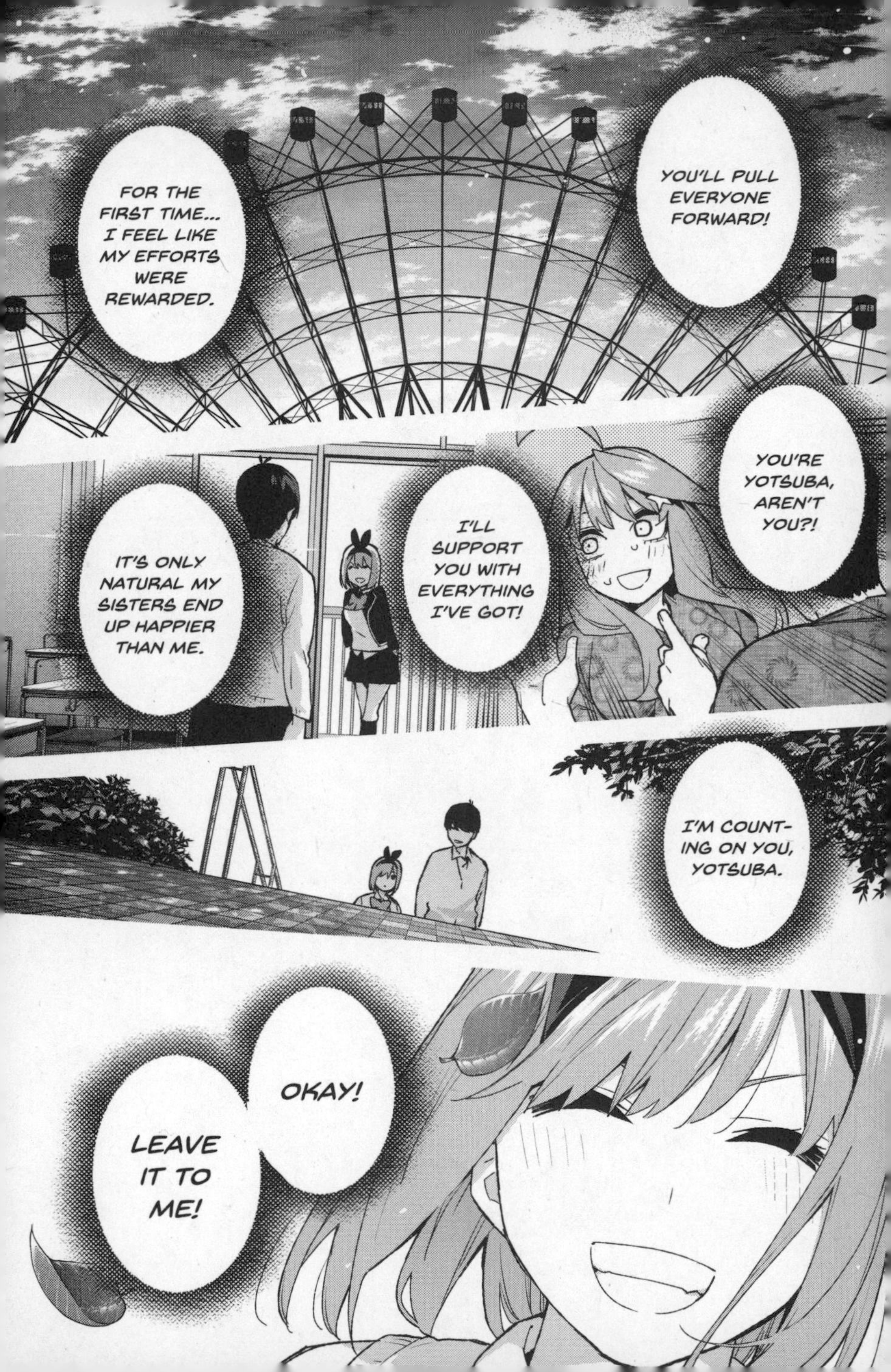
YOU'LL PULL EVERYONE FORWARD!
FOR THE FIRST TIME... I FEEL LIKE MY EFFORTS WERE REWARDED.
YOU'RE YOTSUBA, AREN'T YOU?!
I'LL SUPPORT YOU WITH EVERYTHING I'VE GOT!
IT'S ONLY NATURAL MY SISTERS END UP HAPPIER THAN ME.
I'M COUNTING-ING ON YOU, YOTSUBA.
OKAY!
LEAVE IT TO ME!

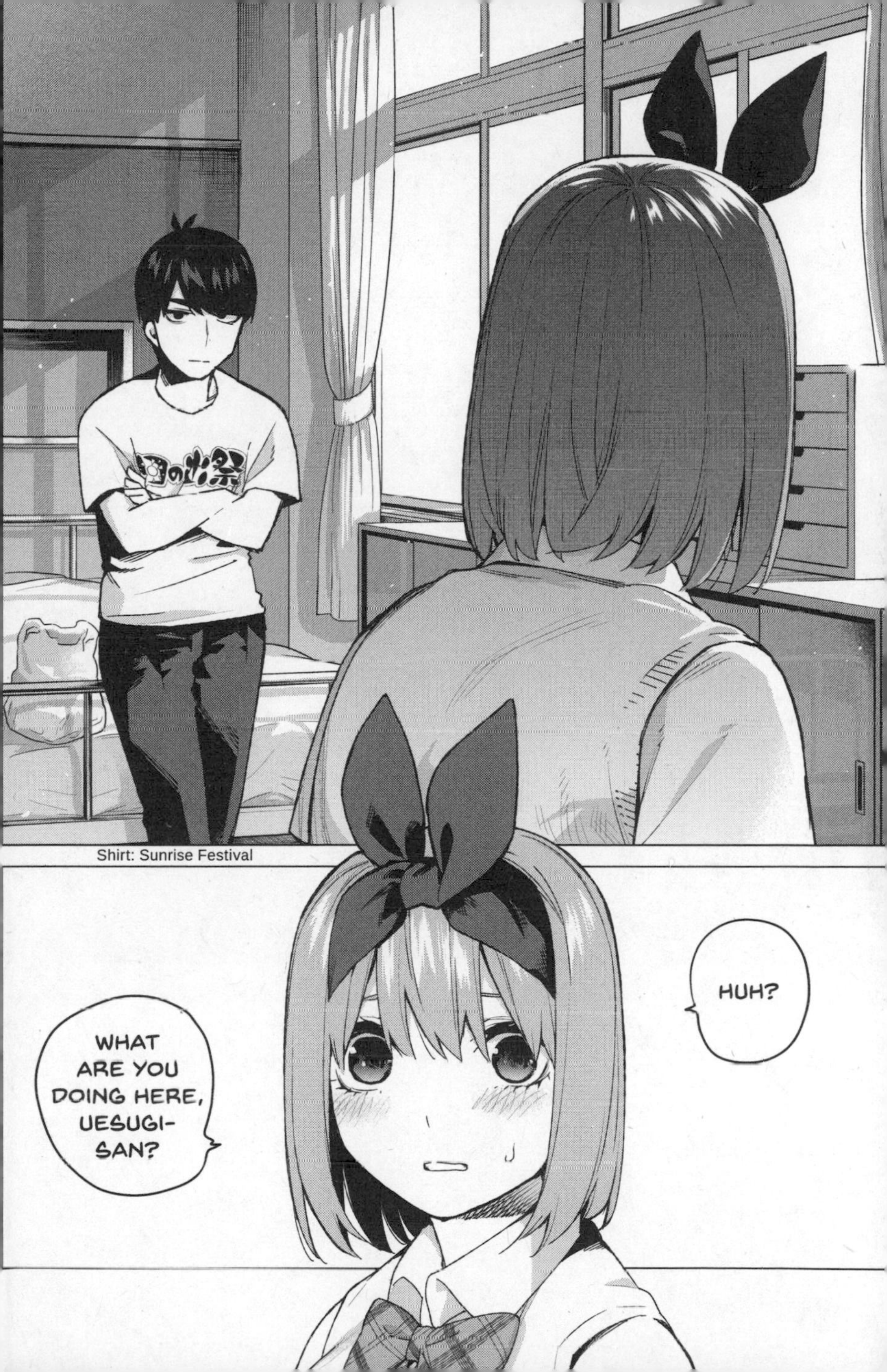
Shirt: Sunrise Festival
HUH?
WHAT ARE YOU DOING HERE, UESUGI-SAN?

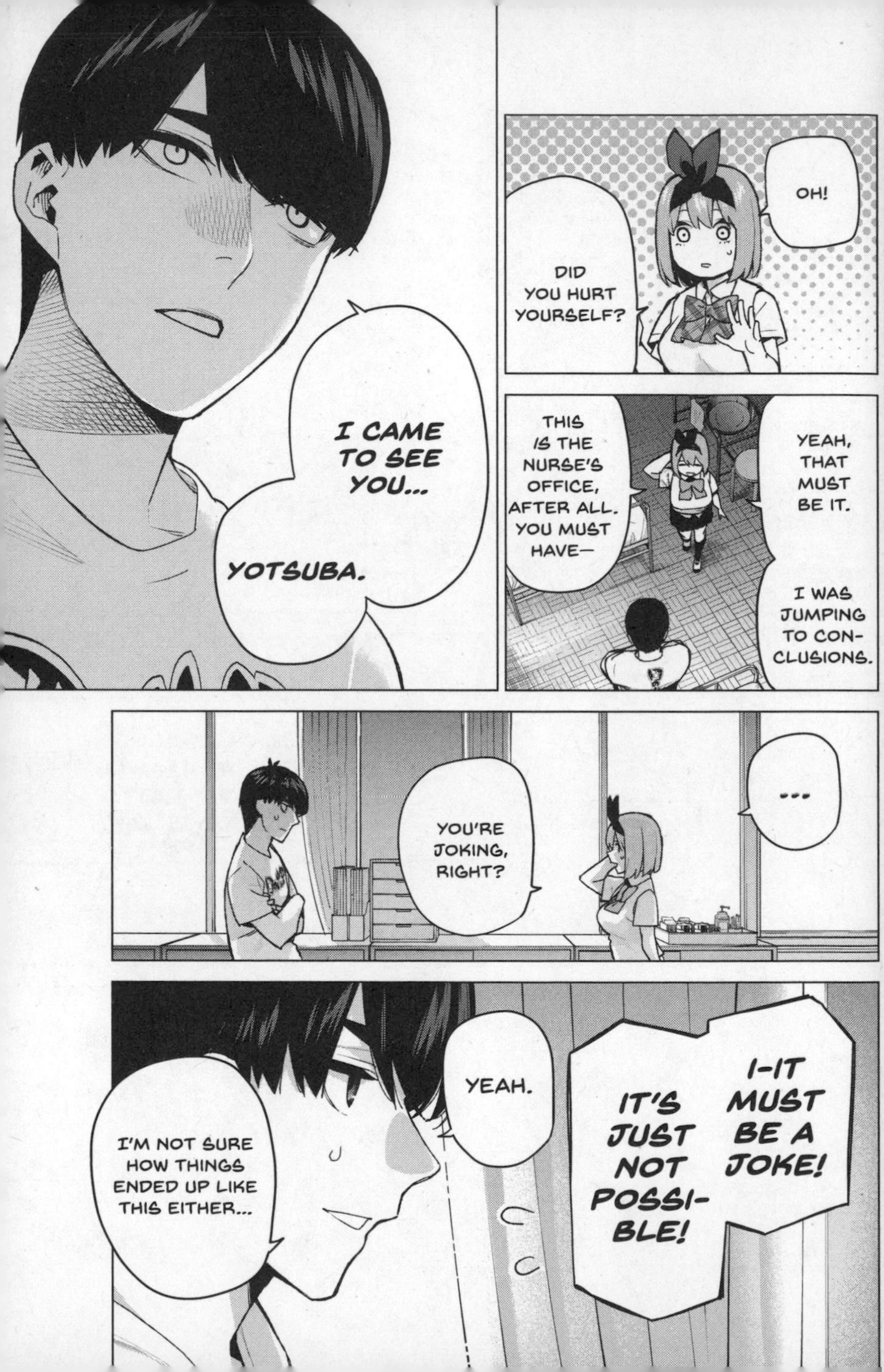
OH!
DID YOU HURT YOURSELF?
YEAH, THAT MUST BE IT.
I WAS JUMPING TO CON-CLUSIONS.
THIS IS THE NURSE'S OFFICE, AFTER ALL. YOU MUST HAVE—
I CAME TO SEE YOU...
YOTSUBA.
...
YOU'RE JOKING, RIGHT?
I-IT MUST BE A JOKE!
IT'S JUST NOT POSSI-BLE!
YEAH.
I'M NOT SURE HOW THINGS ENDED UP LIKE THIS EITHER...

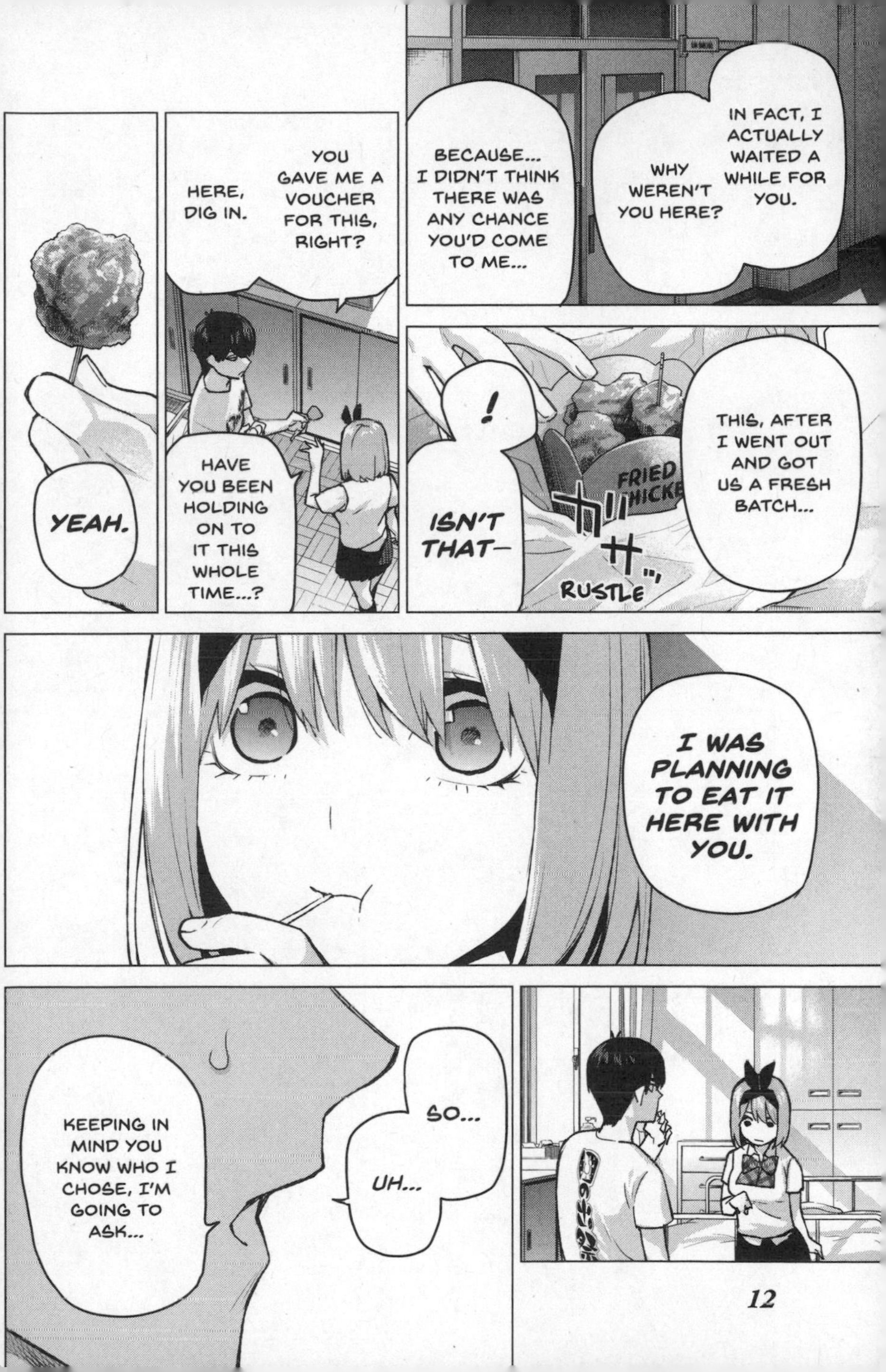
IN FACT, I ACTUALLY WAITED A WHILE FOR YOU.
WHY WEREN'T YOU HERE?
BECAUSE... I DIDN'T THINK THERE WAS ANY CHANCE YOU'D COME TO ME...
THIS, AFTER I WENT OUT AND GOT US A FRESH BATCH...
!
ISN'T THAT—
RUSTLE
YOU GAVE ME A VOUCHER FOR THIS, RIGHT?
HERE, DIG IN.
HAVE YOU BEEN HOLDING ON TO IT THIS WHOLE TIME...?
YEAH.
I WAS PLANNING TO EAT IT HERE WITH YOU.
SO...
UH...
KEEPING IN MIND YOU KNOW WHO I CHOSE, I'M GOING TO ASK...

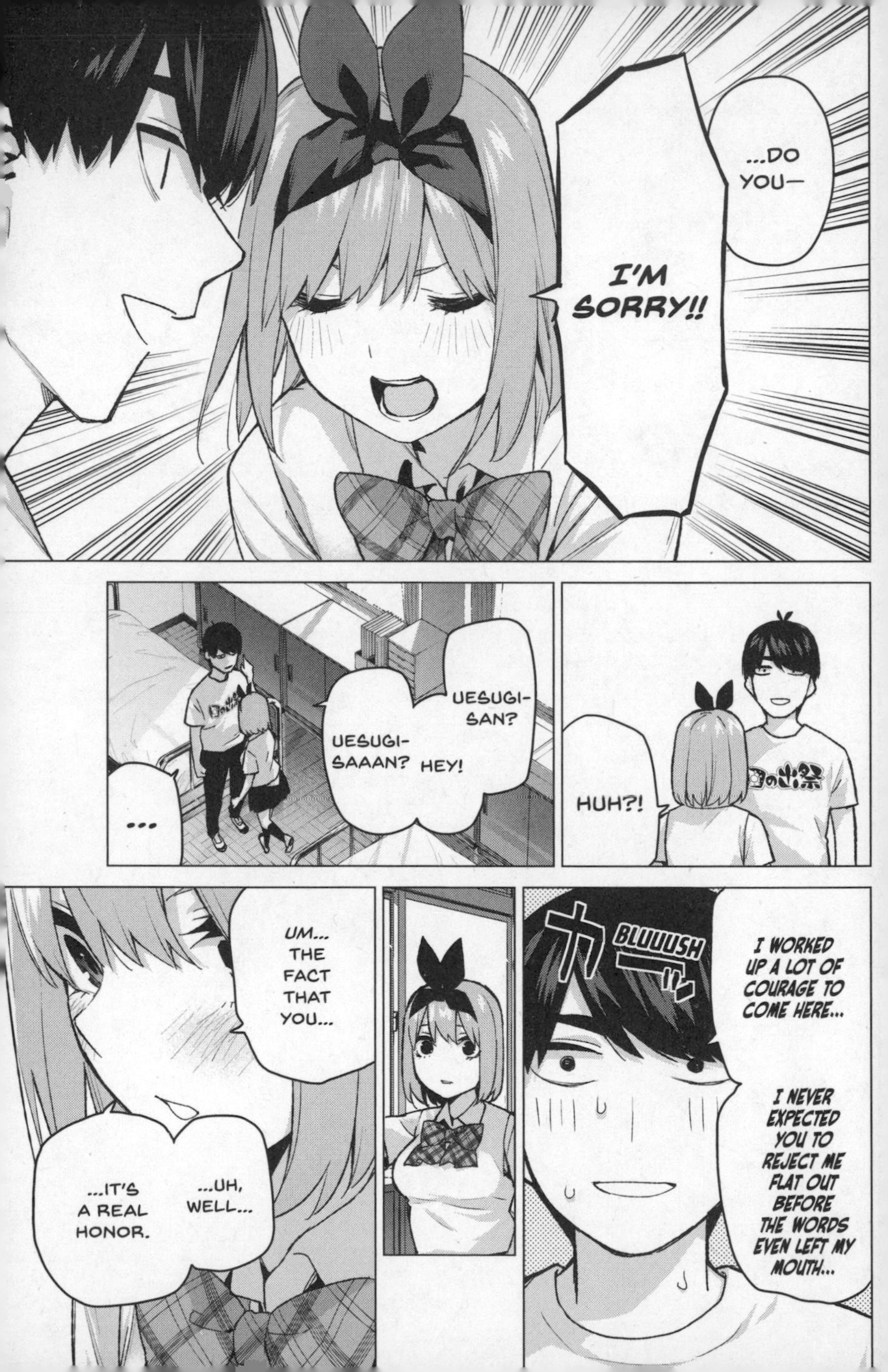
...DO YOU—
I'M SORRY!!
HUH?!
UESUGI-SAN?
UESUGI-SAAAN? HEY!
...
BLUUUSH
ホーッ
I WORKED UP A LOT OF COURAGE TO COME HERE...
I NEVER EXPECTED YOU TO REJECT ME FLAT OUT BEFORE THE WORDS EVEN LEFT MY MOUTH...
UM... THE FACT THAT YOU...
...UH, WELL...
...IT'S A REAL HONOR.

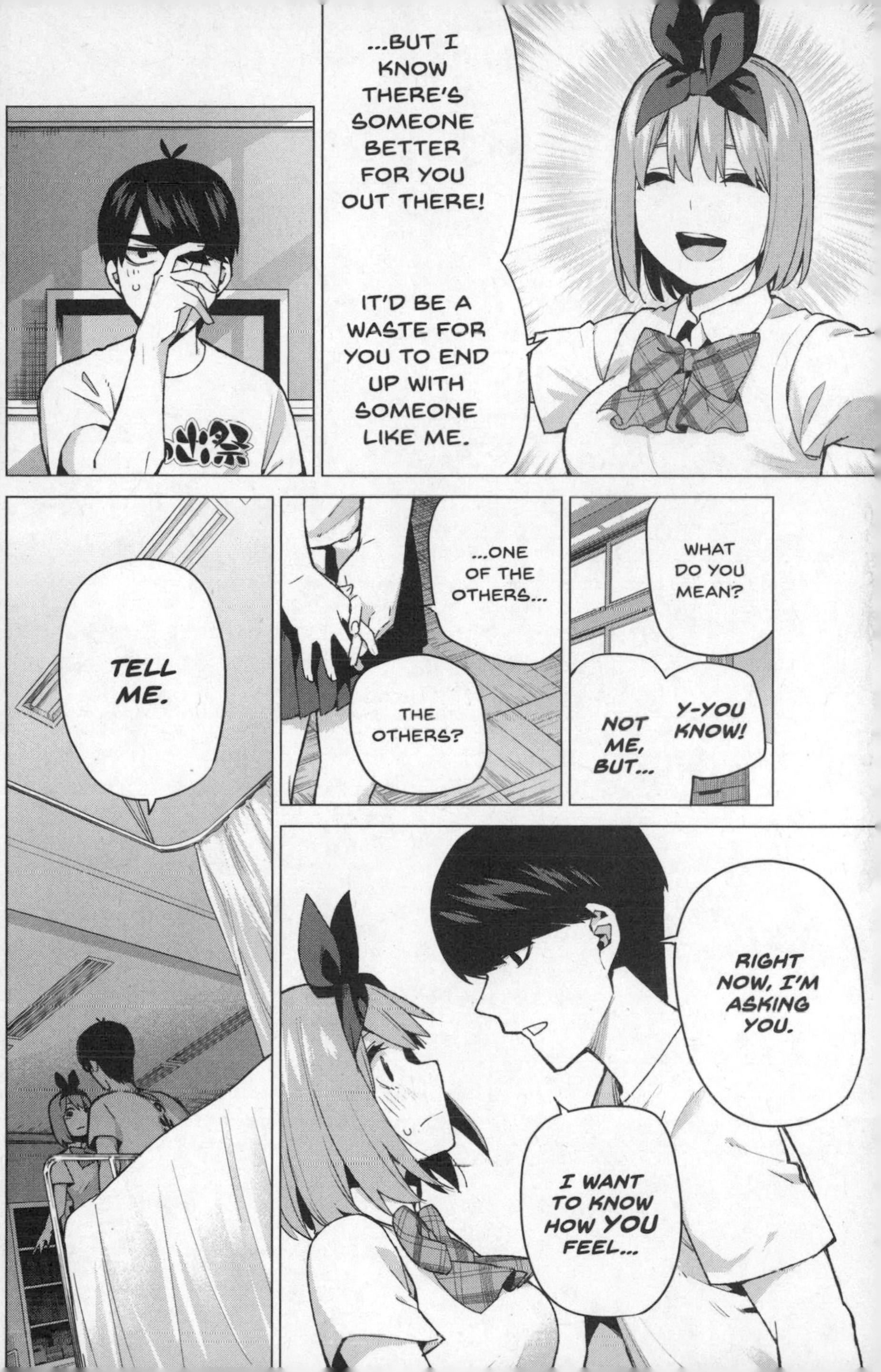
...BUT I KNOW THERE'S SOMEONE BETTER FOR YOU OUT THERE!
IT'D BE A WASTE FOR YOU TO END UP WITH SOMEONE LIKE ME.
WHAT DO YOU MEAN?
Y-YOU KNOW!
NOT ME, BUT...
...ONE OF THE OTHERS...
THE OTHERS?
RIGHT NOW, I'M ASKING YOU.
I WANT TO KNOW HOW YOU FEEL...
TELL ME.

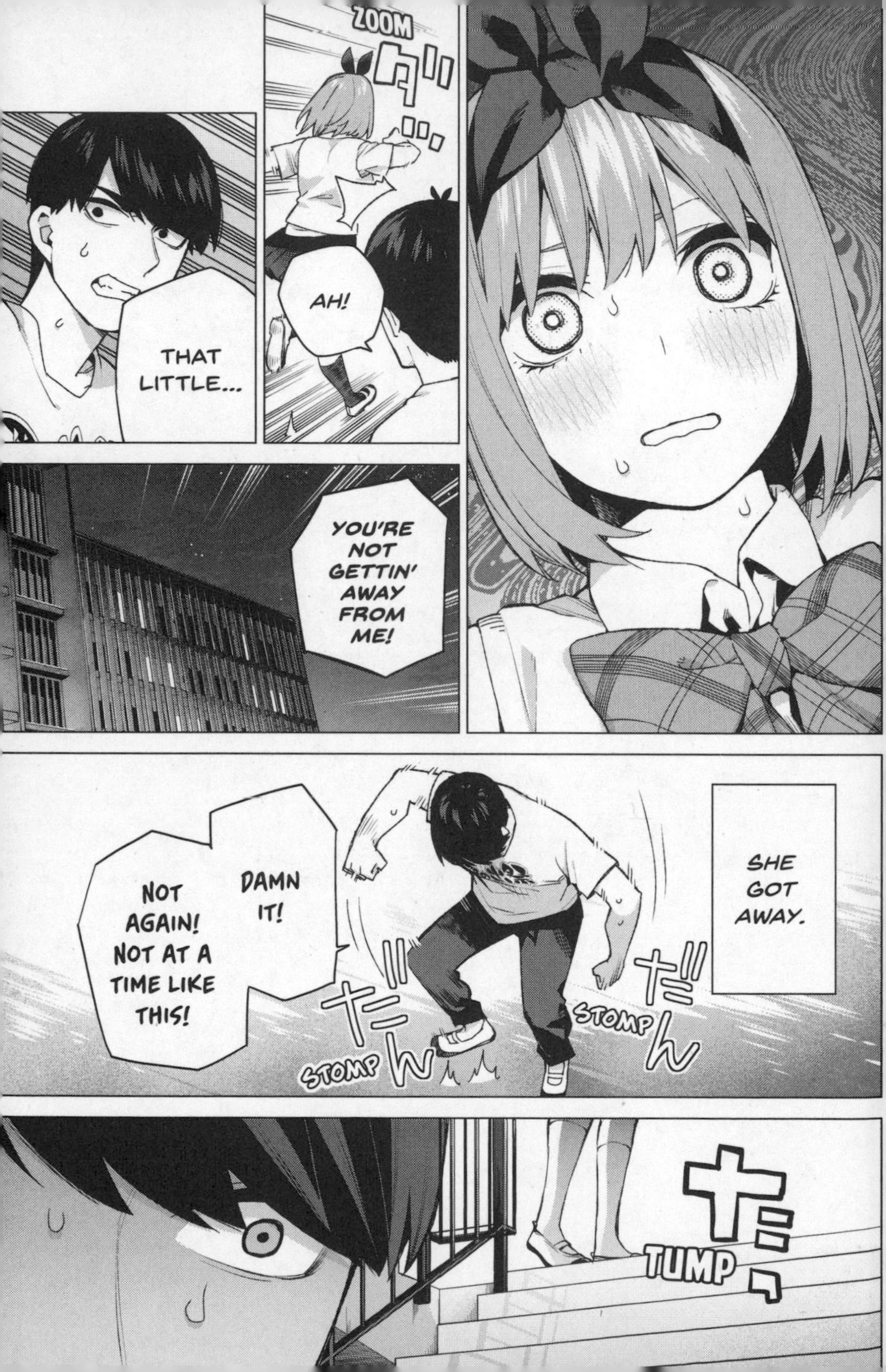
ZOOM
AH!
THAT LITTLE...
YOU'RE NOT GETTIN' AWAY FROM ME!
SHE GOT AWAY.
STOMP
STOMP
DAMN IT!
NOT AGAIN! NOT AT A TIME LIKE THIS!
TUMP

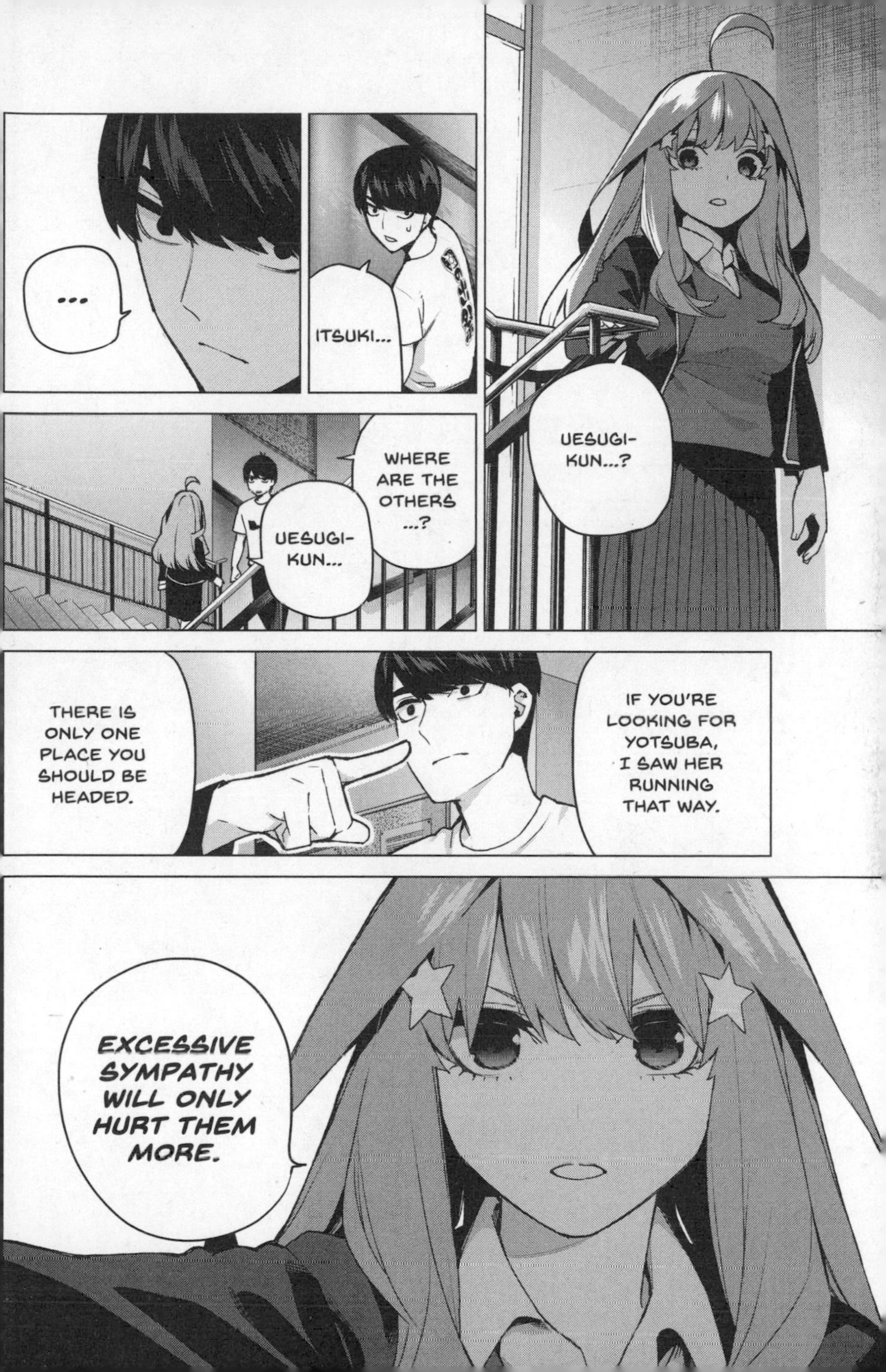

UESUGI-KUN...?
ITSUKI...
...
WHERE ARE THE OTHERS ...?
UESUGI-KUN...
IF YOU'RE LOOKING FOR YOTSUBA, I SAW HER RUNNING THAT WAY.
THERE IS ONLY ONE PLACE YOU SHOULD BE HEADED.
EXCESSIVE SYMPATHY WILL ONLY HURT THEM MORE.

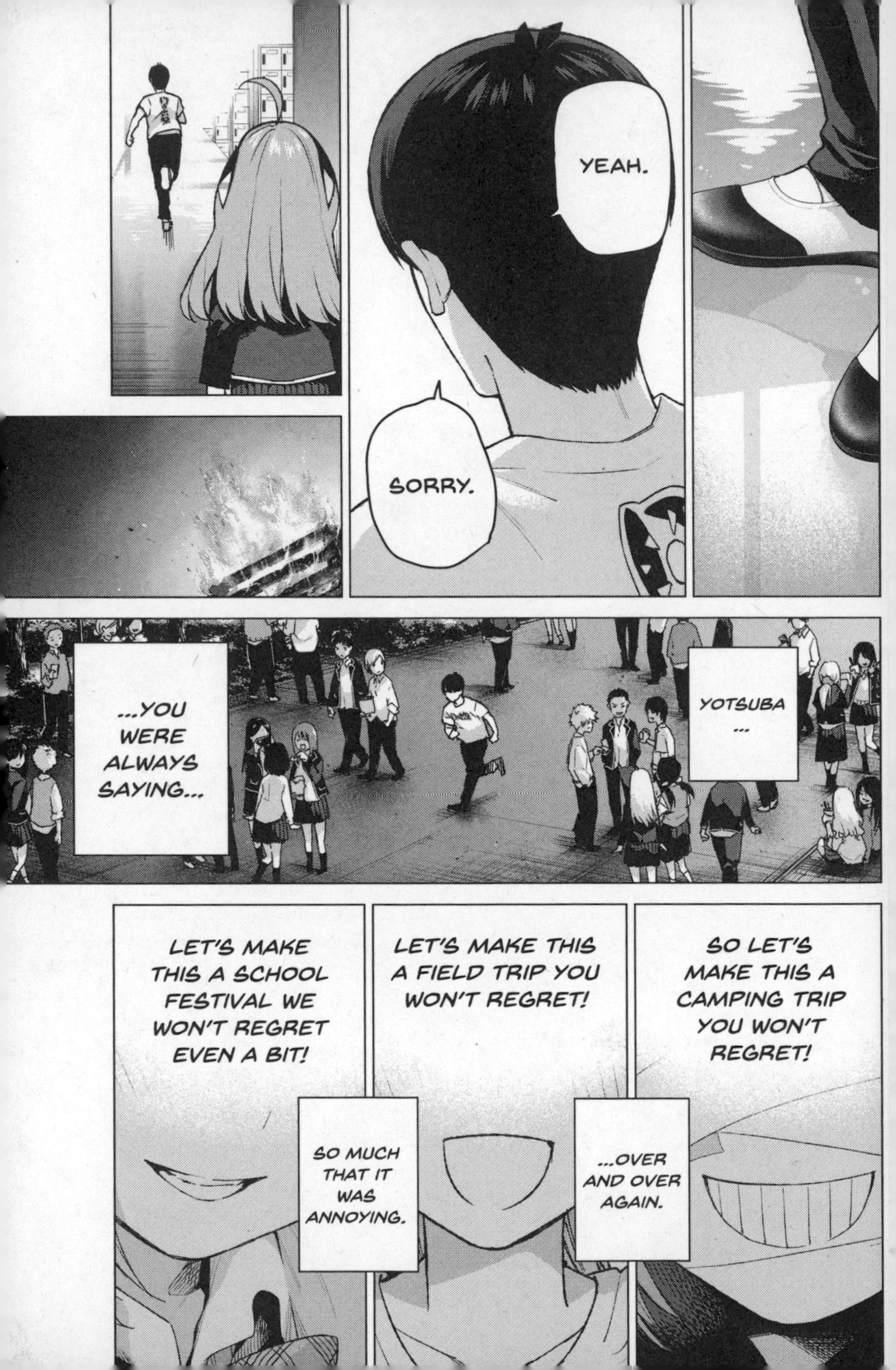

YEAH.
SORRY.
YOTSUBA...
...YOU WERE ALWAYS SAYING...
SO LET'S MAKE THIS A CAMPING TRIP YOU WON'T REGRET!
...OVER AND OVER AGAIN.
LET'S MAKE THIS A FIELD TRIP YOU WON'T REGRET!
SO MUCH THAT IT WAS ANNOYING.
LET'S MAKE THIS A SCHOOL FESTIVAL WE WON'T REGRET EVEN A BIT!

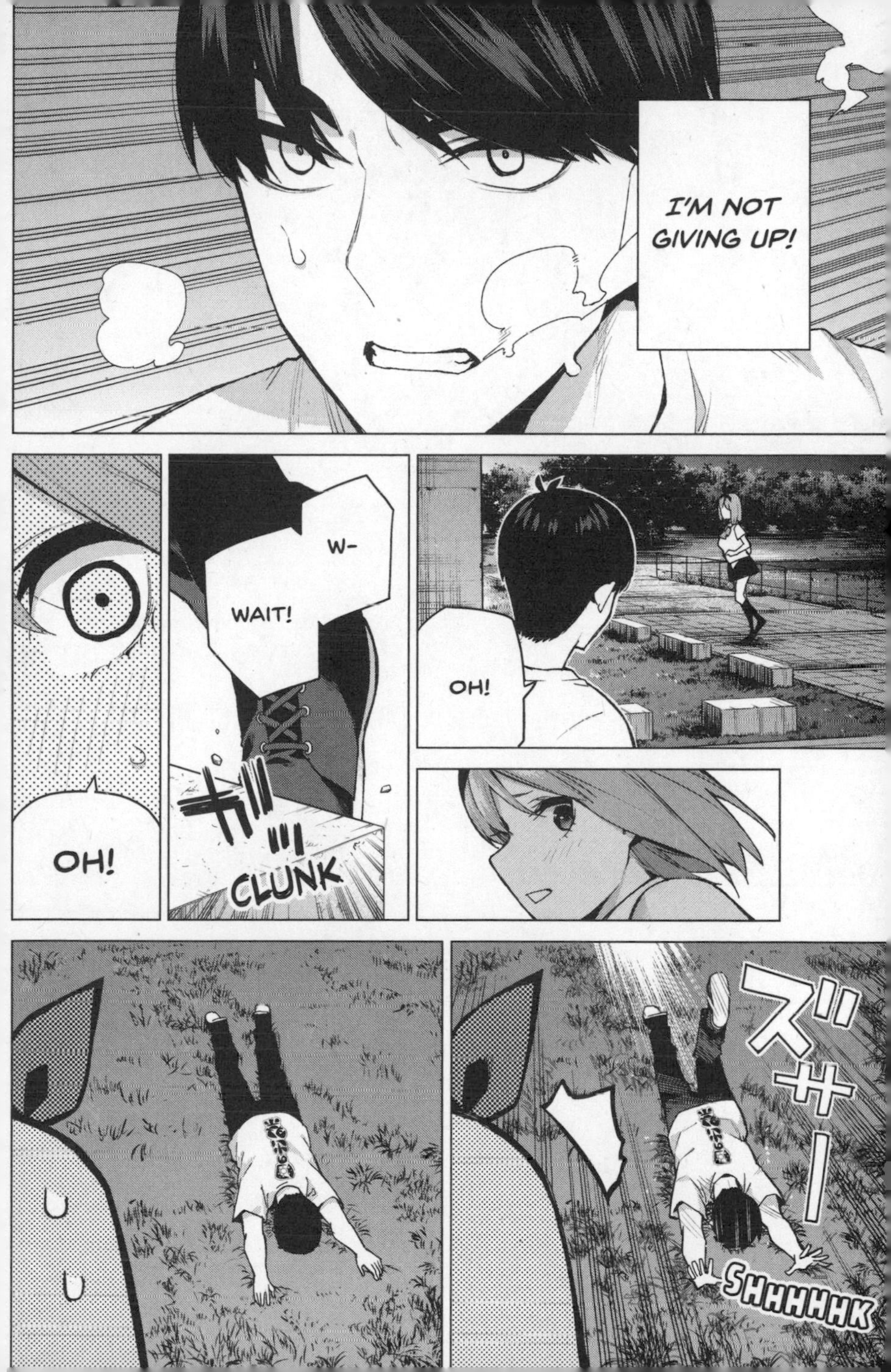
I'M NOT GIVING UP!
OH!
W-
WAIT!
CLUNK
OH!
SHHHHHK

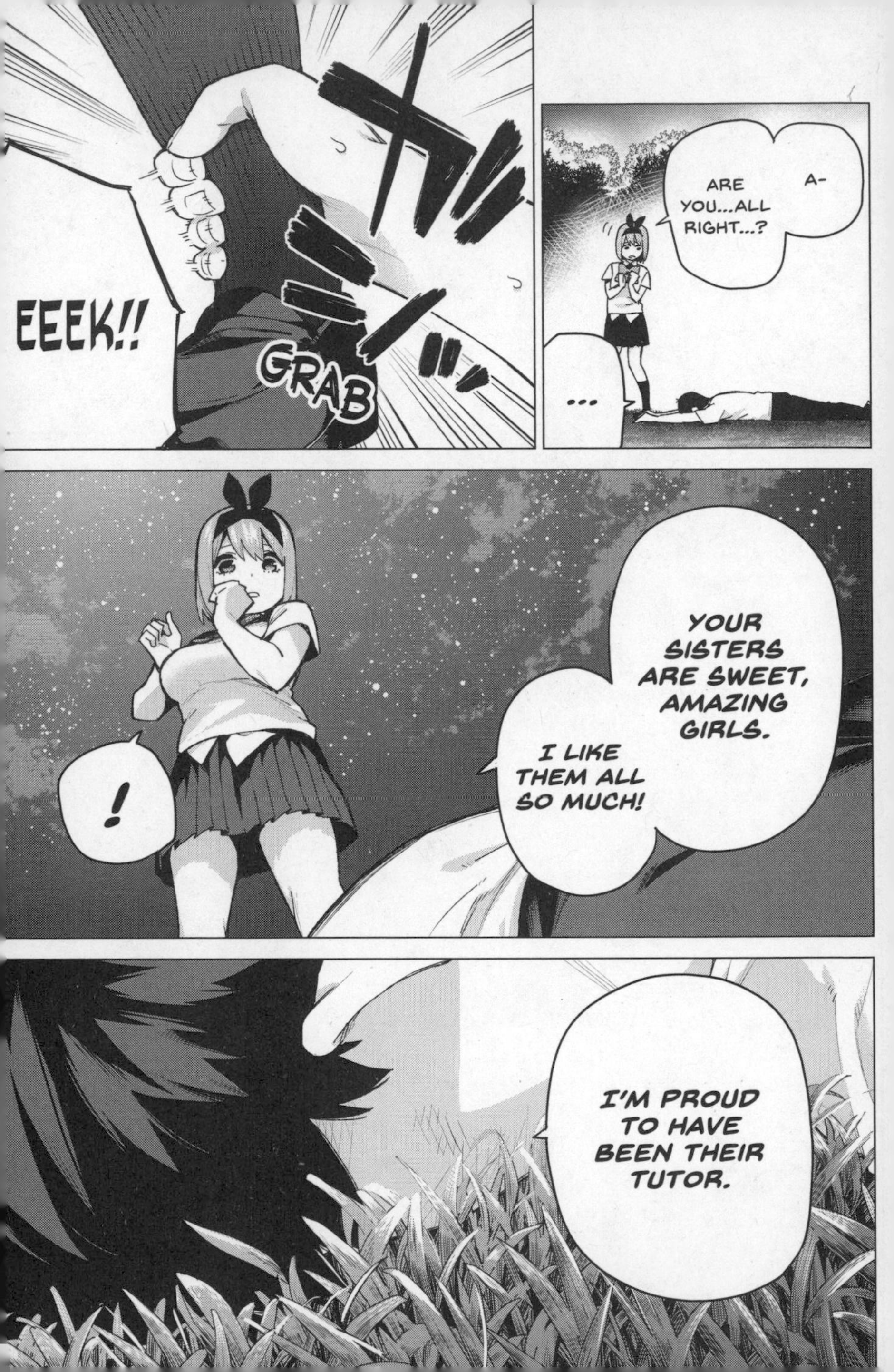
A-
ARE YOU...ALL RIGHT...?
...
EEEK!!
GRAB
YOUR SISTERS ARE SWEET, AMAZING GIRLS.
I LIKE THEM ALL SO MUCH!
!
I'M PROUD TO HAVE BEEN THEIR TUTOR.

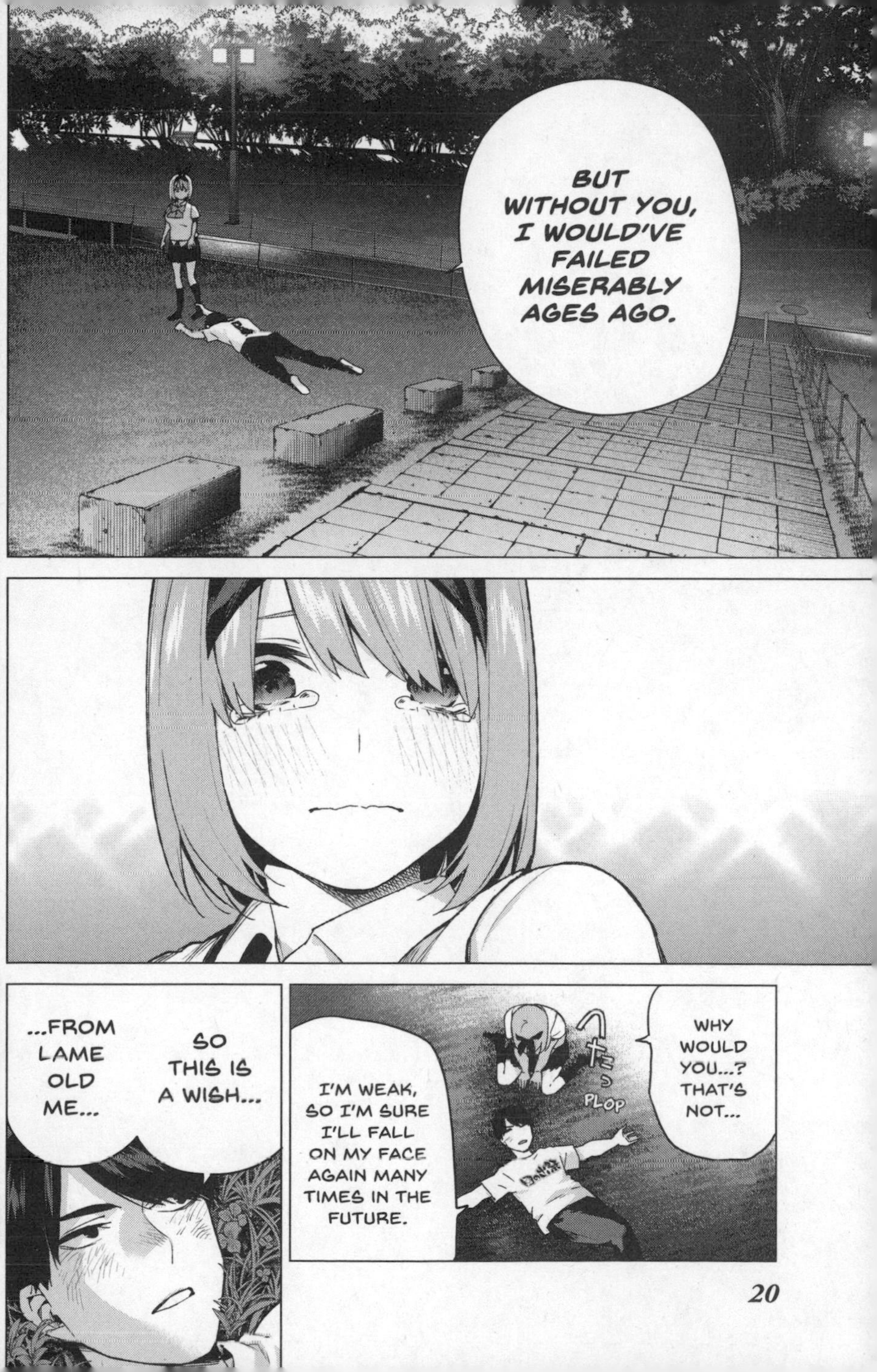
BUT WITHOUT YOU, I WOULD'VE FAILED MISERABLY AGES AGO.
WHY WOULD YOU...? THAT'S NOT...
PLOP
I'M WEAK, SO I'M SURE I'LL FALL ON MY FACE AGAIN MANY TIMES IN THE FUTURE.
SO THIS IS A WISH...
...FROM LAME OLD ME...

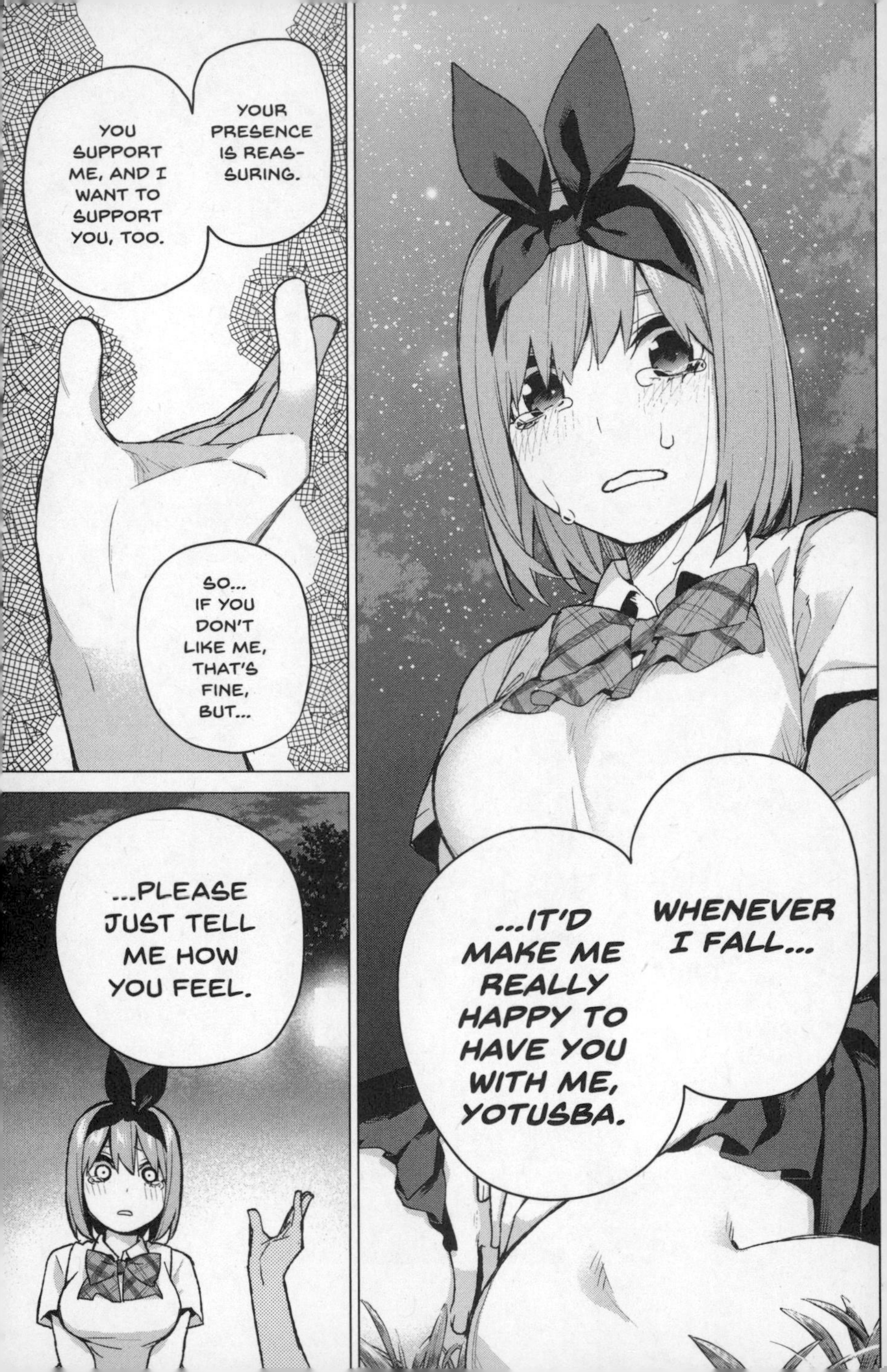
WHENEVER I FALL...
...IT'D MAKE ME REALLY HAPPY TO HAVE YOU WITH ME, YOTUSBA.
YOUR PRESENCE IS REAS-SURING.
YOU SUPPORT ME, AND I WANT TO SUPPORT YOU, TOO.
SO... IF YOU DON'T LIKE ME, THAT'S FINE, BUT...
...PLEASE JUST TELL ME HOW YOU FEEL.

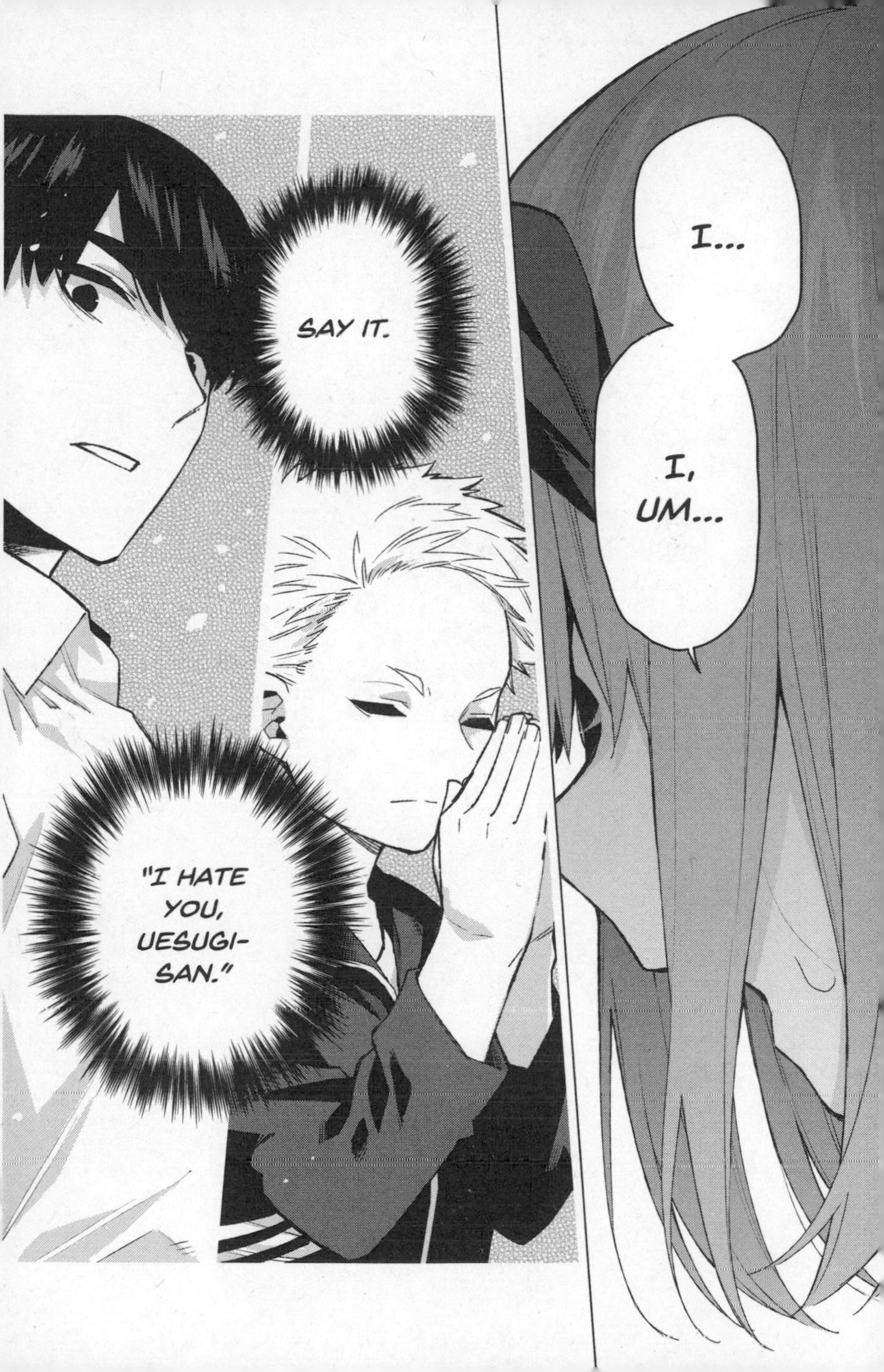
I...
I, UM...
SAY IT.
"I HATE YOU, UESUGI-SAN."

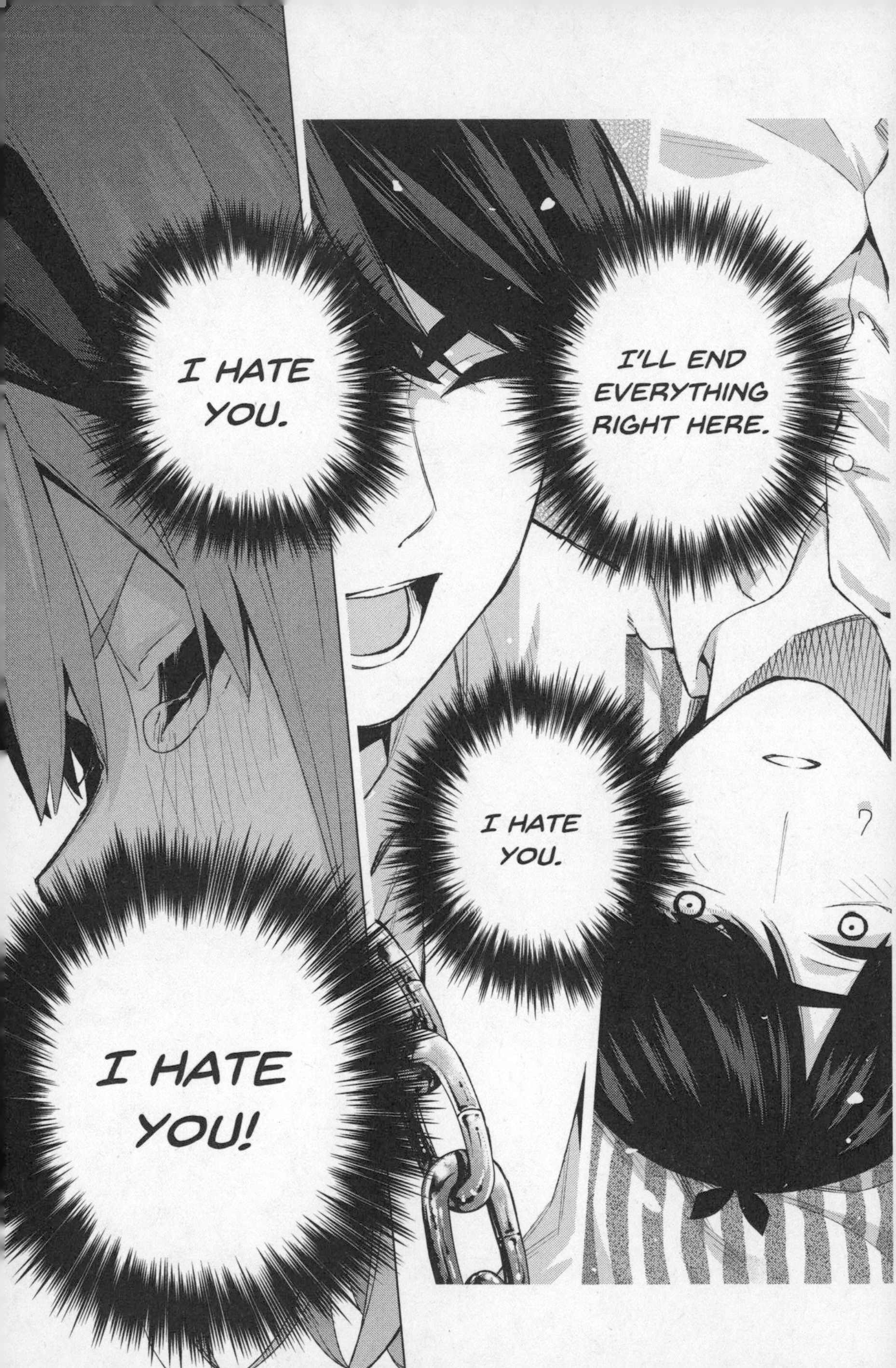
I'LL END EVERYTHING RIGHT HERE.
I HATE YOU.
I HATE YOU.
I HATE YOU!

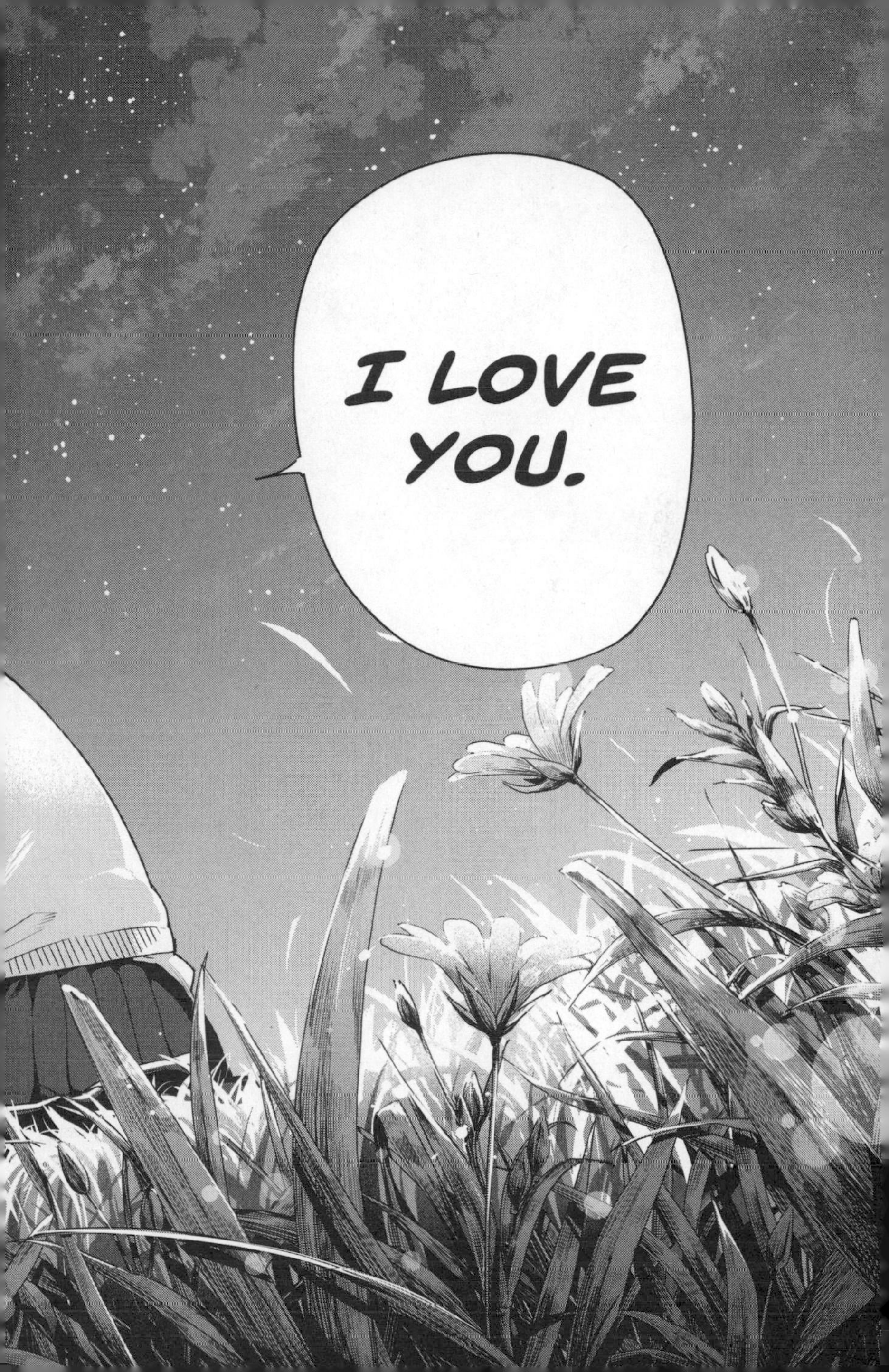
I LOVE YOU.

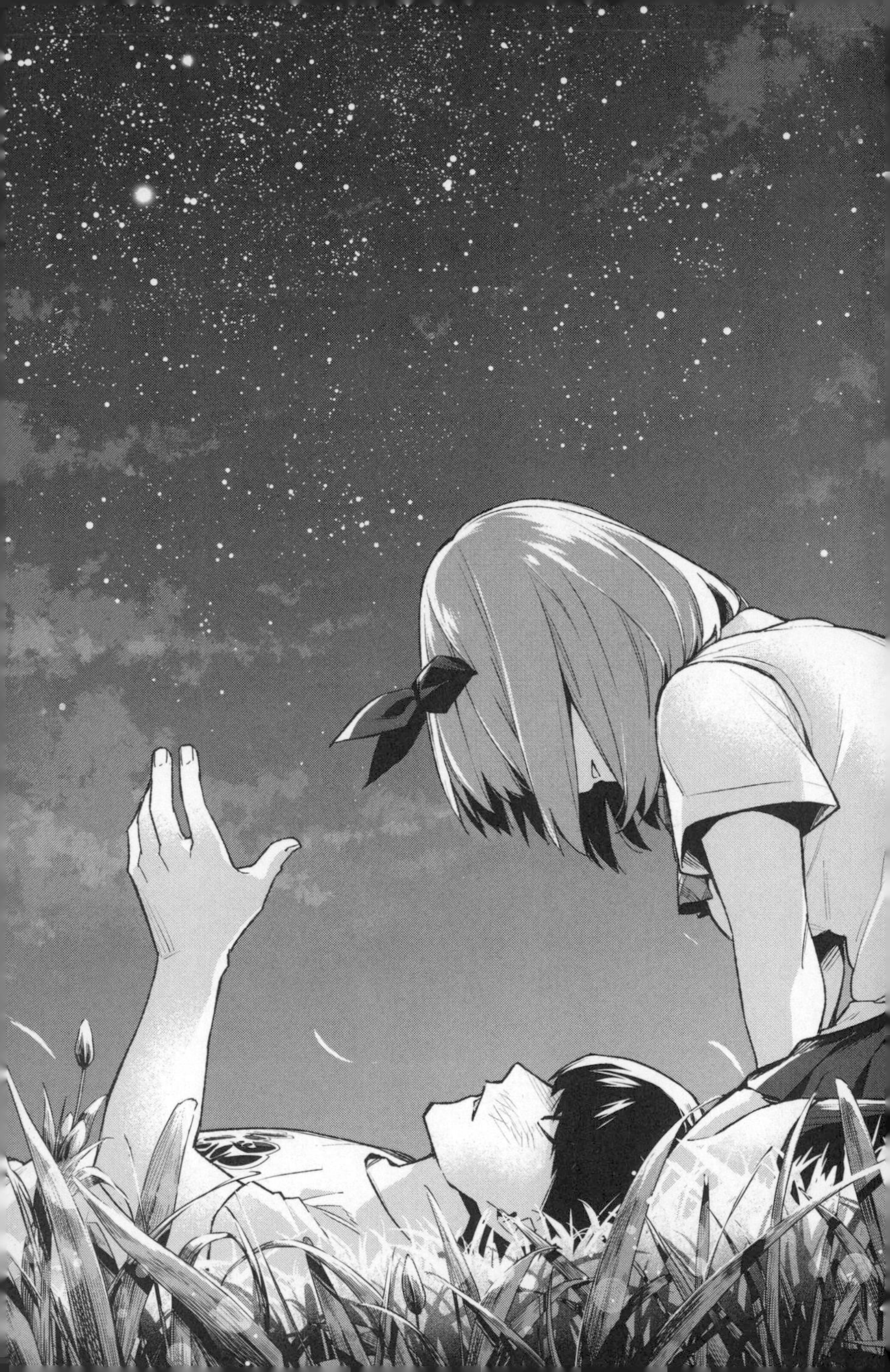

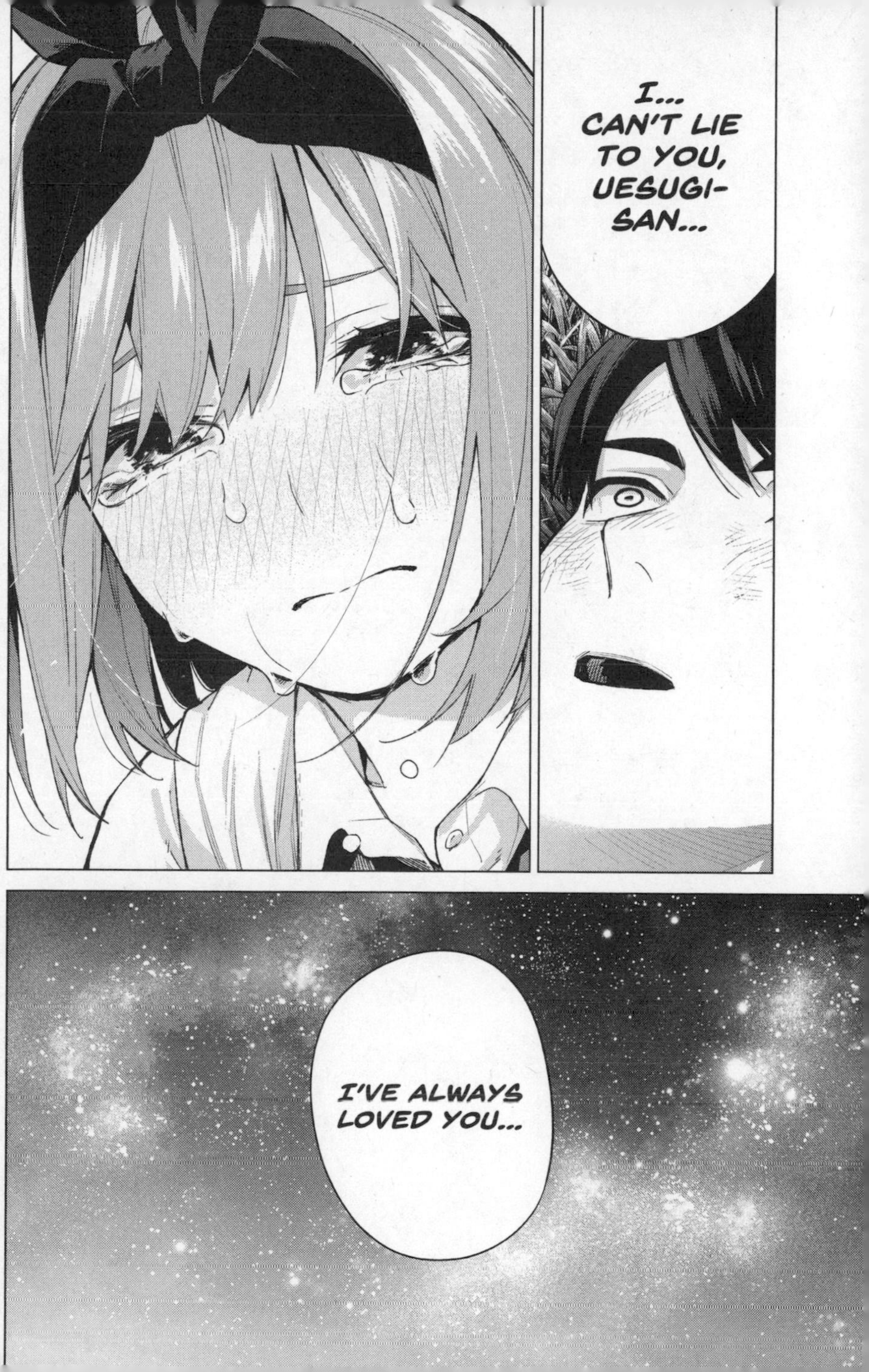
I... CAN'T LIE TO YOU, UESUGI-SAN...
I'VE ALWAYS LOVED YOU...

CHAPTER 115
FIVE MORNINGS

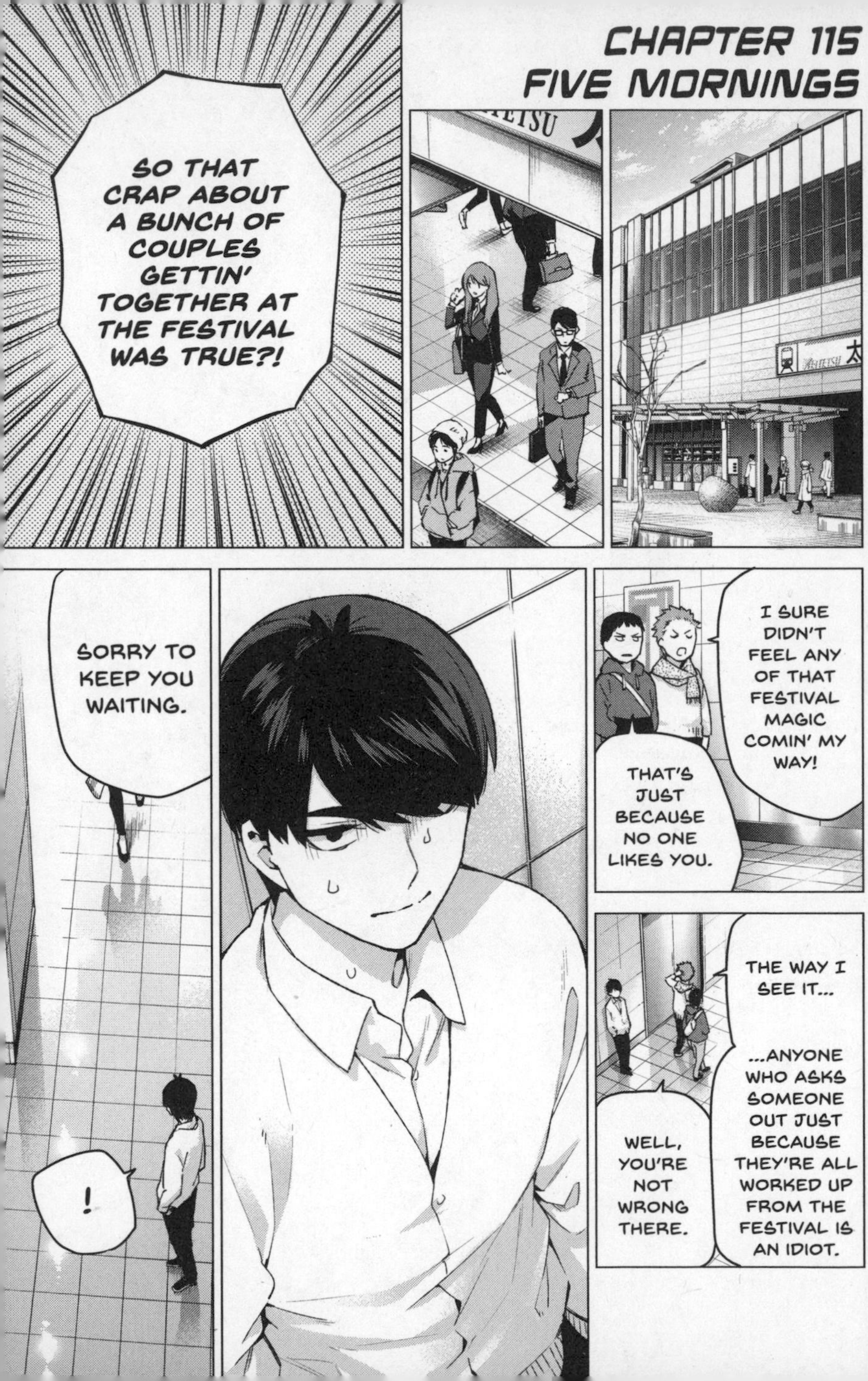
SO THAT CRAP ABOUT A BUNCH OF COUPLES GETTIN' TOGETHER AT THE FESTIVAL WAS TRUE?!
I SURE DIDN'T FEEL ANY OF THAT FESTIVAL MAGIC COMIN' MY WAY!
THAT'S JUST BECAUSE NO ONE LIKES YOU.
THE WAY I SEE IT...
...ANYONE WHO ASKS SOMEONE OUT JUST BECAUSE THEY'RE ALL WORKED UP FROM THE FESTIVAL IS AN IDIOT.
WELL, YOU'RE NOT WRONG THERE.
SORRY TO KEEP YOU WAITING.
!

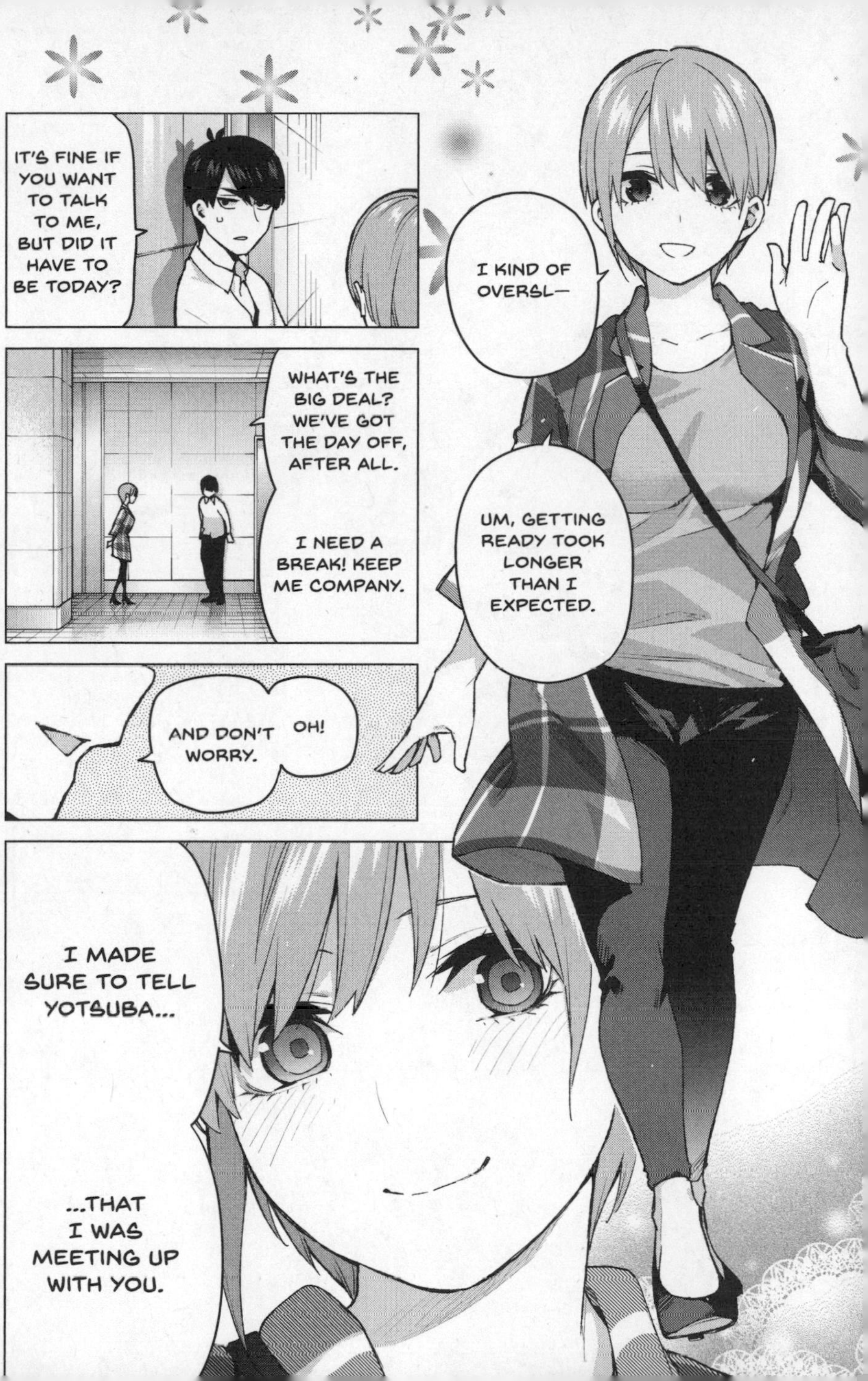
I KIND OF OVERSL—
UM, GETTING READY TOOK LONGER THAN I EXPECTED.
IT'S FINE IF YOU WANT TO TALK TO ME, BUT DID IT HAVE TO BE TODAY?
WHAT'S THE BIG DEAL? WE'VE GOT THE DAY OFF, AFTER ALL.
I NEED A BREAK! KEEP ME COMPANY.
OH!
AND DON'T WORRY.
I MADE SURE TO TELL YOTSUBA...
...THAT I WAS MEETING UP WITH YOU.

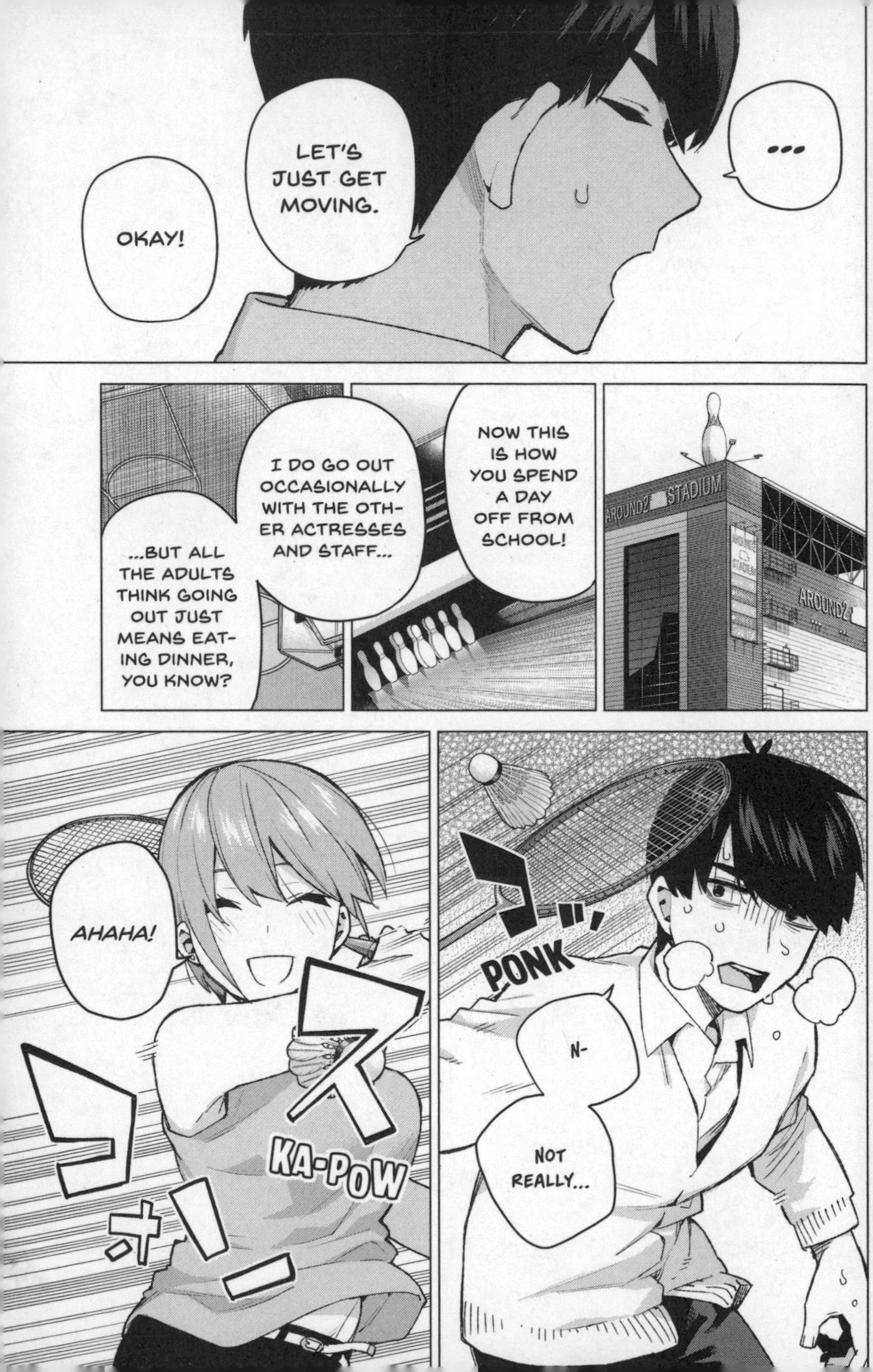
...
LET'S JUST GET MOVING.
OKAY!
NOW THIS IS HOW YOU SPEND A DAY OFF FROM SCHOOL!
I DO GO OUT OCCASIONALLY WITH THE OTHER ACTRESSES AND STAFF...
...BUT ALL THE ADULTS THINK GOING OUT JUST MEANS EATING DINNER, YOU KNOW?
PONK
N-
NOT REALLY...
AHAHA!
KA-POW

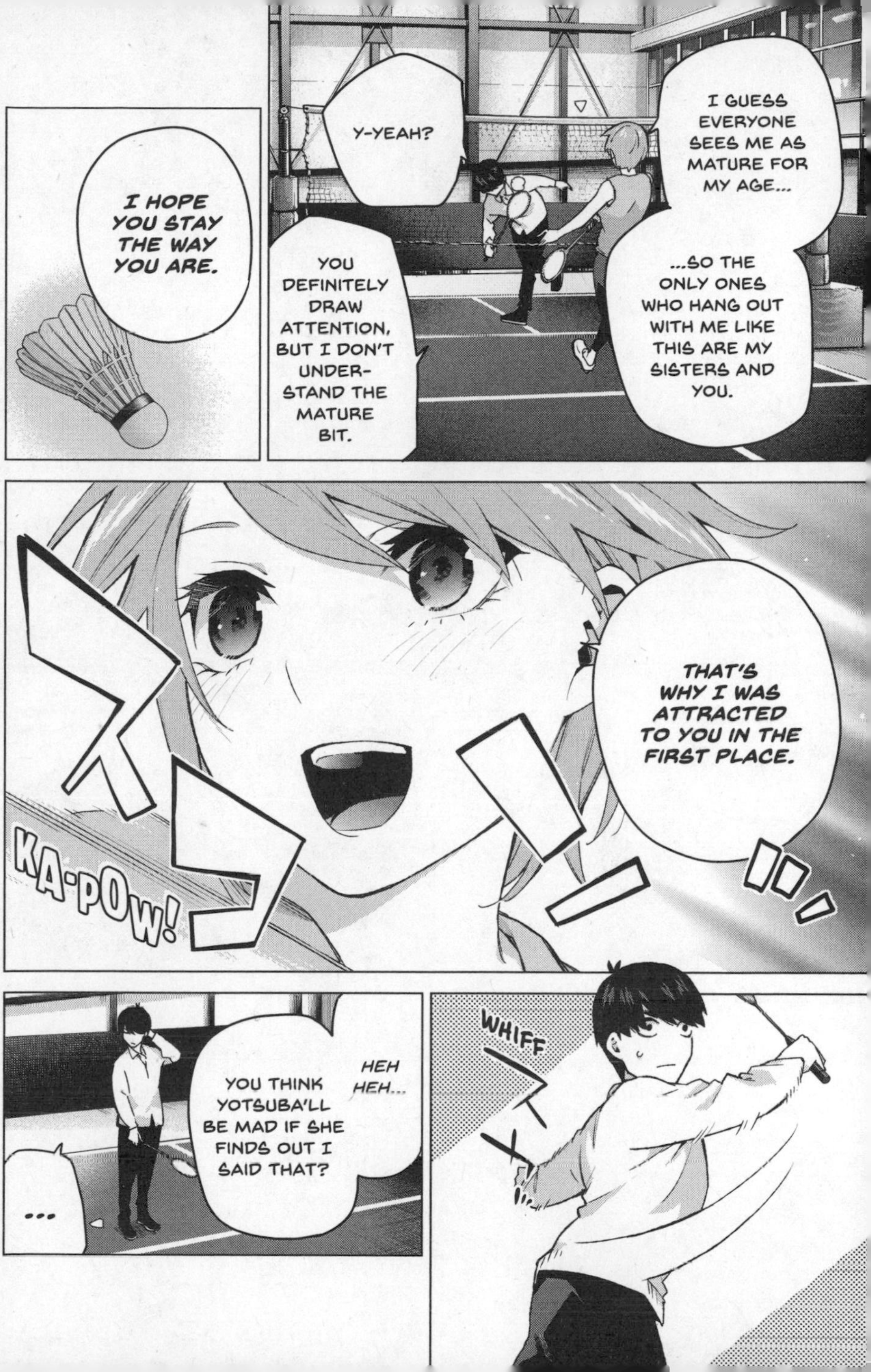
I GUESS EVERYONE SEES ME AS MATURE FOR MY AGE...
Y-YEAH?
...SO THE ONLY ONES WHO HANG OUT WITH ME LIKE THIS ARE MY SISTERS AND YOU.
YOU DEFINITELY DRAW ATTENTION, BUT I DON'T UNDER-STAND THE MATURE BIT.
I HOPE YOU STAY THE WAY YOU ARE.
THAT'S WHY I WAS ATTRACTED TO YOU IN THE FIRST PLACE.
KA-POW!
WHIFF
HEH HEH...
YOU THINK YOTSUBA'LL BE MAD IF SHE FINDS OUT I SAID THAT?
...

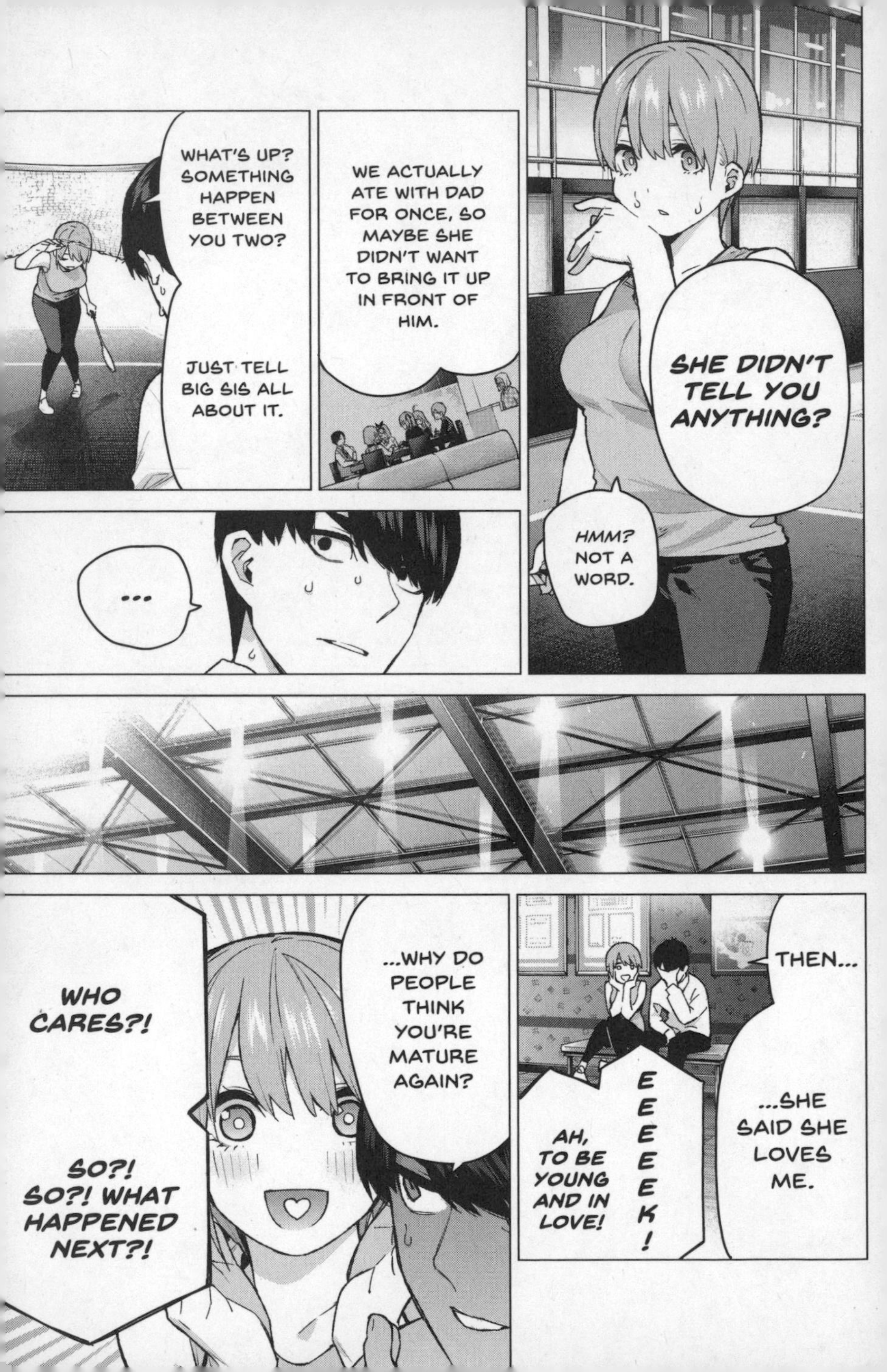
SHE DIDN'T TELL YOU ANYTHING?
HMM? NOT A WORD.
WE ACTUALLY ATE WITH DAD FOR ONCE, SO MAYBE SHE DIDN'T WANT TO BRING IT UP IN FRONT OF HIM.
WHAT'S UP? SOMETHING HAPPEN BETWEEN YOU TWO?
JUST TELL BIG SIS ALL ABOUT IT.
...
THEN...
...SHE SAID SHE LOVES ME.
EEEEEEK!
AH, TO BE YOUNG AND IN LOVE!
...WHY DO PEOPLE THINK YOU'RE MATURE AGAIN?
WHO CARES?!
SO?! SO?! WHAT HAPPENED NEXT?!

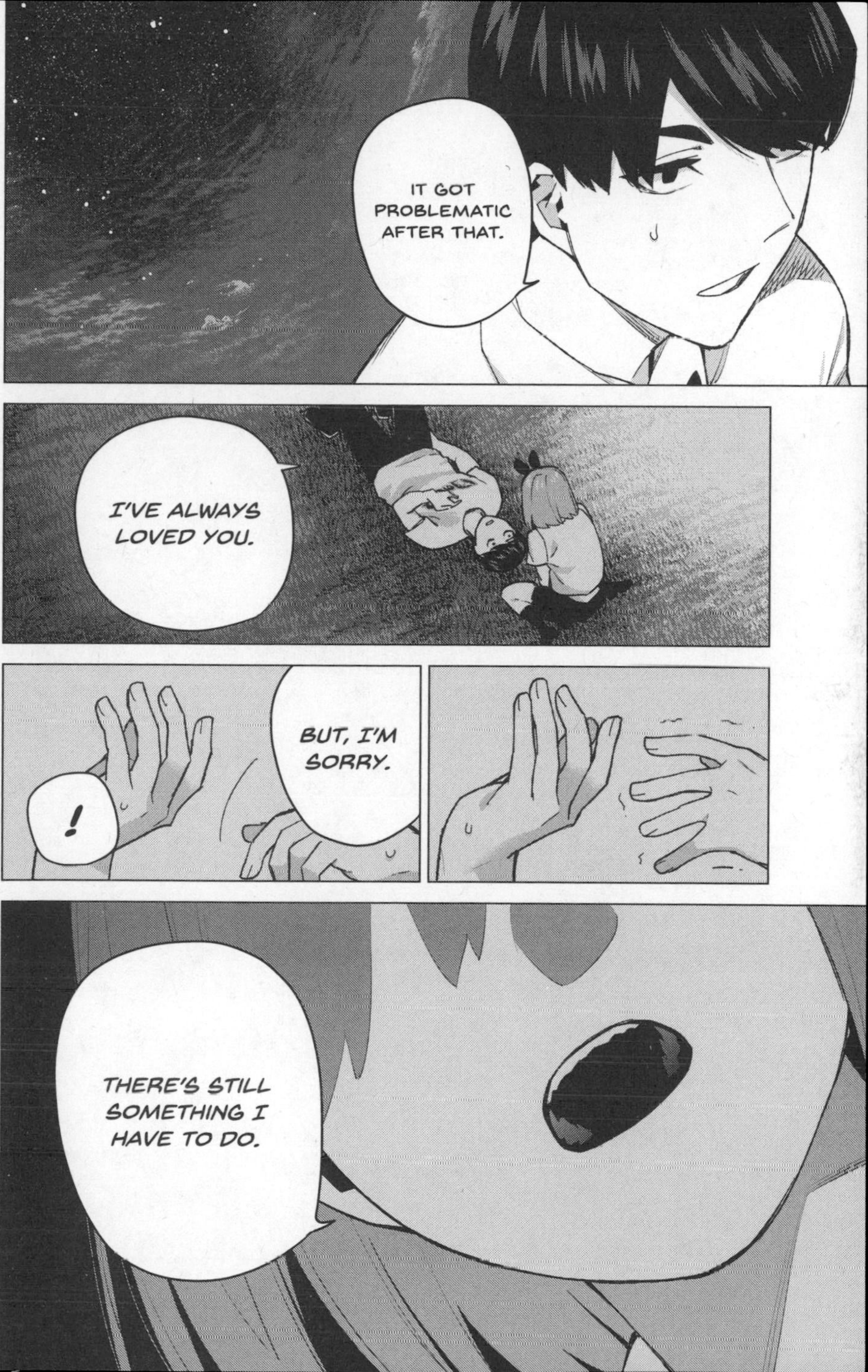
IT GOT PROBLEMATIC AFTER THAT.
I'VE ALWAYS LOVED YOU.
BUT, I'M SORRY.
!
THERE'S STILL SOMETHING I HAVE TO DO.

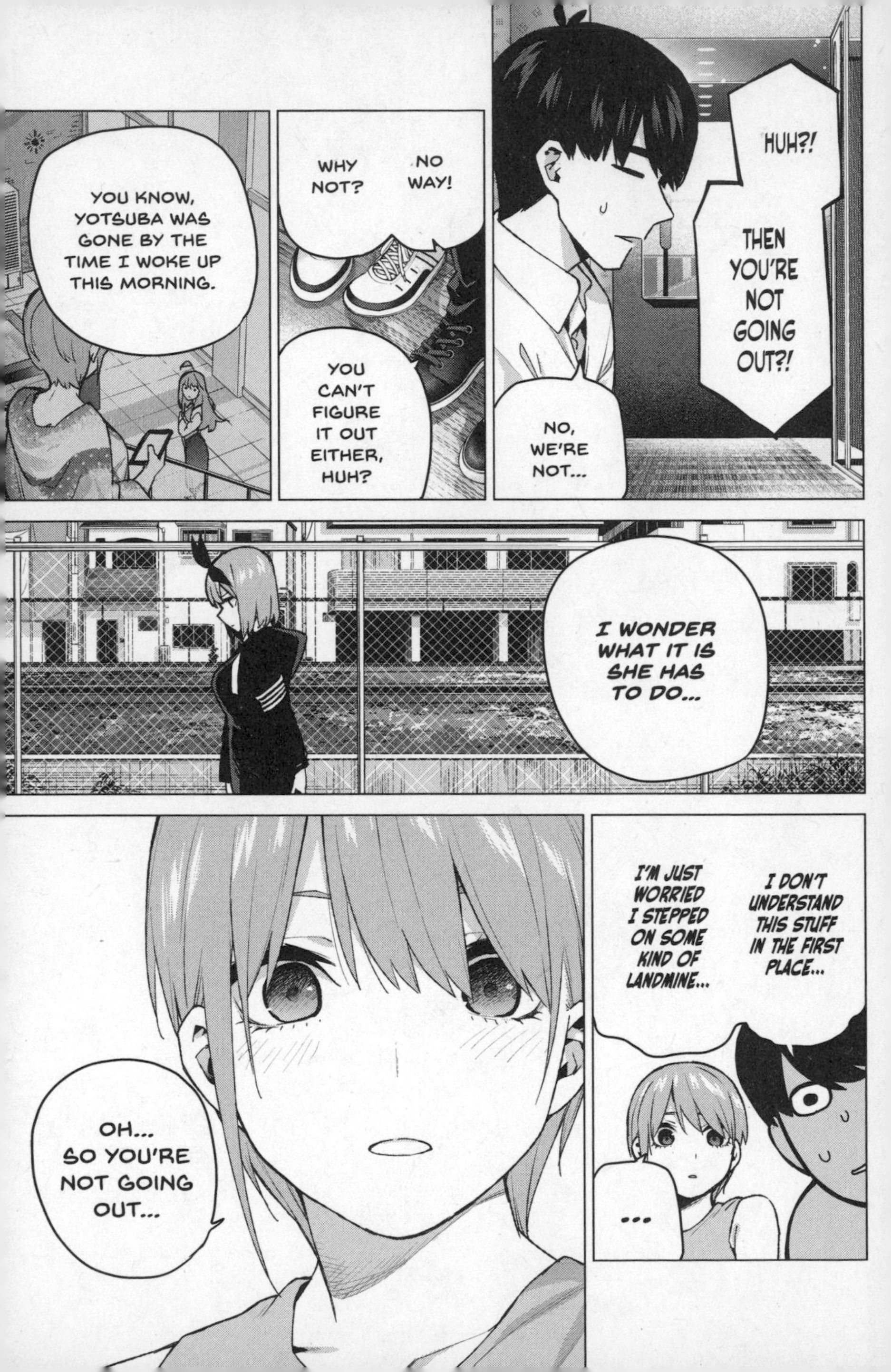
HUH?!
THEN YOU'RE NOT GOING OUT?!
NO, WE'RE NOT...
NO WAY!
WHY NOT?
YOU CAN'T FIGURE IT OUT EITHER, HUH?
YOU KNOW, YOTSUBA WAS GONE BY THE TIME I WOKE UP THIS MORNING.
I WONDER WHAT IT IS SHE HAS TO DO...
I DON'T UNDERSTAND THIS STUFF IN THE FIRST PLACE...
I'M JUST WORRIED I STEPPED ON SOME KIND OF LANDMINE...
...
OH... SO YOU'RE NOT GOING OUT...

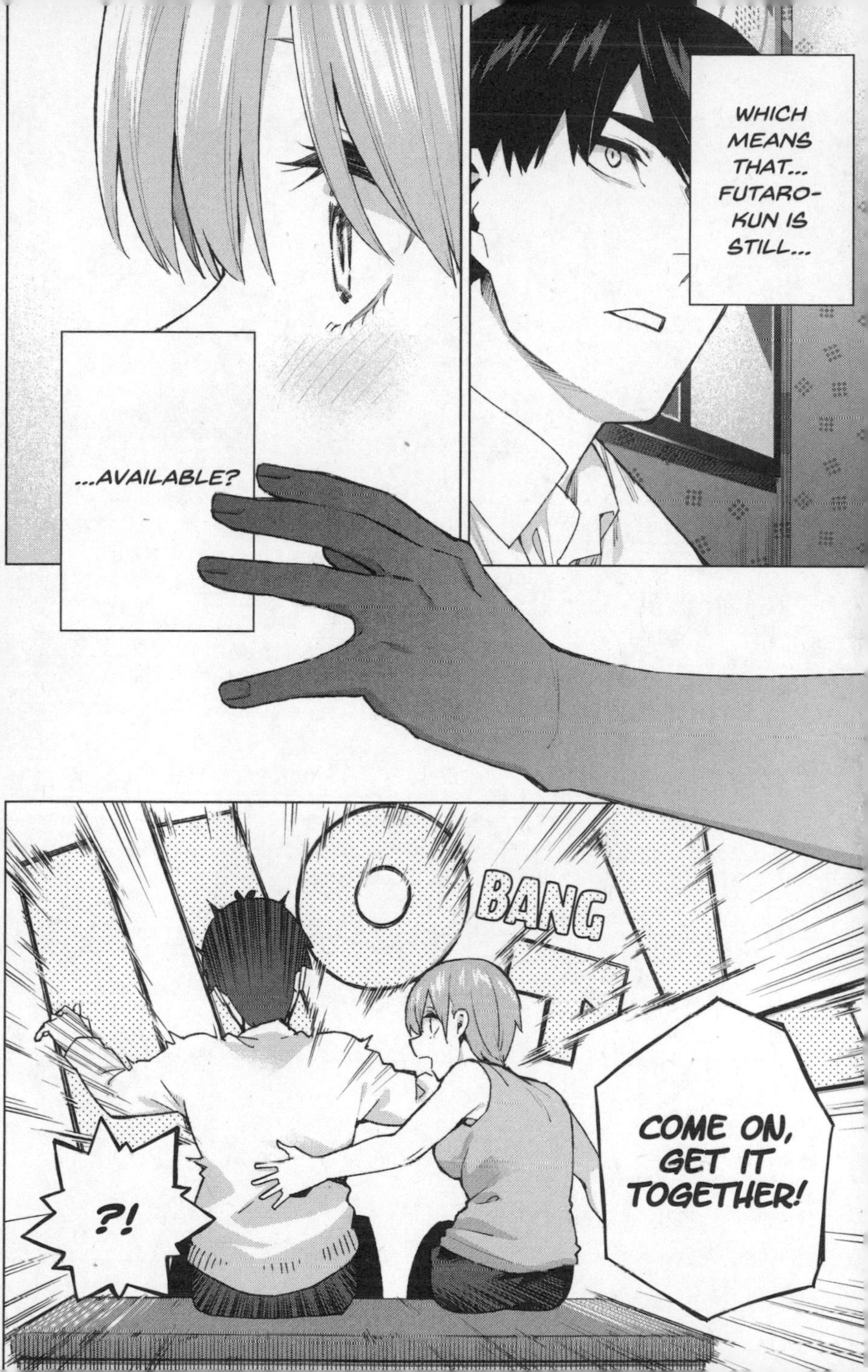
WHICH MEANS THAT... FUTARO-KUN IS STILL...
...AVAILABLE?
BANG
COME ON, GET IT TOGETHER!
?!

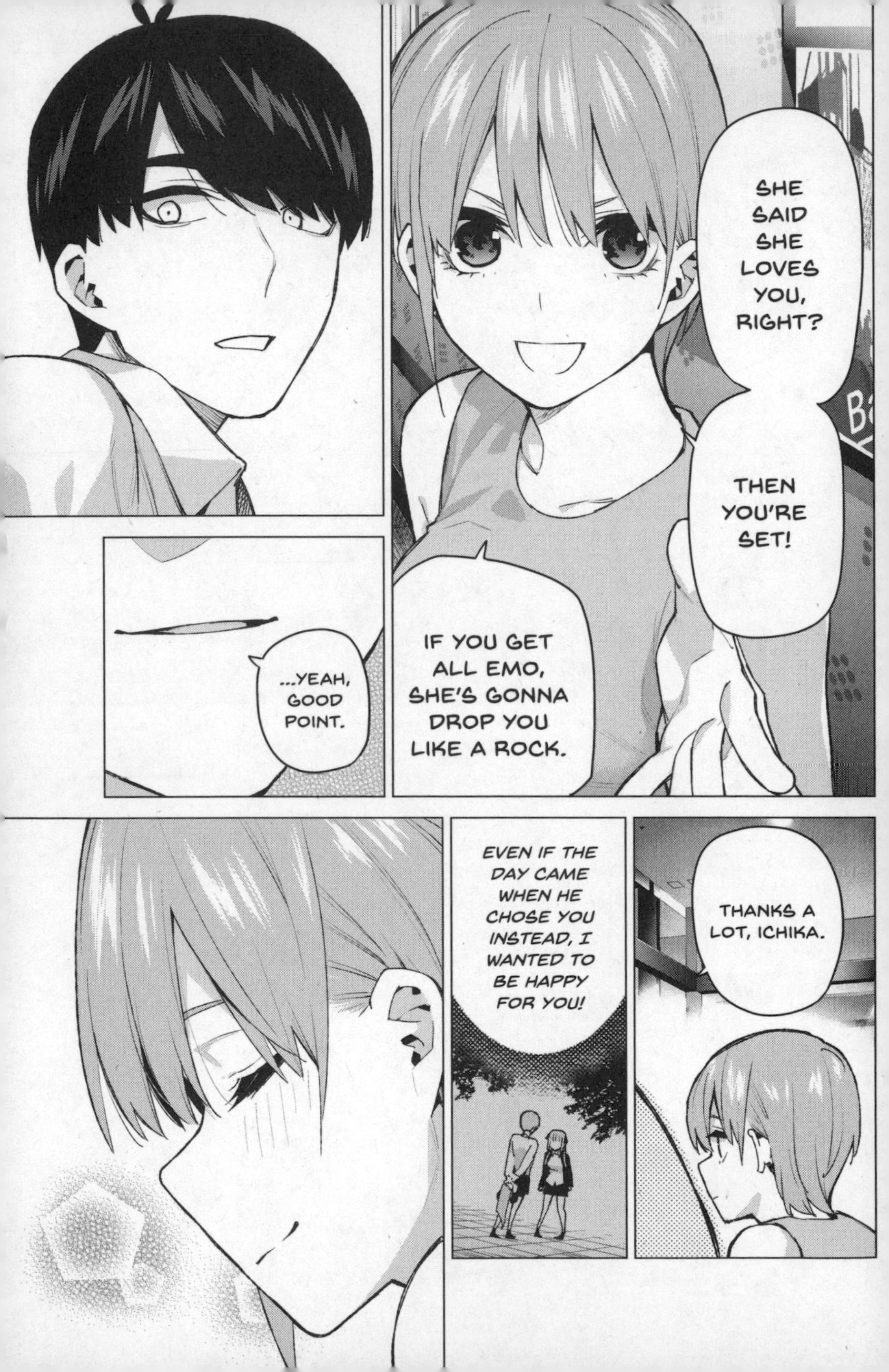
SHE SAID SHE LOVES YOU, RIGHT?
THEN YOU'RE SET!
IF YOU GET ALL EMO, SHE'S GONNA DROP YOU LIKE A ROCK.
...YEAH, GOOD POINT.
THANKS A LOT, ICHIKA.
EVEN IF THE DAY CAME WHEN HE CHOSE YOU INSTEAD, I WANTED TO BE HAPPY FOR YOU!

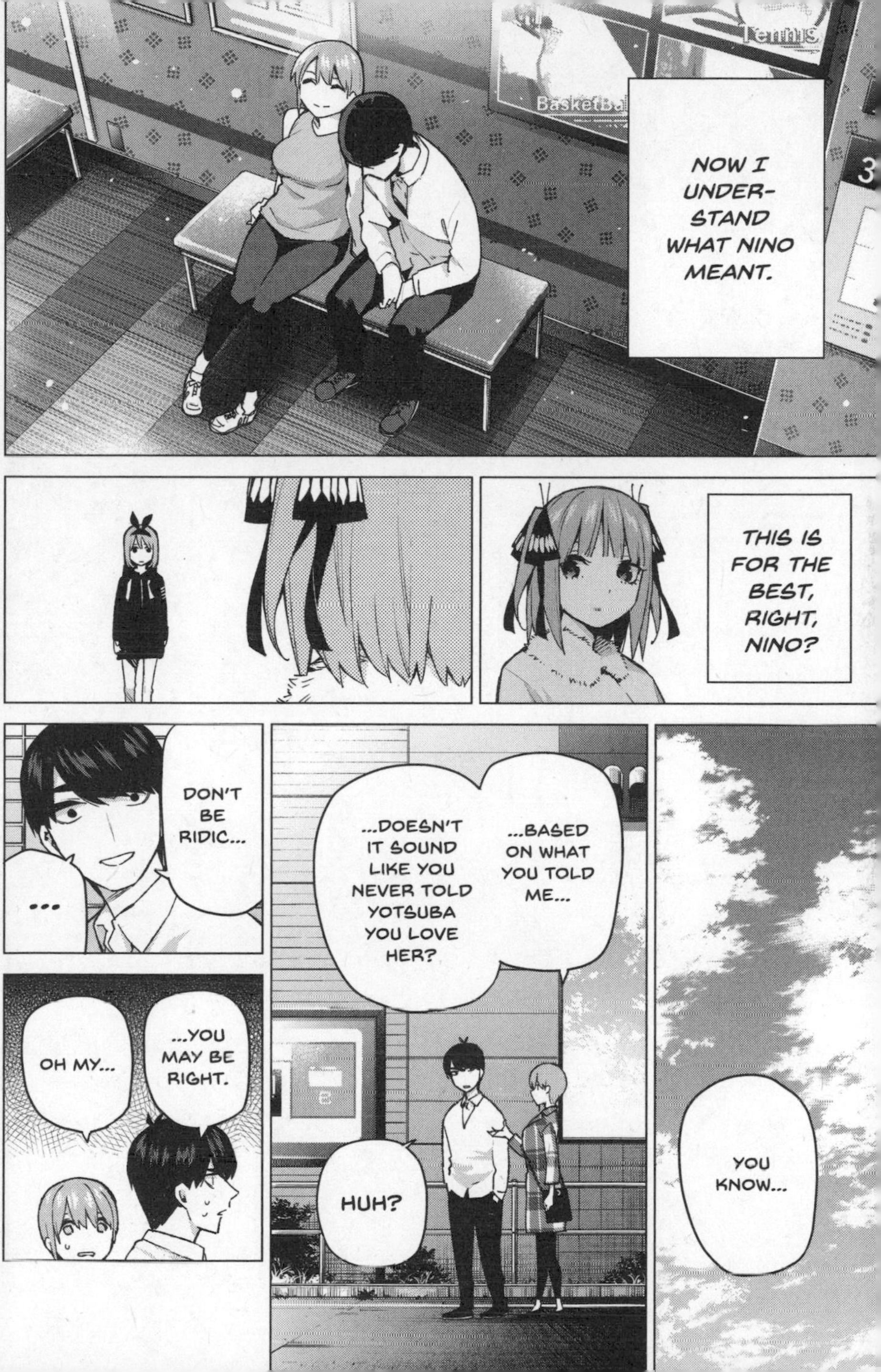
NOW I UNDER-STAND WHAT NINO MEANT.
THIS IS FOR THE BEST, RIGHT, NINO?
YOU KNOW...
...BASED ON WHAT YOU TOLD ME...
...DOESN'T IT SOUND LIKE YOU NEVER TOLD YOTSUBA YOU LOVE HER?
HUH?
DON'T BE RIDIC...
...
...YOU MAY BE RIGHT.
OH MY...

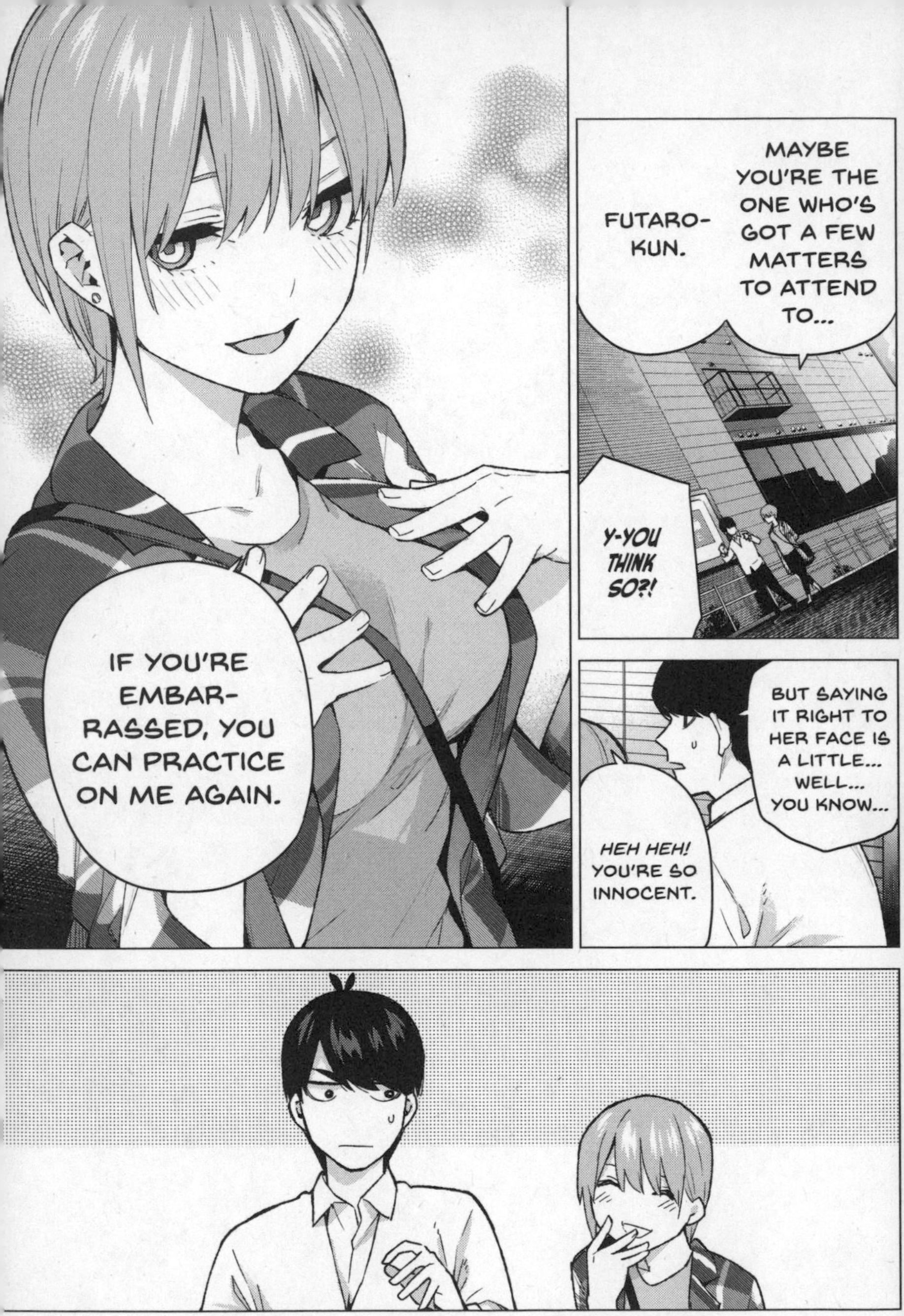
MAYBE YOU'RE THE ONE WHO'S GOT A FEW MATTERS TO ATTEND TO...
FUTARO-KUN.
Y-YOU THINK SO?!
BUT SAYING IT RIGHT TO HER FACE IS A LITTLE... WELL... YOU KNOW...
HEH HEH! YOU'RE SO INNOCENT.
IF YOU'RE EMBARRASSED, YOU CAN PRACTICE ON ME AGAIN.

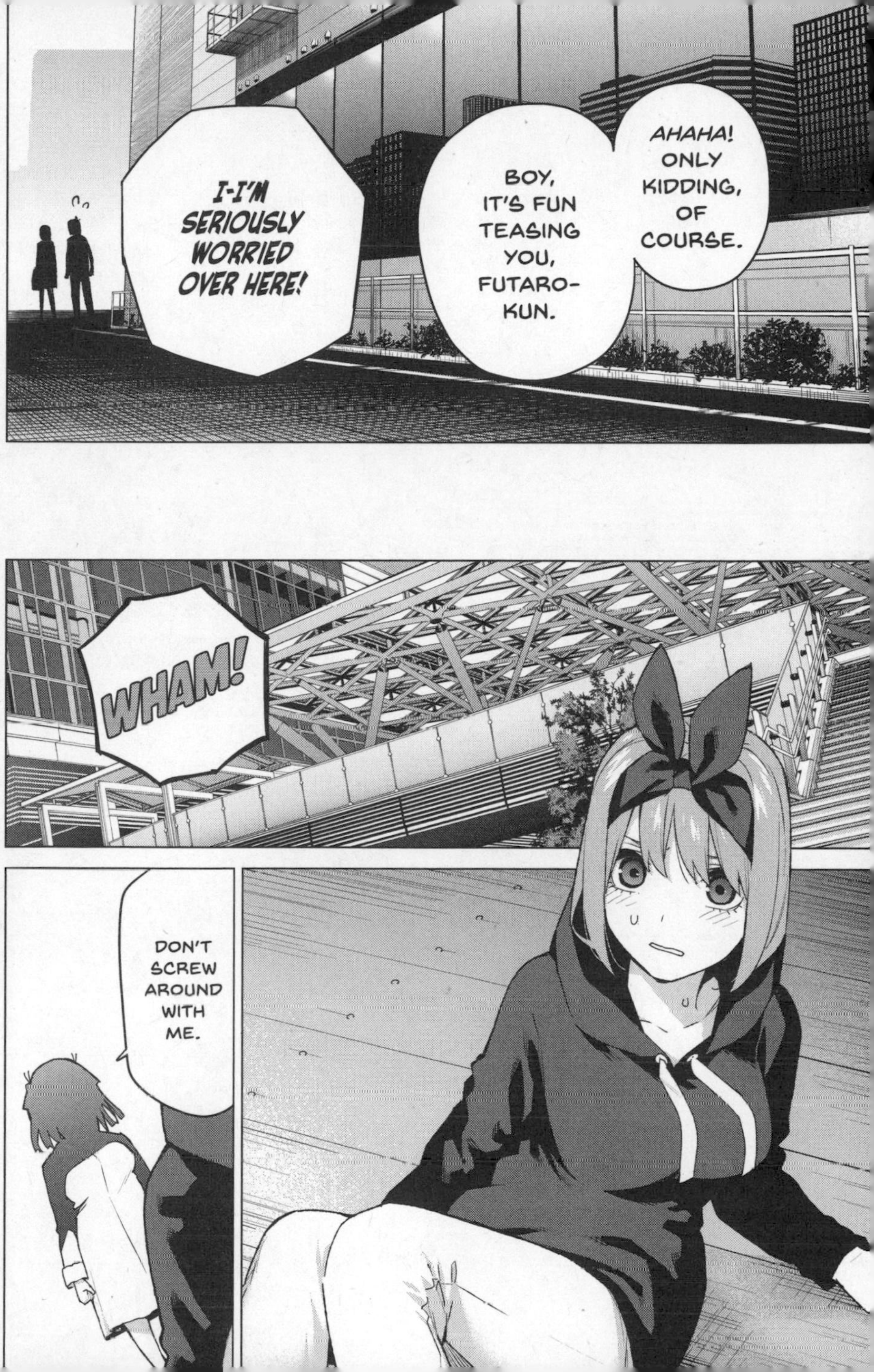
AHAHA! ONLY KIDDING, OF COURSE.
BOY, IT'S FUN TEASING YOU, FUTARO-KUN.
I-I'M SERIOUSLY WORRIED OVER HERE!
WHAM!
DON'T SCREW AROUND WITH ME.

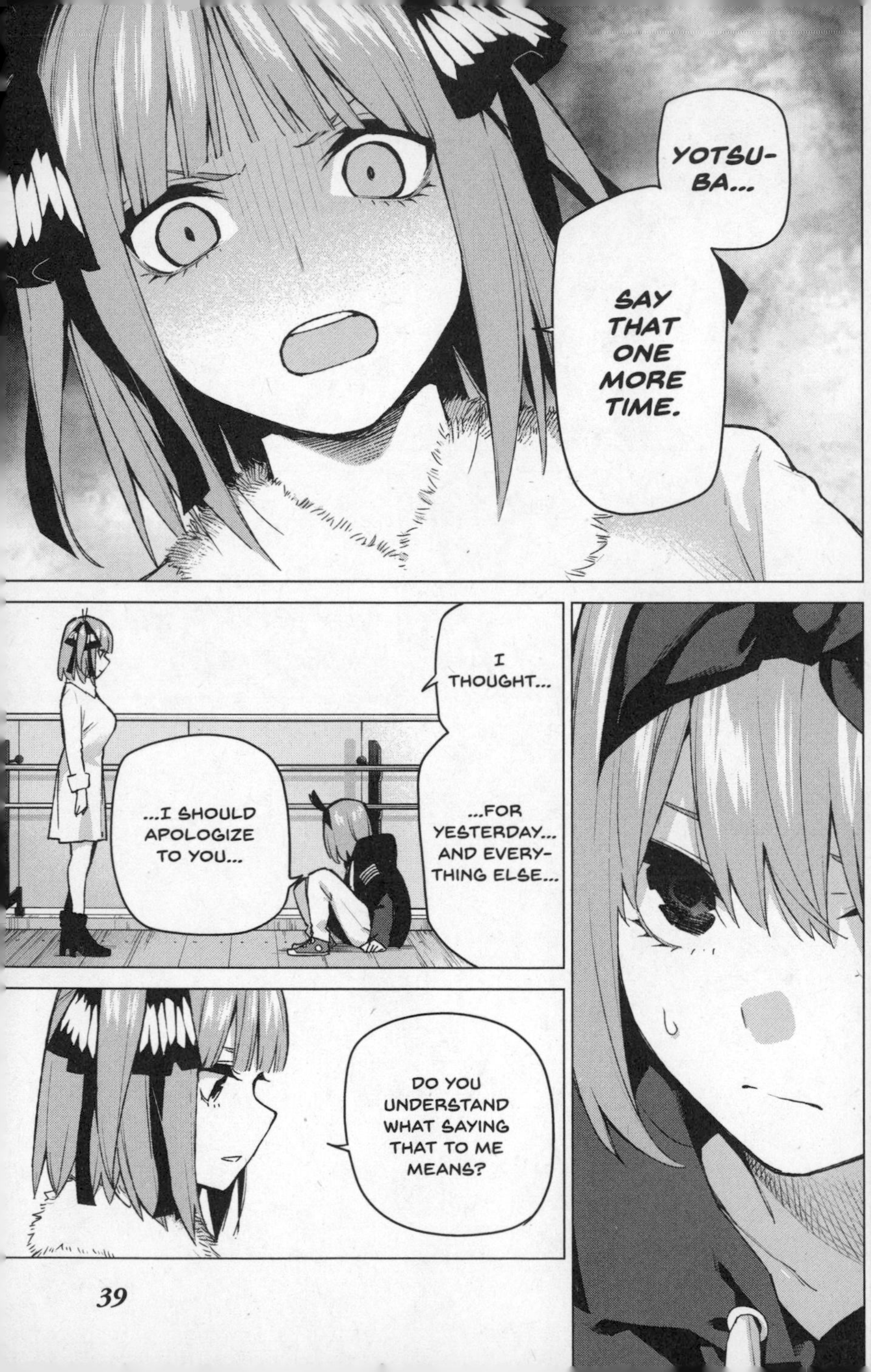
YOTSU-BA...
SAY THAT ONE MORE TIME.
I THOUGHT...
...FOR YESTERDAY... AND EVERY-THING ELSE...
...I SHOULD APOLOGIZE TO YOU...
DO YOU UNDERSTAND WHAT SAYING THAT TO ME MEANS?

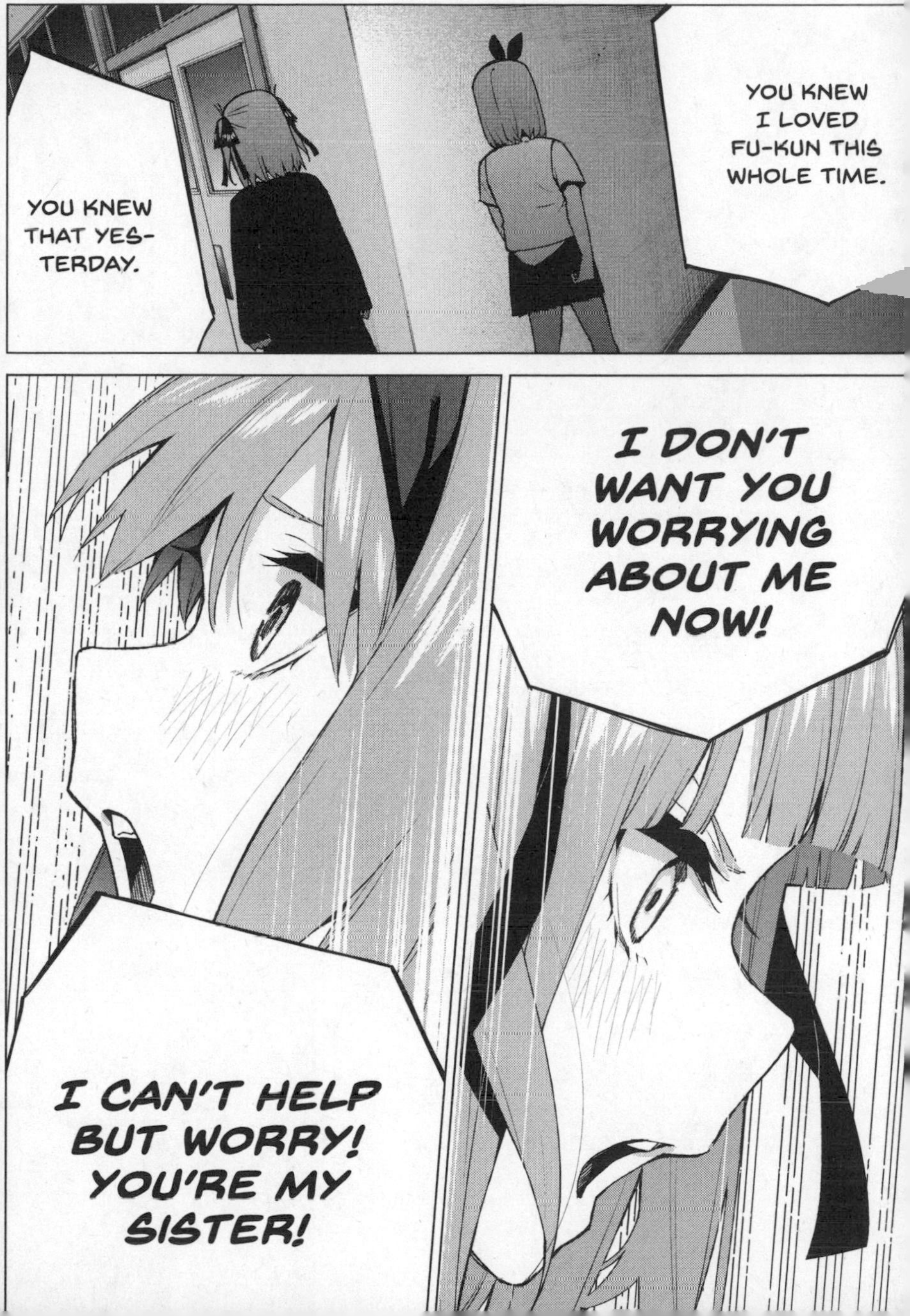
YOU KNEW I LOVED FU-KUN THIS WHOLE TIME.
YOU KNEW THAT YES-TERDAY.
I DON'T WANT YOU WORRYING ABOUT ME NOW!
I CAN'T HELP BUT WORRY! YOU'RE MY SISTER!

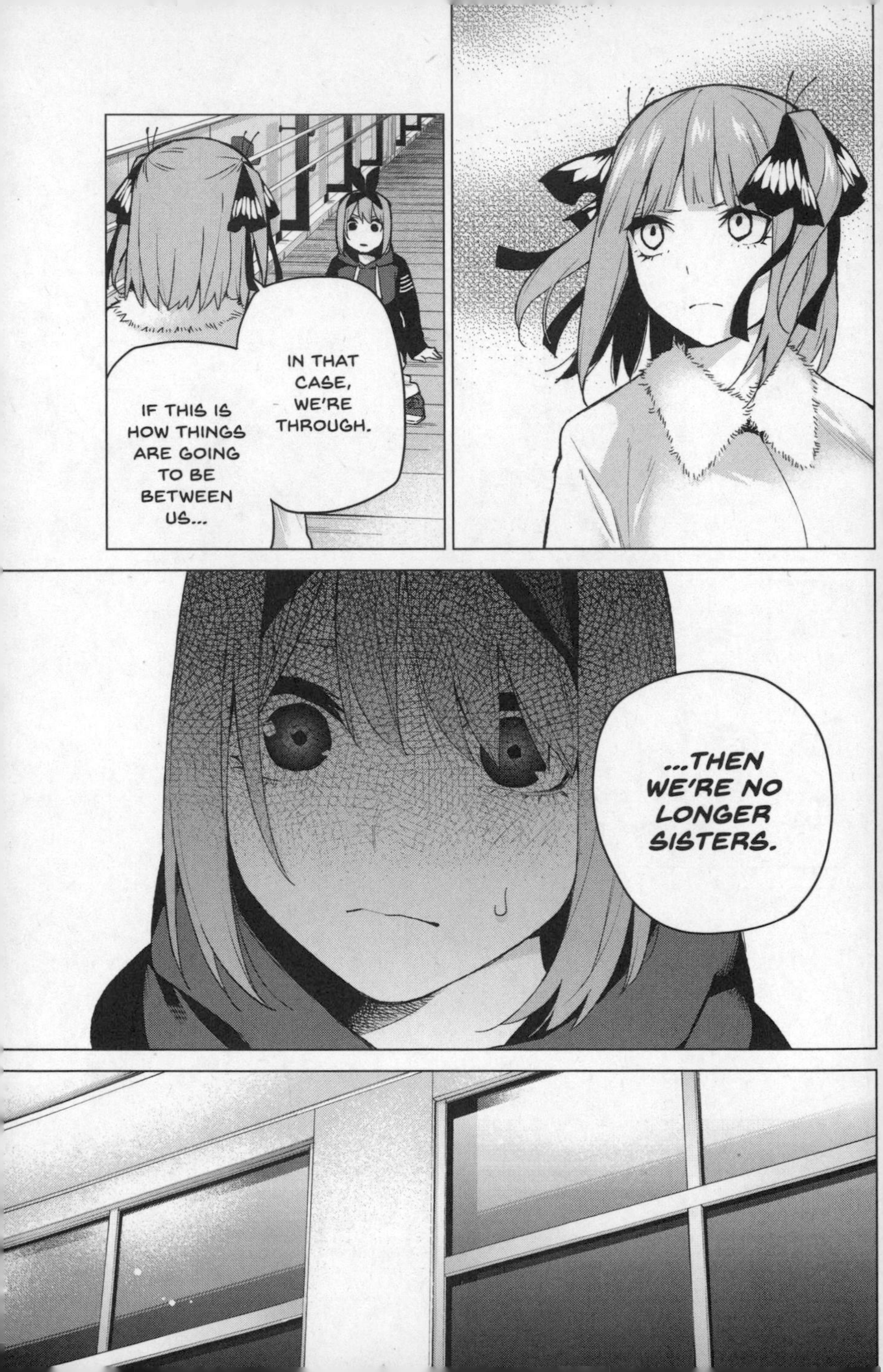
IN THAT CASE, WE'RE THROUGH.
IF THIS IS HOW THINGS ARE GOING TO BE BETWEEN US...
...THEN WE'RE NO LONGER SISTERS.

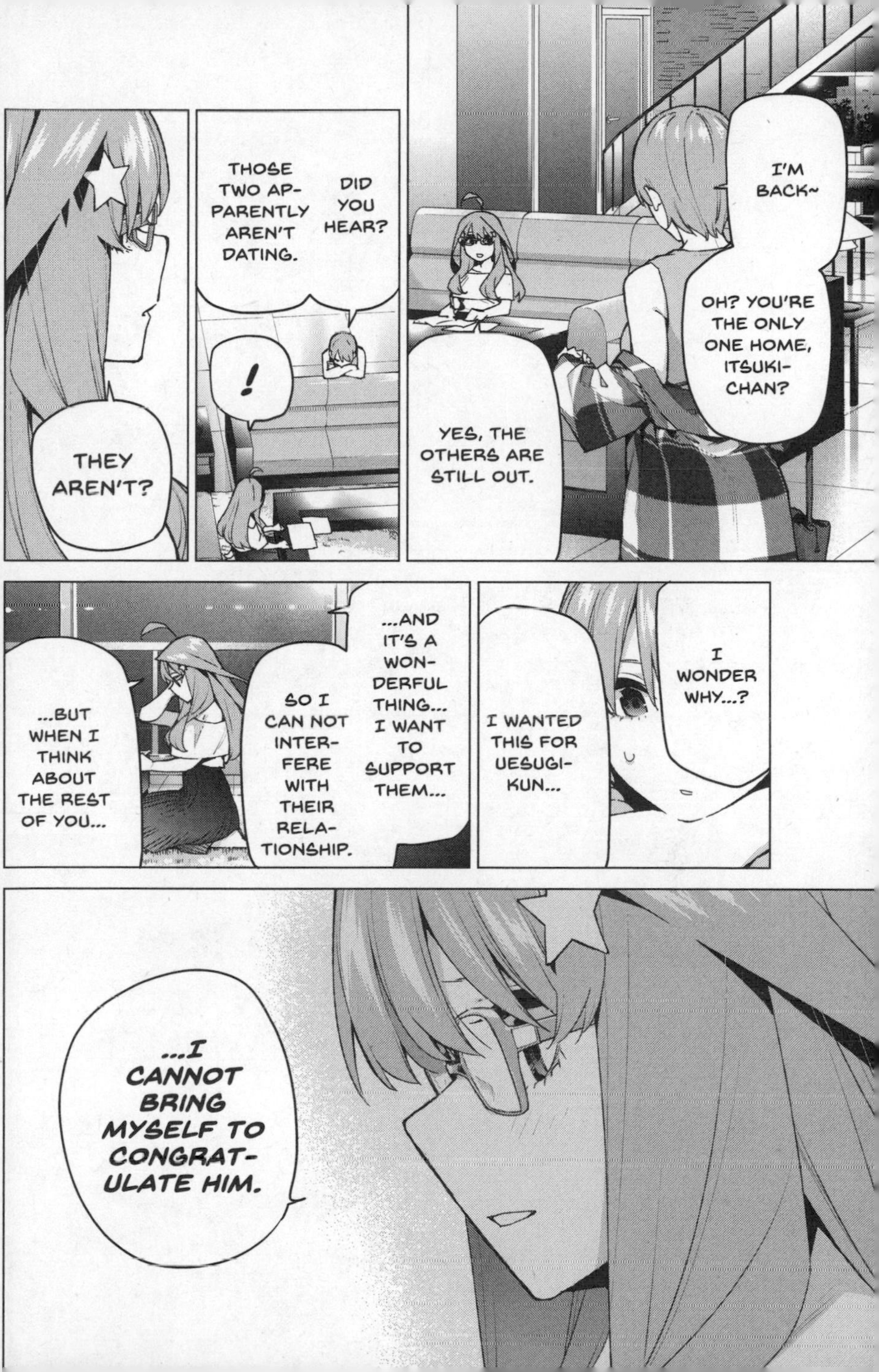
I'M BACK~
OH? YOU'RE THE ONLY ONE HOME, ITSUKI-CHAN?
YES, THE OTHERS ARE STILL OUT.
DID YOU HEAR?
THOSE TWO APPARENTLY AREN'T DATING.
!
THEY AREN'T?
I WONDER WHY...?
I WANTED THIS FOR UESUGI-KUN...
...AND IT'S A WONDERFUL THING... I WANT TO SUPPORT THEM...
SO I CAN NOT INTERFERE WITH THEIR RELATIONSHIP.
...BUT WHEN I THINK ABOUT THE REST OF YOU...
...I CANNOT BRING MYSELF TO CONGRATULATE HIM.

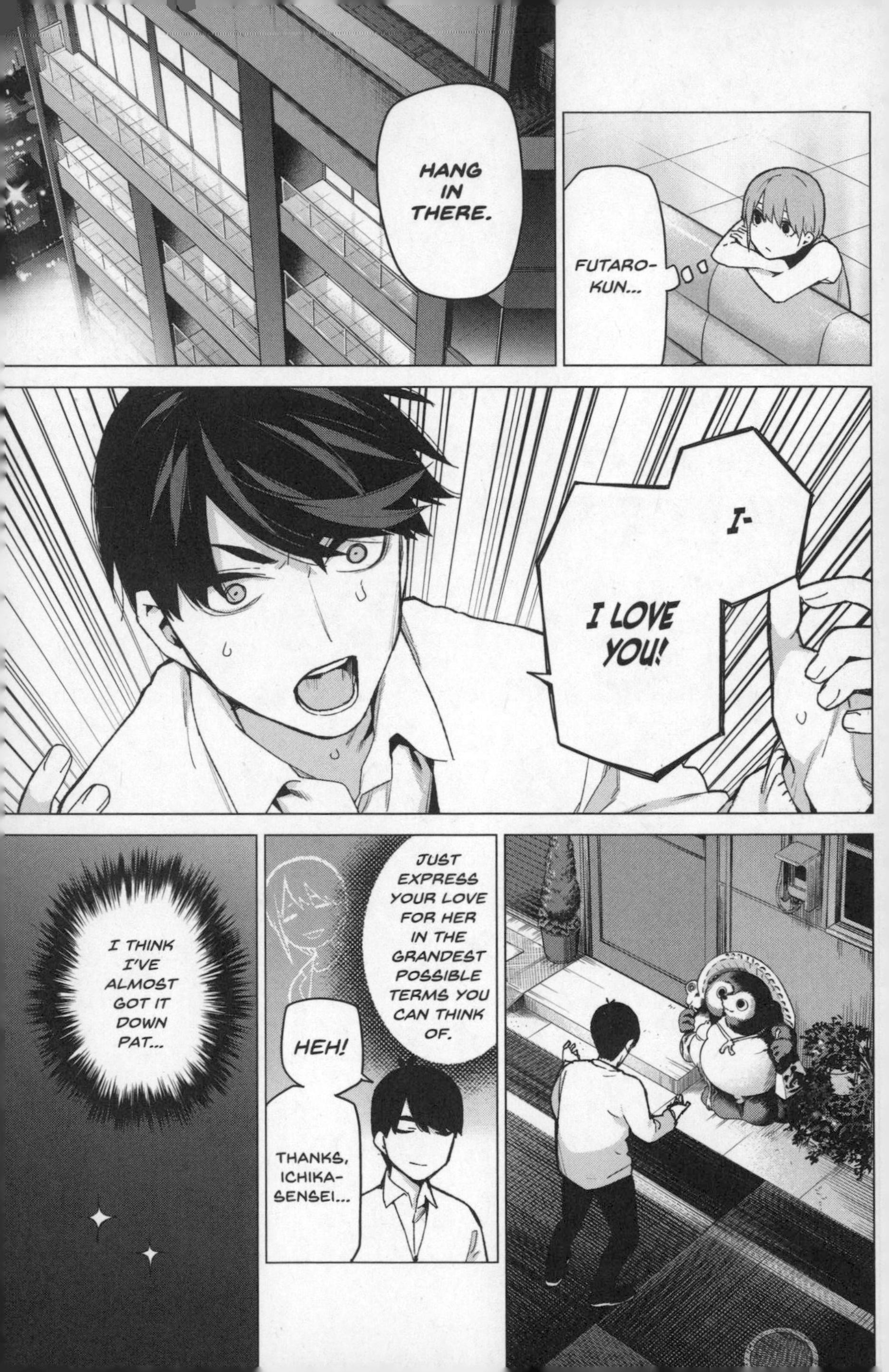
FUTARO-KUN...
HANG IN THERE.
I-
I LOVE YOU!
JUST EXPRESS YOUR LOVE FOR HER IN THE GRANDEST POSSIBLE TERMS YOU CAN THINK OF.
HEH!
THANKS, ICHIKA-SENSEI...
I THINK I'VE ALMOST GOT IT DOWN PAT...

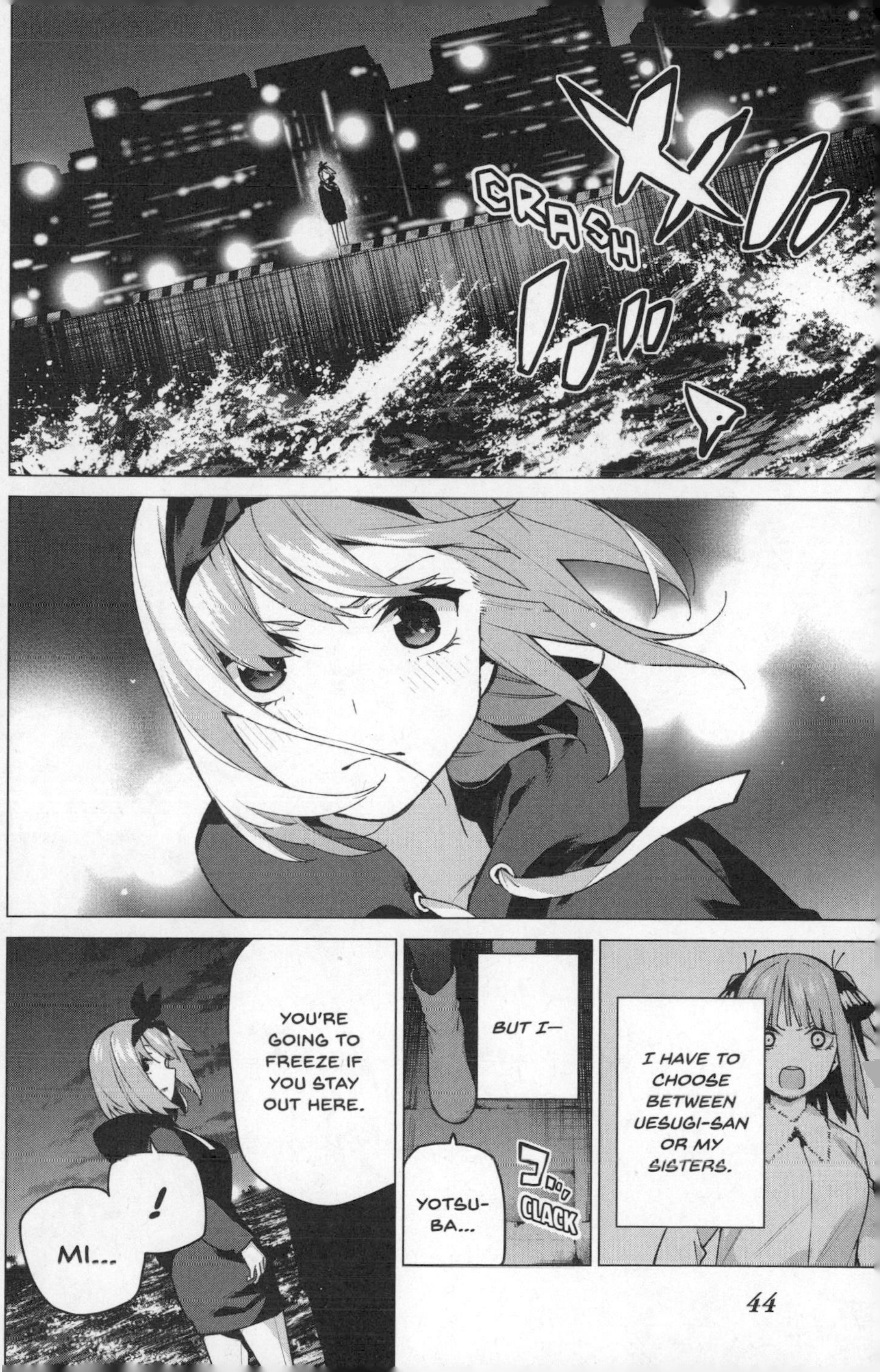
CRASH
I HAVE TO CHOOSE BETWEEN UESUGI-SAN OR MY SISTERS.
BUT I—
CLACK
YOTSU-BA...
YOU'RE GOING TO FREEZE IF YOU STAY OUT HERE.
!
MI...

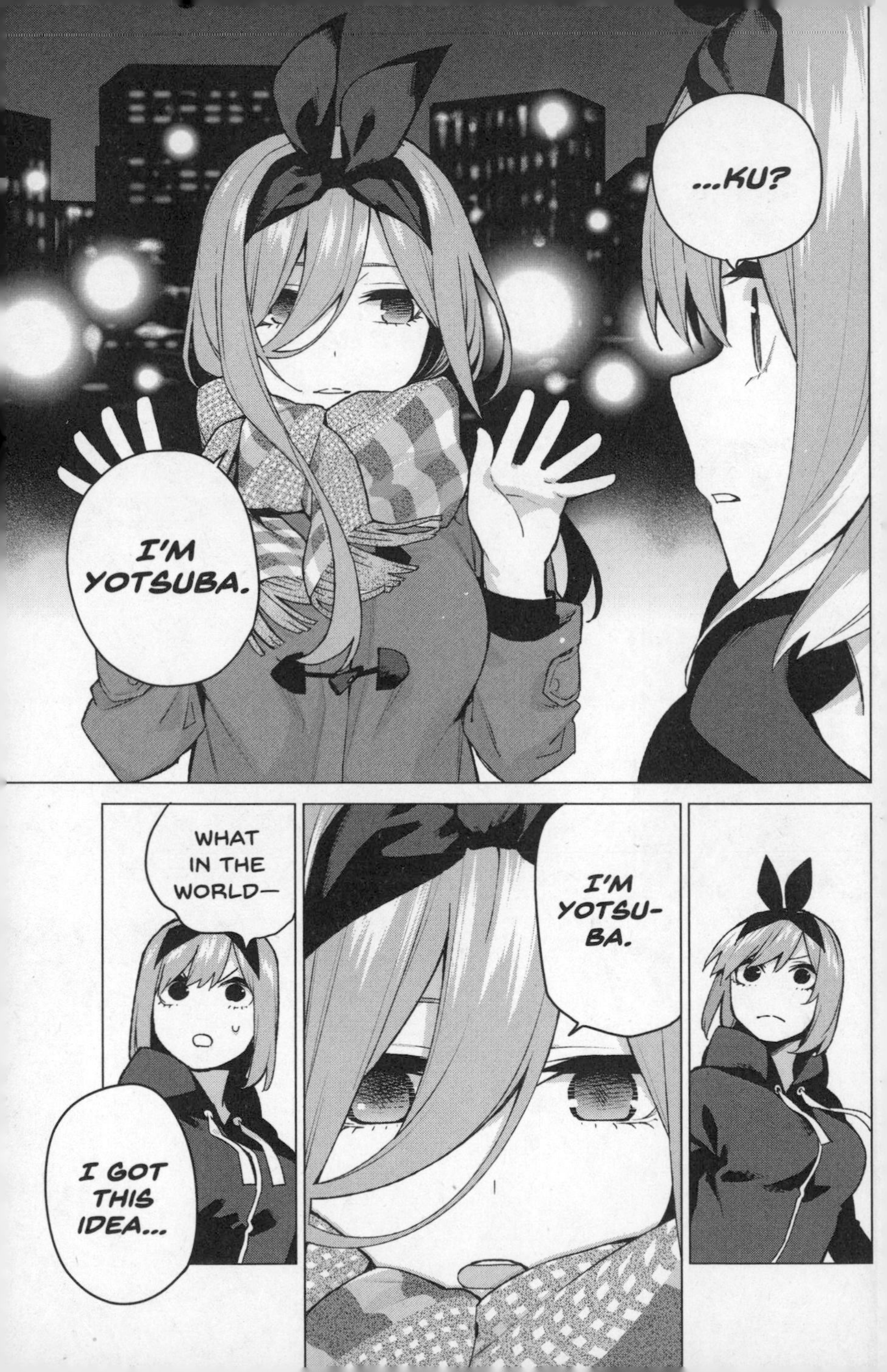
...KU?
I'M YOTSUBA.
I'M YOTSU-BA.
WHAT IN THE WORLD—
I GOT THIS IDEA...

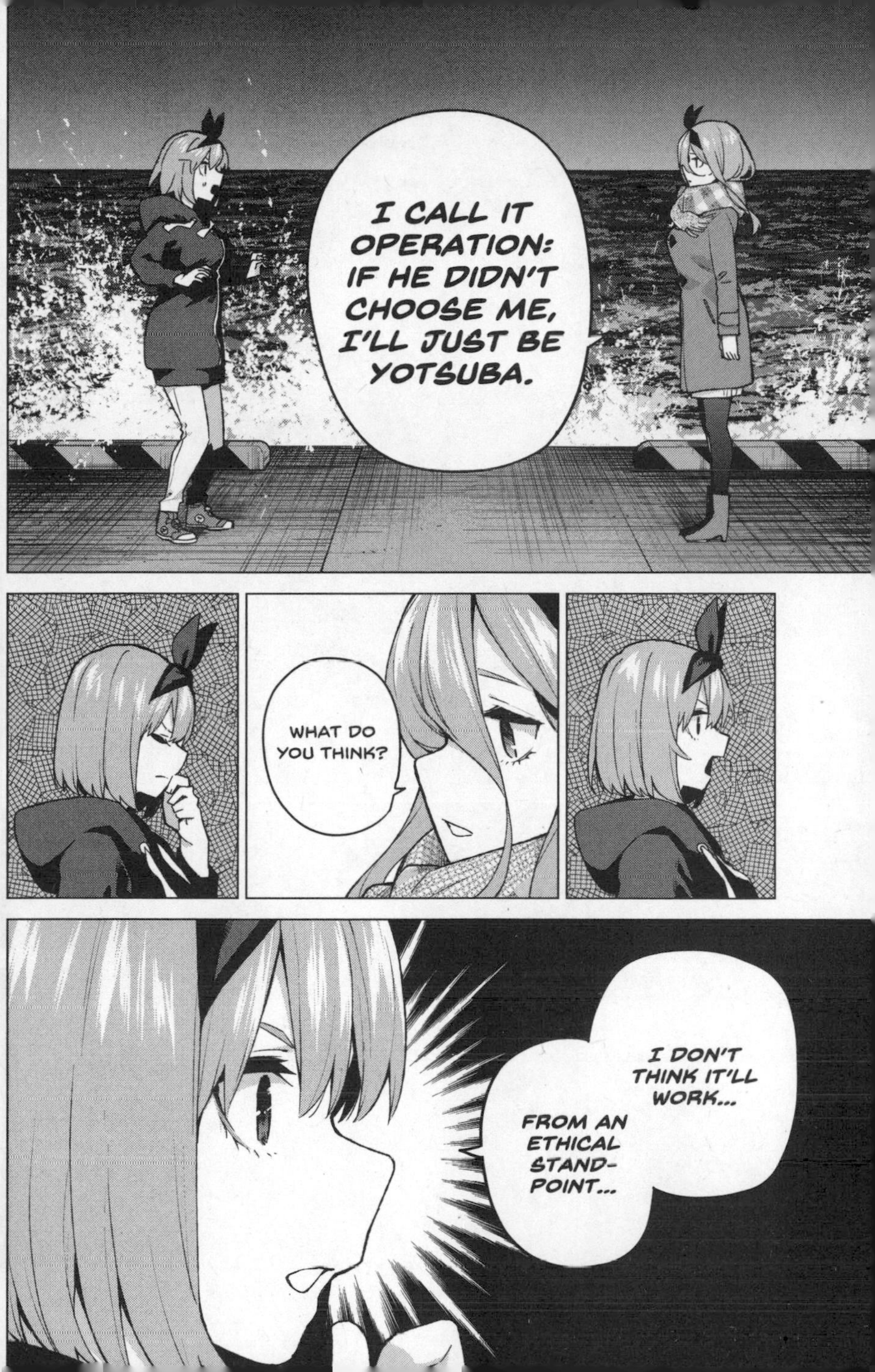
I CALL IT OPERATION: IF HE DIDN'T CHOOSE ME, I'LL JUST BE YOTSUBA.
WHAT DO YOU THINK?
I DON'T THINK IT'LL WORK...
FROM AN ETHICAL STAND-POINT...

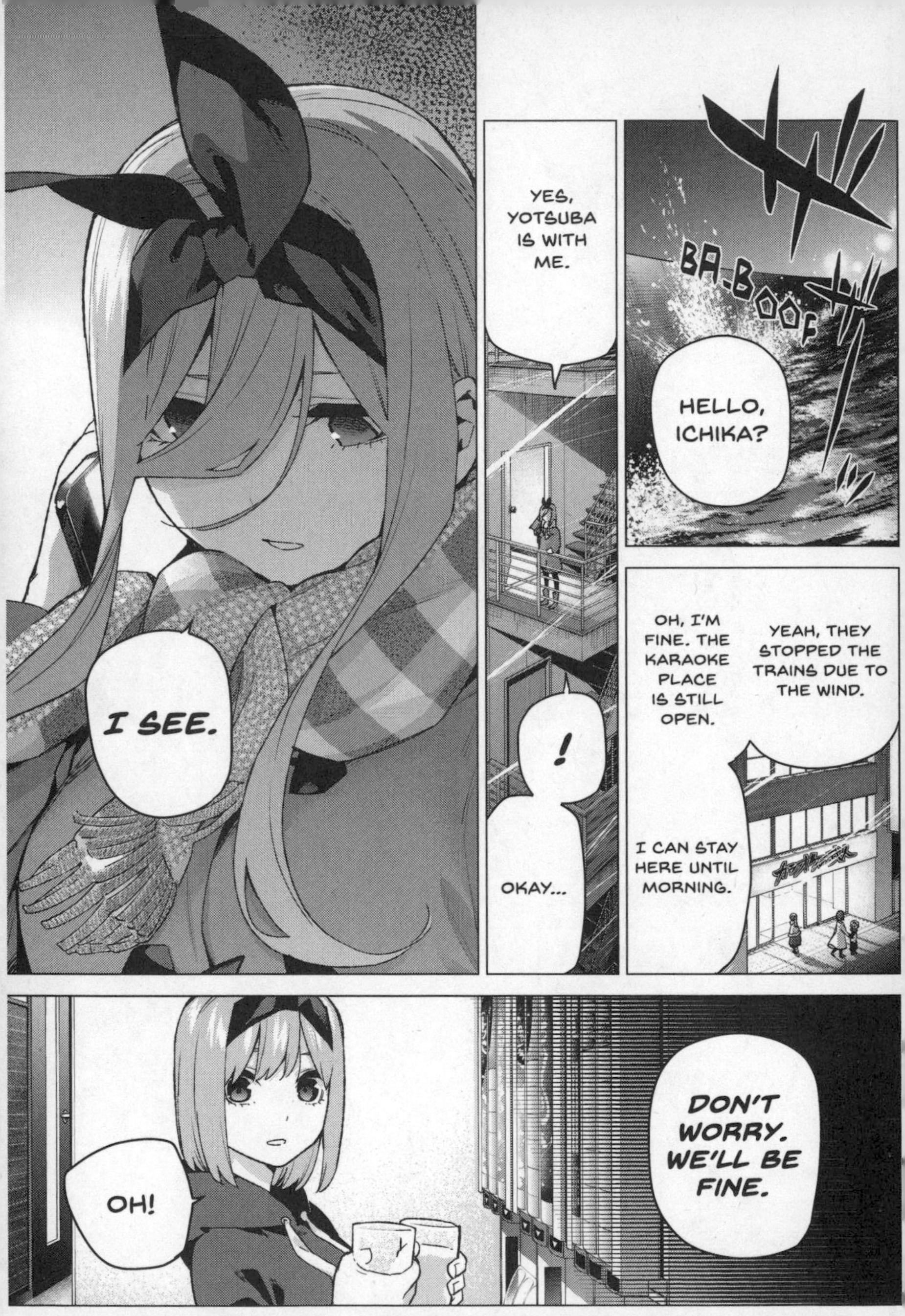
BA-BOOF
HELLO, ICHIKA?
YEAH, THEY STOPPED THE TRAINS DUE TO THE WIND.
OH, I'M FINE. THE KARAOKE PLACE IS STILL OPEN.
I CAN STAY HERE UNTIL MORNING.
YES, YOTSUBA IS WITH ME.
!
OKAY...
I SEE.
DON'T WORRY. WE'LL BE FINE.
OH!

CHAPTER 116 FIVE HOURS, ONE ROOM

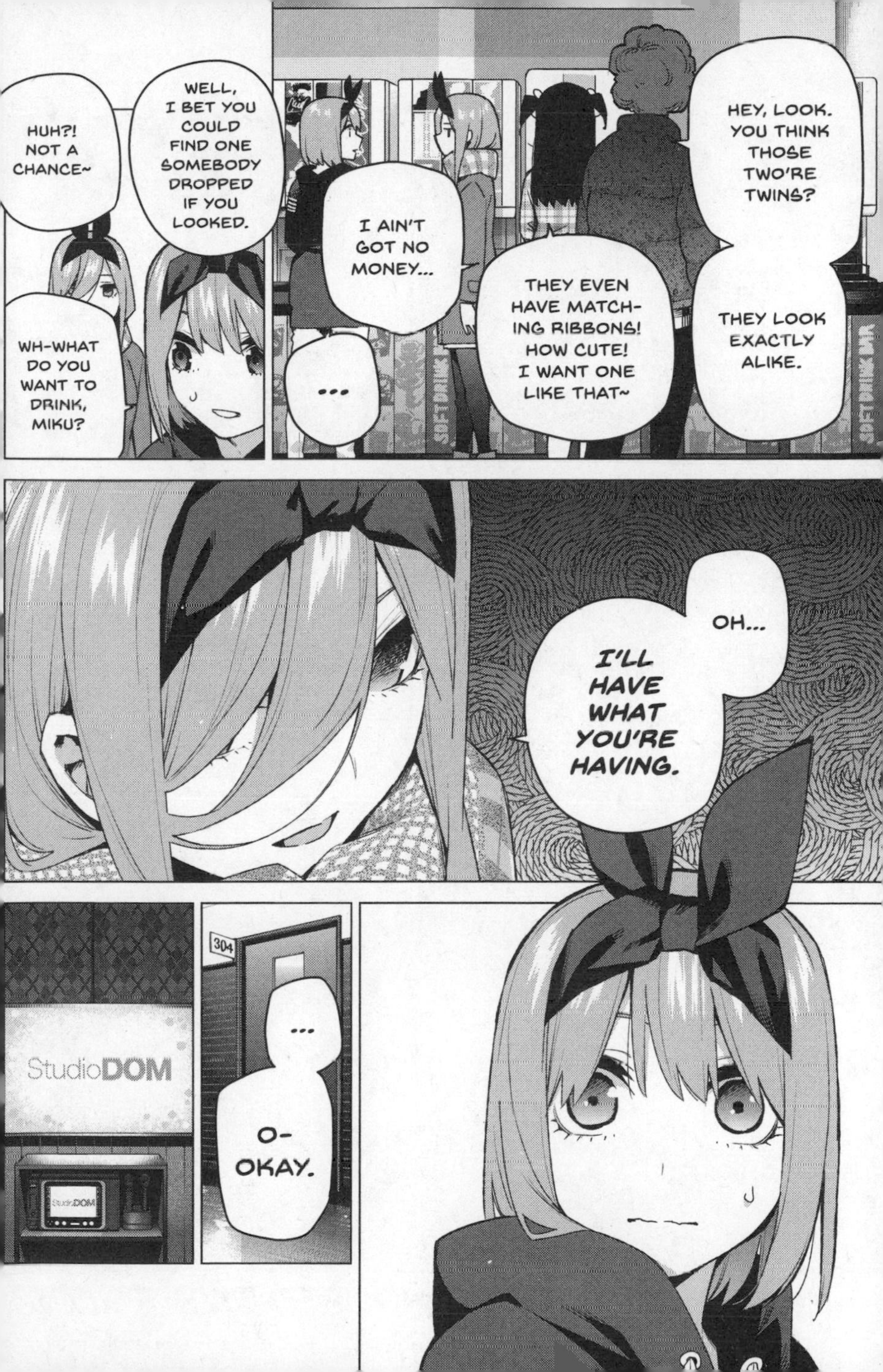
HEY, LOOK. YOU THINK THOSE TWO'RE TWINS?
THEY LOOK EXACTLY ALIKE.
THEY EVEN HAVE MATCHING RIBBONS! HOW CUTE! I WANT ONE LIKE THAT~
I AIN'T GOT NO MONEY...
...
WELL, I BET YOU COULD FIND ONE SOMEBODY DROPPED IF YOU LOOKED.
HUH?! NOT A CHANCE~
WH-WHAT DO YOU WANT TO DRINK, MIKU?
OH... I'LL HAVE WHAT YOU'RE HAVING.
304
...
O-OKAY.
StudioDOM
StudioDOM

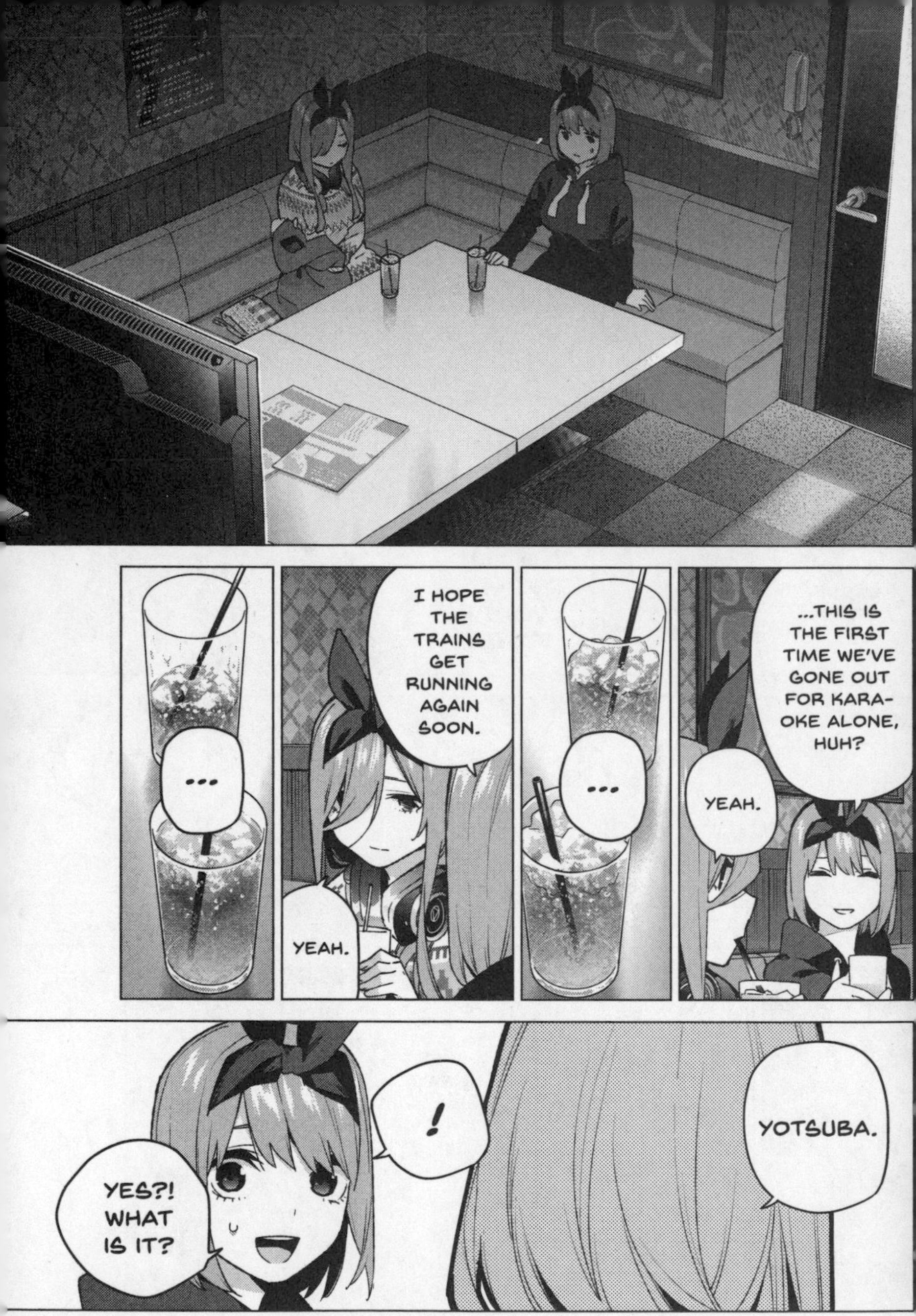
...THIS IS THE FIRST TIME WE'VE GONE OUT FOR KARA-OKE ALONE, HUH?
YEAH.
...
I HOPE THE TRAINS GET RUNNING AGAIN SOON.
YEAH.
...
YOTSUBA.
!
YES?! WHAT IS IT?

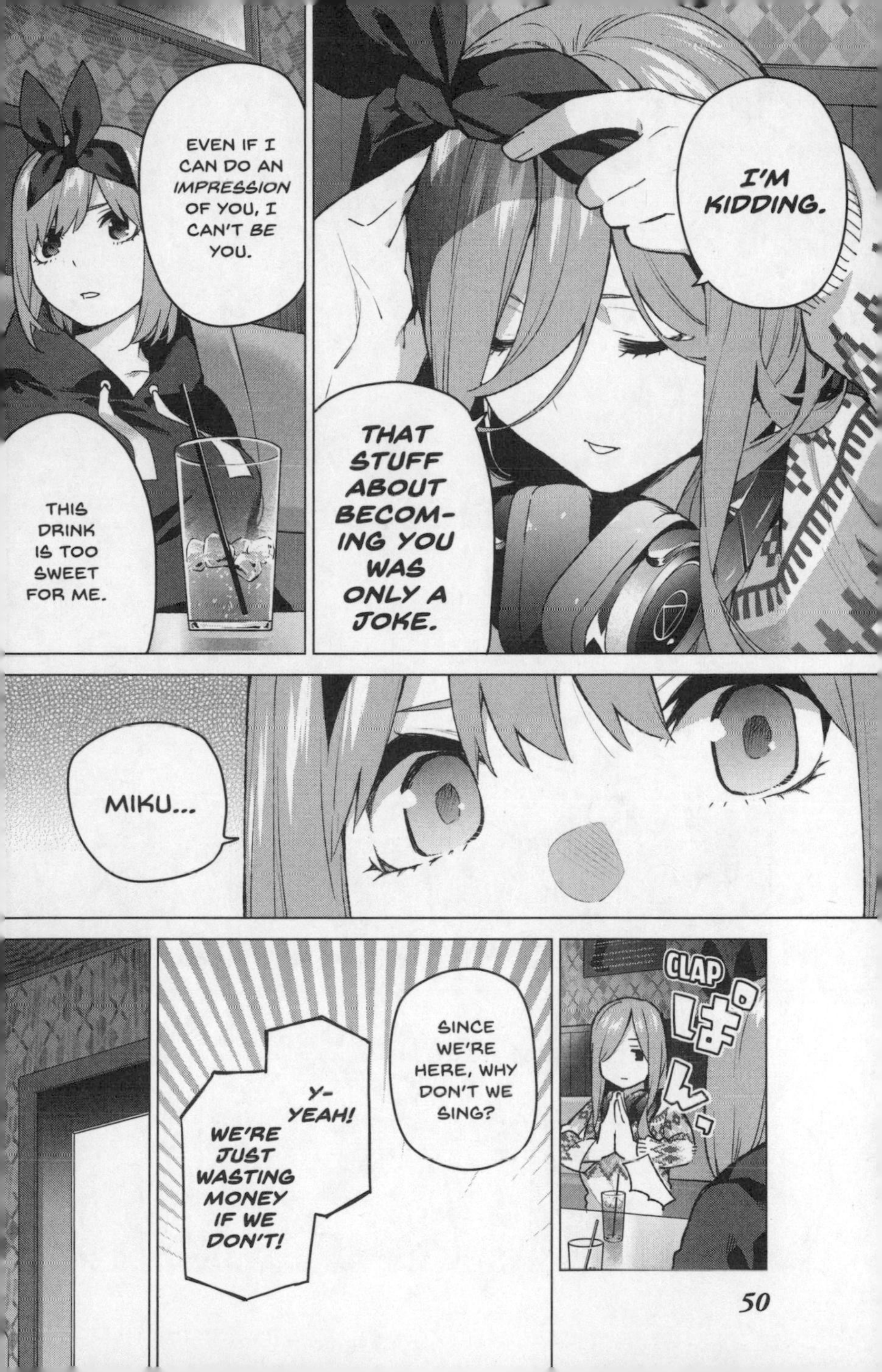
I'M KIDDING.
THAT STUFF ABOUT BECOMING YOU WAS ONLY A JOKE.
EVEN IF I CAN DO AN IMPRESSION OF YOU, I CAN'T BE YOU.
THIS DRINK IS TOO SWEET FOR ME.
MIKU...
CLAP
ぽん,
SINCE WE'RE HERE, WHY DON'T WE SING?
Y-YEAH! WE'RE JUST WASTING MONEY IF WE DON'T!

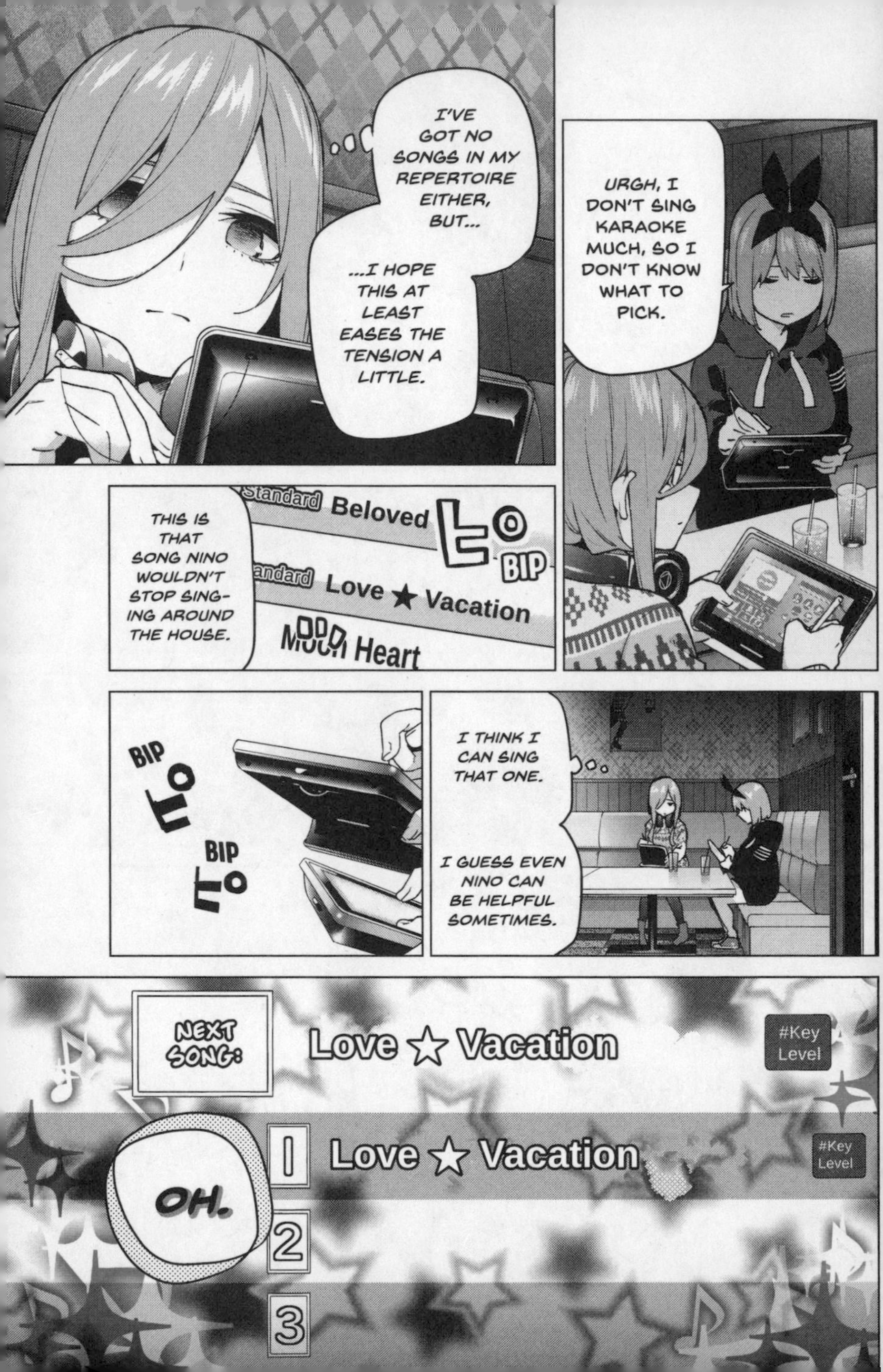

URGH, I DON'T SING KARAOKE MUCH, SO I DON'T KNOW WHAT TO PICK.
I'VE GOT NO SONGS IN MY REPERTOIRE EITHER, BUT...
...I HOPE THIS AT LEAST EASES THE TENSION A LITTLE.
Standard Beloved
BIP
Standard Love ★ Vacation
Heart
THIS IS THAT SONG NINO WOULDN'T STOP SING-ING AROUND THE HOUSE.
I THINK I CAN SING THAT ONE.
I GUESS EVEN NINO CAN BE HELPFUL SOMETIMES.
BIP
BIP
NEXT SONG:
Love ☆ Vacation
#Key Level
OH.
1
Love ☆ Vacation
#Key Level
2
3

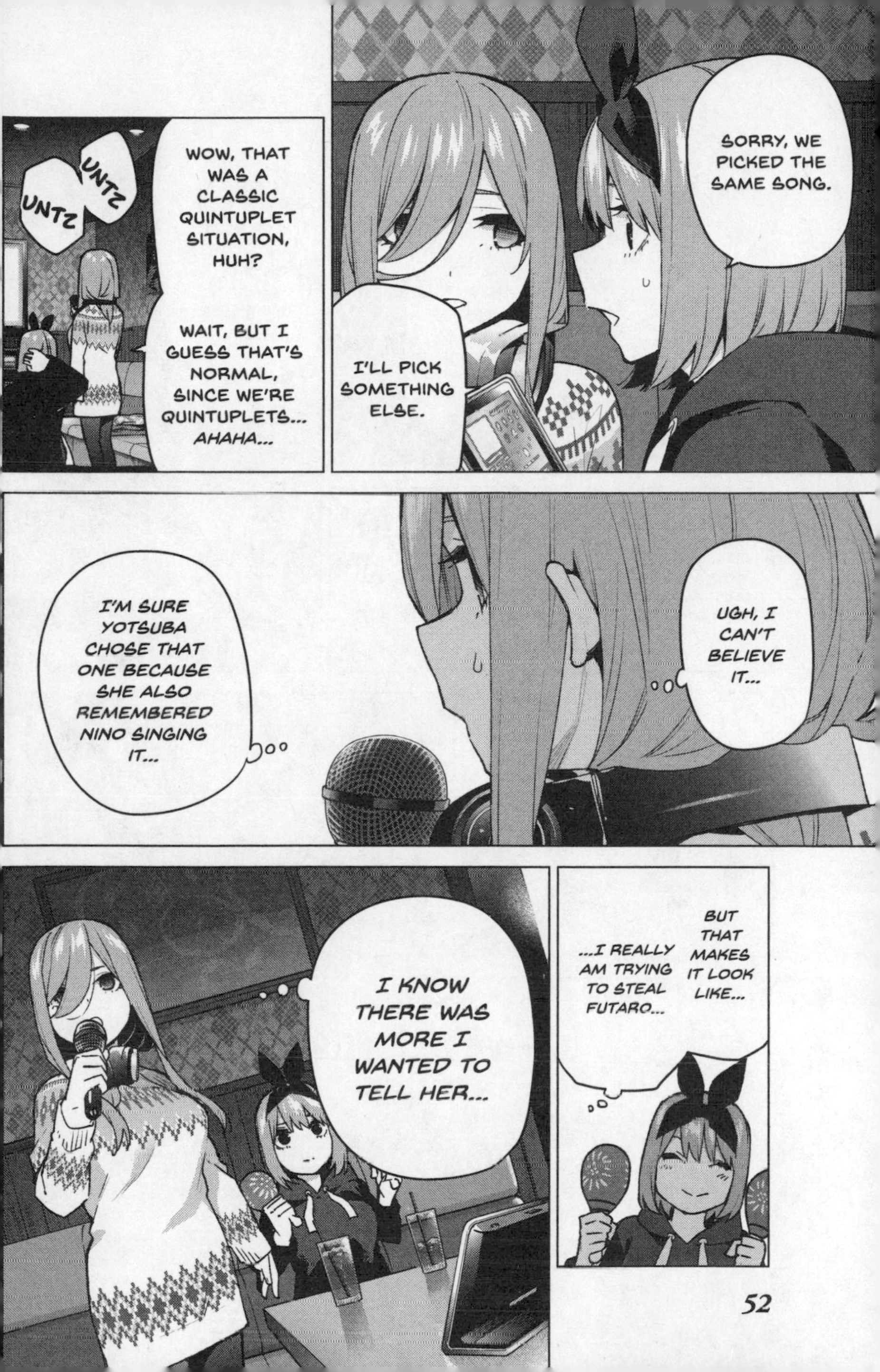
SORRY, WE PICKED THE SAME SONG.
I'LL PICK SOMETHING ELSE.
UNTZ
UNTZ
WOW, THAT WAS A CLASSIC QUINTUPLET SITUATION, HUH?
WAIT, BUT I GUESS THAT'S NORMAL, SINCE WE'RE QUINTUPLETS... AHAHA...
UGH, I CAN'T BELIEVE IT...
I'M SURE YOTSUBA CHOSE THAT ONE BECAUSE SHE ALSO REMEMBERED NINO SINGING IT...
BUT THAT MAKES IT LOOK LIKE...
...I REALLY AM TRYING TO STEAL FUTARO...
I KNOW THERE WAS MORE I WANTED TO TELL HER...

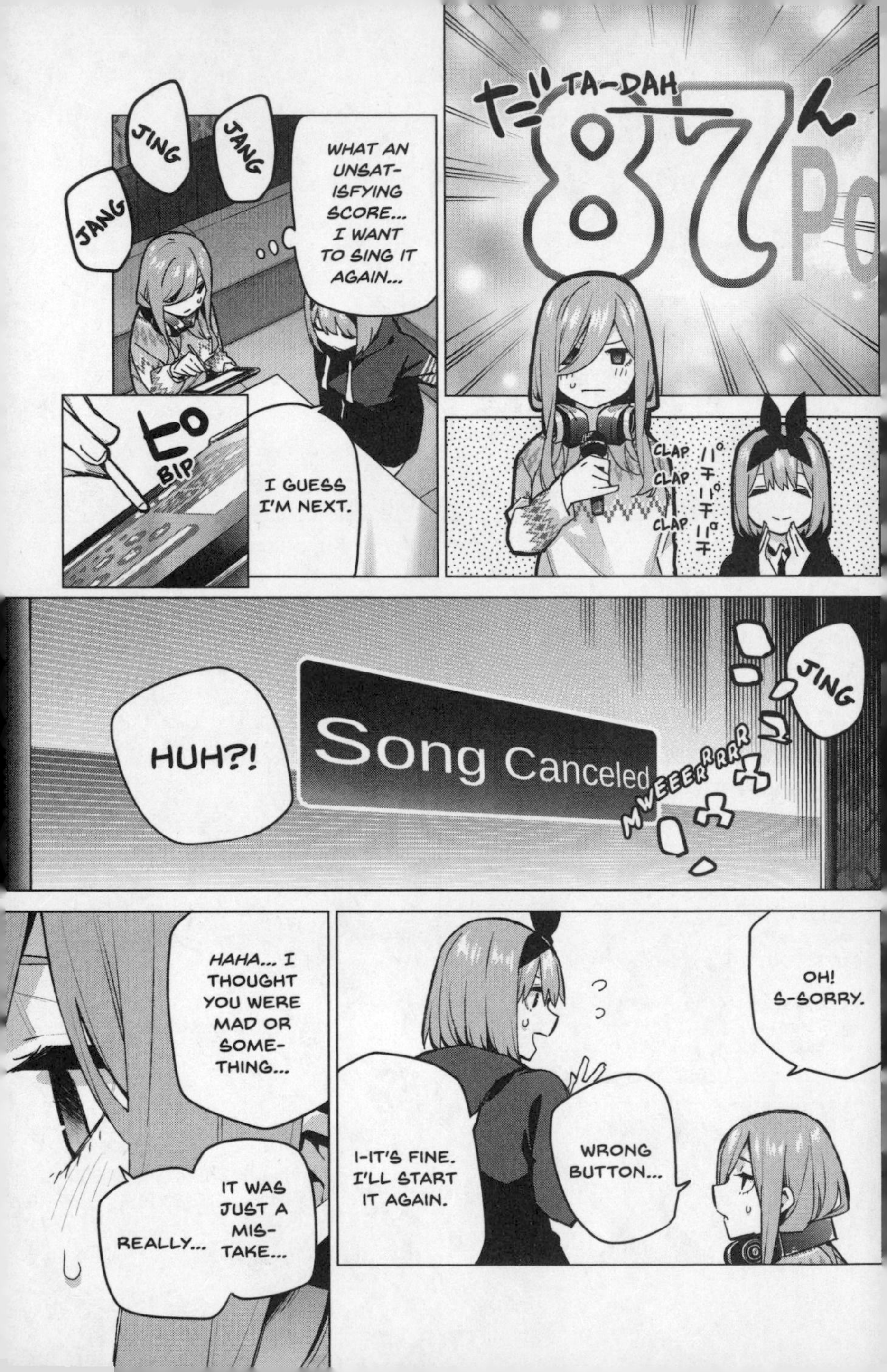
TA-DAH
87 Po
JANG
JING
JANG
WHAT AN UNSATISFYING SCORE... I WANT TO SING IT AGAIN...
CLAP CLAP CLAP
BIP
I GUESS I'M NEXT.
JING
MWEEERRRR
Song Canceled
HUH?!
OH! S-SORRY.
WRONG BUTTON...
I-IT'S FINE. I'LL START IT AGAIN.
HAHA... I THOUGHT YOU WERE MAD OR SOMETHING...
IT WAS JUST A MISTAKE...
REALLY...

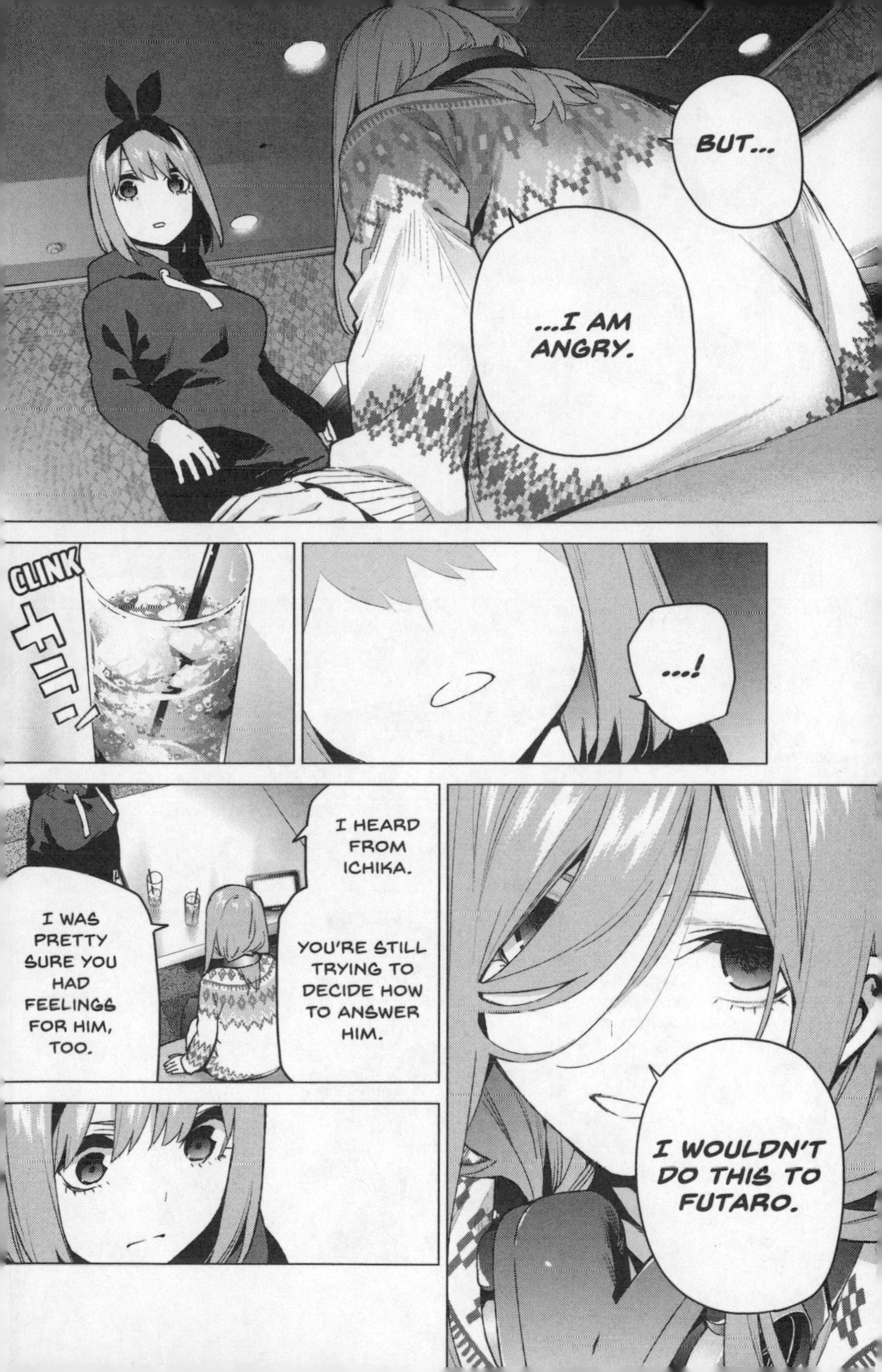
BUT...
...I AM ANGRY.
...!
CLINK
I WOULDN'T DO THIS TO FUTARO.
I HEARD FROM ICHIKA.
YOU'RE STILL TRYING TO DECIDE HOW TO ANSWER HIM.
I WAS PRETTY SURE YOU HAD FEELINGS FOR HIM, TOO.

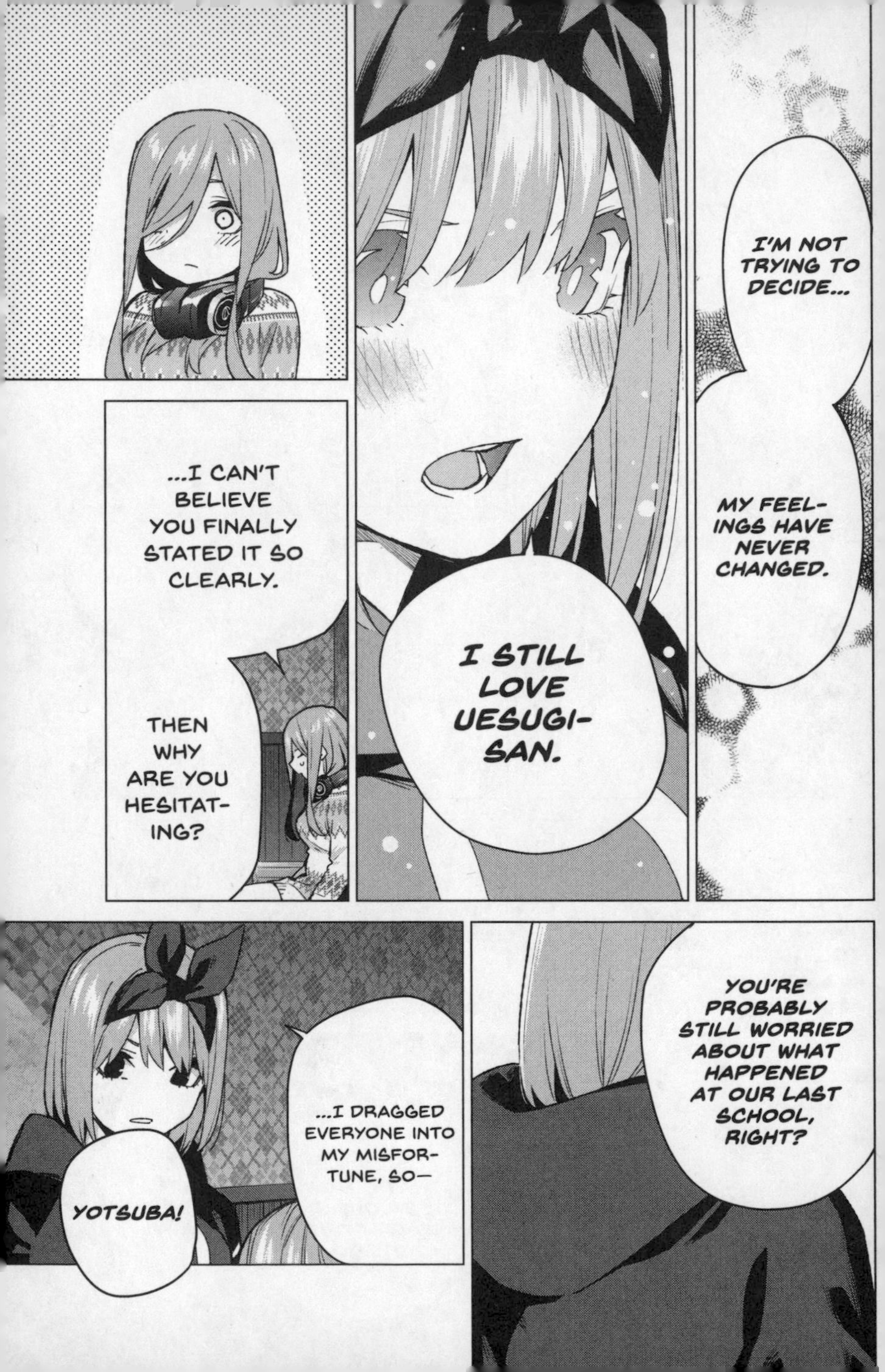
I'M NOT TRYING TO DECIDE...
MY FEEL- INGS HAVE NEVER CHANGED.
I STILL LOVE UESUGI- SAN.
...I CAN'T BELIEVE YOU FINALLY STATED IT SO CLEARLY.
THEN WHY ARE YOU HESITAT- ING?
YOU'RE PROBABLY STILL WORRIED ABOUT WHAT HAPPENED AT OUR LAST SCHOOL, RIGHT?
...I DRAGGED EVERYONE INTO MY MISFOR- TUNE, SO—
YOTSUBA!

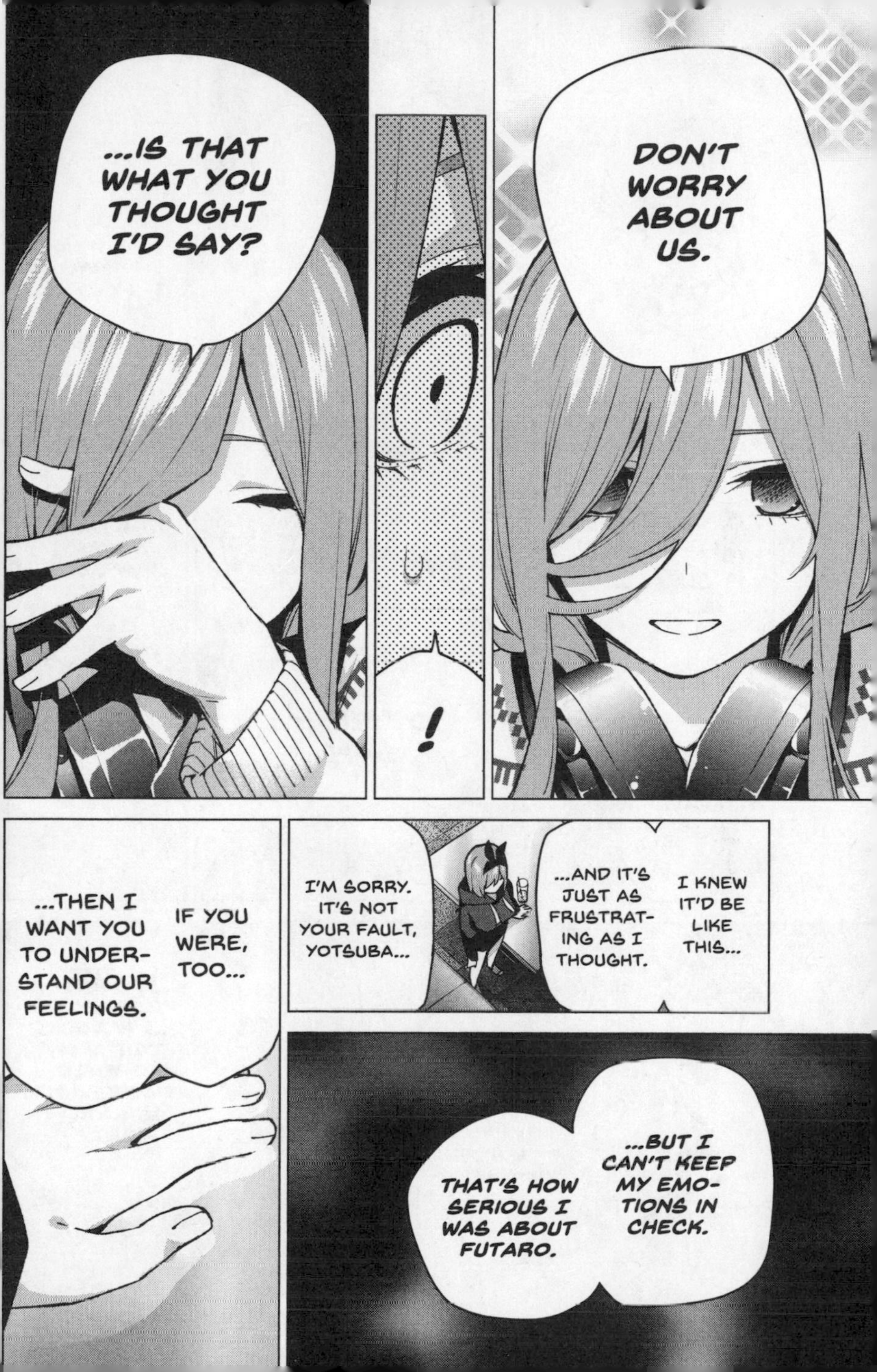
DON'T WORRY ABOUT US.
!
...IS THAT WHAT YOU THOUGHT I'D SAY?
I KNEW IT'D BE LIKE THIS...
...AND IT'S JUST AS FRUSTRATING AS I THOUGHT.
I'M SORRY. IT'S NOT YOUR FAULT, YOTSUBA...
...BUT I CAN'T KEEP MY EMOTIONS IN CHECK.
THAT'S HOW SERIOUS I WAS ABOUT FUTARO.
IF YOU WERE, TOO...
...THEN I WANT YOU TO UNDERSTAND OUR FEELINGS.

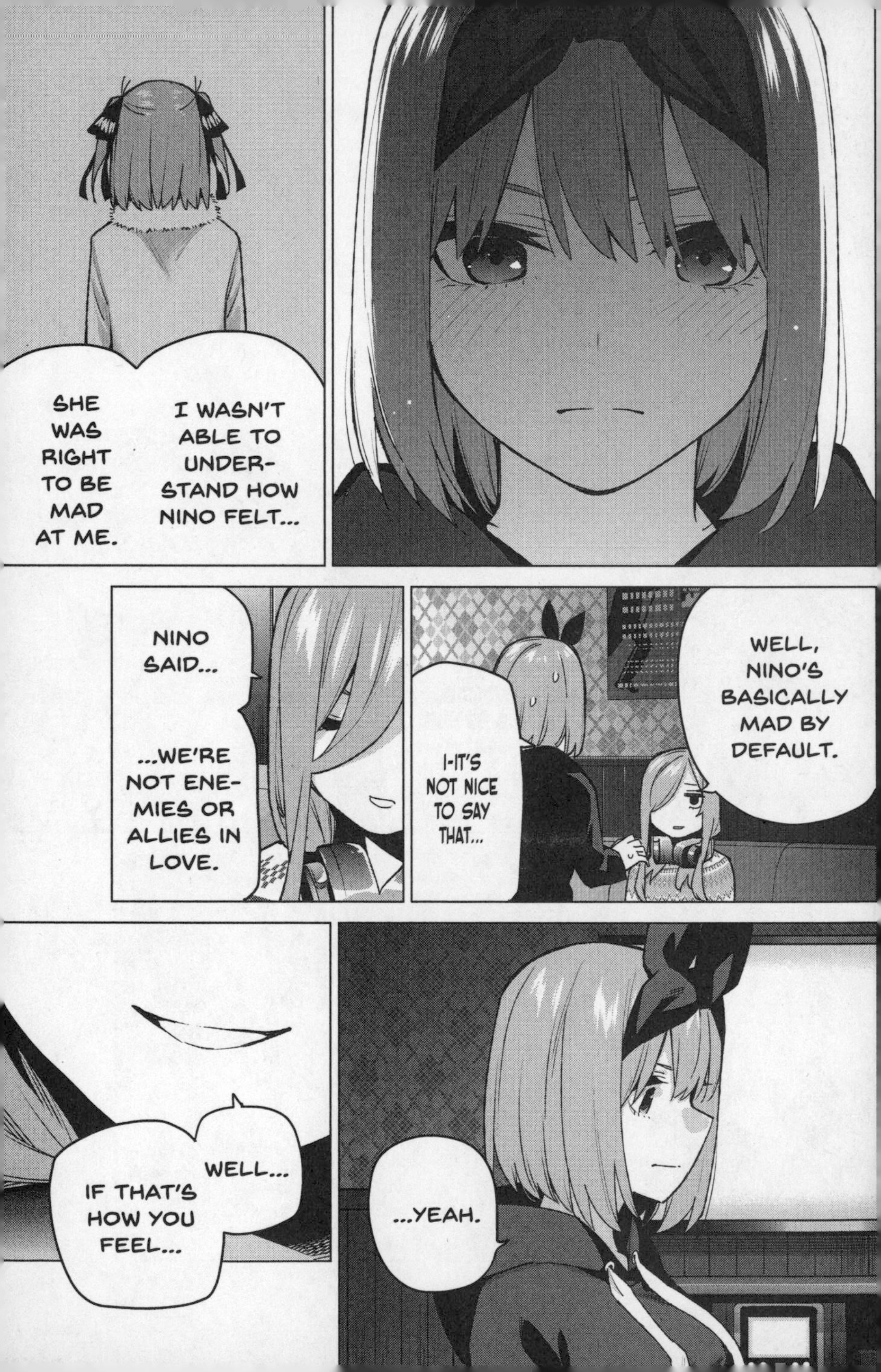
I WASN'T ABLE TO UNDERSTAND HOW NINO FELT...
SHE WAS RIGHT TO BE MAD AT ME.
WELL, NINO'S BASICALLY MAD BY DEFAULT.
I-IT'S NOT NICE TO SAY THAT...
NINO SAID...
...WE'RE NOT ENEMIES OR ALLIES IN LOVE.
...YEAH.
WELL... IF THAT'S HOW YOU FEEL...

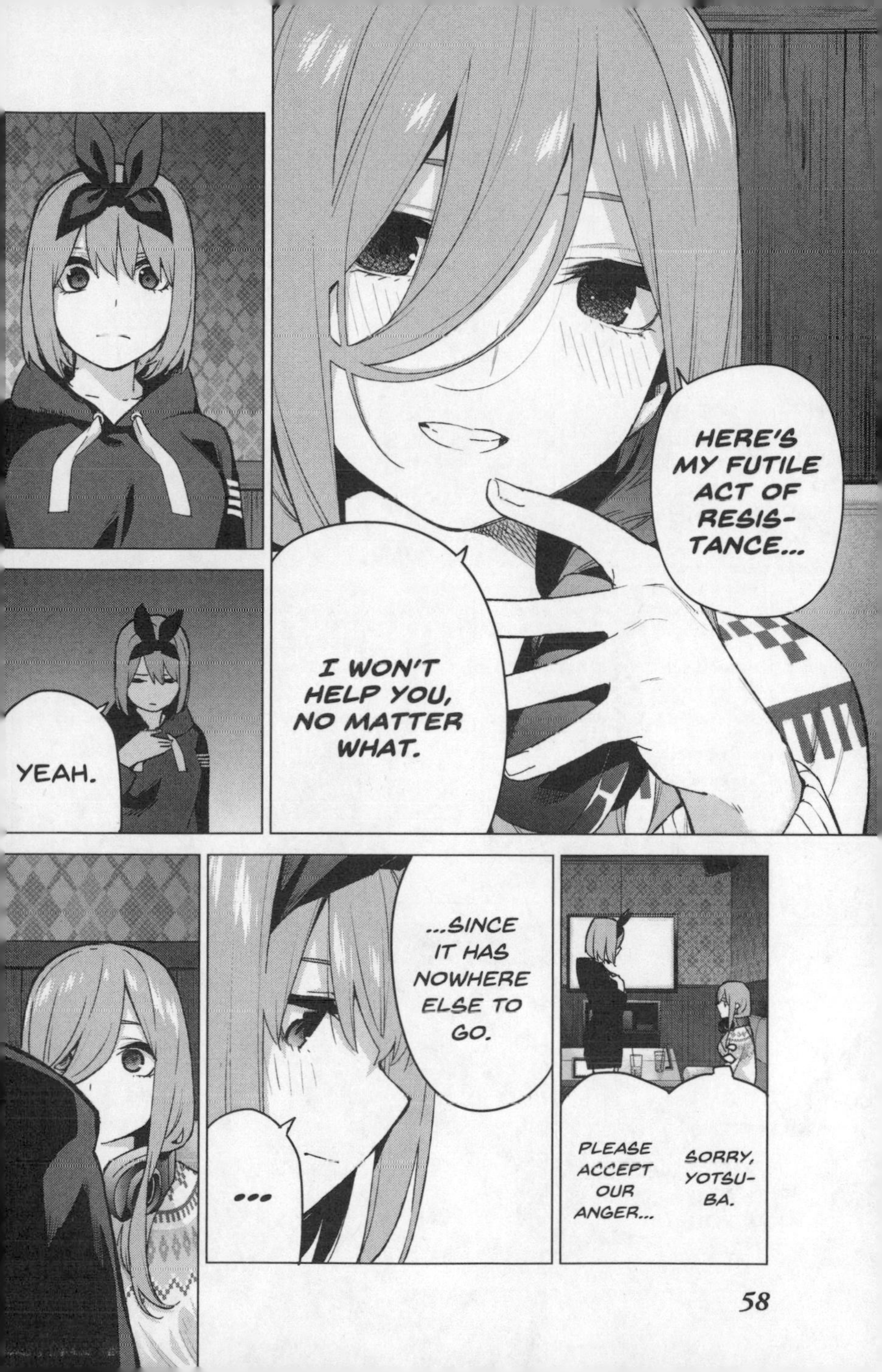
HERE'S MY FUTILE ACT OF RESISTANCE...
I WON'T HELP YOU, NO MATTER WHAT.
YEAH.
SORRY, YOTSUBA.
PLEASE ACCEPT OUR ANGER...
...SINCE IT HAS NOWHERE ELSE TO GO.
...

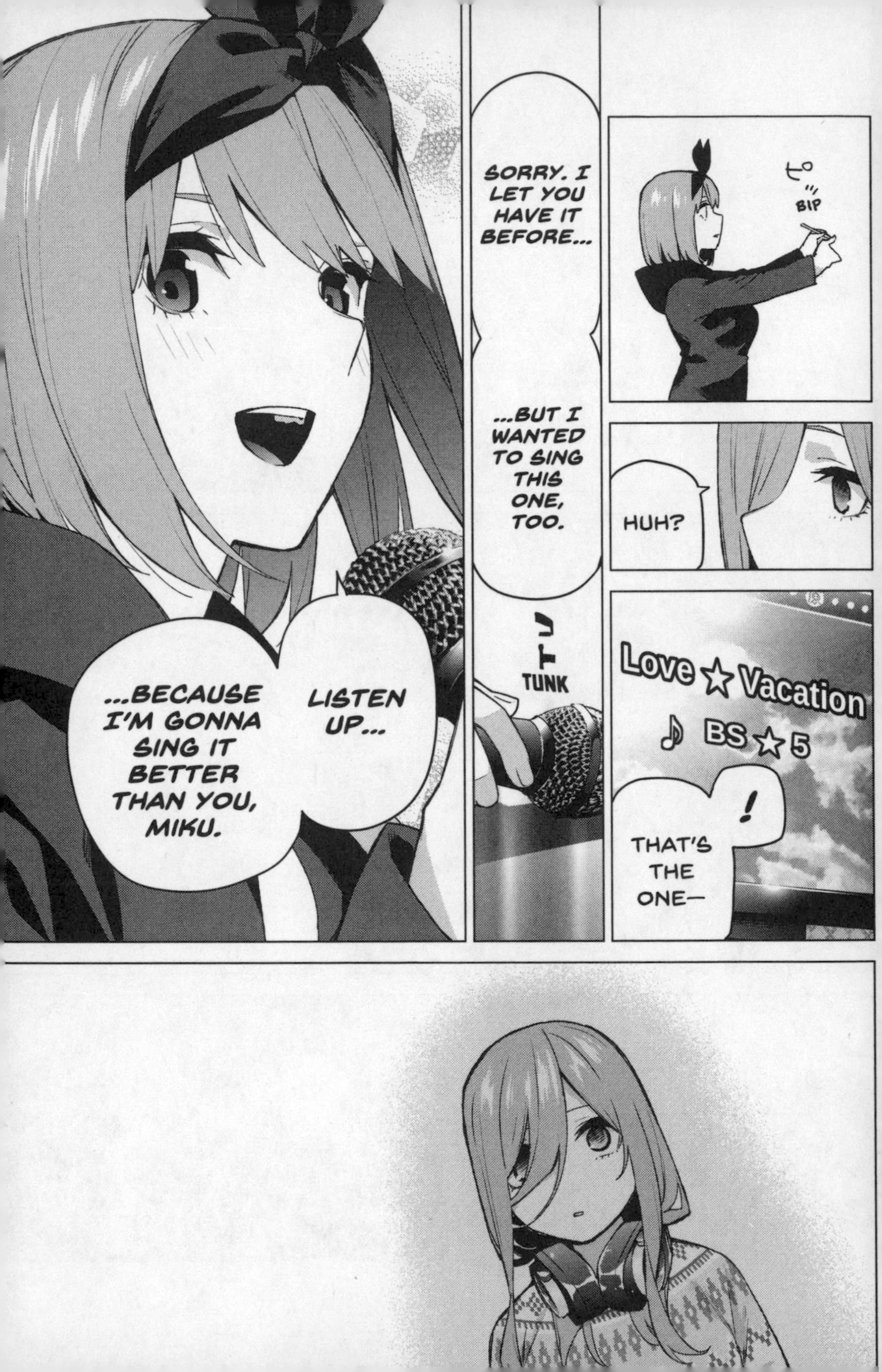
ピ
BIP
HUH?
Love ☆ Vacation
♪ BS ☆ 5
!
THAT'S THE ONE—
SORRY. I LET YOU HAVE IT BEFORE...
...BUT I WANTED TO SING THIS ONE, TOO.
TUNK
LISTEN UP...
...BECAUSE I'M GONNA SING IT BETTER THAN YOU, MIKU.

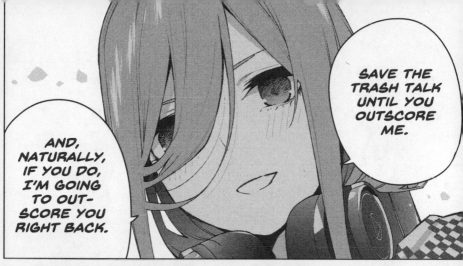

SAVE THE TRASH TALK UNTIL YOU OUTSCORE ME.

AND, NATURALLY, IF YOU DO, I'M GOING TO OUTSCORE YOU RIGHT BACK.

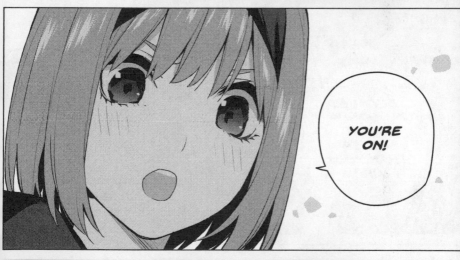

YOU'RE ON!

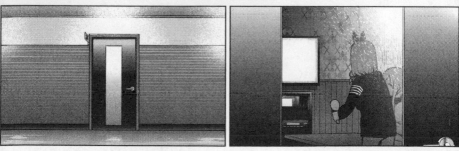

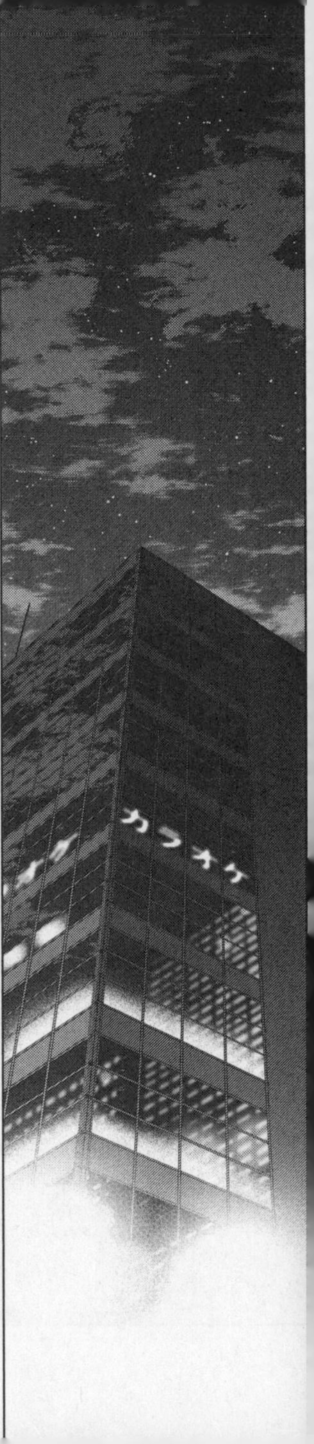

カラオケ

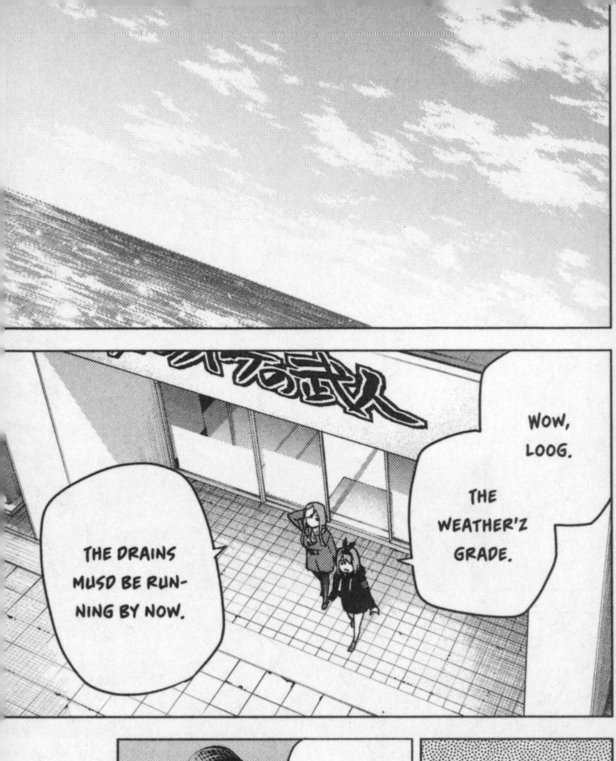

WOW, LOOG.
THE WEATHER'Z GRADE.
THE DRAINS MUSD BE RUN-NING BY NOW.
COUGH!
SINGING ALL NIGHT WRECKED OUR VOICES.
YEP! EVERYONE'S GONNA LAUGH AT US WHEN WE GET HOME.
SO WHAT DO YOU WANT TO DO?
STAY OUT?

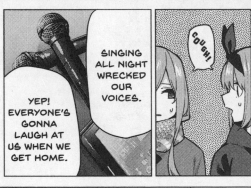

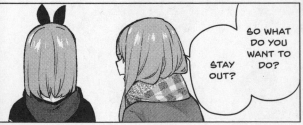

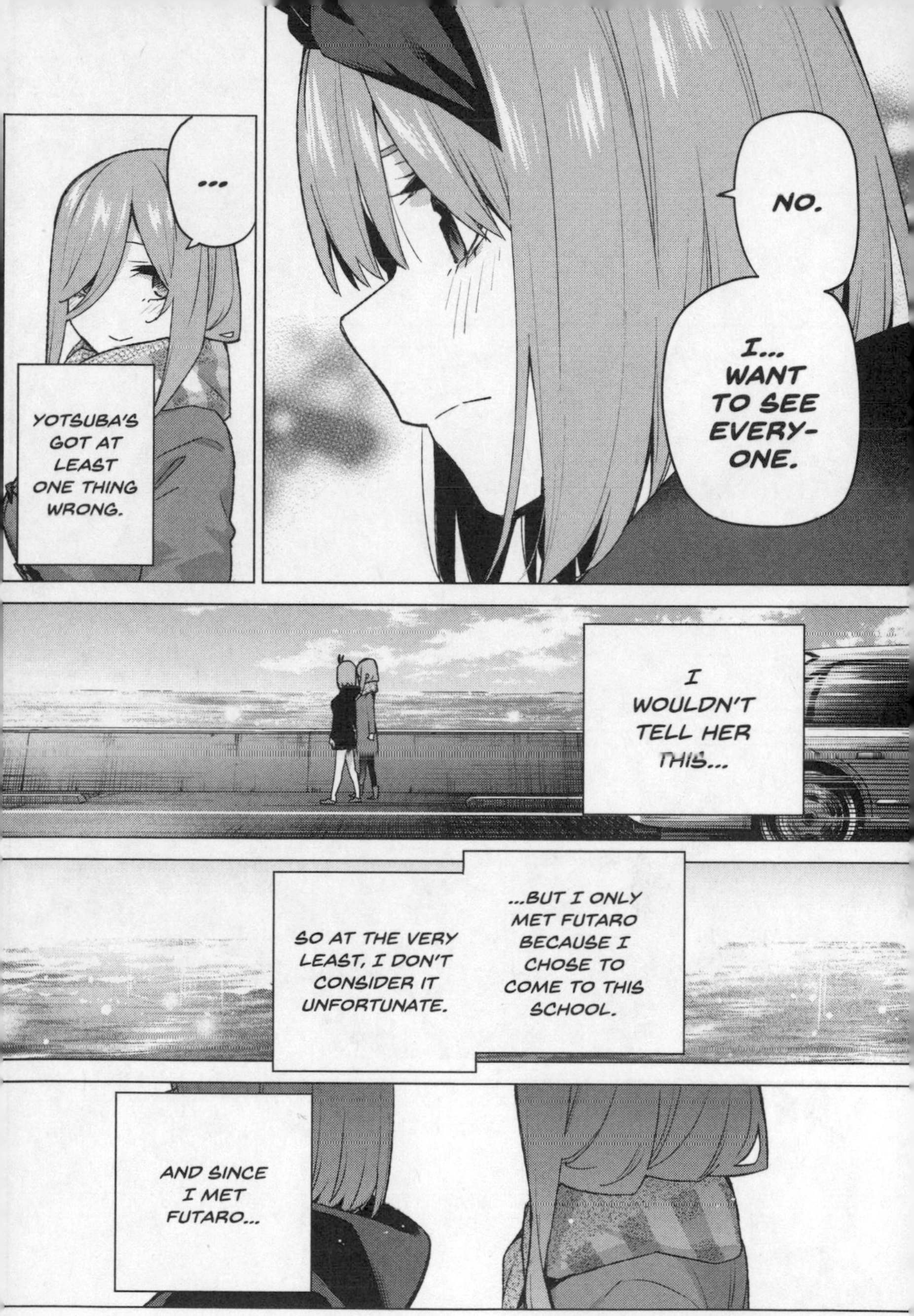
NO.
I... WANT TO SEE EVERY-ONE.
...
YOTSUBA'S GOT AT LEAST ONE THING WRONG.
I WOULDN'T TELL HER THIS...
...BUT I ONLY MET FUTARO BECAUSE I CHOSE TO COME TO THIS SCHOOL.
SO AT THE VERY LEAST, I DON'T CONSIDER IT UNFORTUNATE.
AND SINCE I MET FUTARO...

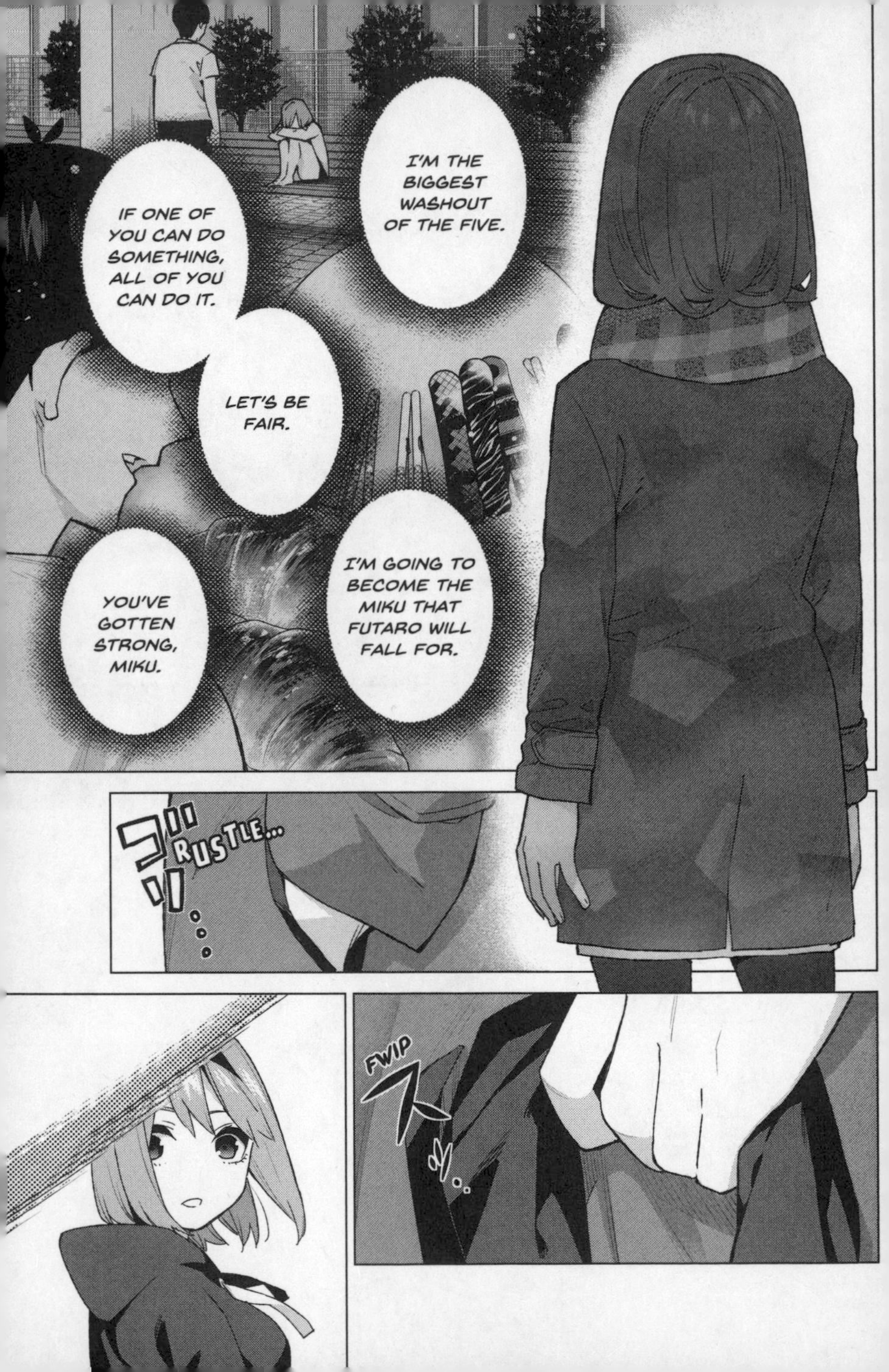
I'M THE BIGGEST WASHOUT OF THE FIVE.
IF ONE OF YOU CAN DO SOMETHING, ALL OF YOU CAN DO IT.
LET'S BE FAIR.
I'M GOING TO BECOME THE MIKU THAT FUTARO WILL FALL FOR.
YOU'VE GOTTEN STRONG, MIKU.
RUSTLE...
FWIP

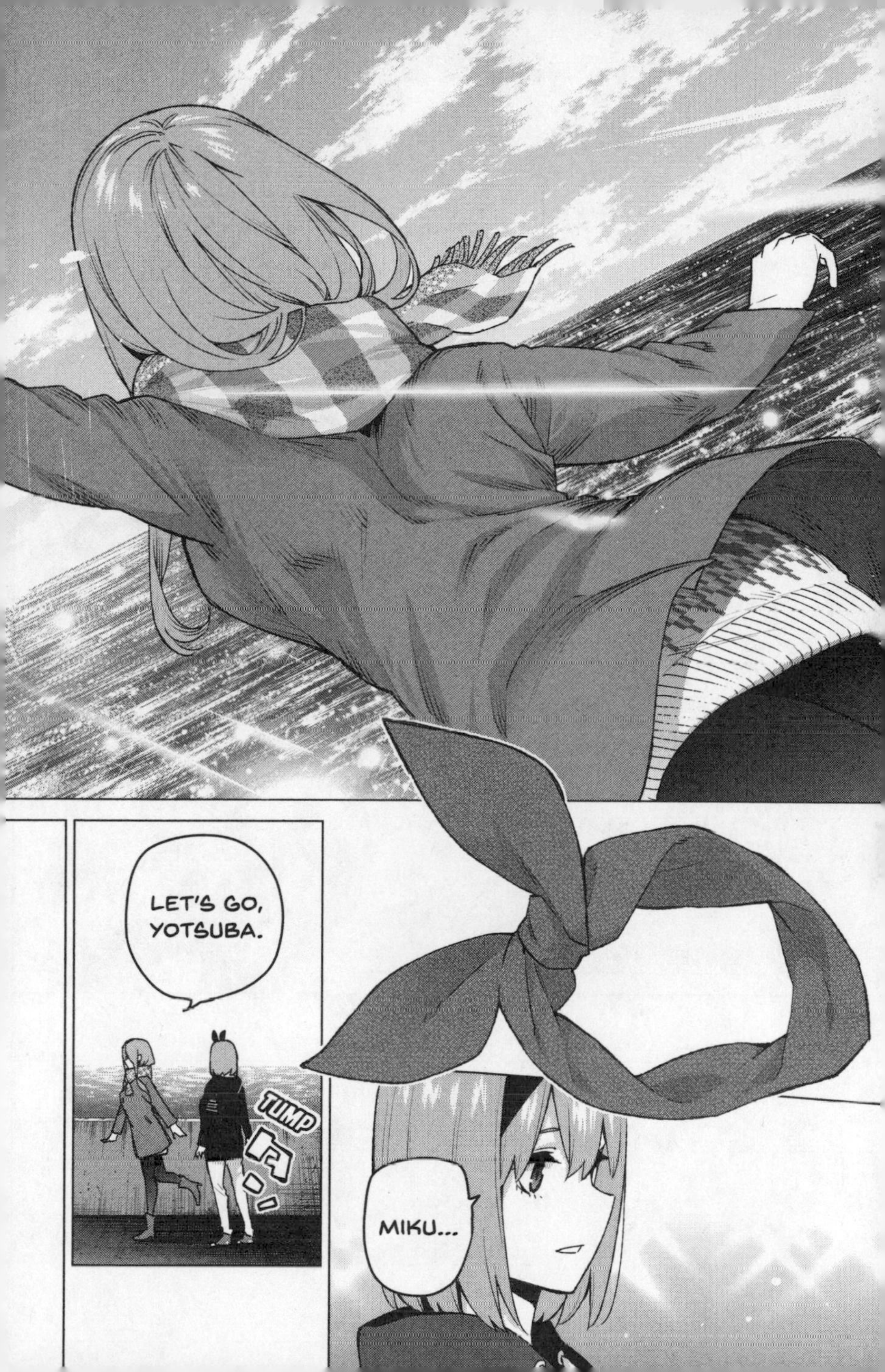
MIKU...
LET'S GO, YOTSUBA.
TUMP

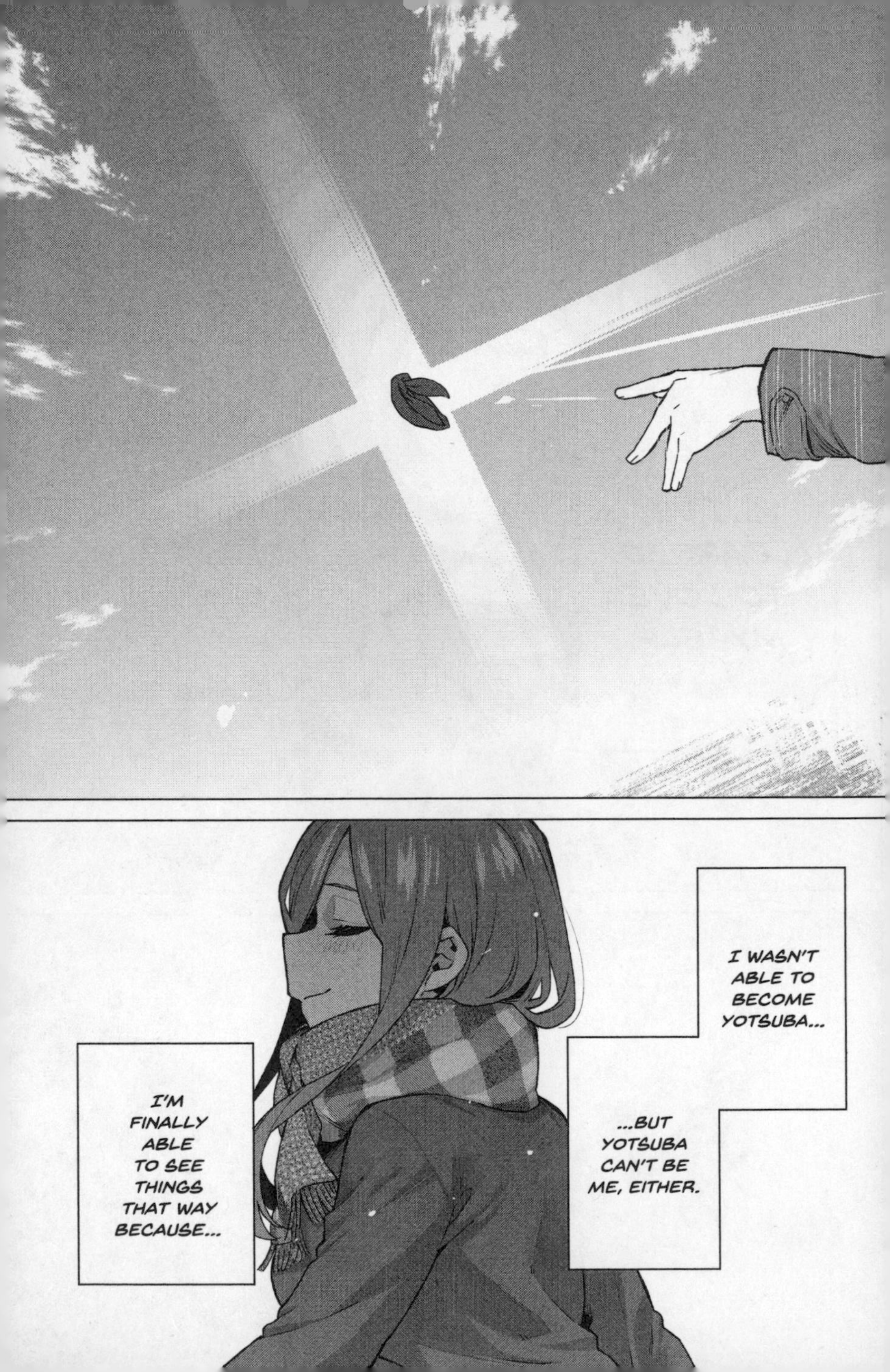
I WASN'T ABLE TO BECOME YOTSUBA...
...BUT YOTSUBA CAN'T BE ME, EITHER.
I'M FINALLY ABLE TO SEE THINGS THAT WAY BECAUSE...

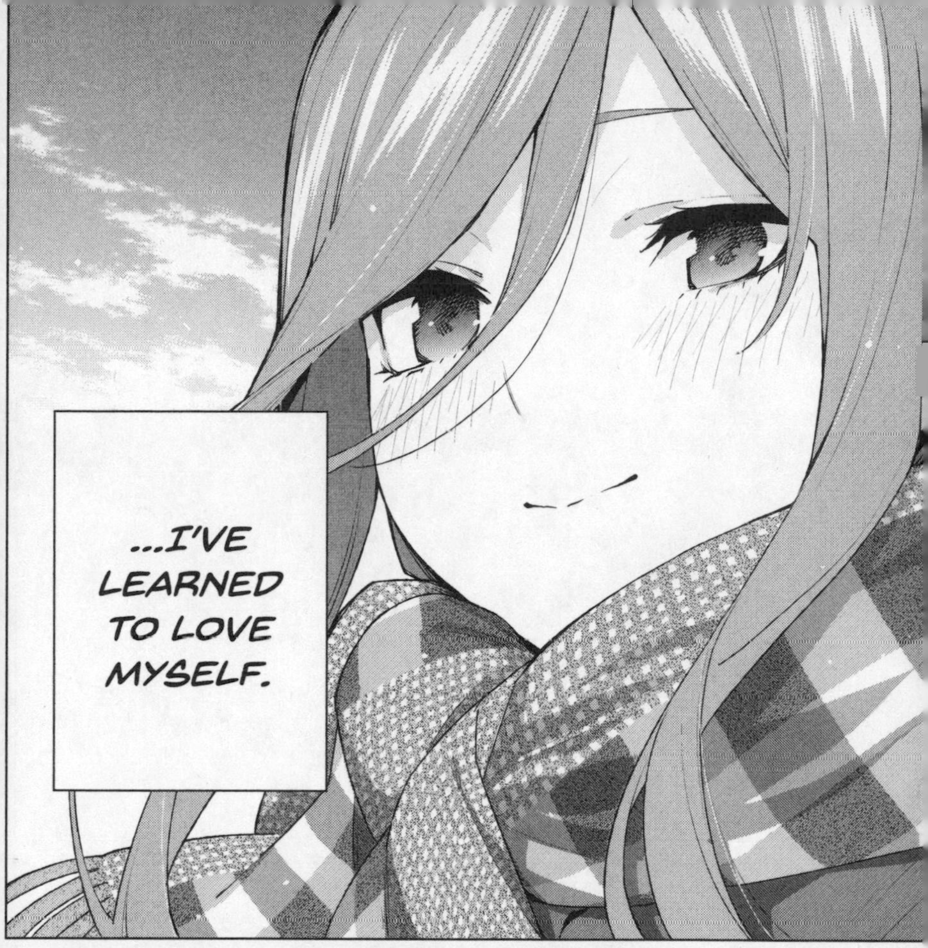
...I'VE LEARNED TO LOVE MYSELF.

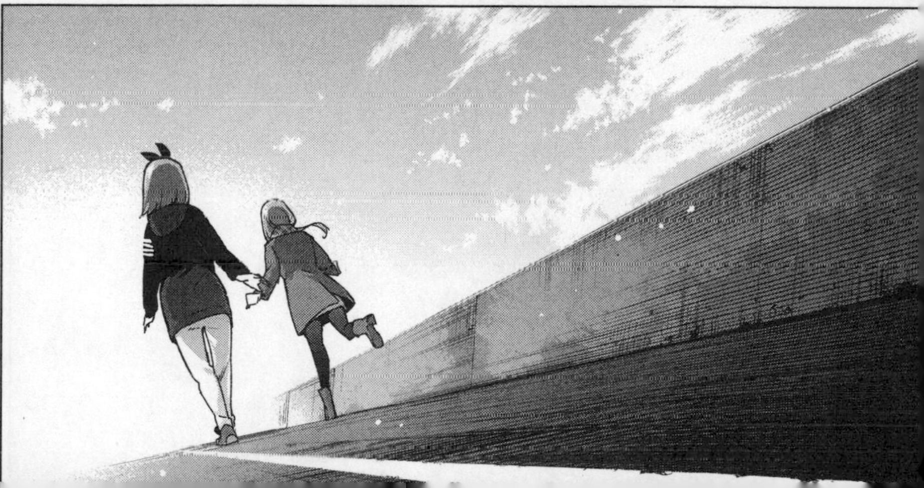

CHAPTER 117
FIVE-ALARM LUNCHTIME

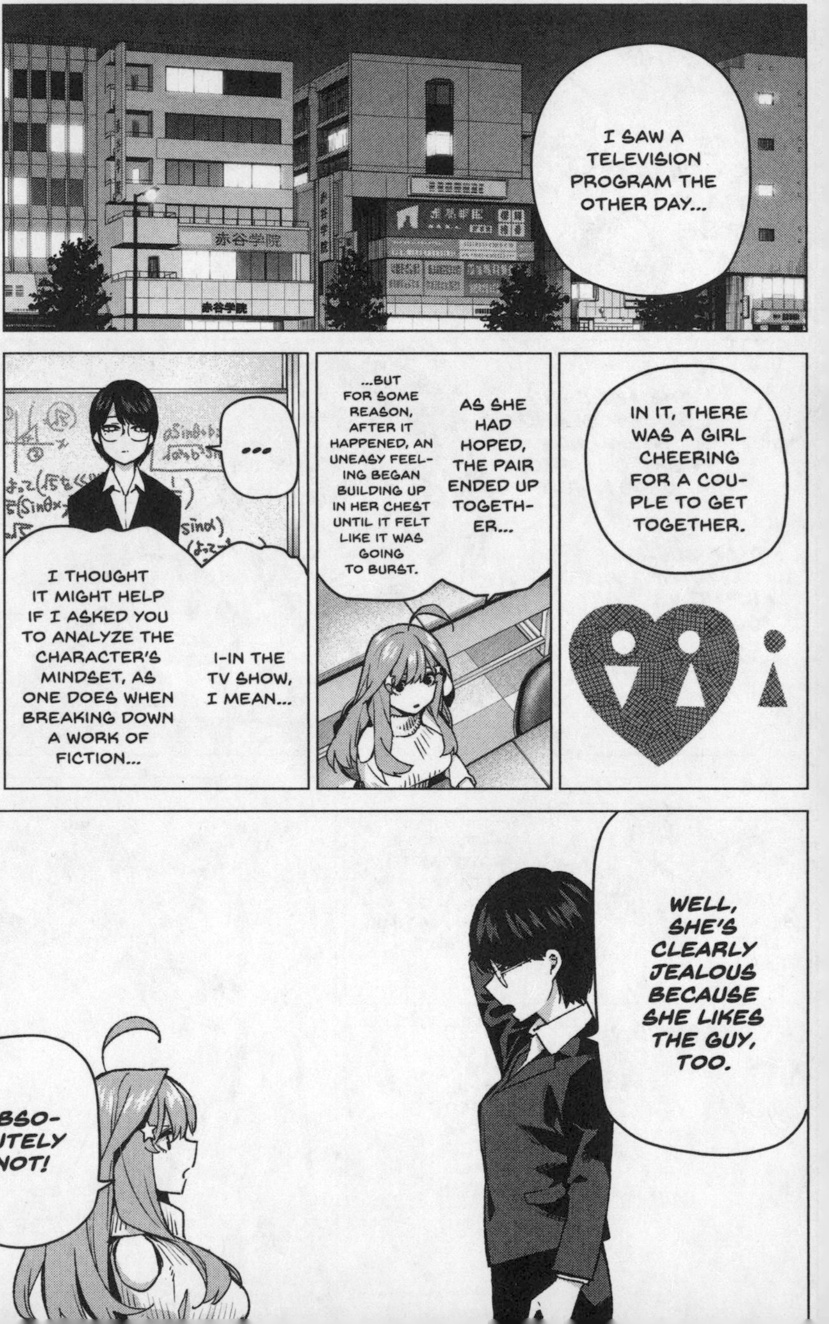
I SAW A TELEVISION PROGRAM THE OTHER DAY...
IN IT, THERE WAS A GIRL CHEERING FOR A COUPLE TO GET TOGETHER.
AS SHE HAD HOPED, THE PAIR ENDED UP TOGETHER...
...BUT FOR SOME REASON, AFTER IT HAPPENED, AN UNEASY FEELING BEGAN BUILDING UP IN HER CHEST UNTIL IT FELT LIKE IT WAS GOING TO BURST.
...
I-IN THE TV SHOW, I MEAN...
I THOUGHT IT MIGHT HELP IF I ASKED YOU TO ANALYZE THE CHARACTER'S MINDSET, AS ONE DOES WHEN BREAKING DOWN A WORK OF FICTION...
WELL, SHE'S CLEARLY JEALOUS BECAUSE SHE LIKES THE GUY, TOO.
ABSOLUTELY NOT!

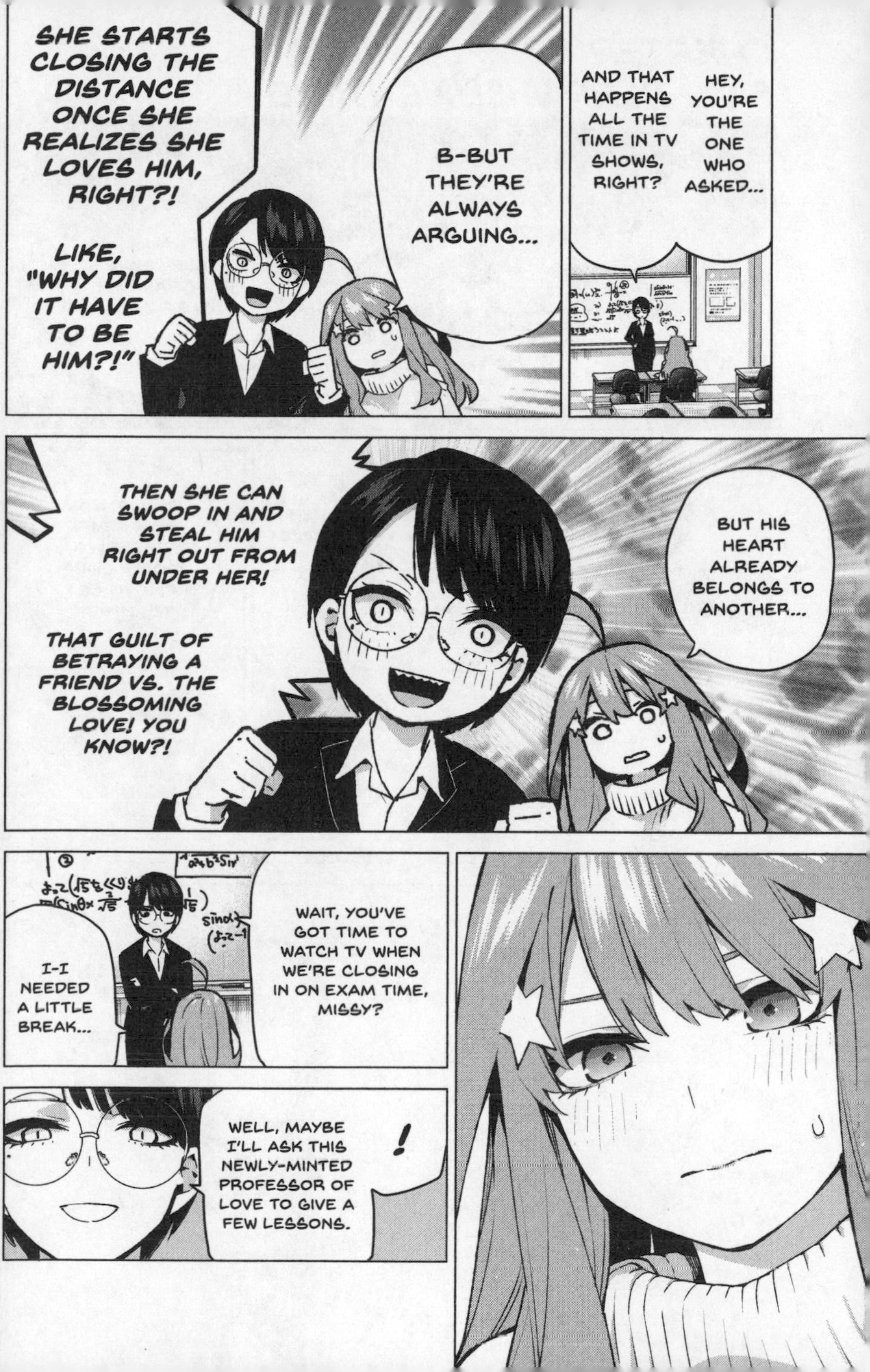
HEY, YOU'RE THE ONE WHO ASKED...
AND THAT HAPPENS ALL THE TIME IN TV SHOWS, RIGHT?
B-BUT THEY'RE ALWAYS ARGUING...
SHE STARTS CLOSING THE DISTANCE ONCE SHE REALIZES SHE LOVES HIM, RIGHT?!
LIKE, "WHY DID IT HAVE TO BE HIM?!"
BUT HIS HEART ALREADY BELONGS TO ANOTHER...
THEN SHE CAN SWOOP IN AND STEAL HIM RIGHT OUT FROM UNDER HER!
THAT GUILT OF BETRAYING A FRIEND VS. THE BLOSSOMING LOVE! YOU KNOW?!
WAIT, YOU'VE GOT TIME TO WATCH TV WHEN WE'RE CLOSING IN ON EXAM TIME, MISSY?
I-I NEEDED A LITTLE BREAK...
!
WELL, MAYBE I'LL ASK THIS NEWLY-MINTED PROFESSOR OF LOVE TO GIVE A FEW LESSONS.

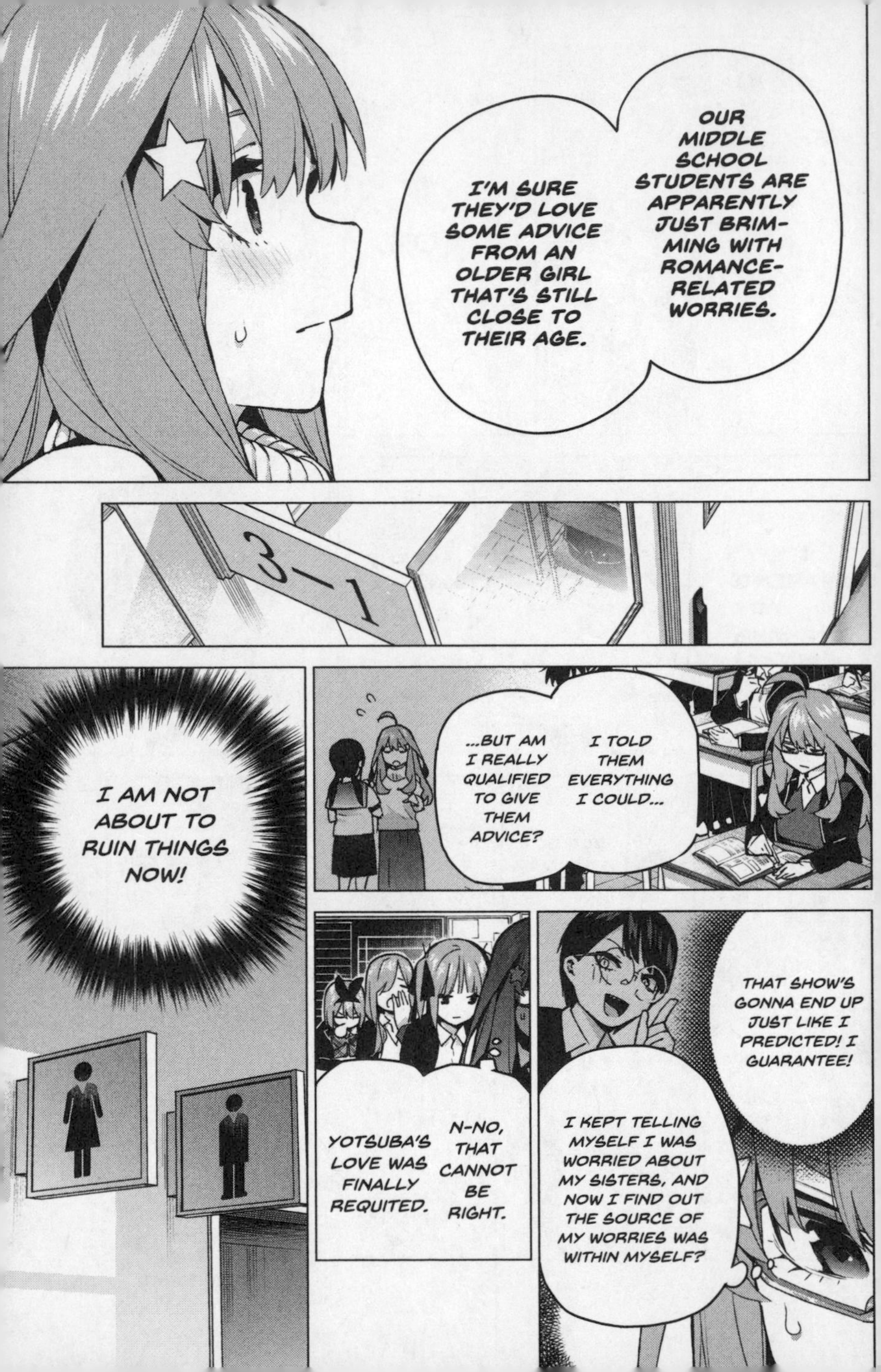
OUR MIDDLE SCHOOL STUDENTS ARE APPARENTLY JUST BRIMMING WITH ROMANCE-RELATED WORRIES.
I'M SURE THEY'D LOVE SOME ADVICE FROM AN OLDER GIRL THAT'S STILL CLOSE TO THEIR AGE.
3-1
I TOLD THEM EVERYTHING I COULD...
...BUT AM I REALLY QUALIFIED TO GIVE THEM ADVICE?
THAT SHOW'S GONNA END UP JUST LIKE I PREDICTED! I GUARANTEE!
I KEPT TELLING MYSELF I WAS WORRIED ABOUT MY SISTERS, AND NOW I FIND OUT THE SOURCE OF MY WORRIES WAS WITHIN MYSELF?
N-NO, THAT CANNOT BE RIGHT.
YOTSUBA'S LOVE WAS FINALLY REQUITED.
I AM NOT ABOUT TO RUIN THINGS NOW!

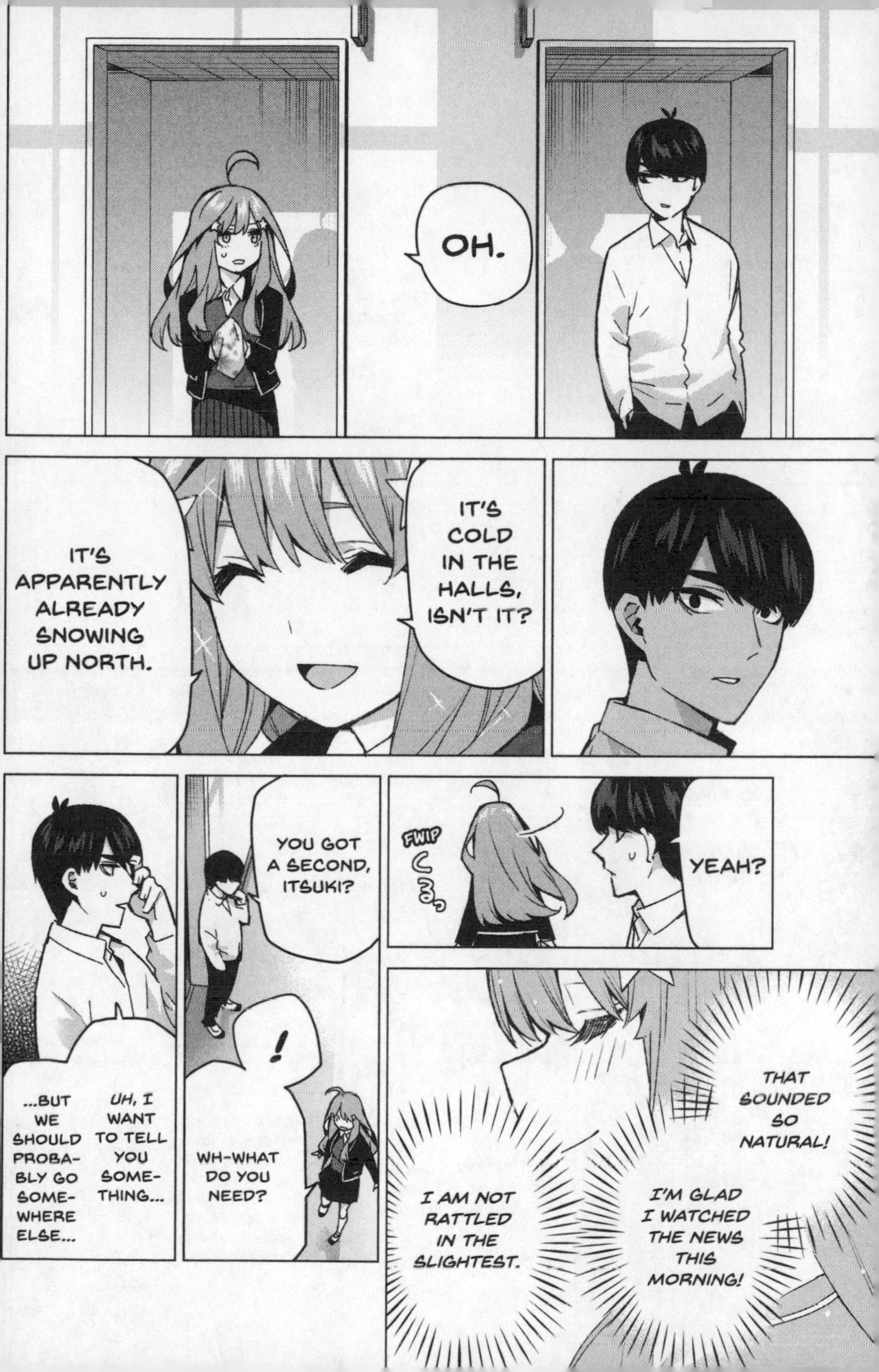
OH.
IT'S COLD IN THE HALLS, ISN'T IT?
IT'S APPARENTLY ALREADY SNOWING UP NORTH.
YEAH?
FWIP
THAT SOUNDED SO NATURAL!
I'M GLAD I WATCHED THE NEWS THIS MORNING!
I AM NOT RATTLED IN THE SLIGHTEST.
YOU GOT A SECOND, ITSUKI?
!
WH-WHAT DO YOU NEED?
UH, I WANT TO TELL YOU SOME-THING...
...BUT WE SHOULD PROBA-BLY GO SOME-WHERE ELSE...

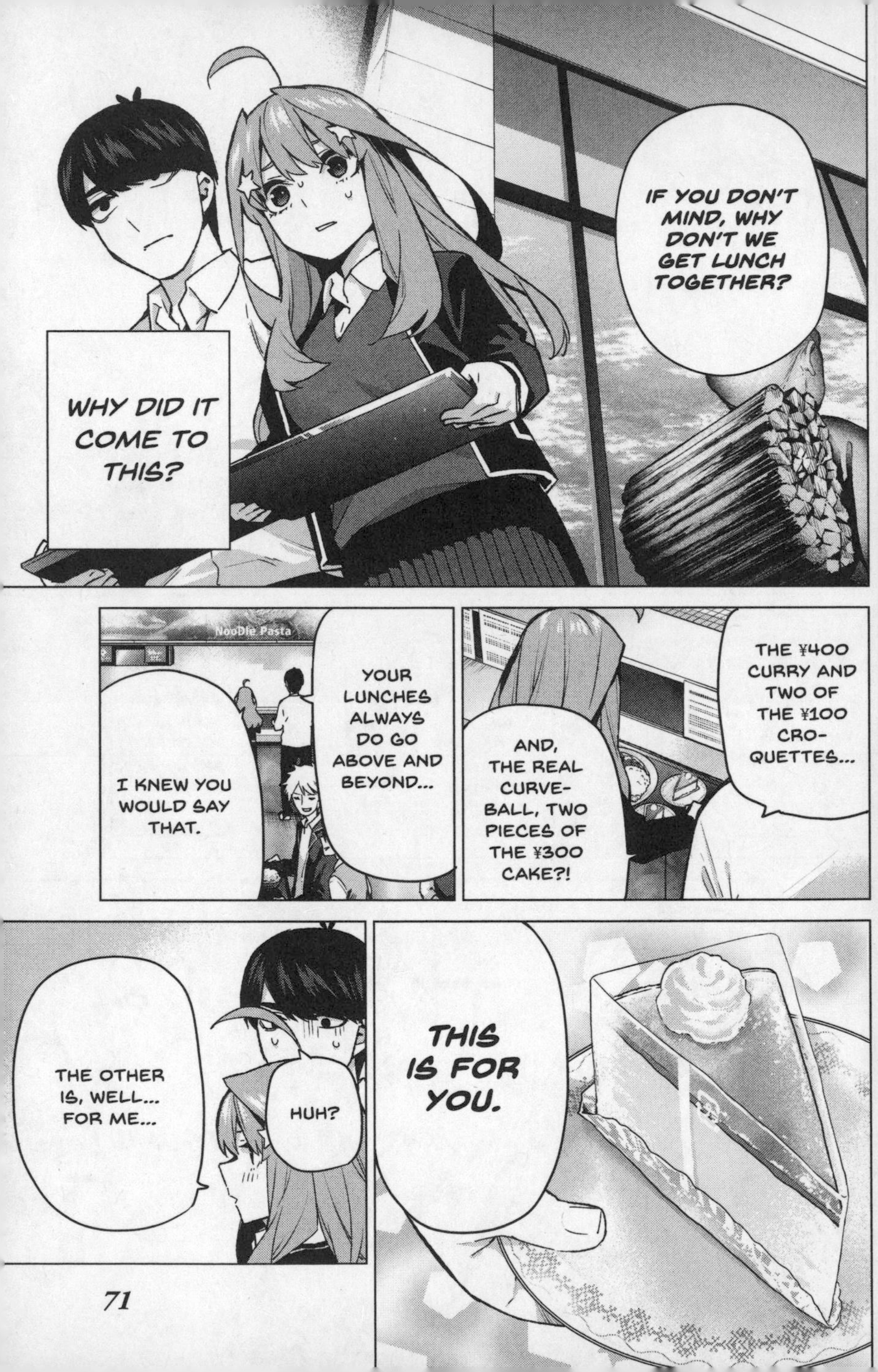

IF YOU DON'T MIND, WHY DON'T WE GET LUNCH TOGETHER?
WHY DID IT COME TO THIS?
THE ¥400 CURRY AND TWO OF THE ¥100 CRO-QUETTES...
AND, THE REAL CURVE-BALL, TWO PIECES OF THE ¥300 CAKE?!
NooDle Pasta
YOUR LUNCHES ALWAYS DO GO ABOVE AND BEYOND...
I KNEW YOU WOULD SAY THAT.
THIS IS FOR YOU.
HUH?
THE OTHER IS, WELL... FOR ME...

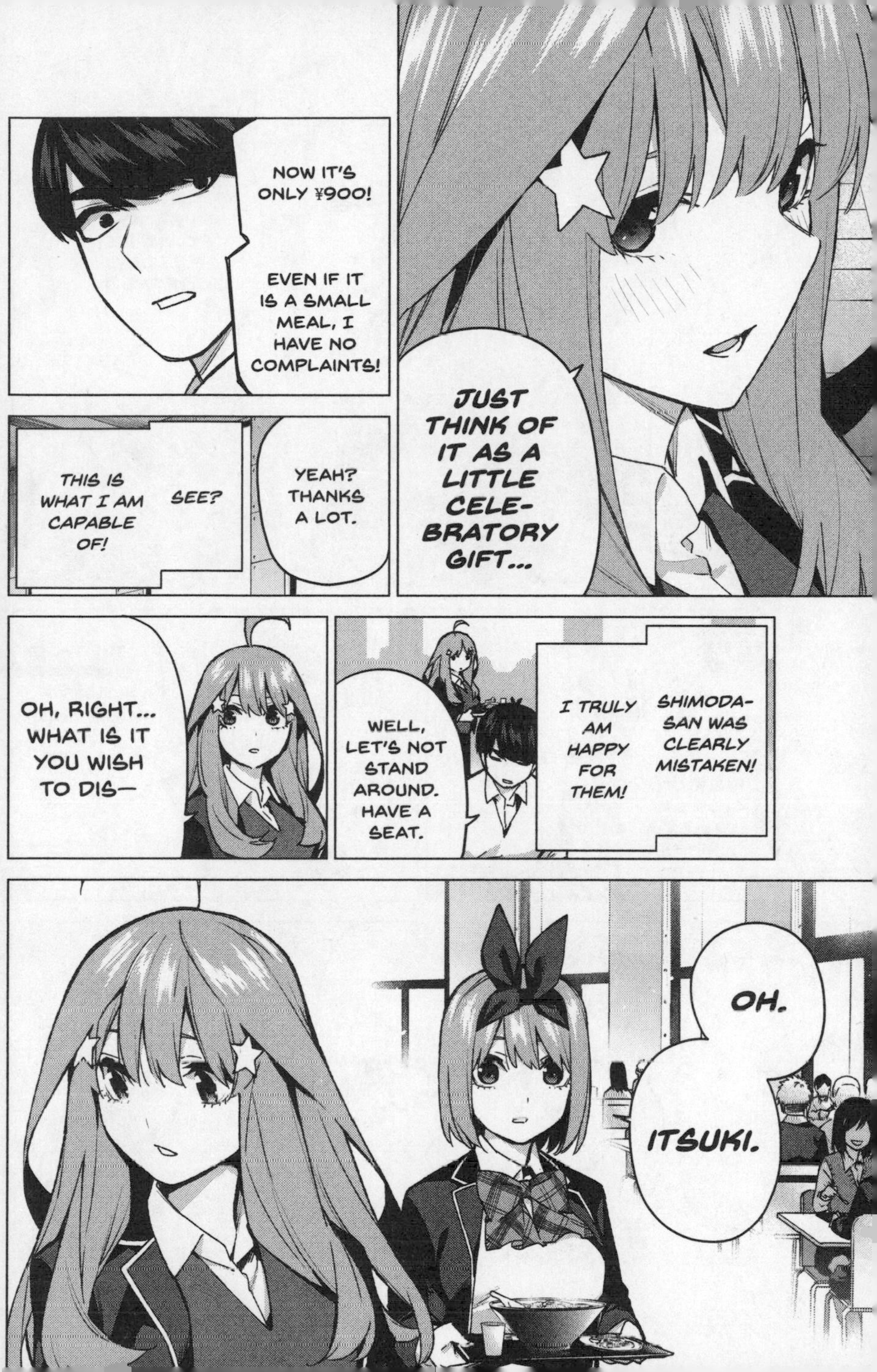
JUST THINK OF IT AS A LITTLE CELE-BRATORY GIFT...
NOW IT'S ONLY ¥900!
EVEN IF IT IS A SMALL MEAL, I HAVE NO COMPLAINTS!
YEAH? THANKS A LOT.
SEE?
THIS IS WHAT I AM CAPABLE OF!
SHIMODA-SAN WAS CLEARLY MISTAKEN!
I TRULY AM HAPPY FOR THEM!
WELL, LET'S NOT STAND AROUND. HAVE A SEAT.
OH, RIGHT... WHAT IS IT YOU WISH TO DIS—
OH.
ITSUKI.

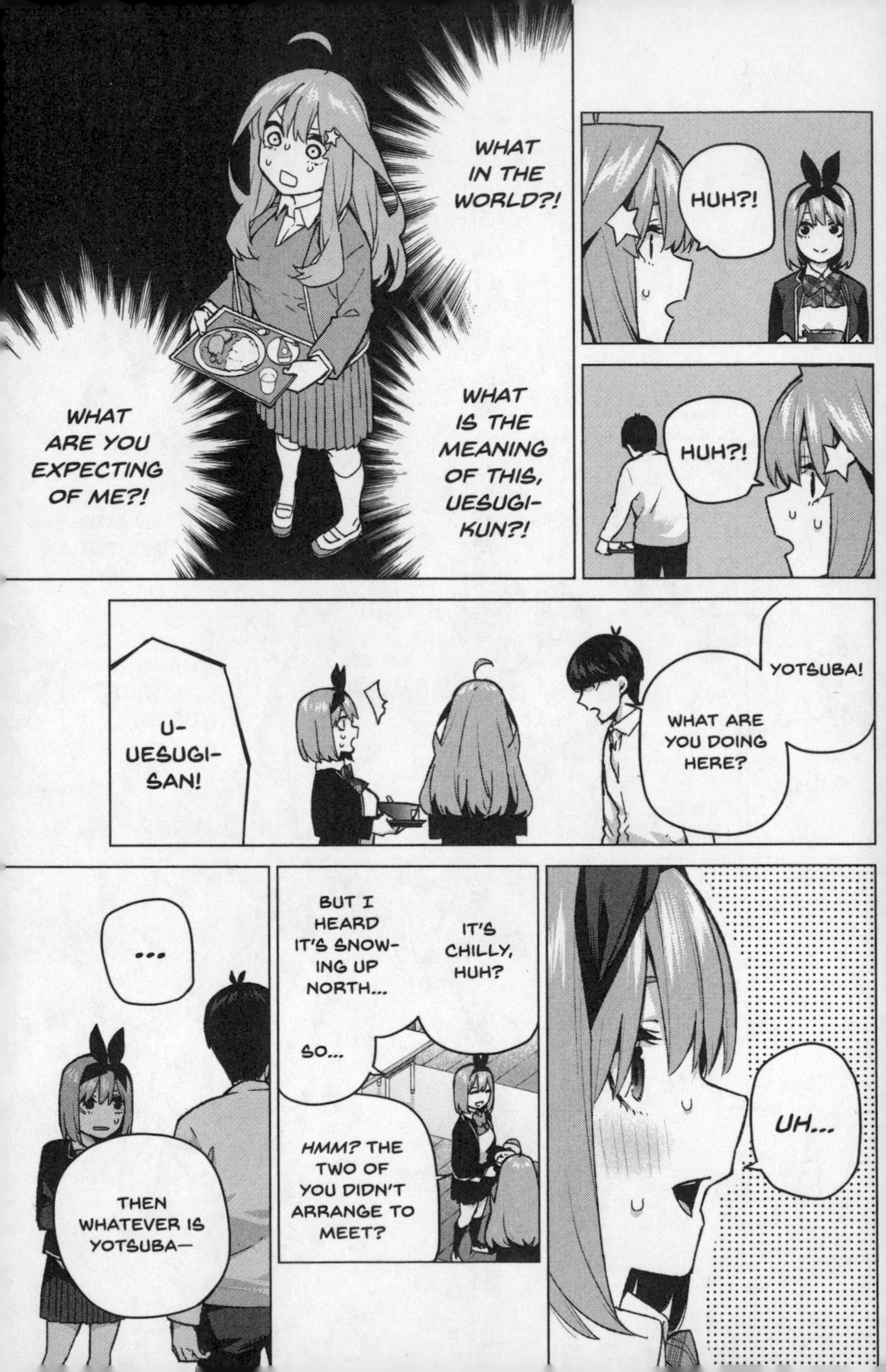
HUH?!
HUH?!
WHAT IN THE WORLD?!
WHAT IS THE MEANING OF THIS, UESUGI-KUN?!
WHAT ARE YOU EXPECTING OF ME?!
YOTSUBA!
WHAT ARE YOU DOING HERE?
U-UESUGI-SAN!
UH...
IT'S CHILLY, HUH?
BUT I HEARD IT'S SNOWING UP NORTH...
SO...
HMM? THE TWO OF YOU DIDN'T ARRANGE TO MEET?
...
THEN WHATEVER IS YOTSUBA—

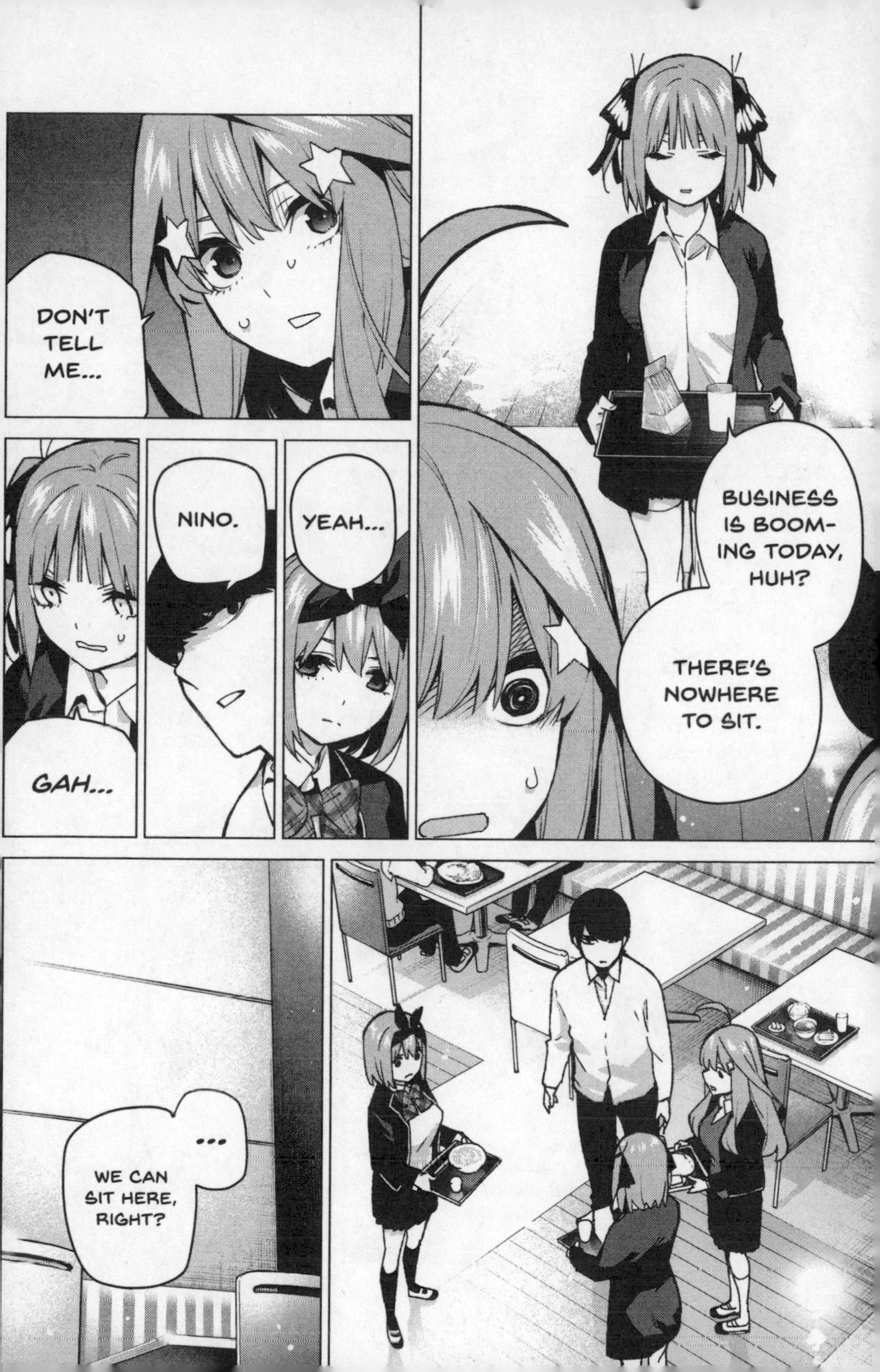
BUSINESS IS BOOMING TODAY, HUH?
THERE'S NOWHERE TO SIT.
DON'T TELL ME...
YEAH...
NINO.
GAH...
...
WE CAN SIT HERE, RIGHT?

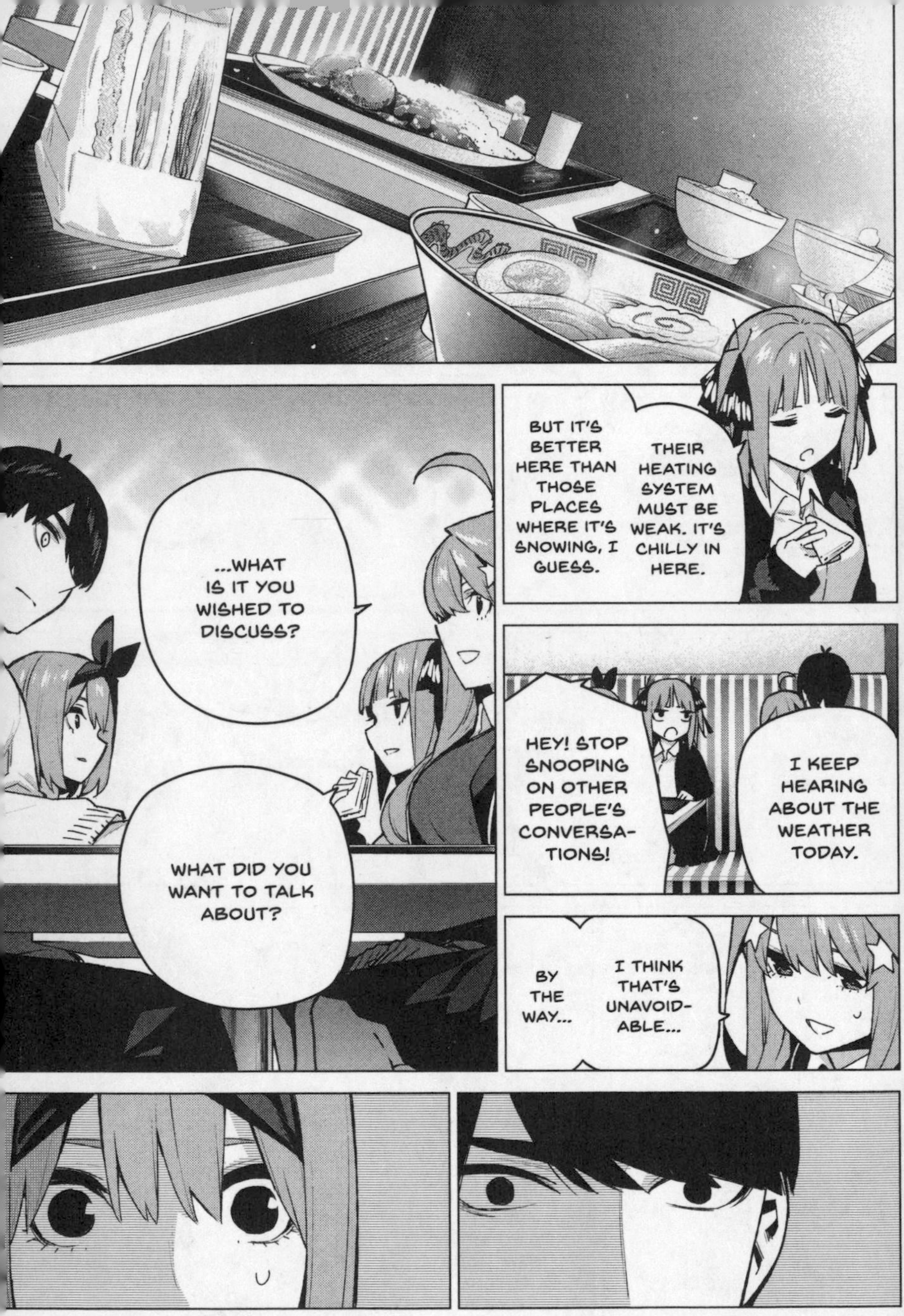
THEIR HEATING SYSTEM MUST BE WEAK. IT'S CHILLY IN HERE.
BUT IT'S BETTER HERE THAN THOSE PLACES WHERE IT'S SNOWING, I GUESS.
I KEEP HEARING ABOUT THE WEATHER TODAY.
HEY! STOP SNOOPING ON OTHER PEOPLE'S CONVERSA-TIONS!
I THINK THAT'S UNAVOID-ABLE...
BY THE WAY...
...WHAT IS IT YOU WISHED TO DISCUSS?
WHAT DID YOU WANT TO TALK ABOUT?

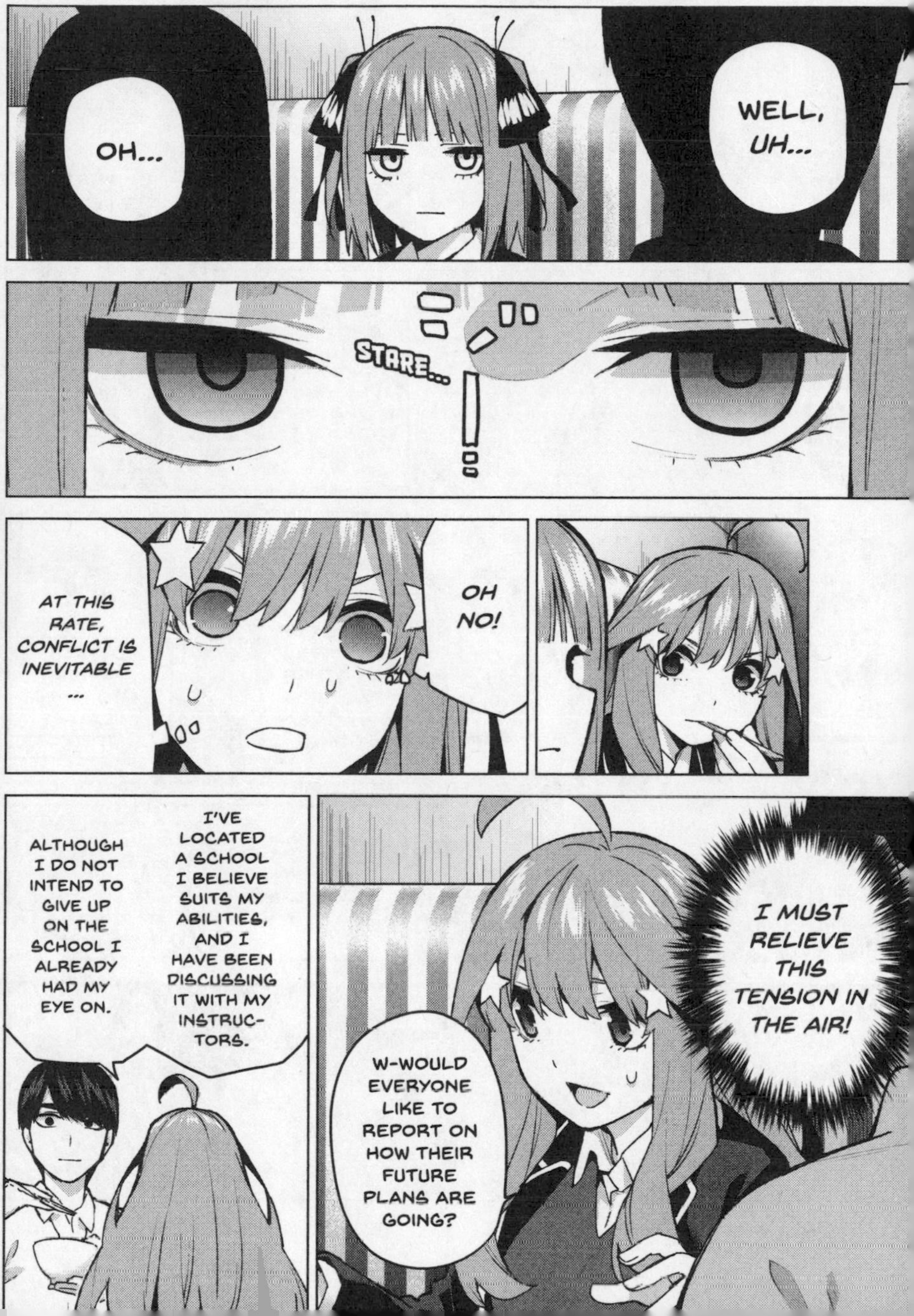
WELL, UH...
OH...
STARE...
OH NO!
AT THIS RATE, CONFLICT IS INEVITABLE...
I MUST RELIEVE THIS TENSION IN THE AIR!
W-WOULD EVERYONE LIKE TO REPORT ON HOW THEIR FUTURE PLANS ARE GOING?
I'VE LOCATED A SCHOOL I BELIEVE SUITS MY ABILITIES, AND I HAVE BEEN DISCUSSING IT WITH MY INSTRUC-TORS.
ALTHOUGH I DO NOT INTEND TO GIVE UP ON THE SCHOOL I ALREADY HAD MY EYE ON.

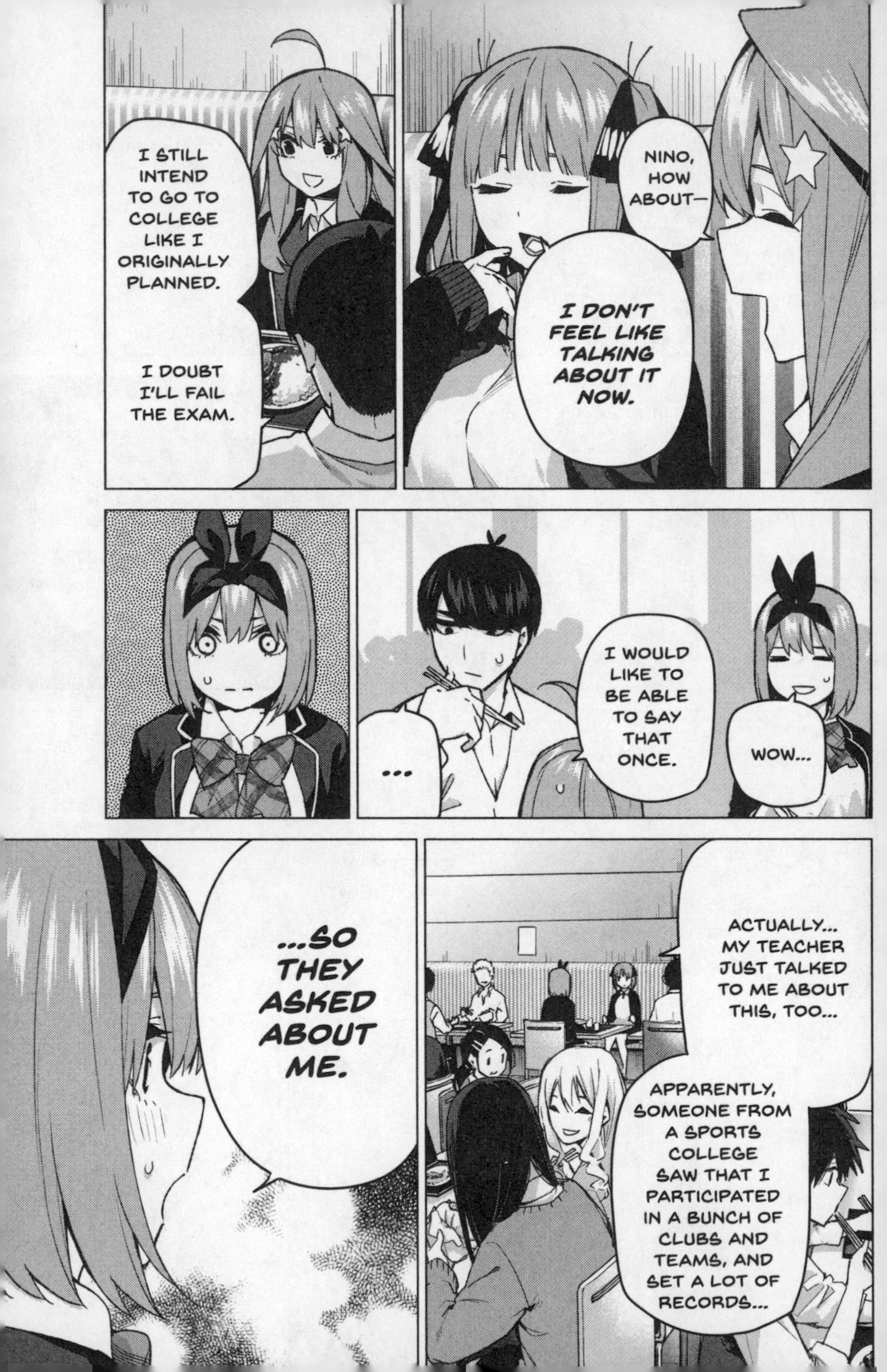
NINO, HOW ABOUT—
I DON'T FEEL LIKE TALKING ABOUT IT NOW.
I STILL INTEND TO GO TO COLLEGE LIKE I ORIGINALLY PLANNED.
I DOUBT I'LL FAIL THE EXAM.
I WOULD LIKE TO BE ABLE TO SAY THAT ONCE.
WOW...
...
ACTUALLY... MY TEACHER JUST TALKED TO ME ABOUT THIS, TOO...
APPARENTLY, SOMEONE FROM A SPORTS COLLEGE SAW THAT I PARTICIPATED IN A BUNCH OF CLUBS AND TEAMS, AND SET A LOT OF RECORDS...
...SO THEY ASKED ABOUT ME.

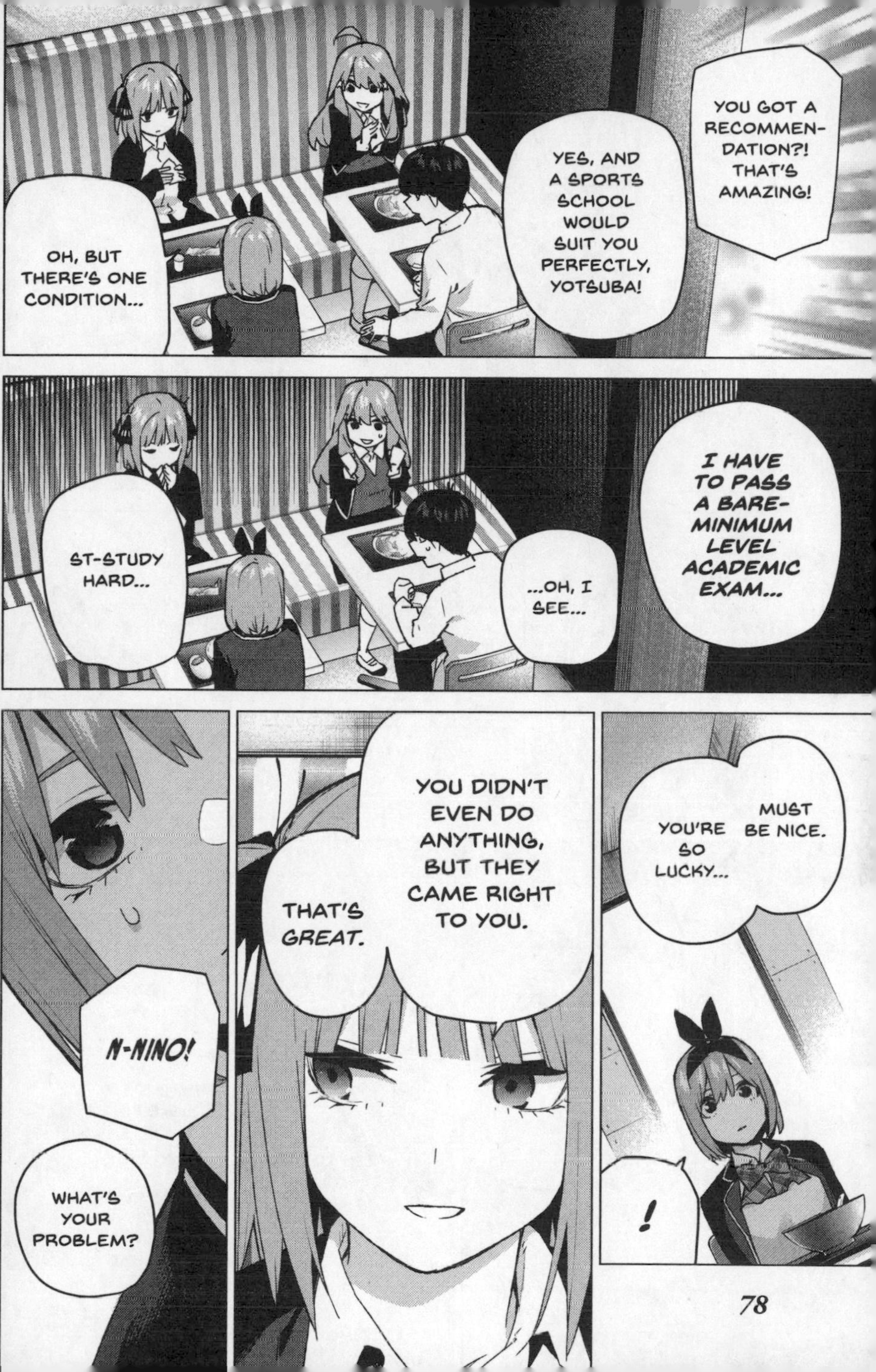
YOU GOT A RECOMMENDATION?! THAT'S AMAZING!
YES, AND A SPORTS SCHOOL WOULD SUIT YOU PERFECTLY, YOTSUBA!
OH, BUT THERE'S ONE CONDITION...
I HAVE TO PASS A BARE-MINIMUM LEVEL ACADEMIC EXAM...
...OH, I SEE...
ST-STUDY HARD...
MUST BE NICE.
YOU'RE SO LUCKY...
!
YOU DIDN'T EVEN DO ANYTHING, BUT THEY CAME RIGHT TO YOU.
THAT'S GREAT.
N-NINO!
WHAT'S YOUR PROBLEM?

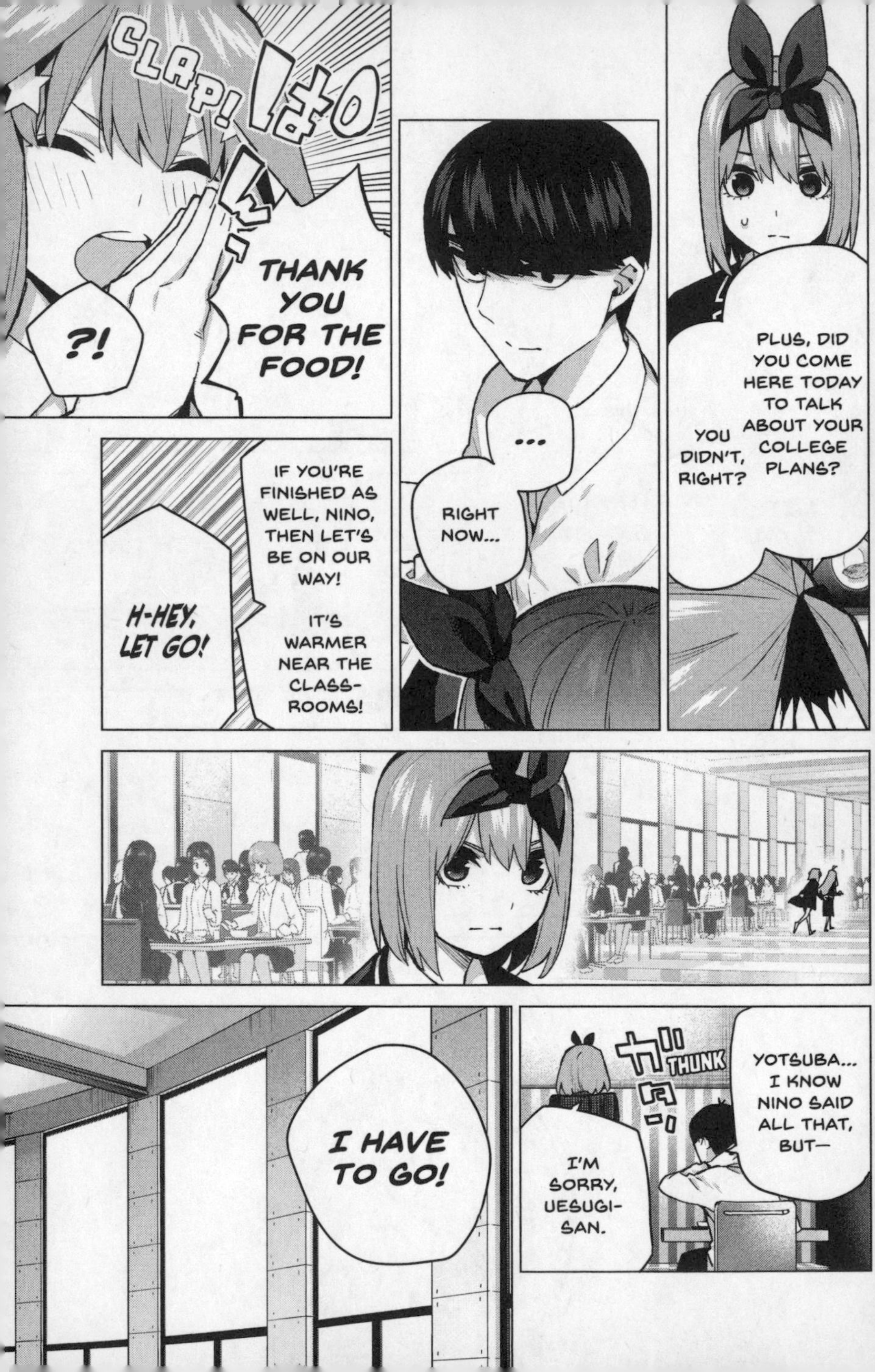
PLUS, DID YOU COME HERE TODAY TO TALK ABOUT YOUR COLLEGE PLANS?
YOU DIDN'T, RIGHT?
...
RIGHT NOW...
CLAP!
THANK YOU FOR THE FOOD!
?!
IF YOU'RE FINISHED AS WELL, NINO, THEN LET'S BE ON OUR WAY!
IT'S WARMER NEAR THE CLASS-ROOMS!
H-HEY, LET GO!
YOTSUBA... I KNOW NINO SAID ALL THAT, BUT—
THUNK
I'M SORRY, UESUGI-SAN.
I HAVE TO GO!

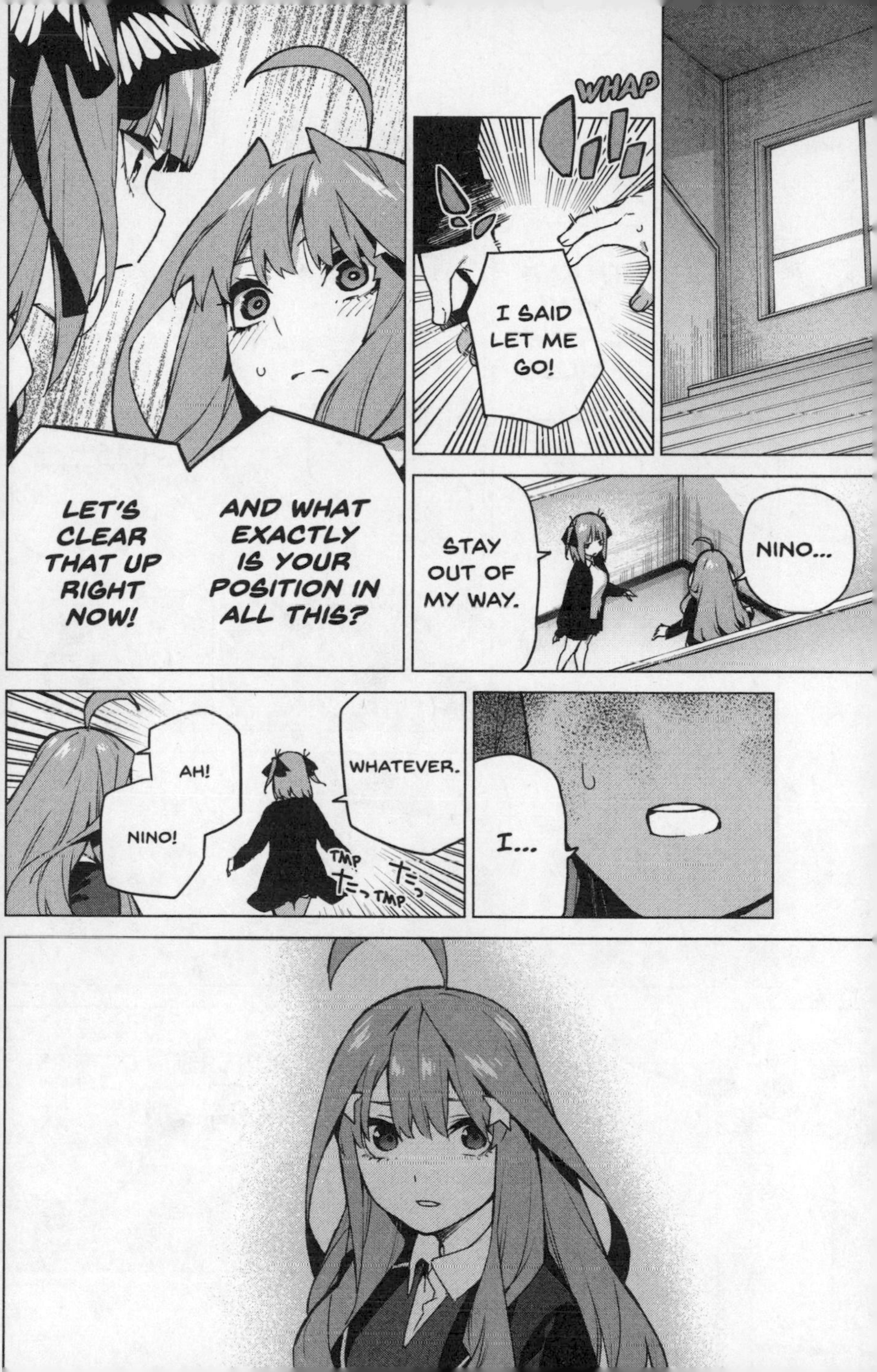
WHAP
I SAID LET ME GO!
NINO...
STAY OUT OF MY WAY.
AND WHAT EXACTLY IS YOUR POSITION IN ALL THIS?
LET'S CLEAR THAT UP RIGHT NOW!
I...
WHATEVER.
AH!
NINO!
TMP
TMP

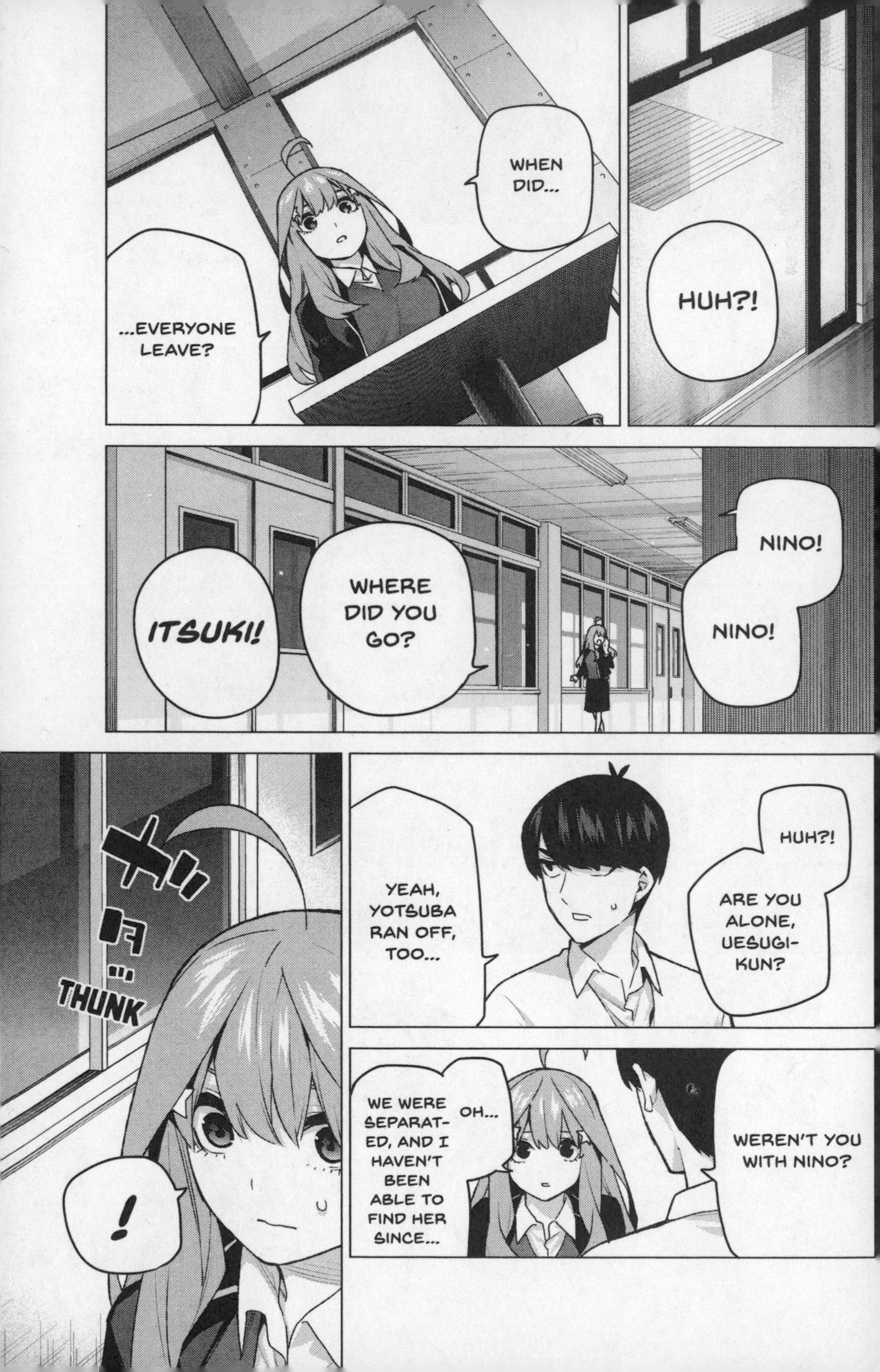
HUH?!
WHEN DID...
...EVERYONE LEAVE?
NINO!
NINO!
WHERE DID YOU GO?
ITSUKI!
HUH?!
ARE YOU ALONE, UESUGI-KUN?
YEAH, YOTSUBA RAN OFF, TOO...
WEREN'T YOU WITH NINO?
OH...
WE WERE SEPARAT-ED, AND I HAVEN'T BEEN ABLE TO FIND HER SINCE...
THUNK
!

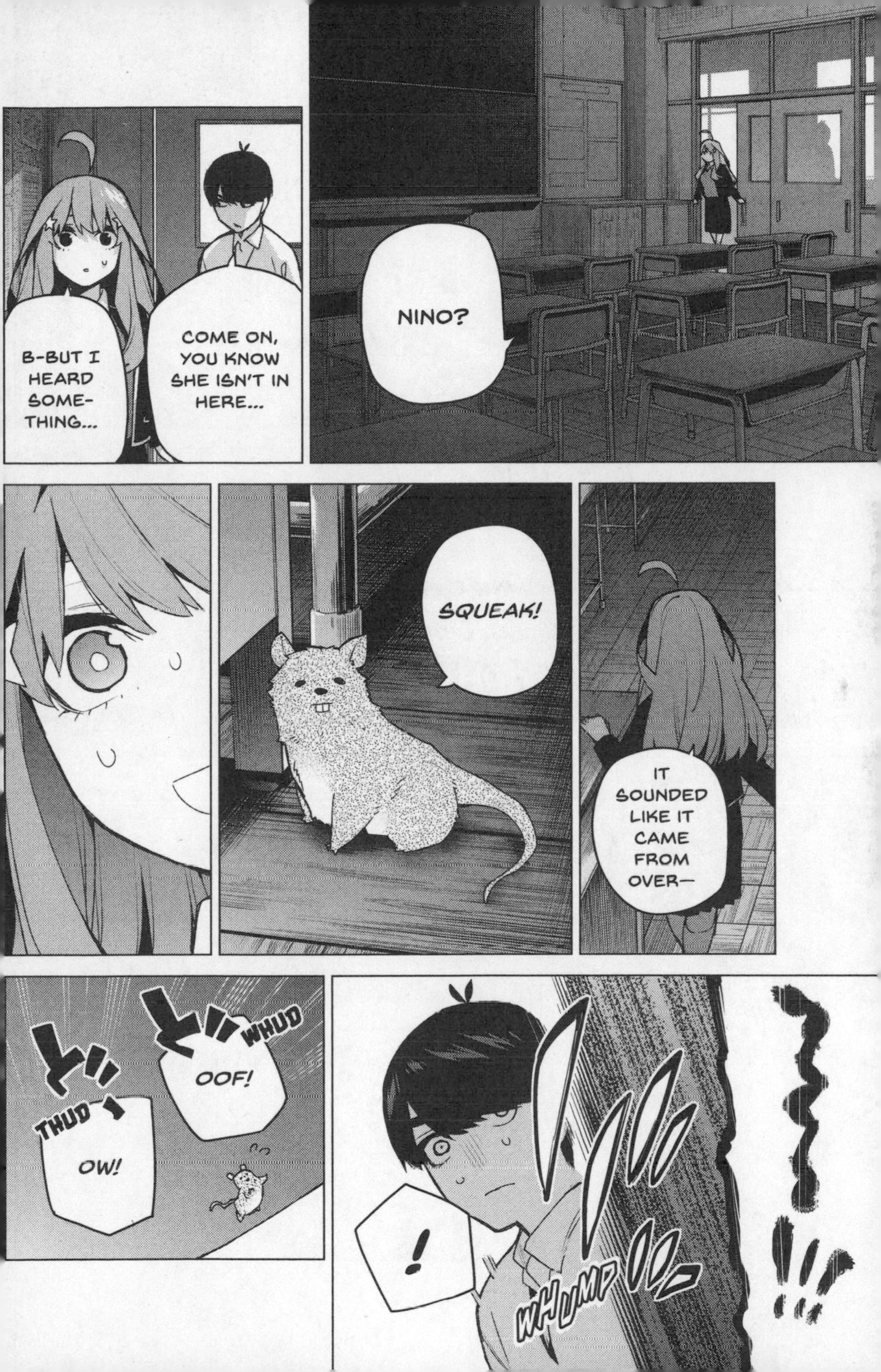
NINO?
COME ON, YOU KNOW SHE ISN'T IN HERE...
B-BUT I HEARD SOME-THING...
IT SOUNDED LIKE IT CAME FROM OVER—
SQUEAK!
!
WHUMP
WHUD
OOF!
THUD
OW!

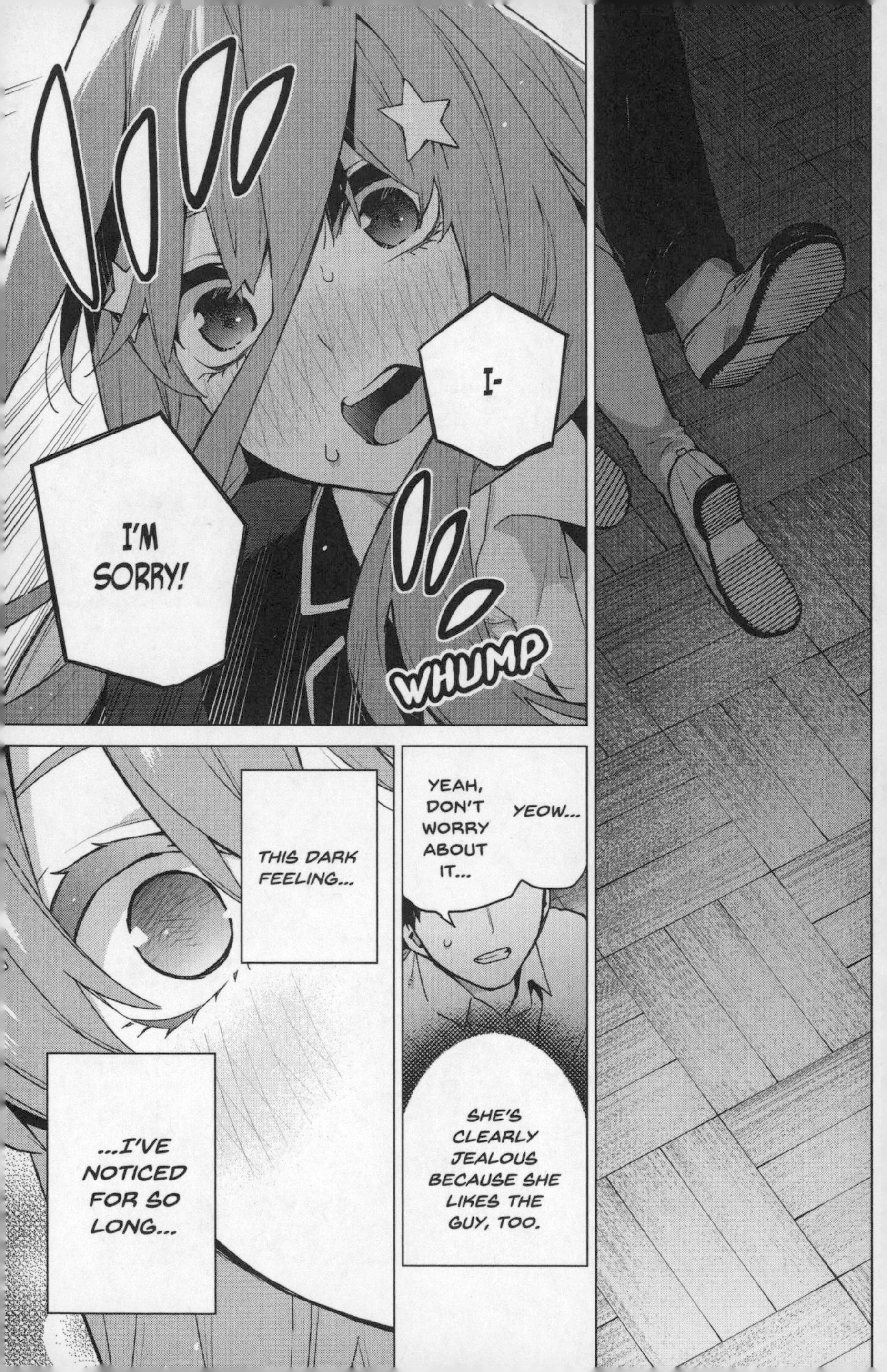
I-
I'M SORRY!
WHUMP
YEOW...
YEAH, DON'T WORRY ABOUT IT...
SHE'S CLEARLY JEALOUS BECAUSE SHE LIKES THE GUY, TOO.
THIS DARK FEELING...
...I'VE NOTICED FOR SO LONG...

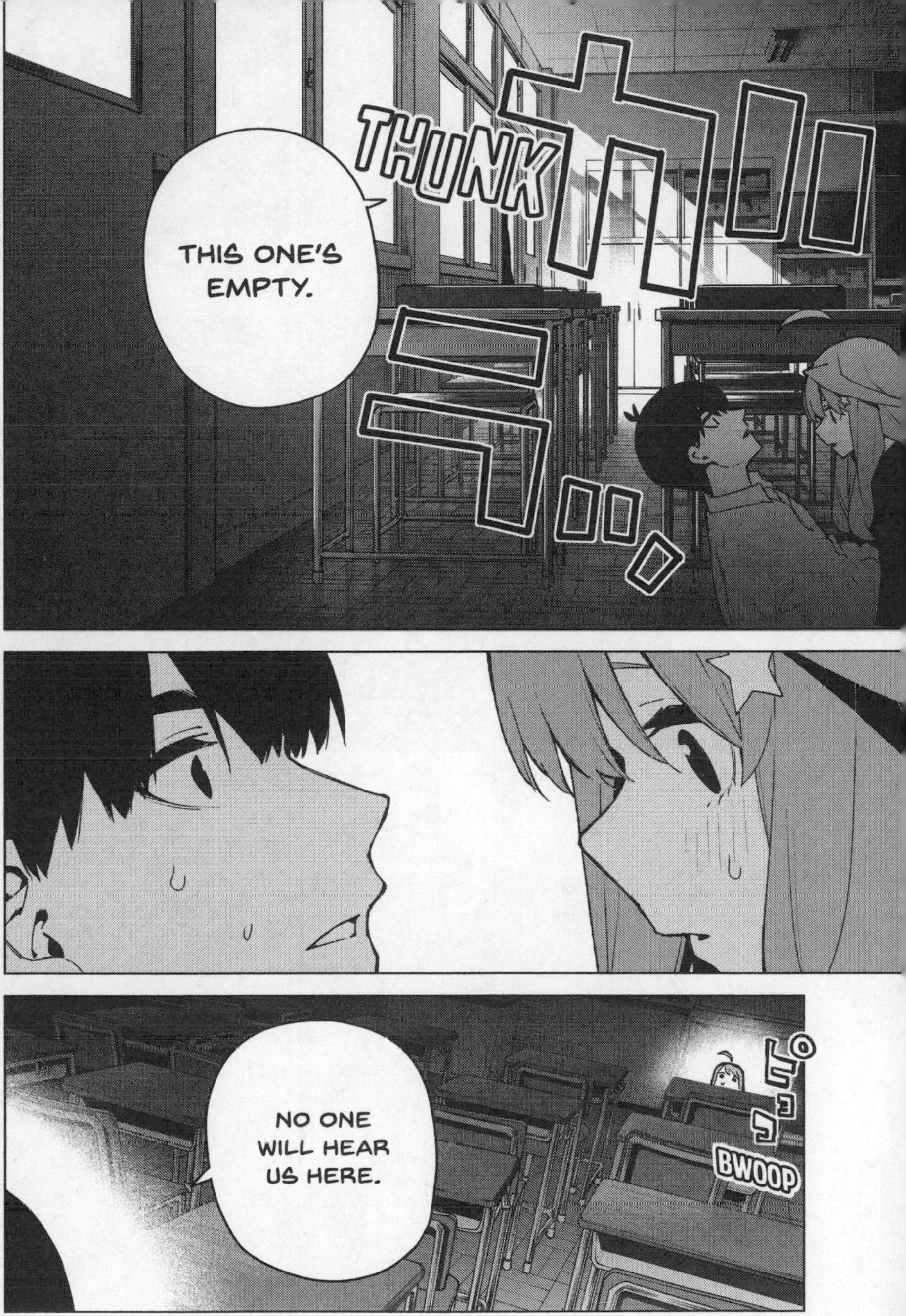
THUNK
THIS ONE'S EMPTY.
ピョコ
BWOOP
NO ONE WILL HEAR US HERE.

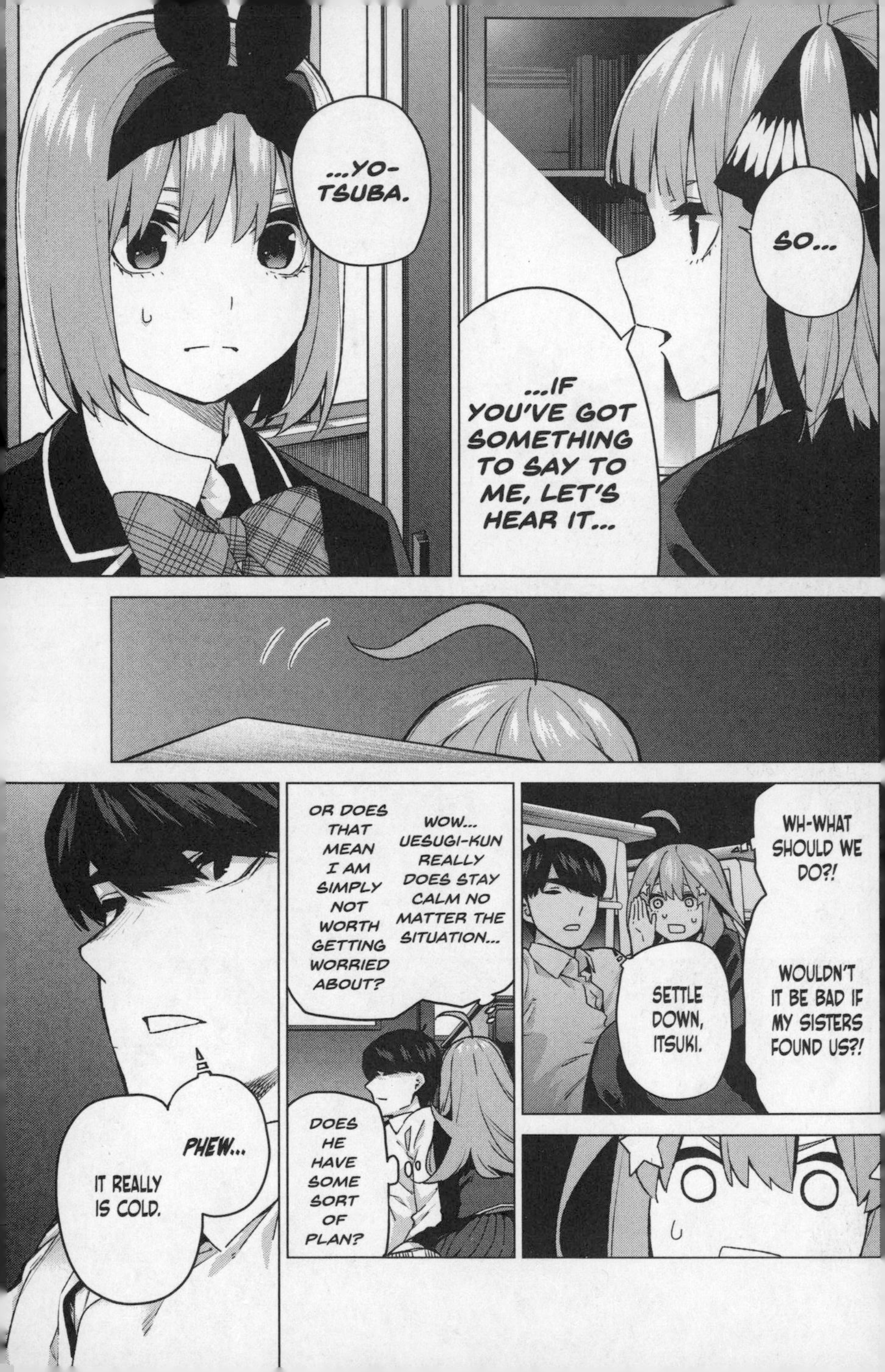
SO...
...IF YOU'VE GOT SOMETHING TO SAY TO ME, LET'S HEAR IT...
...YO-TSUBA.
WH-WHAT SHOULD WE DO?!
WOULDN'T IT BE BAD IF MY SISTERS FOUND US?!
SETTLE DOWN, ITSUKI.
WOW... UESUGI-KUN REALLY DOES STAY CALM NO MATTER THE SITUATION...
OR DOES THAT MEAN I AM SIMPLY NOT WORTH GETTING WORRIED ABOUT?
DOES HE HAVE SOME SORT OF PLAN?
PHEW...
IT REALLY IS COLD.

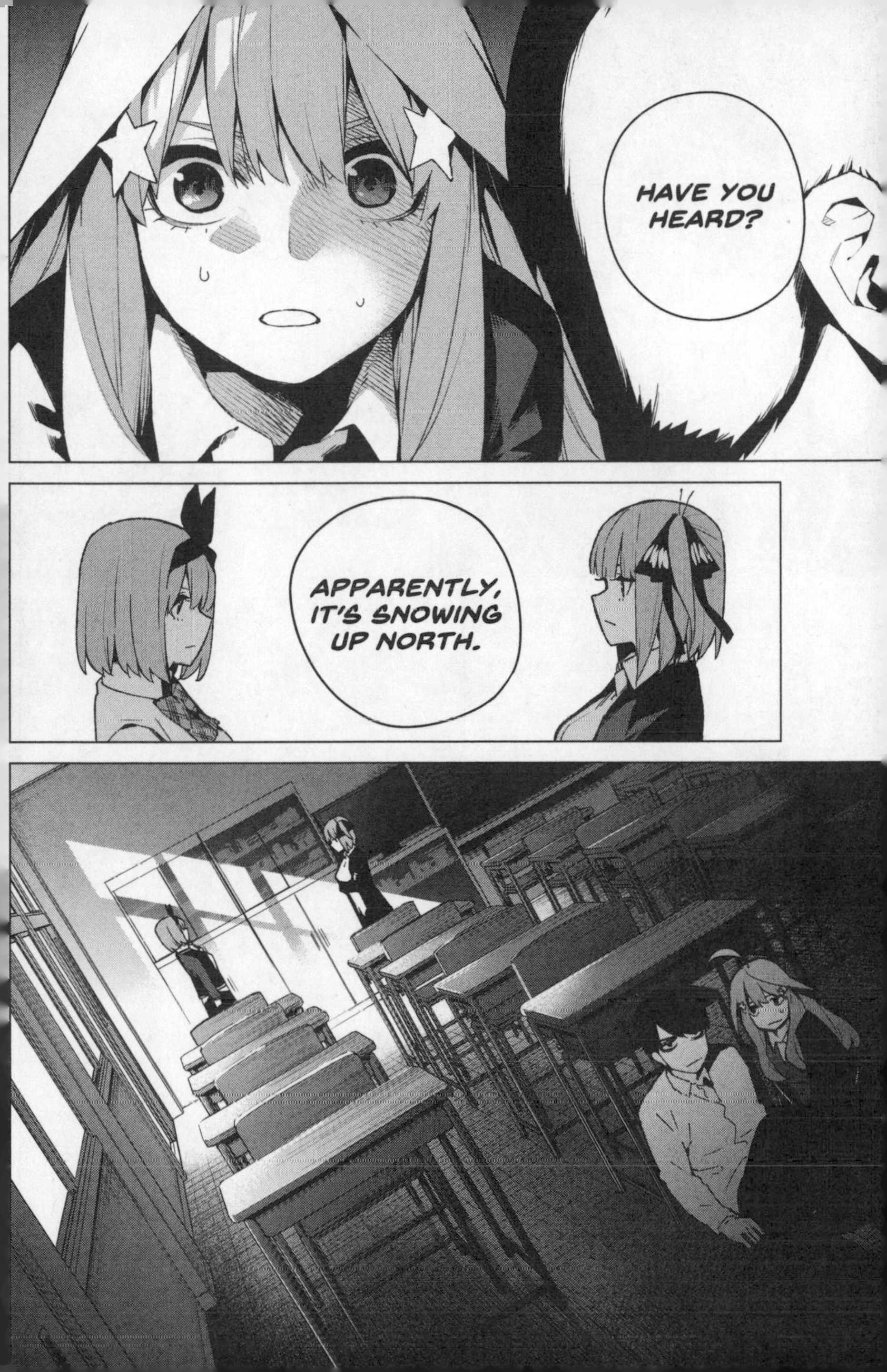
HAVE YOU HEARD?
APPARENTLY, IT'S SNOWING UP NORTH.

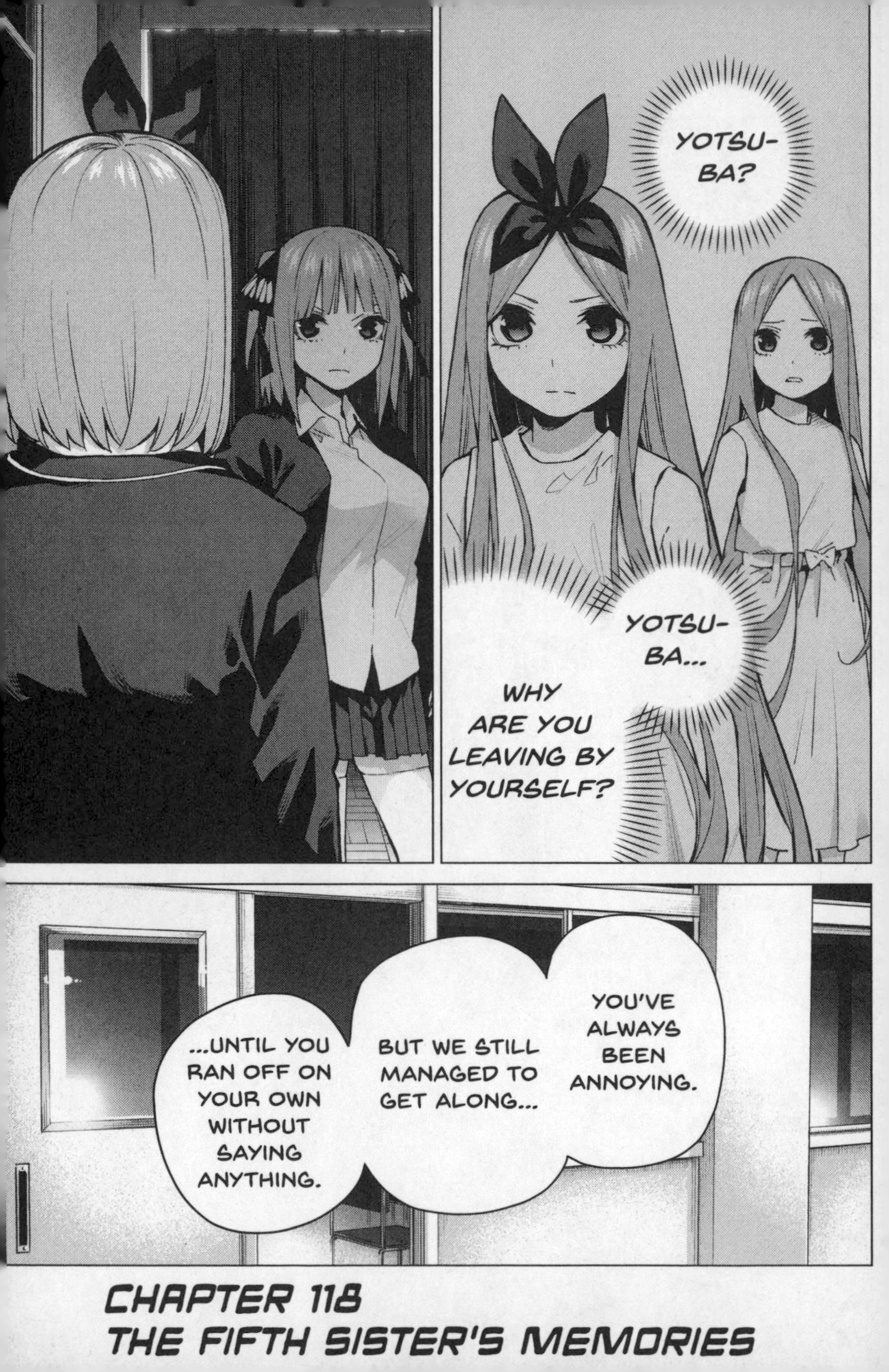
YOTSU-BA?
YOTSU-BA...
WHY ARE YOU LEAVING BY YOURSELF?
YOU'VE ALWAYS BEEN ANNOYING.
BUT WE STILL MANAGED TO GET ALONG...
...UNTIL YOU RAN OFF ON YOUR OWN WITHOUT SAYING ANYTHING.

CHAPTER 118
THE FIFTH SISTER'S MEMORIES

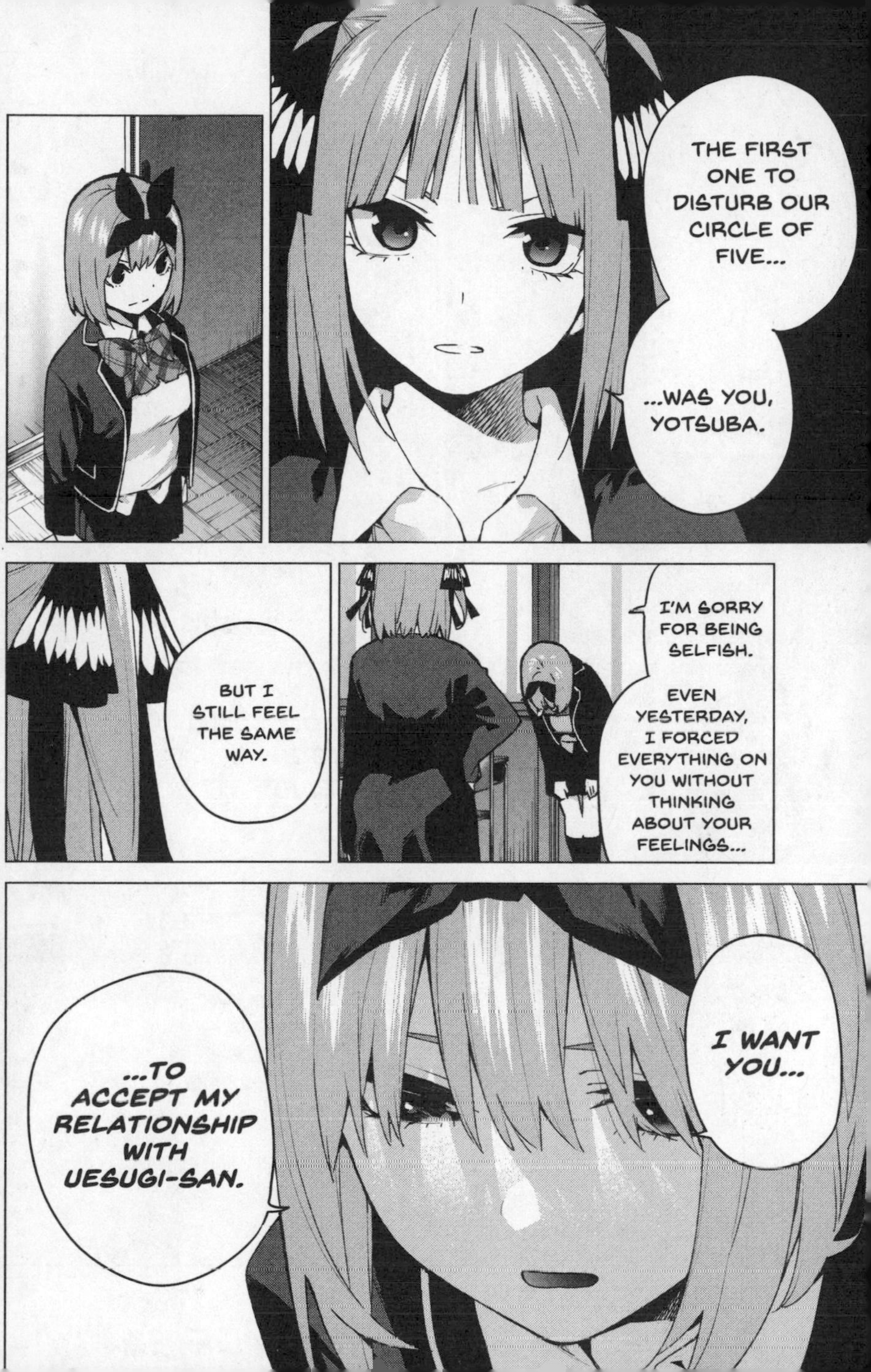
THE FIRST ONE TO DISTURB OUR CIRCLE OF FIVE...
...WAS YOU, YOTSUBA.
I'M SORRY FOR BEING SELFISH.
EVEN YESTERDAY, I FORCED EVERYTHING ON YOU WITHOUT THINKING ABOUT YOUR FEELINGS...
BUT I STILL FEEL THE SAME WAY.
I WANT YOU...
...TO ACCEPT MY RELATIONSHIP WITH UESUGI-SAN.

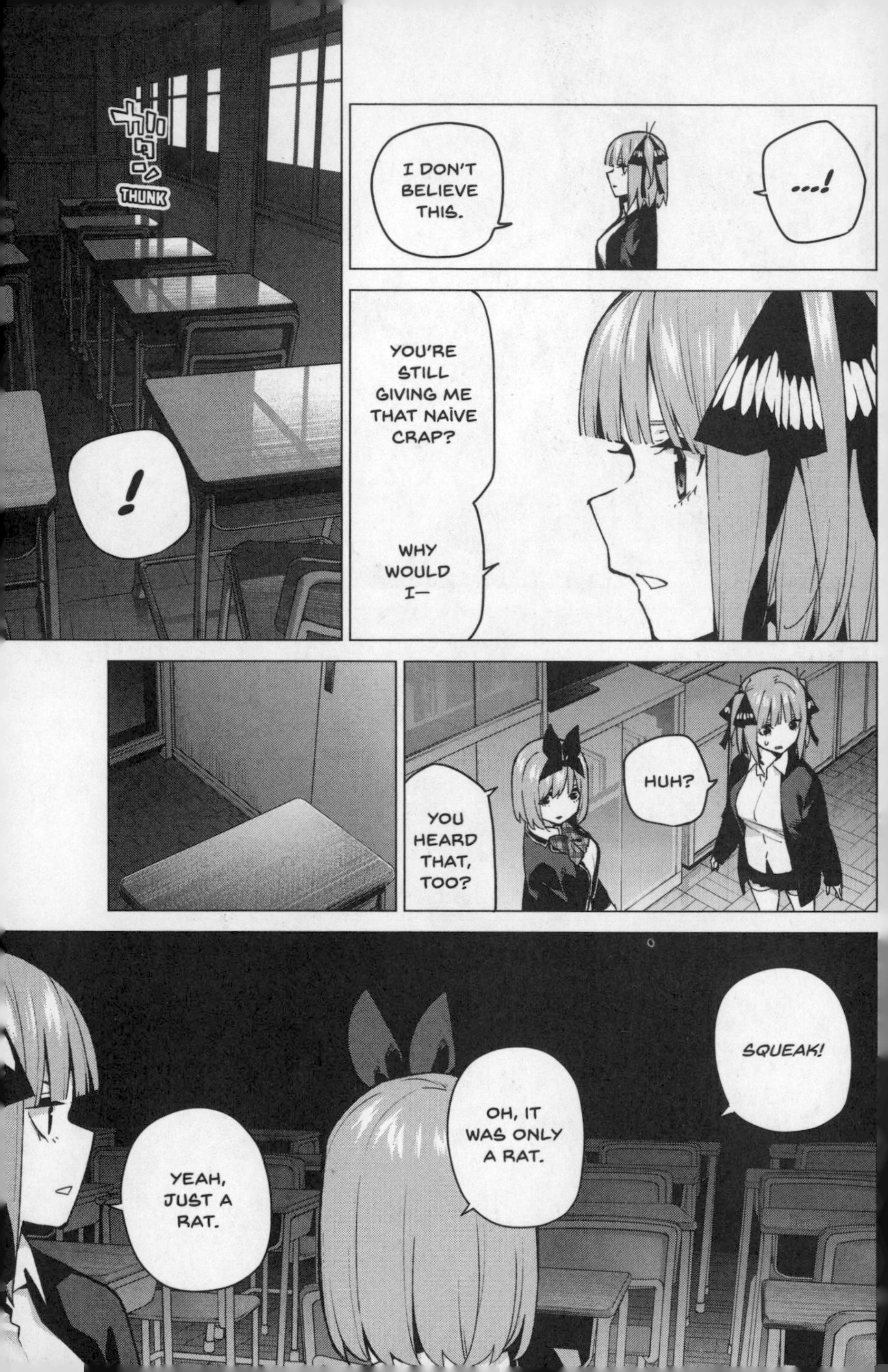
...!
I DON'T BELIEVE THIS.
YOU'RE STILL GIVING ME THAT NAÏVE CRAP?
WHY WOULD I—
THUNK
!
HUH?
YOU HEARD THAT, TOO?
SQUEAK!
OH, IT WAS ONLY A RAT.
YEAH, JUST A RAT.

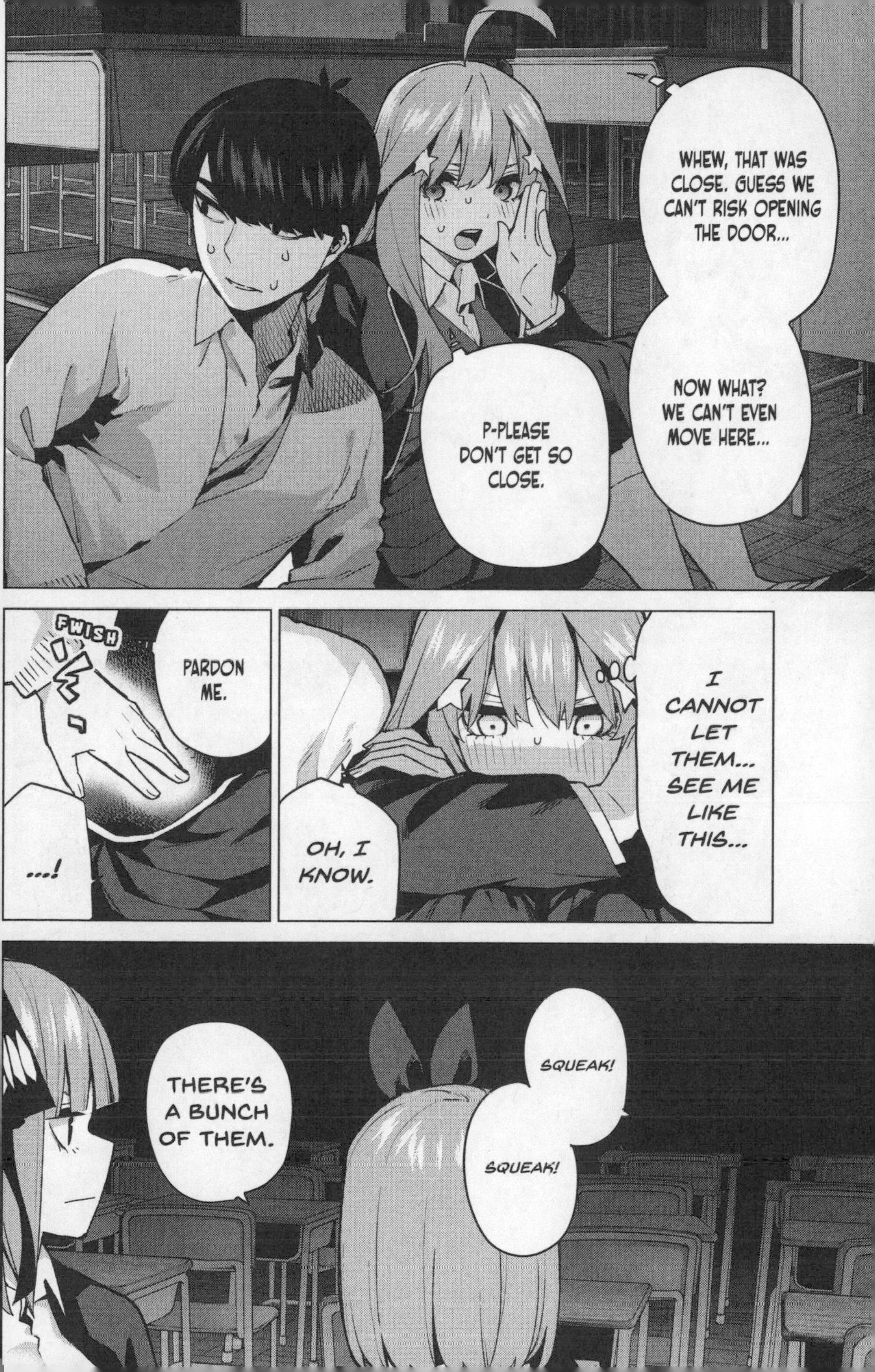
WHEW, THAT WAS CLOSE. GUESS WE CAN'T RISK OPENING THE DOOR...
NOW WHAT? WE CAN'T EVEN MOVE HERE...
P-PLEASE DON'T GET SO CLOSE.
I CANNOT LET THEM... SEE ME LIKE THIS...
OH, I KNOW.
FWISH
PARDON ME.
...!
SQUEAK!
SQUEAK!
THERE'S A BUNCH OF THEM.

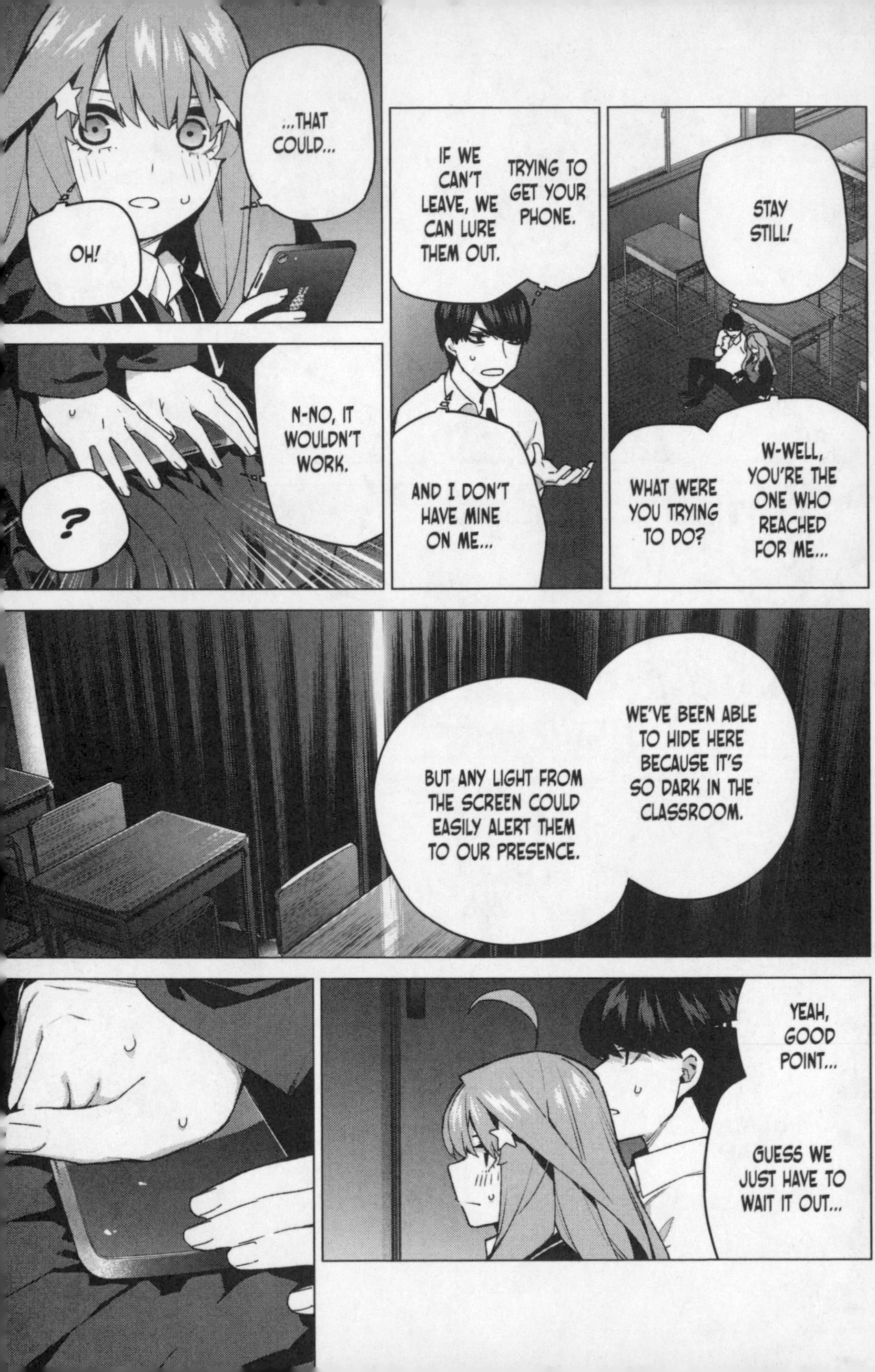
STAY STILL!
W-WELL, YOU'RE THE ONE WHO REACHED FOR ME...
WHAT WERE YOU TRYING TO DO?
TRYING TO GET YOUR PHONE.
IF WE CAN'T LEAVE, WE CAN LURE THEM OUT.
AND I DON'T HAVE MINE ON ME...
...THAT COULD...
OH!
N-NO, IT WOULDN'T WORK.
?
WE'VE BEEN ABLE TO HIDE HERE BECAUSE IT'S SO DARK IN THE CLASSROOM.
BUT ANY LIGHT FROM THE SCREEN COULD EASILY ALERT THEM TO OUR PRESENCE.
YEAH, GOOD POINT...
GUESS WE JUST HAVE TO WAIT IT OUT...

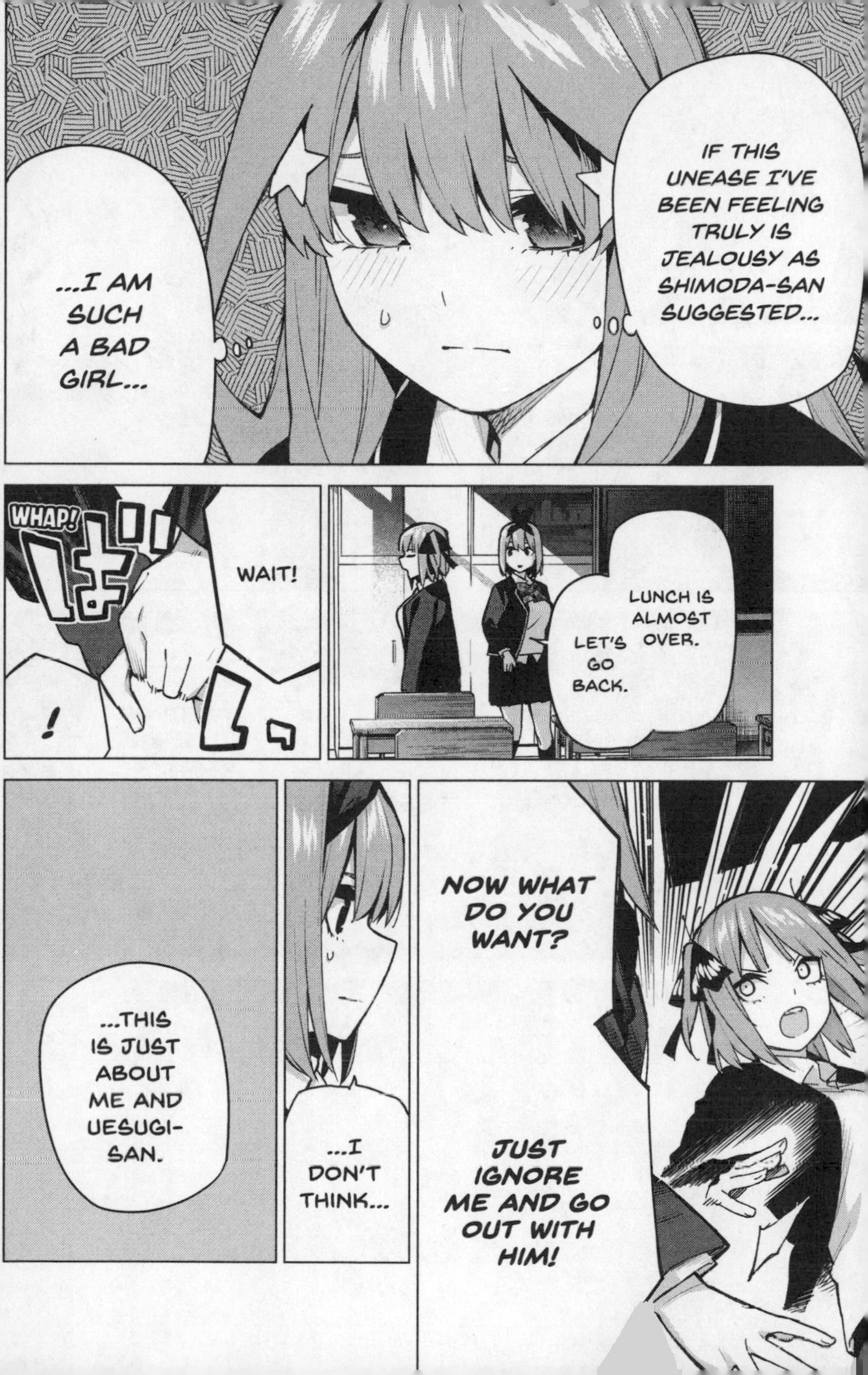
IF THIS UNEASE I'VE BEEN FEELING TRULY IS JEALOUSY AS SHIMODA-SAN SUGGESTED...
...I AM SUCH A BAD GIRL...
LUNCH IS ALMOST OVER. LET'S GO BACK.
WAIT!
WHAP!
NOW WHAT DO YOU WANT?
JUST IGNORE ME AND GO OUT WITH HIM!
...I DON'T THINK...
...THIS IS JUST ABOUT ME AND UESUGI-SAN.

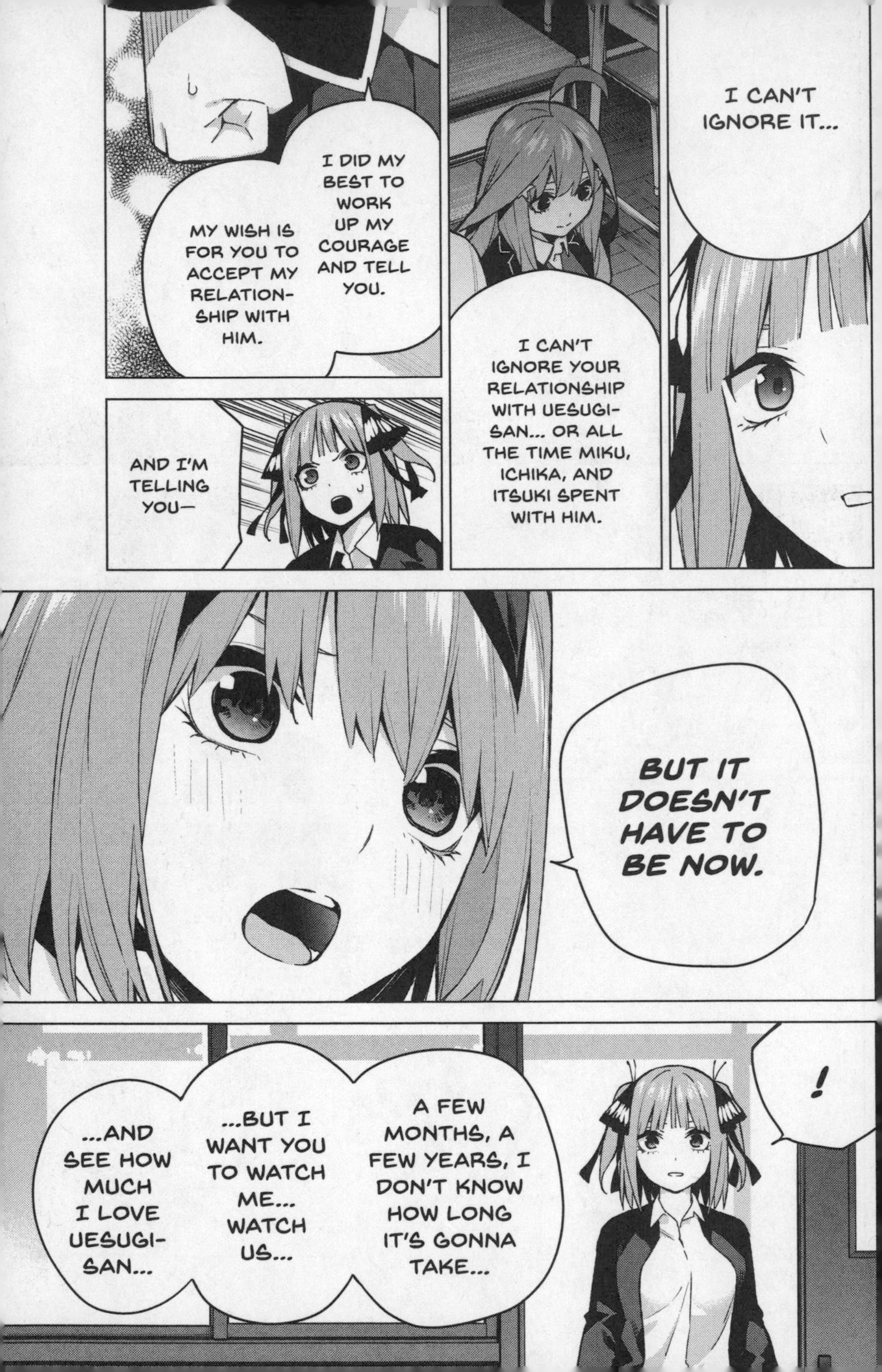
I CAN'T IGNORE IT...
I CAN'T IGNORE YOUR RELATIONSHIP WITH UESUGI-SAN... OR ALL THE TIME MIKU, ICHIKA, AND ITSUKI SPENT WITH HIM.
I DID MY BEST TO WORK UP MY COURAGE AND TELL YOU.
MY WISH IS FOR YOU TO ACCEPT MY RELATIONSHIP WITH HIM.
AND I'M TELLING YOU—
BUT IT DOESN'T HAVE TO BE NOW.
!
A FEW MONTHS, A FEW YEARS, I DON'T KNOW HOW LONG IT'S GONNA TAKE...
...BUT I WANT YOU TO WATCH ME... WATCH US...
...AND SEE HOW MUCH I LOVE UESUGI-SAN...

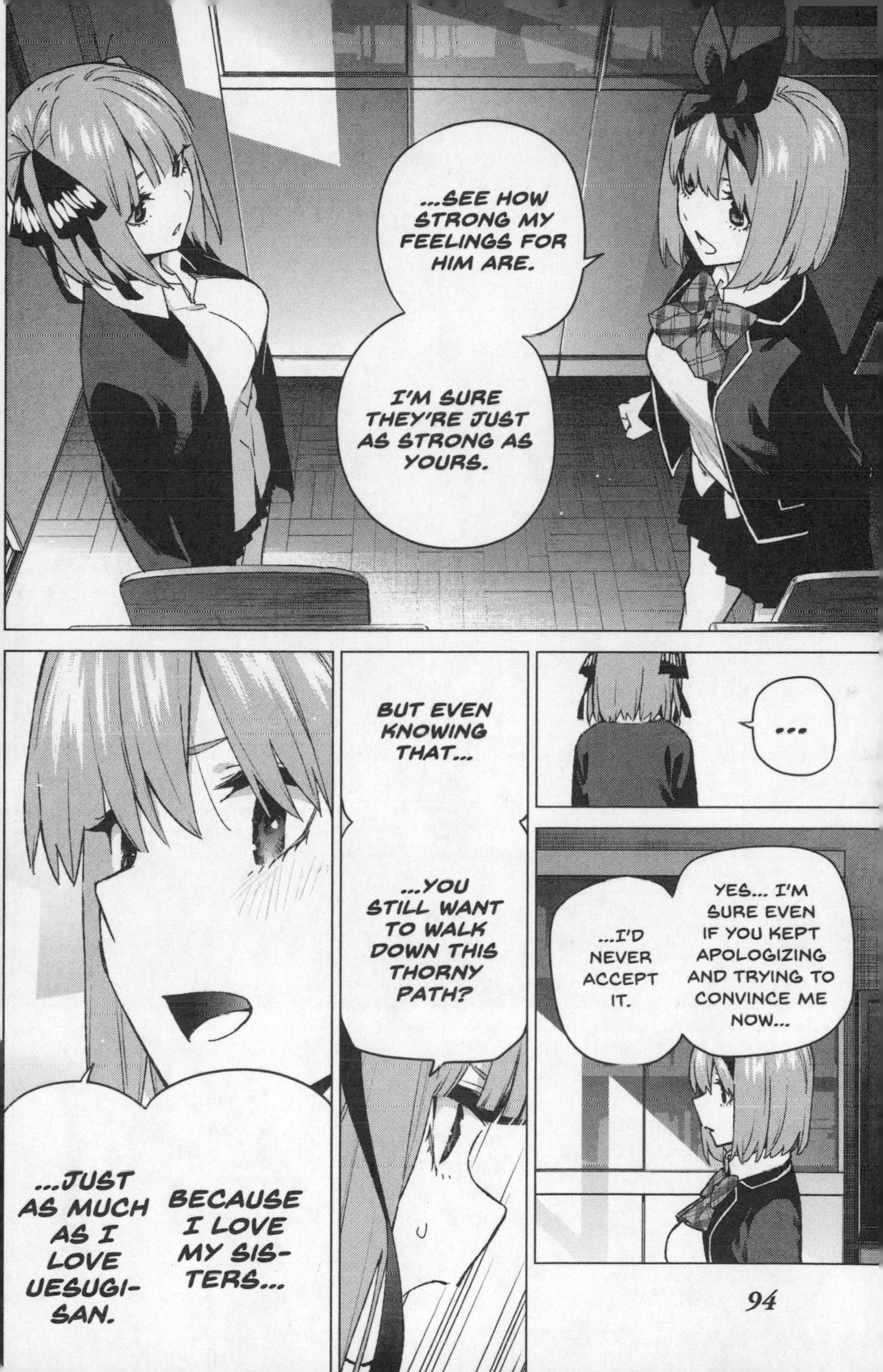
...SEE HOW STRONG MY FEELINGS FOR HIM ARE.
I'M SURE THEY'RE JUST AS STRONG AS YOURS.
...
YES... I'M SURE EVEN IF YOU KEPT APOLOGIZING AND TRYING TO CONVINCE ME NOW...
...I'D NEVER ACCEPT IT.
BUT EVEN KNOWING THAT...
...YOU STILL WANT TO WALK DOWN THIS THORNY PATH?
BECAUSE I LOVE MY SIS-TERS...
...JUST AS MUCH AS I LOVE UESUGI-SAN.

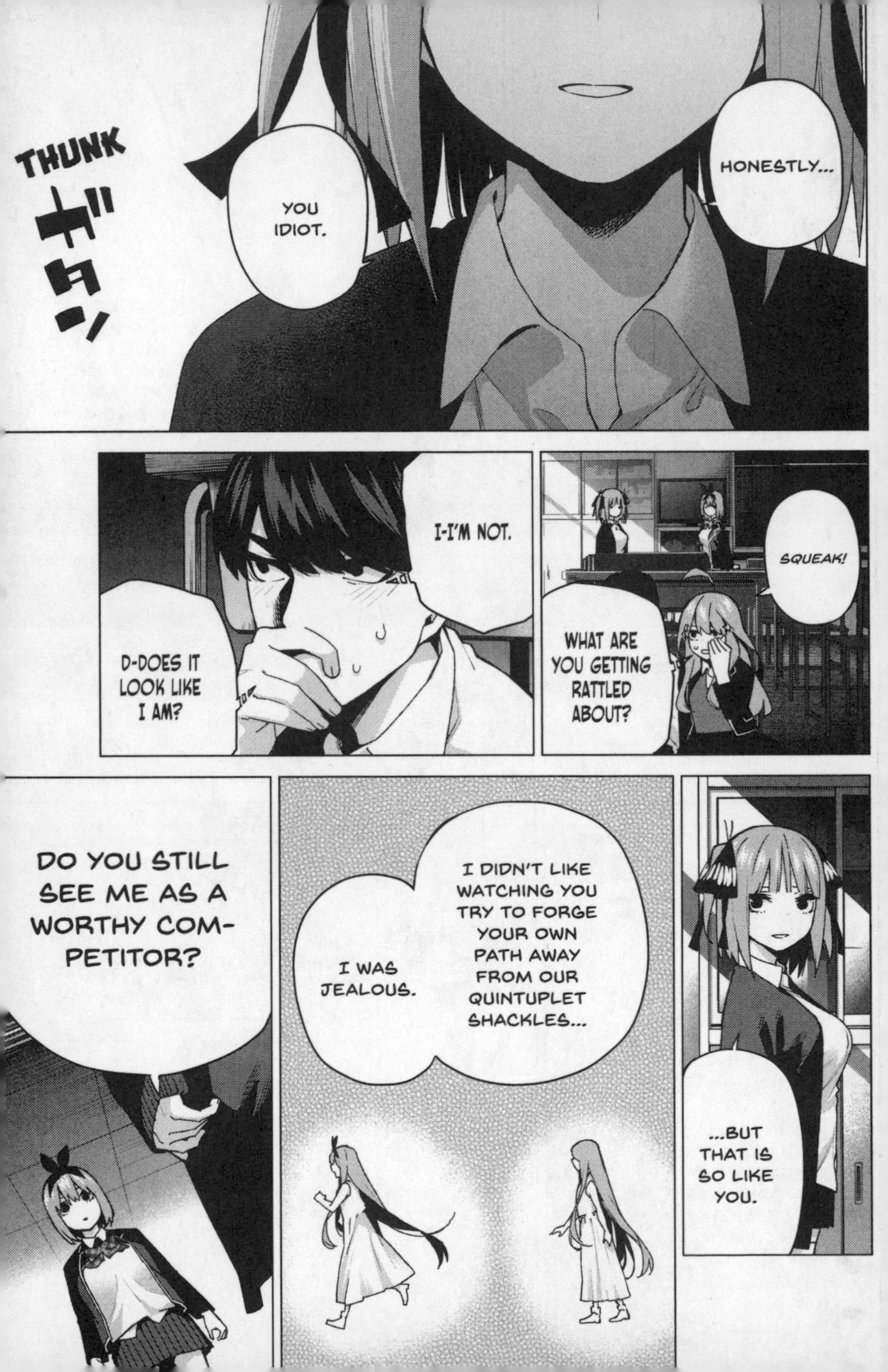
HONESTLY...
YOU IDIOT.
THUNK
ガタッ
SQUEAK!
WHAT ARE YOU GETTING RATTLED ABOUT?
I-I'M NOT.
D-DOES IT LOOK LIKE I AM?
...BUT THAT IS SO LIKE YOU.
I DIDN'T LIKE WATCHING YOU TRY TO FORGE YOUR OWN PATH AWAY FROM OUR QUINTUPLET SHACKLES...
I WAS JEALOUS.
DO YOU STILL SEE ME AS A WORTHY COM-PETITOR?

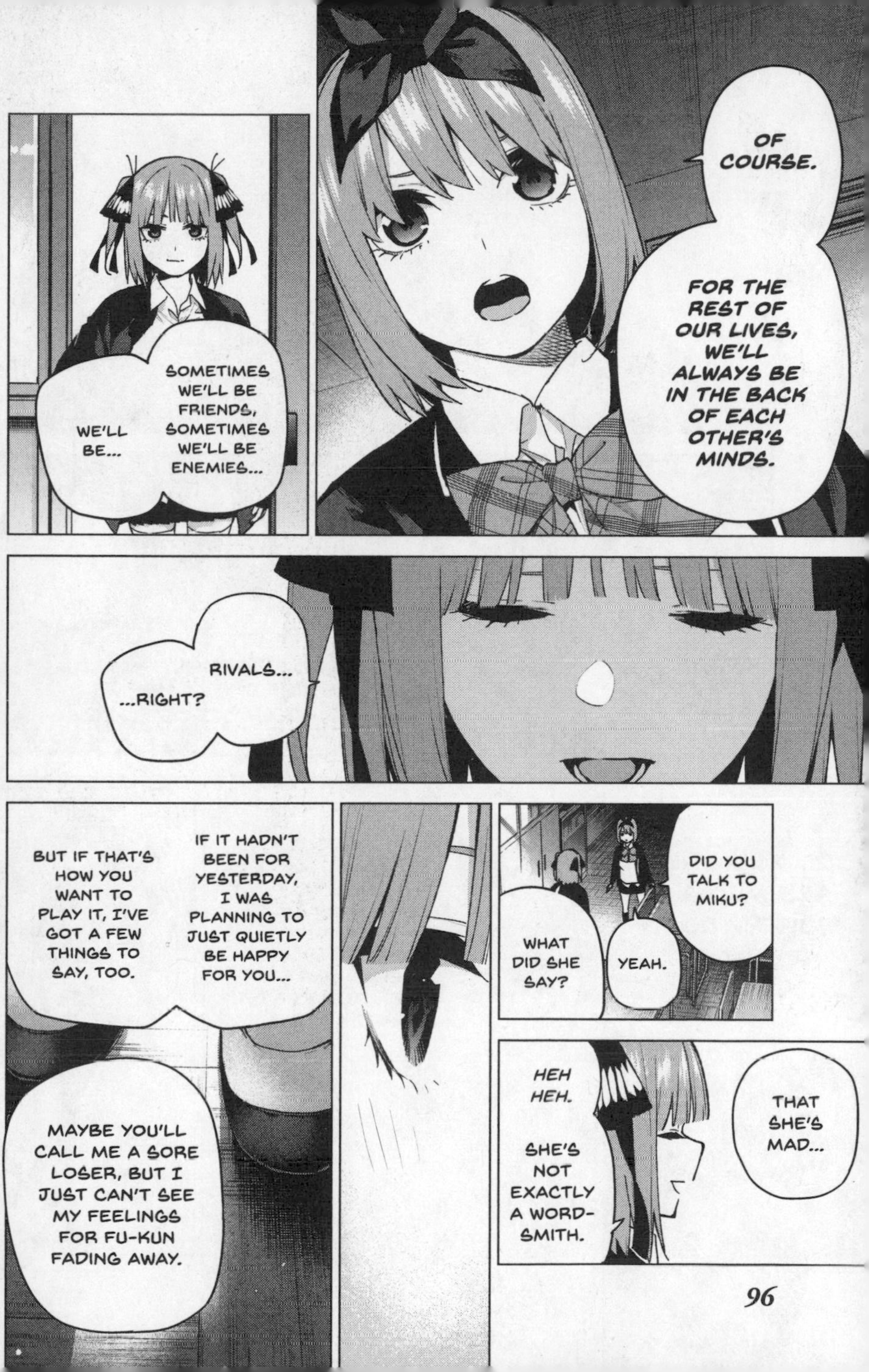
OF COURSE.
FOR THE REST OF OUR LIVES, WE'LL ALWAYS BE IN THE BACK OF EACH OTHER'S MINDS.
SOMETIMES WE'LL BE FRIENDS, SOMETIMES WE'LL BE ENEMIES...
WE'LL BE...
RIVALS...
...RIGHT?
DID YOU TALK TO MIKU?
YEAH.
WHAT DID SHE SAY?
THAT SHE'S MAD...
HEH HEH.
SHE'S NOT EXACTLY A WORD-SMITH.
IF IT HADN'T BEEN FOR YESTERDAY, I WAS PLANNING TO JUST QUIETLY BE HAPPY FOR YOU...
BUT IF THAT'S HOW YOU WANT TO PLAY IT, I'VE GOT A FEW THINGS TO SAY, TOO.
MAYBE YOU'LL CALL ME A SORE LOSER, BUT I JUST CAN'T SEE MY FEELINGS FOR FU-KUN FADING AWAY.

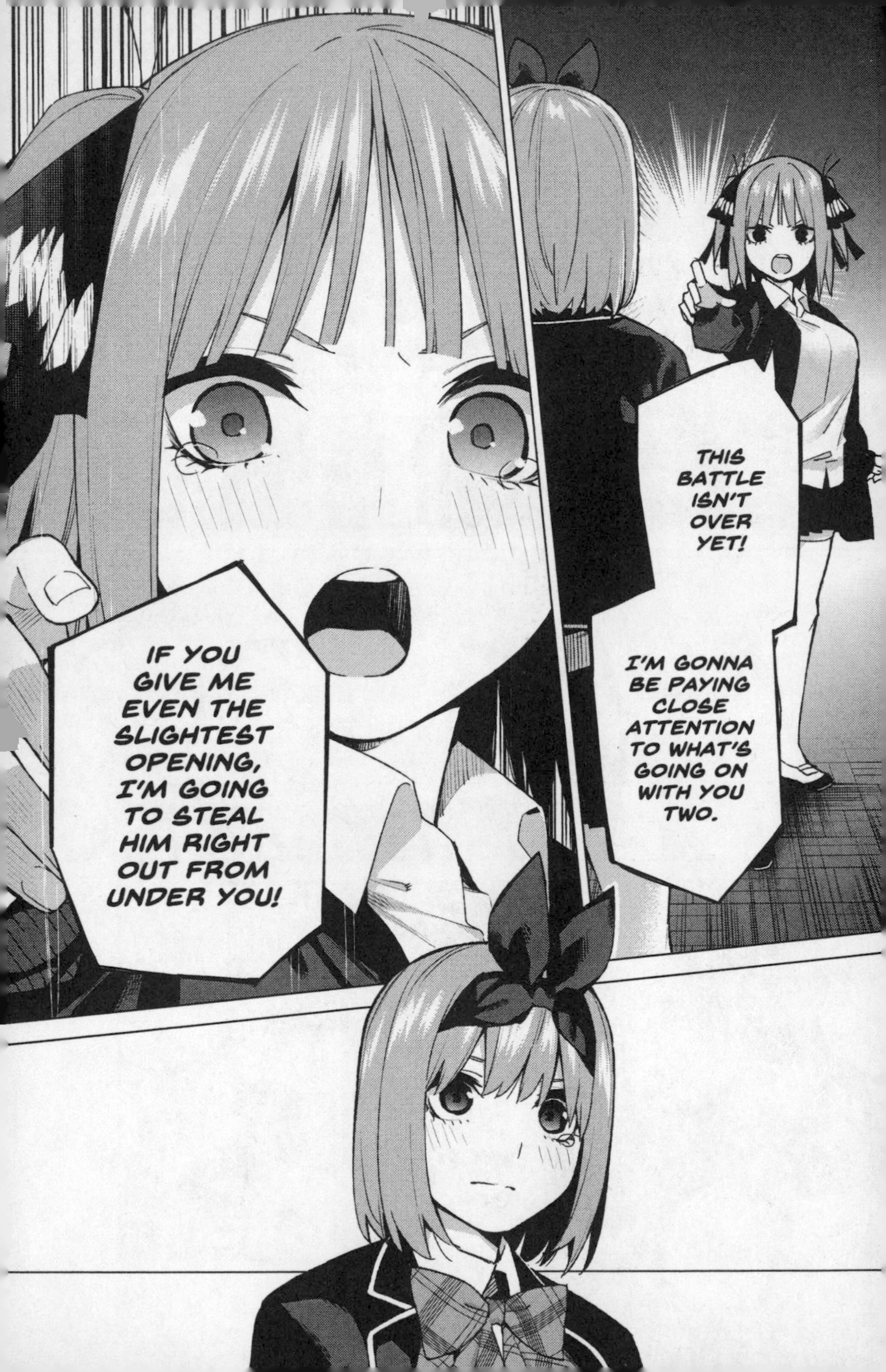
THIS BATTLE ISN'T OVER YET!
I'M GONNA BE PAYING CLOSE ATTENTION TO WHAT'S GOING ON WITH YOU TWO.
IF YOU GIVE ME EVEN THE SLIGHTEST OPENING, I'M GOING TO STEAL HIM RIGHT OUT FROM UNDER YOU!

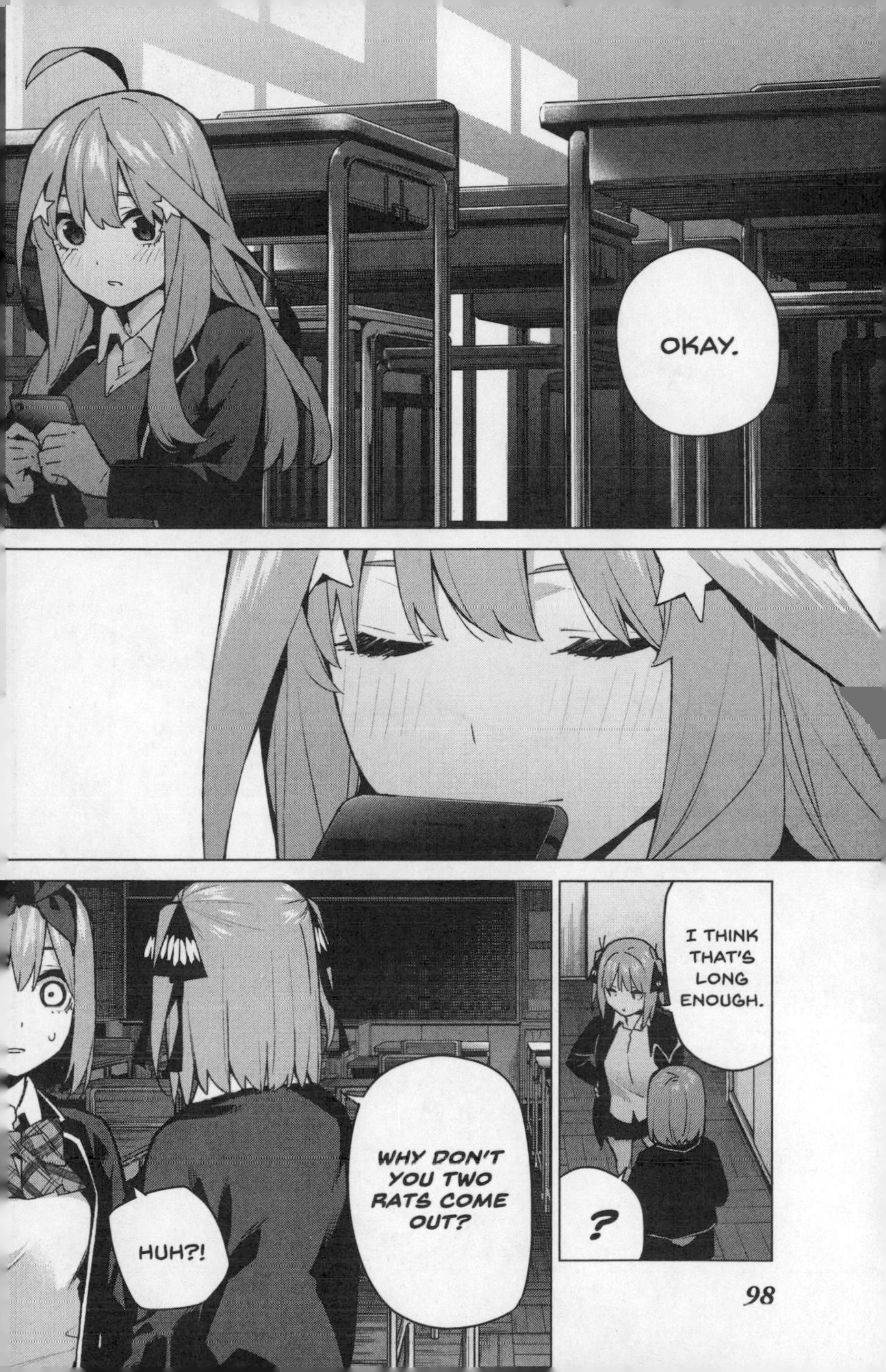
OKAY.
I THINK THAT'S LONG ENOUGH.
?
WHY DON'T YOU TWO RATS COME OUT?
HUH?!

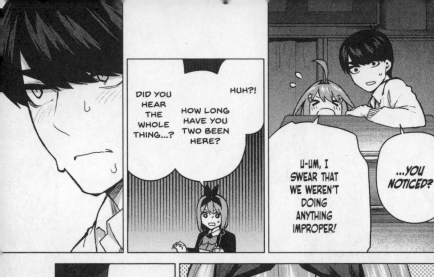

DID YOU HEAR THE WHOLE THING...?

HUH?!

HOW LONG HAVE YOU TWO BEEN HERE?

...YOU NOTICED?

U-UM, I SWEAR THAT WE WEREN'T DOING ANYTHING IMPROPER!

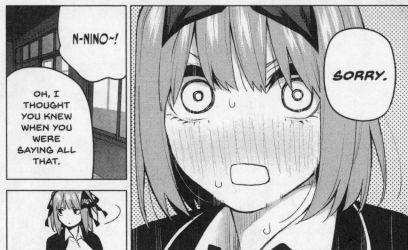

N-NINO~!

OH, I THOUGHT YOU KNEW WHEN YOU WERE SAYING ALL THAT.

SORRY.

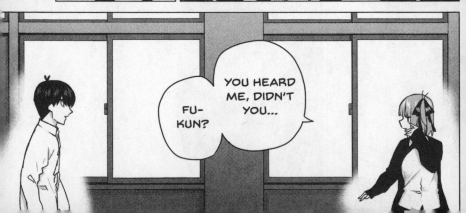

YOU HEARD ME, DIDN'T YOU...

FU-KUN?

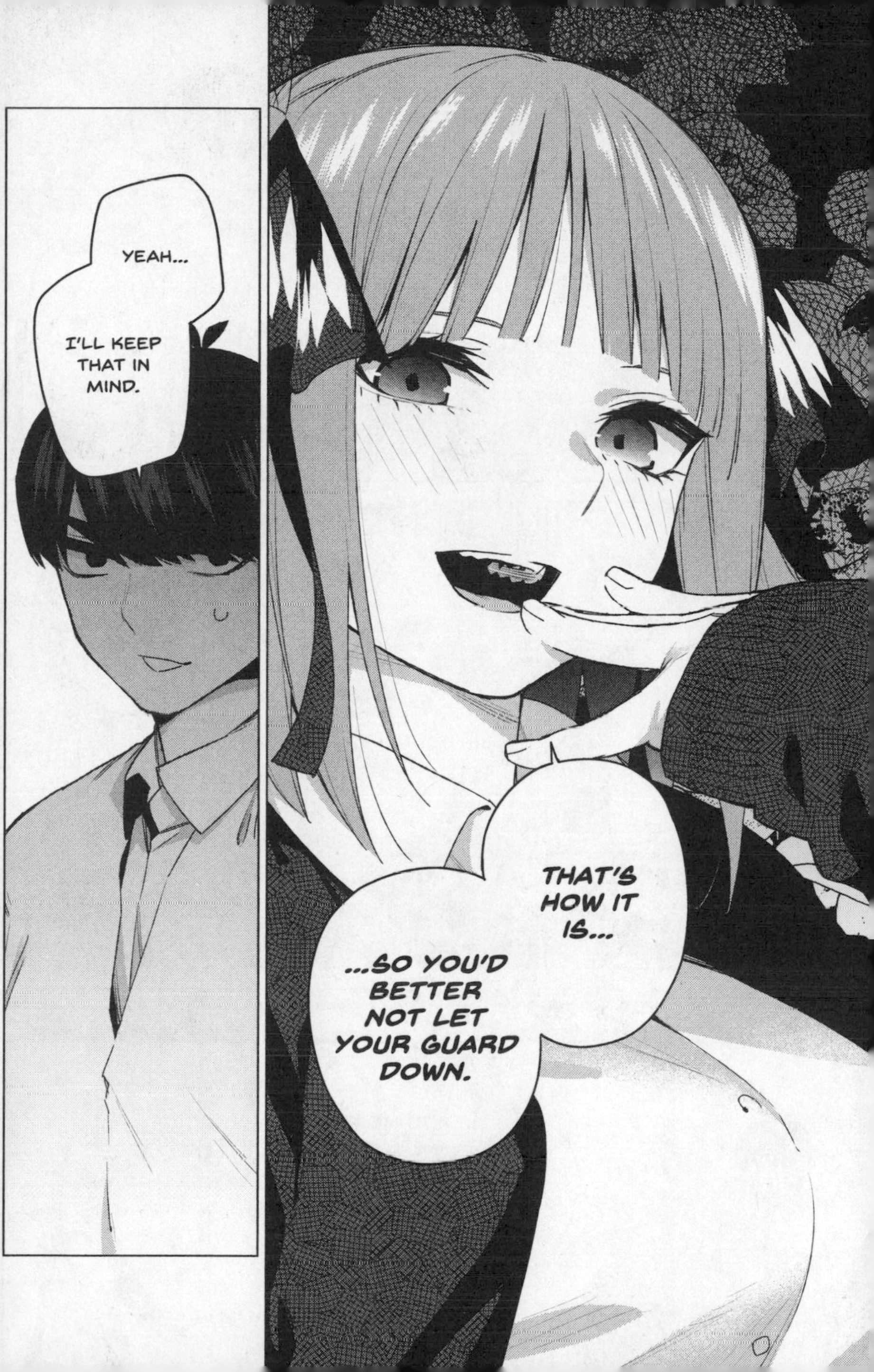
THAT'S HOW IT IS...
...SO YOU'D BETTER NOT LET YOUR GUARD DOWN.
YEAH...
I'LL KEEP THAT IN MIND.

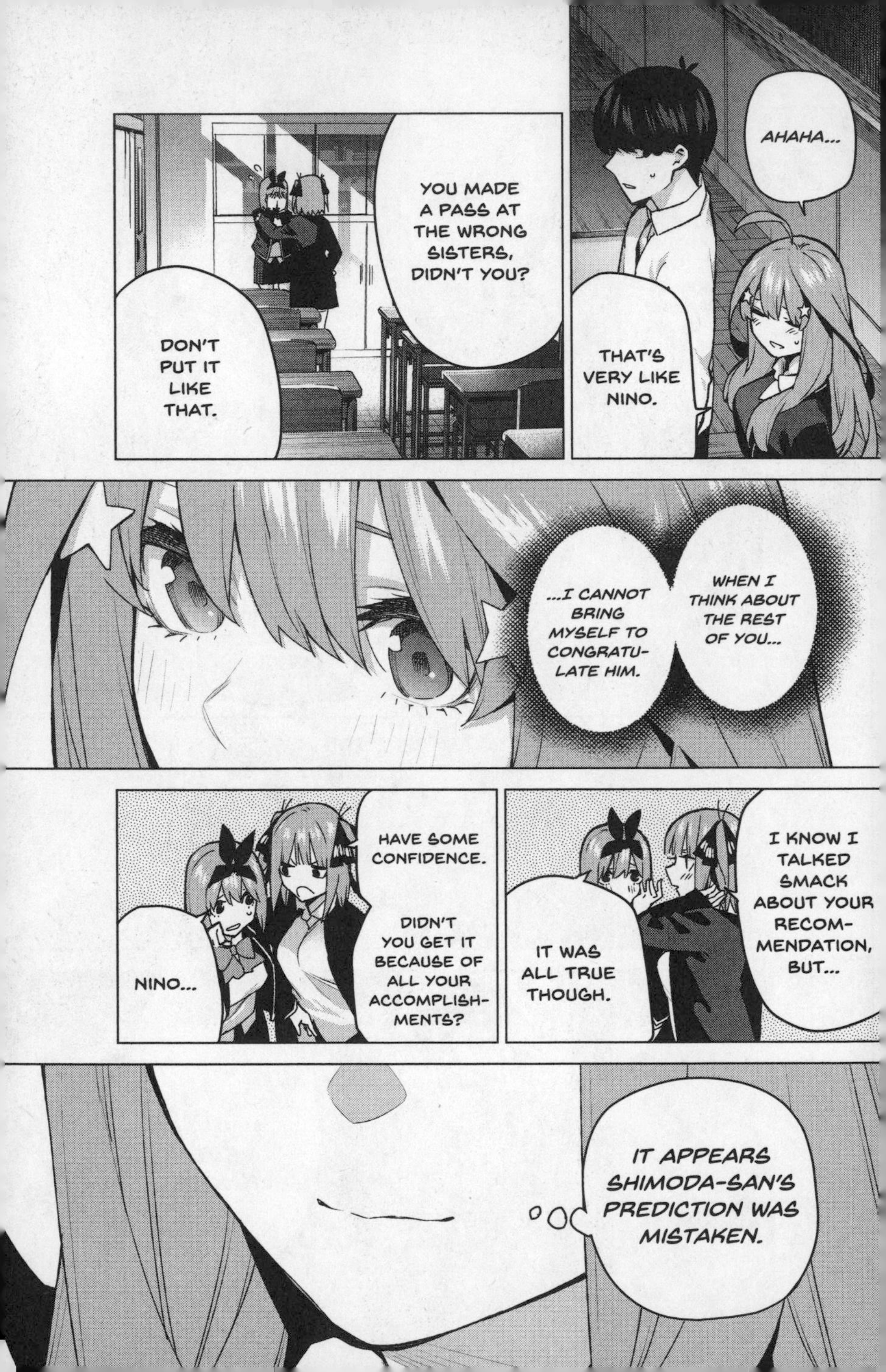
AHAHA...
THAT'S VERY LIKE NINO.
YOU MADE A PASS AT THE WRONG SISTERS, DIDN'T YOU?
DON'T PUT IT LIKE THAT.
WHEN I THINK ABOUT THE REST OF YOU...
...I CANNOT BRING MYSELF TO CONGRATULATE HIM.
I KNOW I TALKED SMACK ABOUT YOUR RECOMMENDATION, BUT...
IT WAS ALL TRUE THOUGH.
HAVE SOME CONFIDENCE.
DIDN'T YOU GET IT BECAUSE OF ALL YOUR ACCOMPLISHMENTS?
NINO...
IT APPEARS SHIMODA-SAN'S PREDICTION WAS MISTAKEN.

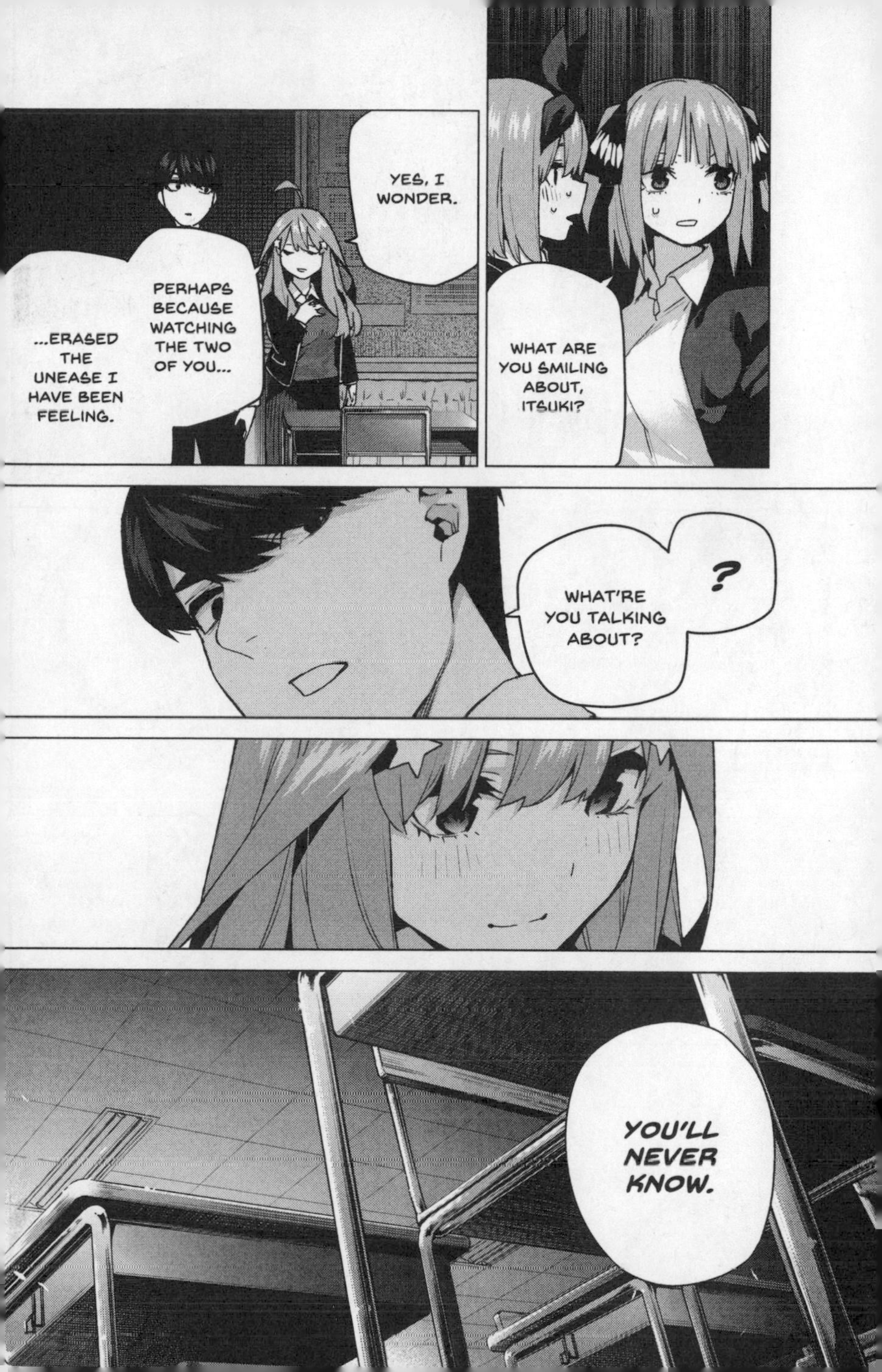
WHAT ARE YOU SMILING ABOUT, ITSUKI?
YES, I WONDER.
PERHAPS BECAUSE WATCHING THE TWO OF YOU...
...ERASED THE UNEASE I HAVE BEEN FEELING.
?
WHAT'RE YOU TALKING ABOUT?
YOU'LL NEVER KNOW.

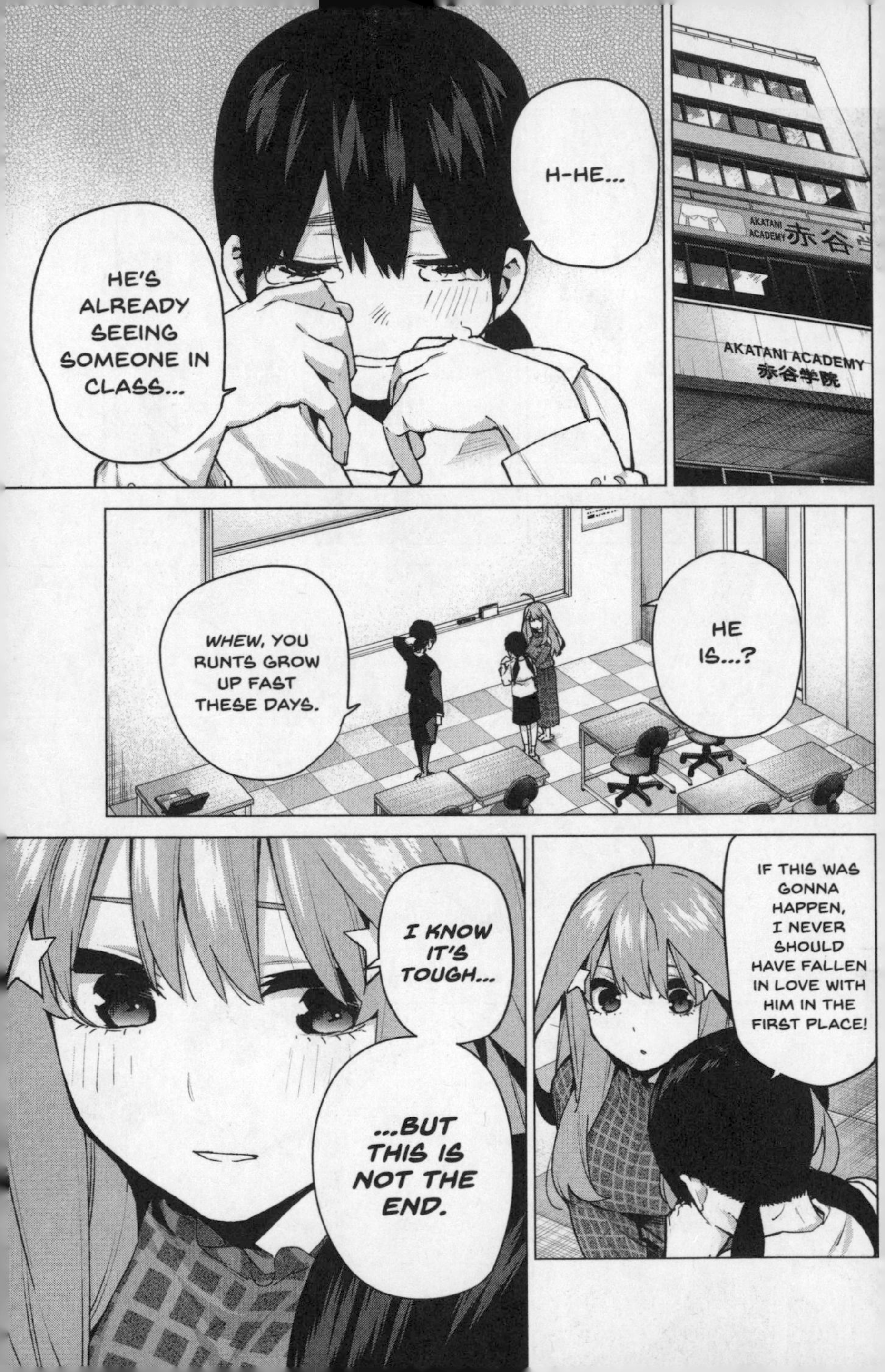
AKATANI ACADEMY 赤谷
AKATANI ACADEMY
赤谷学院
H-HE...
HE'S ALREADY SEEING SOMEONE IN CLASS...
HE IS...?
WHEW, YOU RUNTS GROW UP FAST THESE DAYS.
IF THIS WAS GONNA HAPPEN, I NEVER SHOULD HAVE FALLEN IN LOVE WITH HIM IN THE FIRST PLACE!
I KNOW IT'S TOUGH...
...BUT THIS IS NOT THE END.

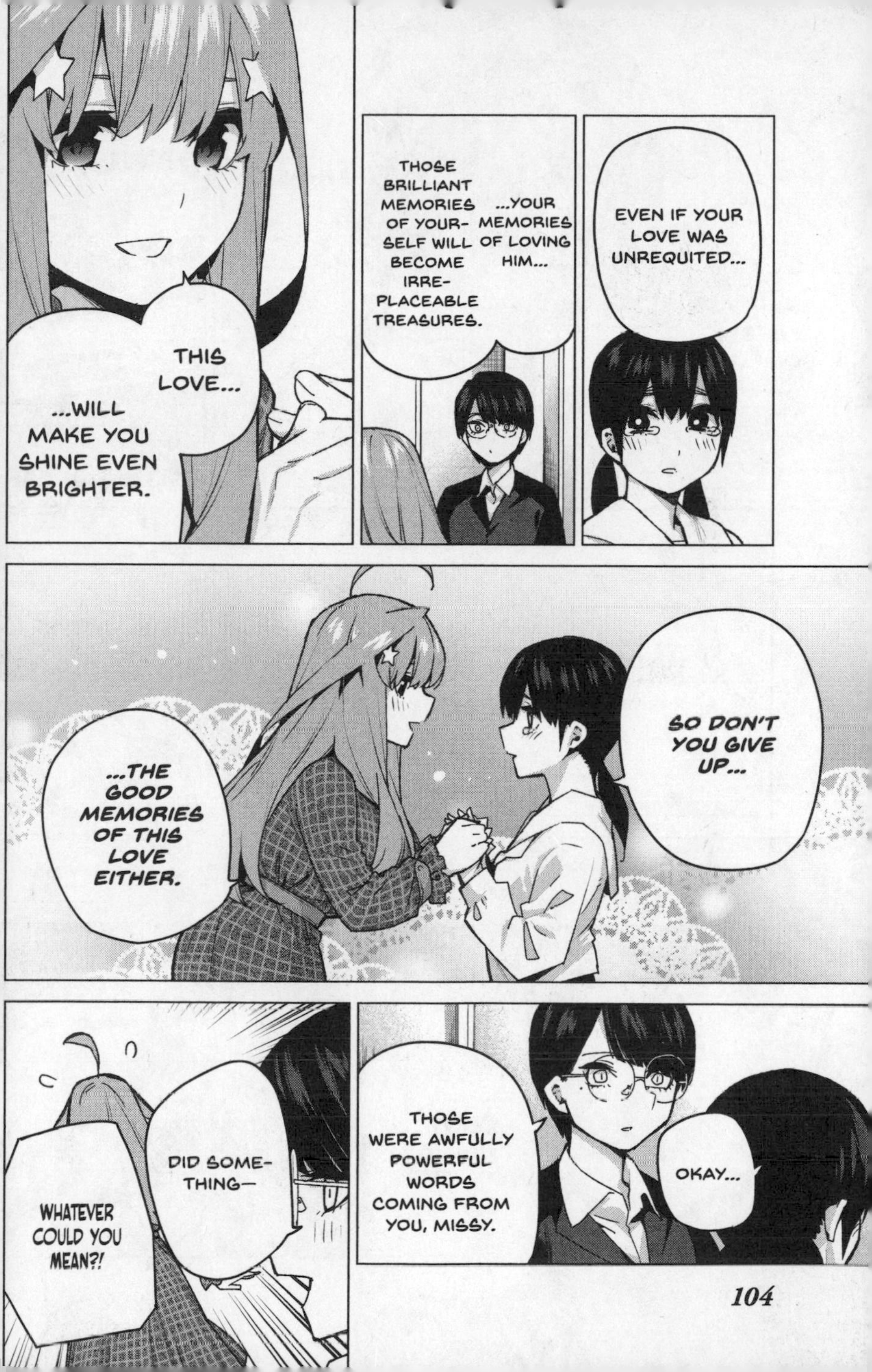
EVEN IF YOUR LOVE WAS UNREQUITED...
...YOUR MEMORIES OF LOVING HIM...
THOSE BRILLIANT MEMORIES OF YOUR-SELF WILL BECOME IRRE-PLACEABLE TREASURES.
THIS LOVE...
...WILL MAKE YOU SHINE EVEN BRIGHTER.
SO DON'T YOU GIVE UP...
...THE GOOD MEMORIES OF THIS LOVE EITHER.
OKAY...
THOSE WERE AWFULLY POWERFUL WORDS COMING FROM YOU, MISSY.
DID SOME-THING—
WHATEVER COULD YOU MEAN?!

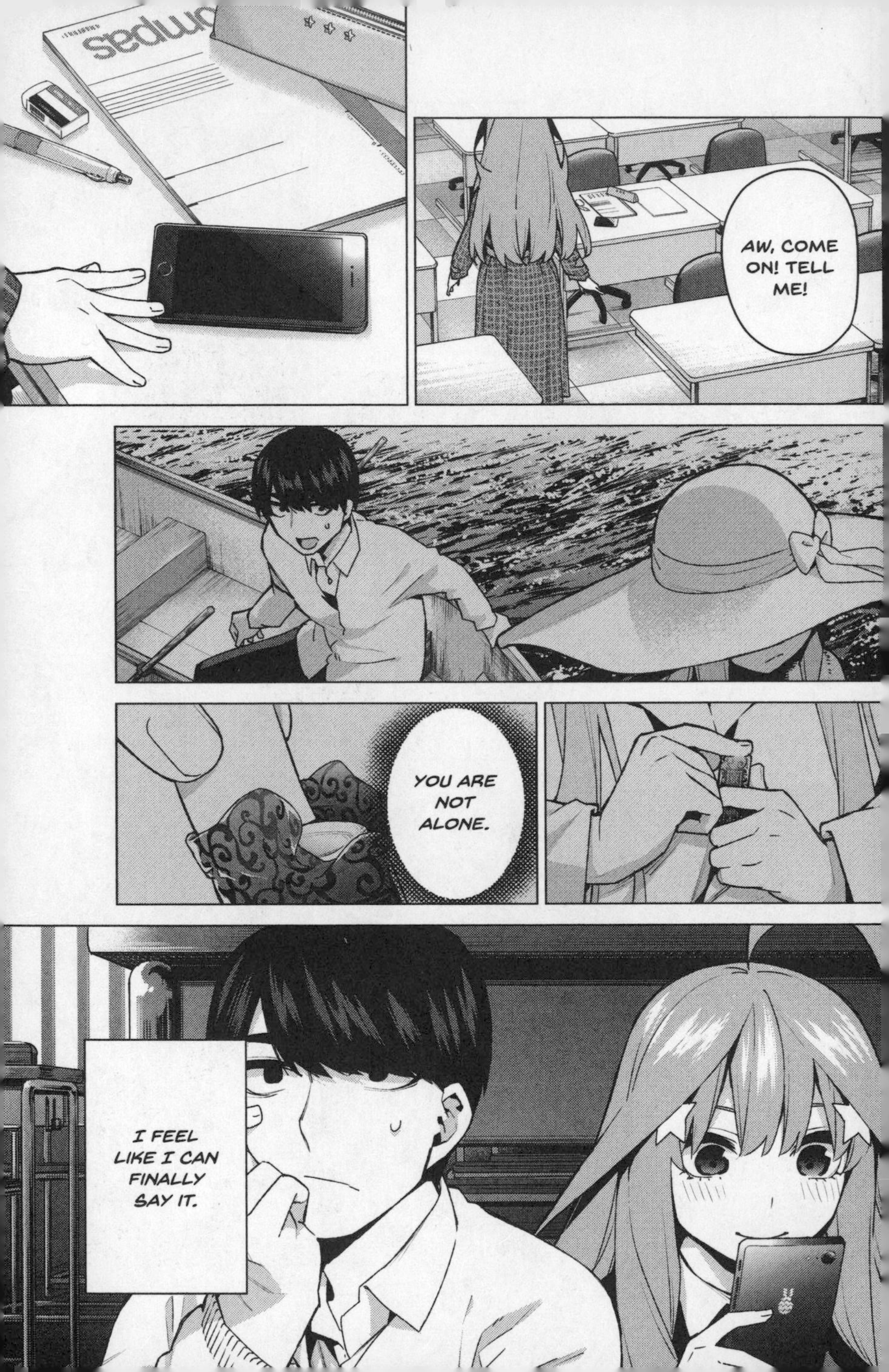
AW, COME ON! TELL ME!
YOU ARE NOT ALONE.
I FEEL LIKE I CAN FINALLY SAY IT.

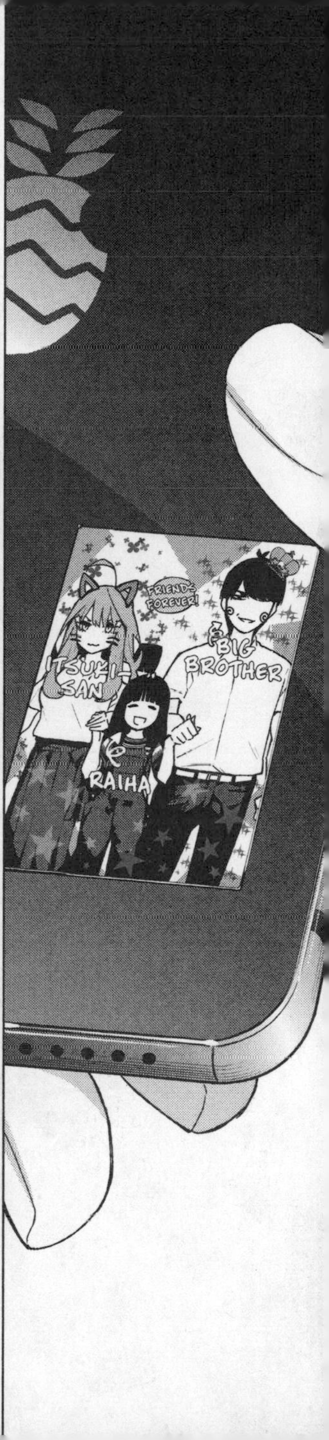
FRIENDS FOREVER!
ITSUKI-SAN
BIG BROTHER
RAIHA
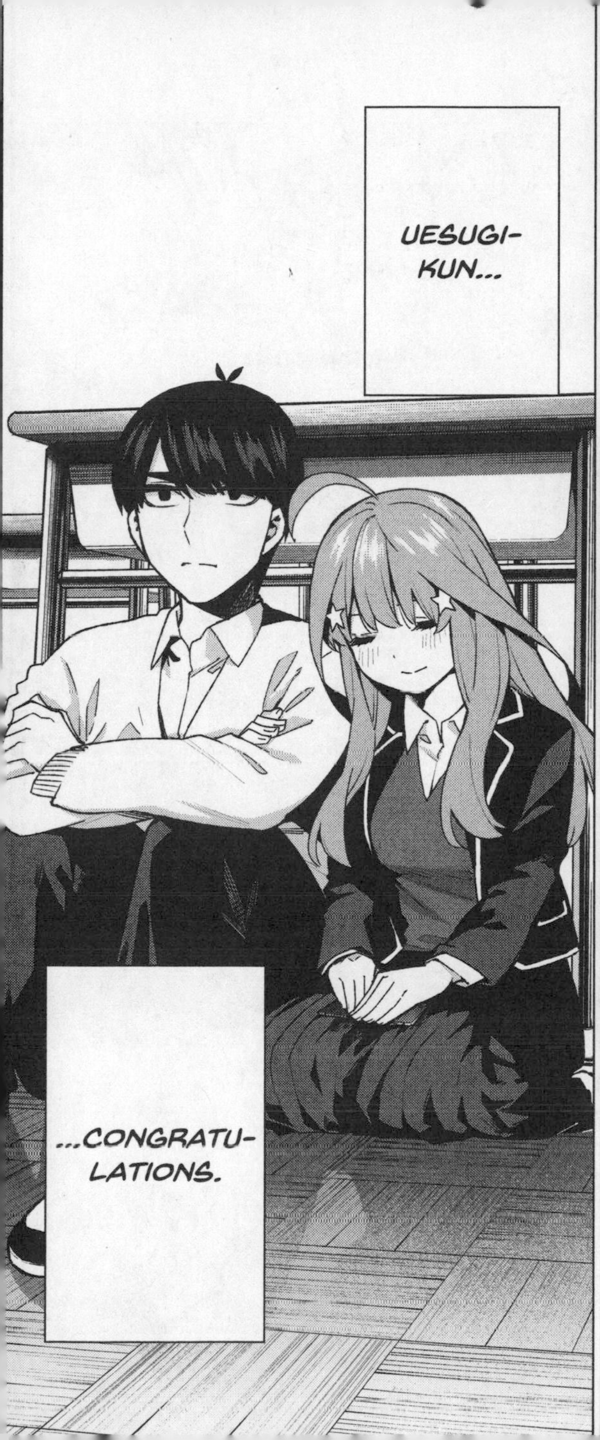
UESUGI-KUN...
...CONGRATU-LATIONS.

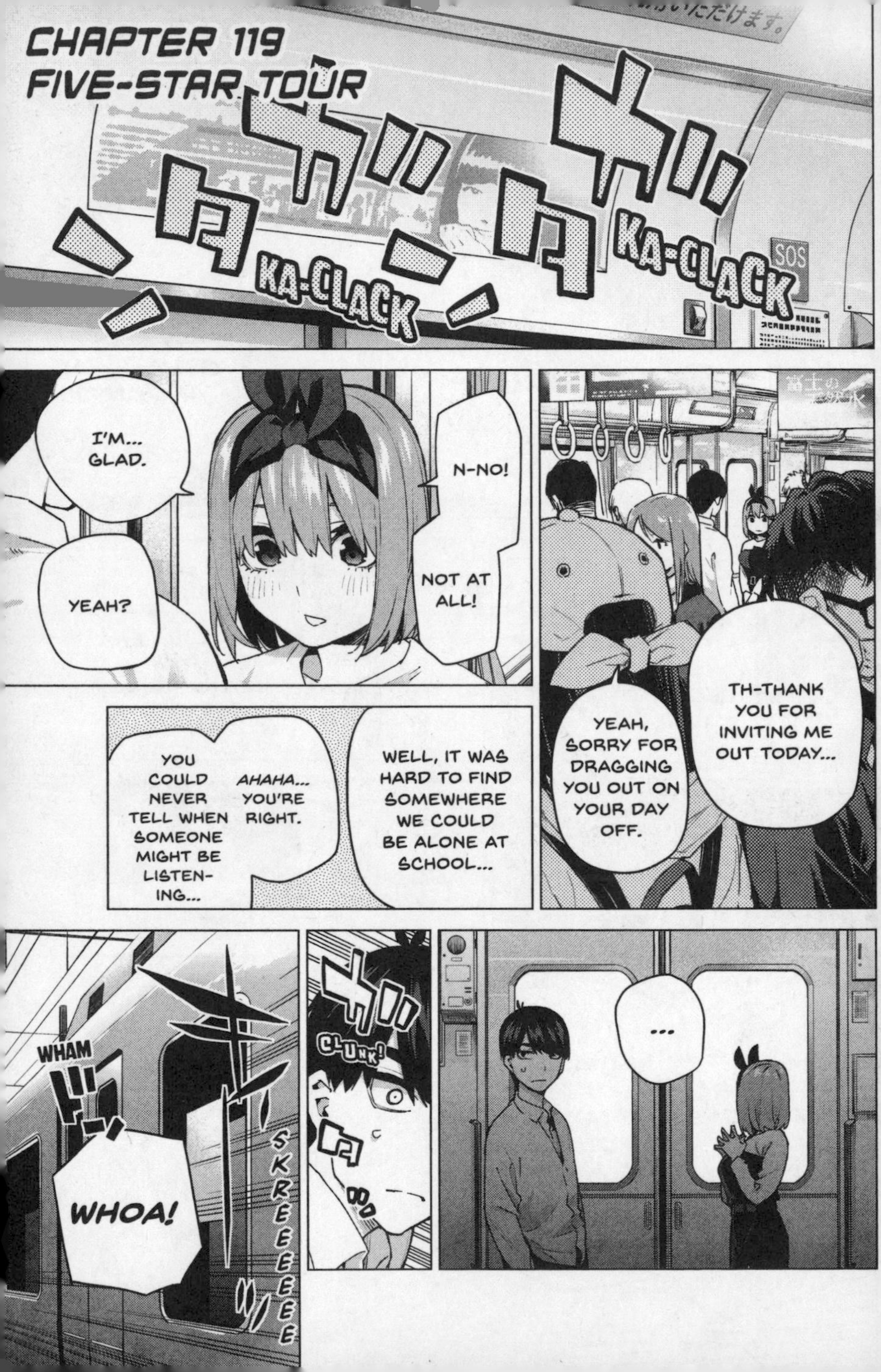

CHAPTER 119
FIVE-STAR TOUR
KA-CLACK
KA-CLACK
TH-THANK YOU FOR INVITING ME OUT TODAY...
YEAH, SORRY FOR DRAGGING YOU OUT ON YOUR DAY OFF.
N-NO!
NOT AT ALL!
I'M... GLAD.
YEAH?
WELL, IT WAS HARD TO FIND SOMEWHERE WE COULD BE ALONE AT SCHOOL...
YOU COULD NEVER TELL WHEN SOMEONE MIGHT BE LISTEN-ING...
AHAHA... YOU'RE RIGHT.
...
CLUNK!
WHAM
WHOA!
SKREEEEEEEE

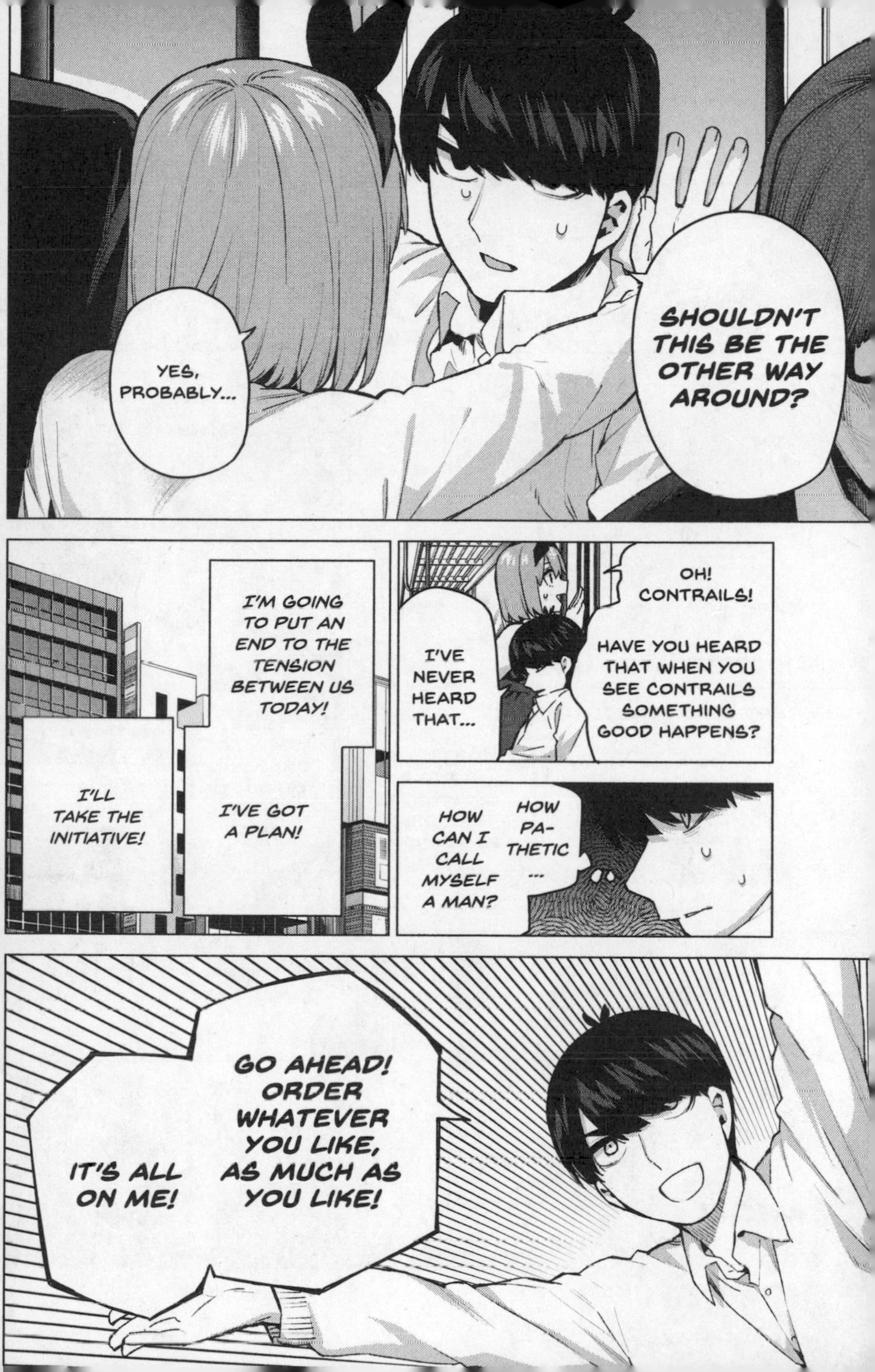
SHOULDN'T THIS BE THE OTHER WAY AROUND?
YES, PROBABLY...
OH! CONTRAILS!
HAVE YOU HEARD THAT WHEN YOU SEE CONTRAILS SOMETHING GOOD HAPPENS?
I'VE NEVER HEARD THAT...
HOW PATHETIC...
HOW CAN I CALL MYSELF A MAN?
I'M GOING TO PUT AN END TO THE TENSION BETWEEN US TODAY!
I'VE GOT A PLAN!
I'LL TAKE THE INITIATIVE!
GO AHEAD! ORDER WHATEVER YOU LIKE, AS MUCH AS YOU LIKE!
IT'S ALL ON ME!

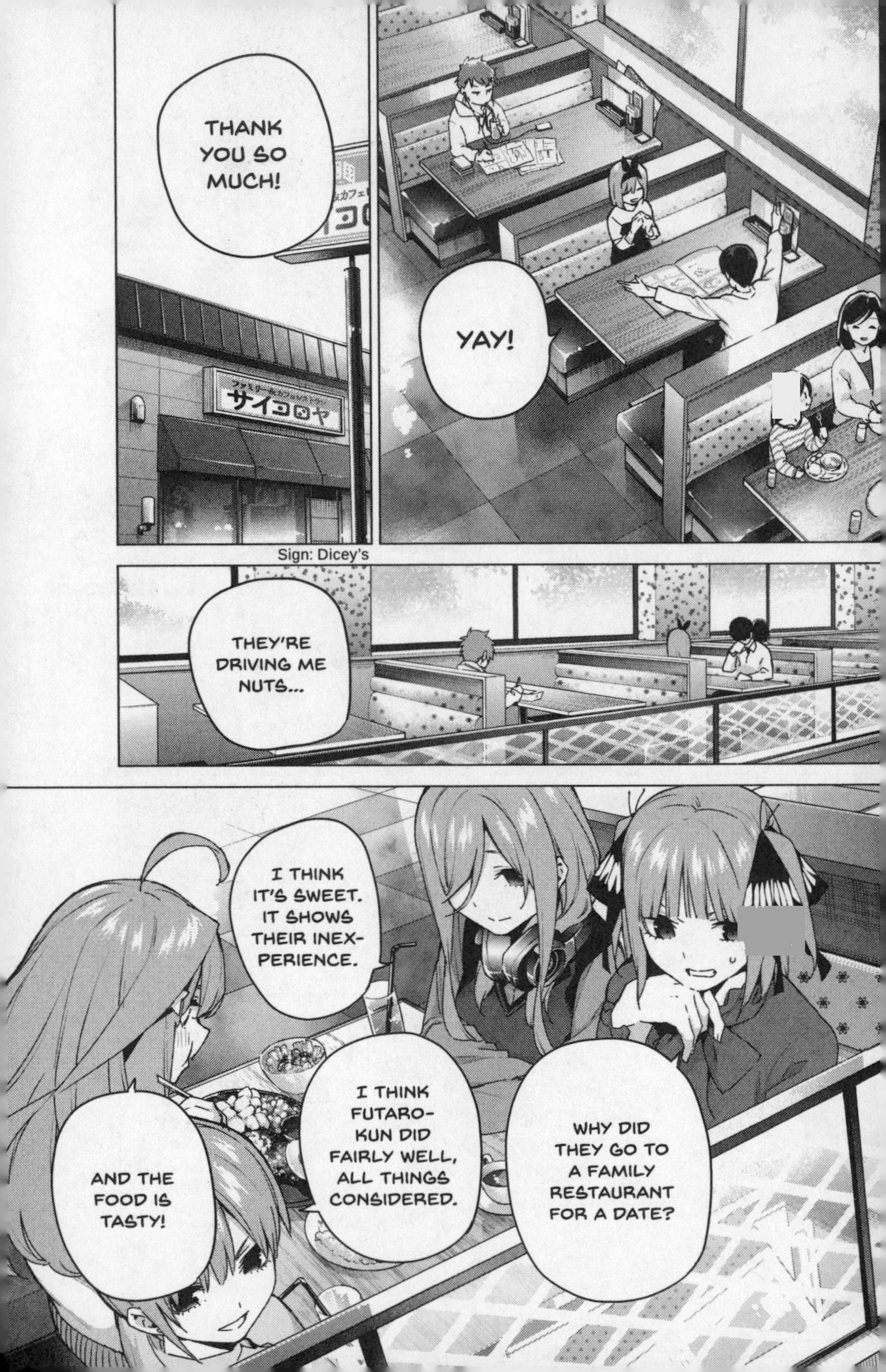
YAY!
THANK YOU SO MUCH!
サイコロヤ
Sign: Dicey's
THEY'RE DRIVING ME NUTS...
WHY DID THEY GO TO A FAMILY RESTAURANT FOR A DATE?
I THINK IT'S SWEET. IT SHOWS THEIR INEXPERIENCE.
I THINK FUTARO-KUN DID FAIRLY WELL, ALL THINGS CONSIDERED.
AND THE FOOD IS TASTY!

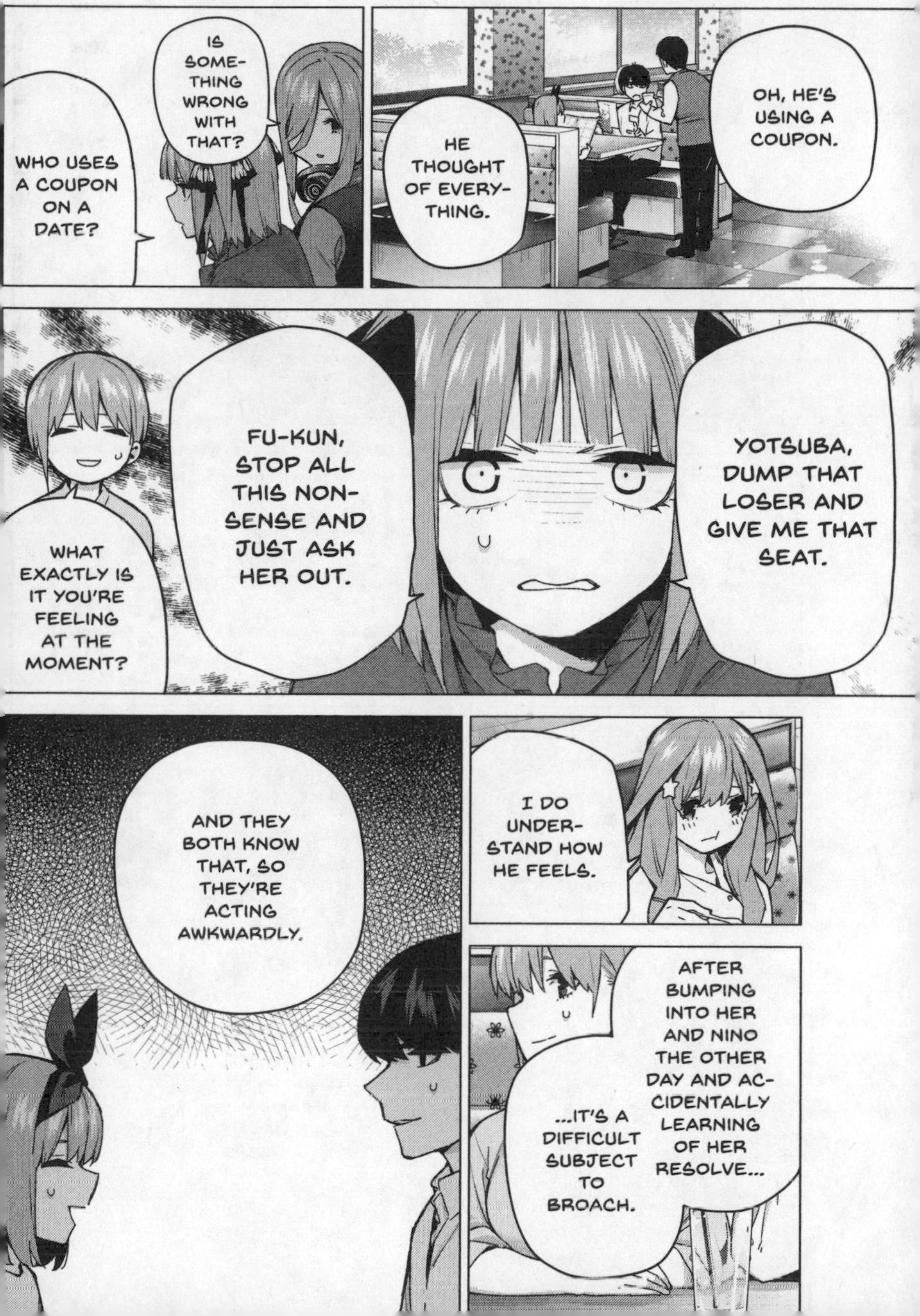
OH, HE'S USING A COUPON.
HE THOUGHT OF EVERYTHING.
IS SOMETHING WRONG WITH THAT?
WHO USES A COUPON ON A DATE?
YOTSUBA, DUMP THAT LOSER AND GIVE ME THAT SEAT.
FU-KUN, STOP ALL THIS NONSENSE AND JUST ASK HER OUT.
WHAT EXACTLY IS IT YOU'RE FEELING AT THE MOMENT?
I DO UNDERSTAND HOW HE FEELS.
AFTER BUMPING INTO HER AND NINO THE OTHER DAY AND ACCIDENTALLY LEARNING OF HER RESOLVE...
...IT'S A DIFFICULT SUBJECT TO BROACH.
AND THEY BOTH KNOW THAT, SO THEY'RE ACTING AWKWARDLY.

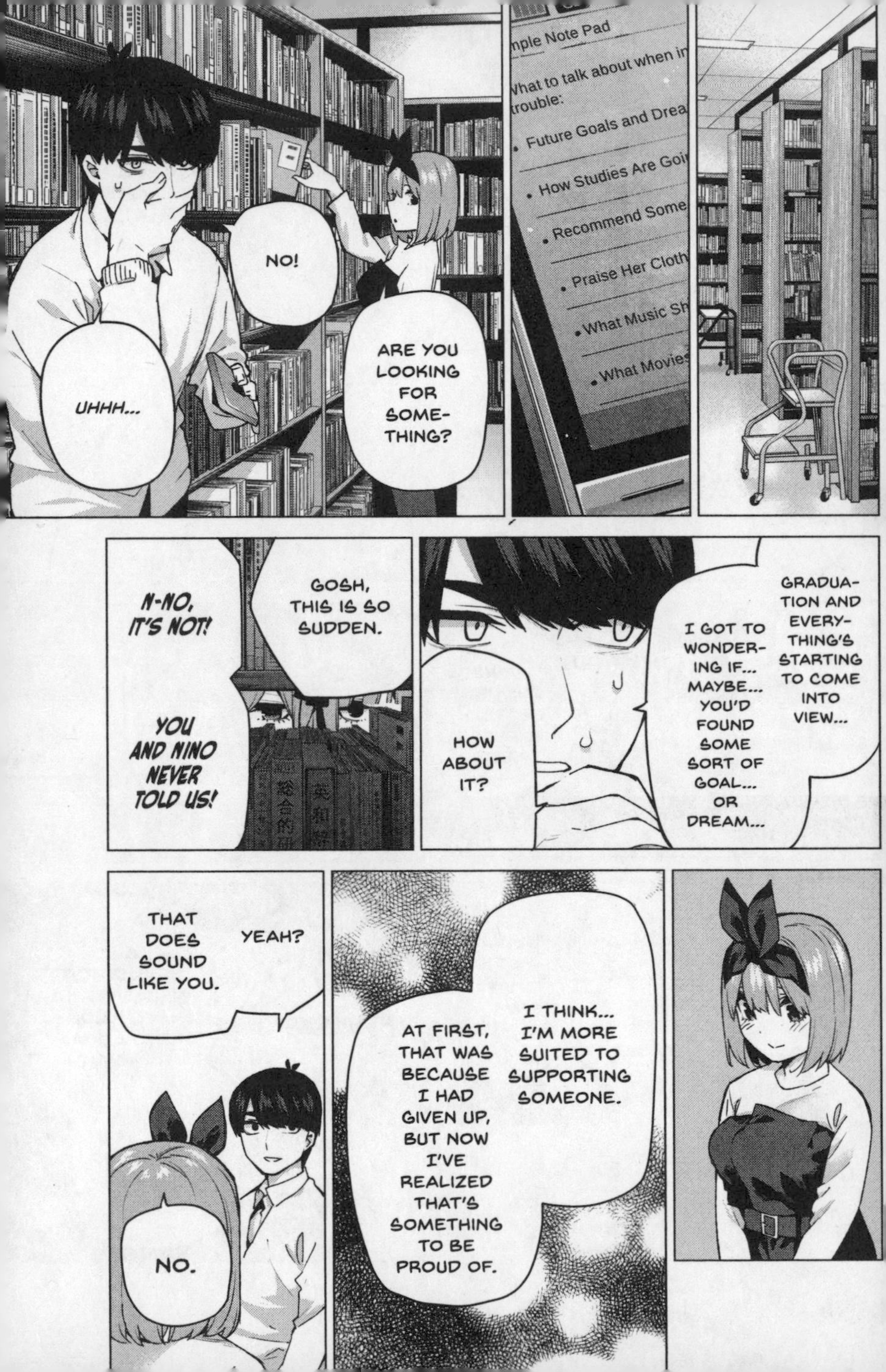

mple Note Pad
What to talk about when in trouble:
Future Goals and Drea
How Studies Are Goi
Recommend Some
Praise Her Cloth
What Music Sh
What Movies
ARE YOU LOOKING FOR SOME-THING?
NO!
UHHH...
GRADUA-TION AND EVERY-THING'S STARTING TO COME INTO VIEW...
I GOT TO WONDER-ING IF... MAYBE... YOU'D FOUND SOME SORT OF GOAL... OR DREAM...
HOW ABOUT IT?
GOSH, THIS IS SO SUDDEN.
N-NO, IT'S NOT!
YOU AND NINO NEVER TOLD US!
I THINK... I'M MORE SUITED TO SUPPORTING SOMEONE.
AT FIRST, THAT WAS BECAUSE I HAD GIVEN UP, BUT NOW I'VE REALIZED THAT'S SOMETHING TO BE PROUD OF.
YEAH?
THAT DOES SOUND LIKE YOU.
NO.

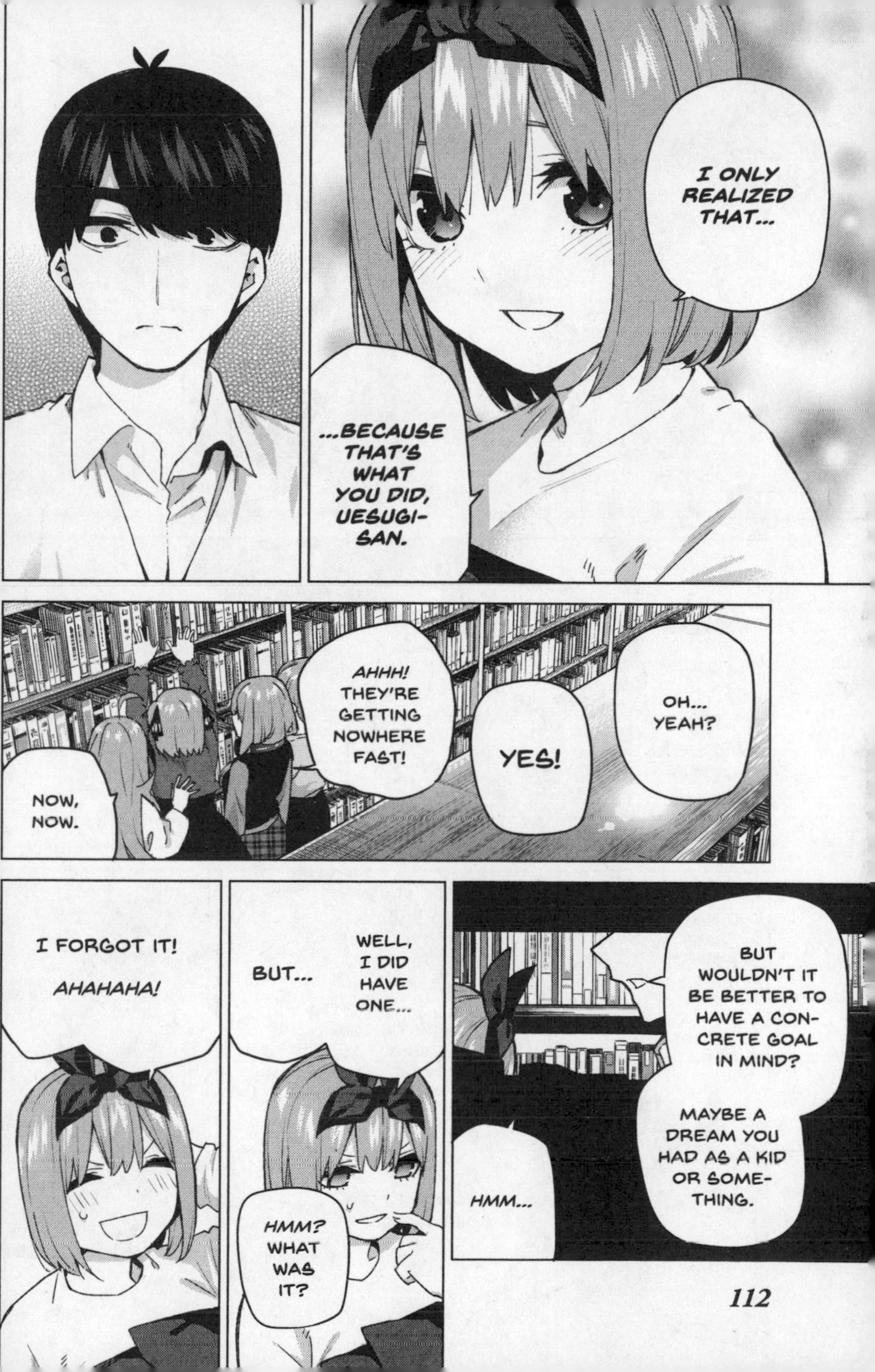
I ONLY REALIZED THAT...
...BECAUSE THAT'S WHAT YOU DID, UESUGI-SAN.
OH... YEAH?
YES!
AHHH! THEY'RE GETTING NOWHERE FAST!
NOW, NOW.
BUT WOULDN'T IT BE BETTER TO HAVE A CONCRETE GOAL IN MIND?
MAYBE A DREAM YOU HAD AS A KID OR SOMETHING.
HMM...
WELL, I DID HAVE ONE...
BUT...
HMM? WHAT WAS IT?
I FORGOT IT!
AHAHAHA!

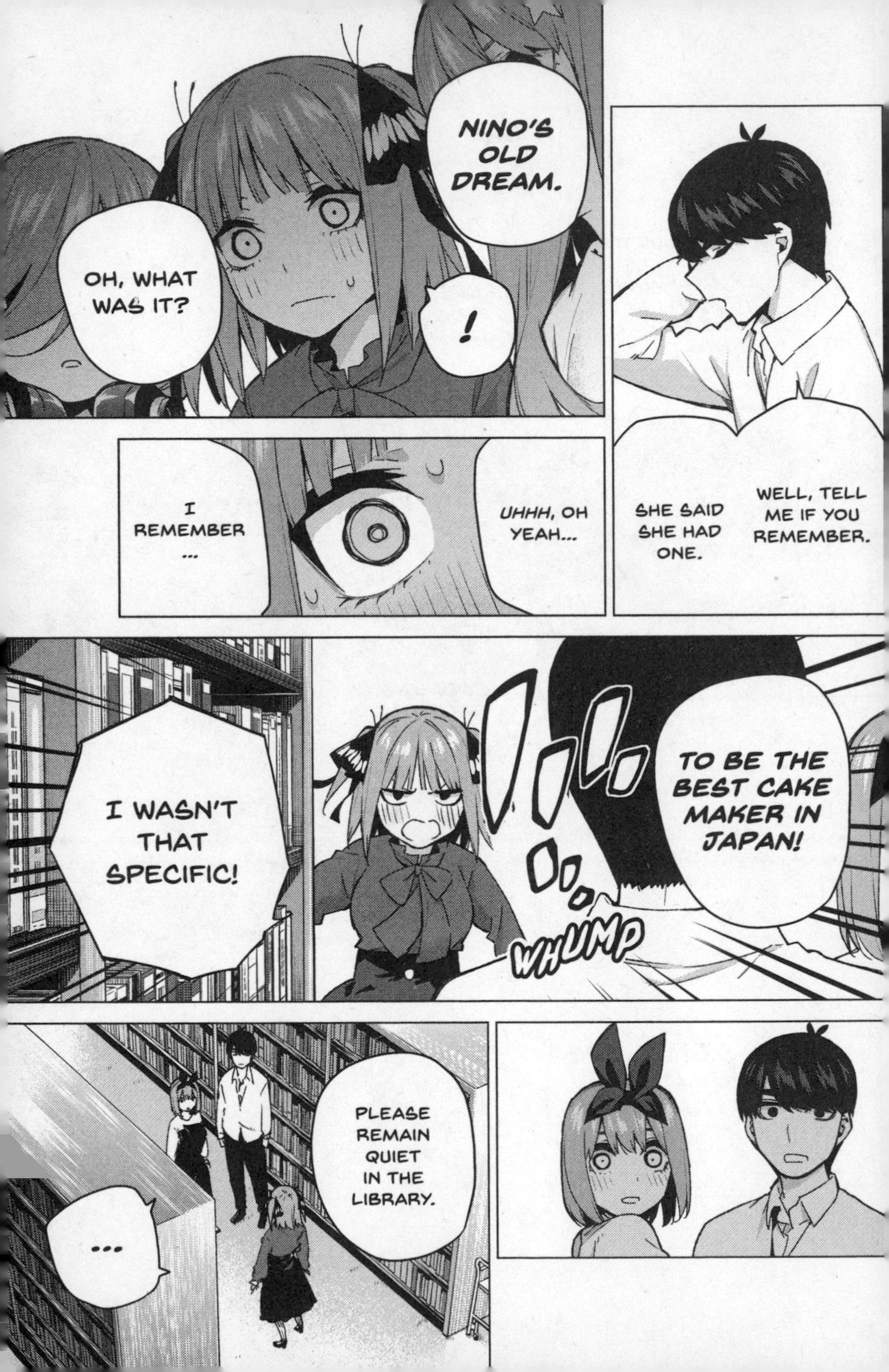
WELL, TELL ME IF YOU REMEMBER.
SHE SAID SHE HAD ONE.
NINO'S OLD DREAM.
OH, WHAT WAS IT?
!
UHHH, OH YEAH...
I REMEMBER ...
TO BE THE BEST CAKE MAKER IN JAPAN!
WHUMP
I WASN'T THAT SPECIFIC!
PLEASE REMAIN QUIET IN THE LIBRARY.
...

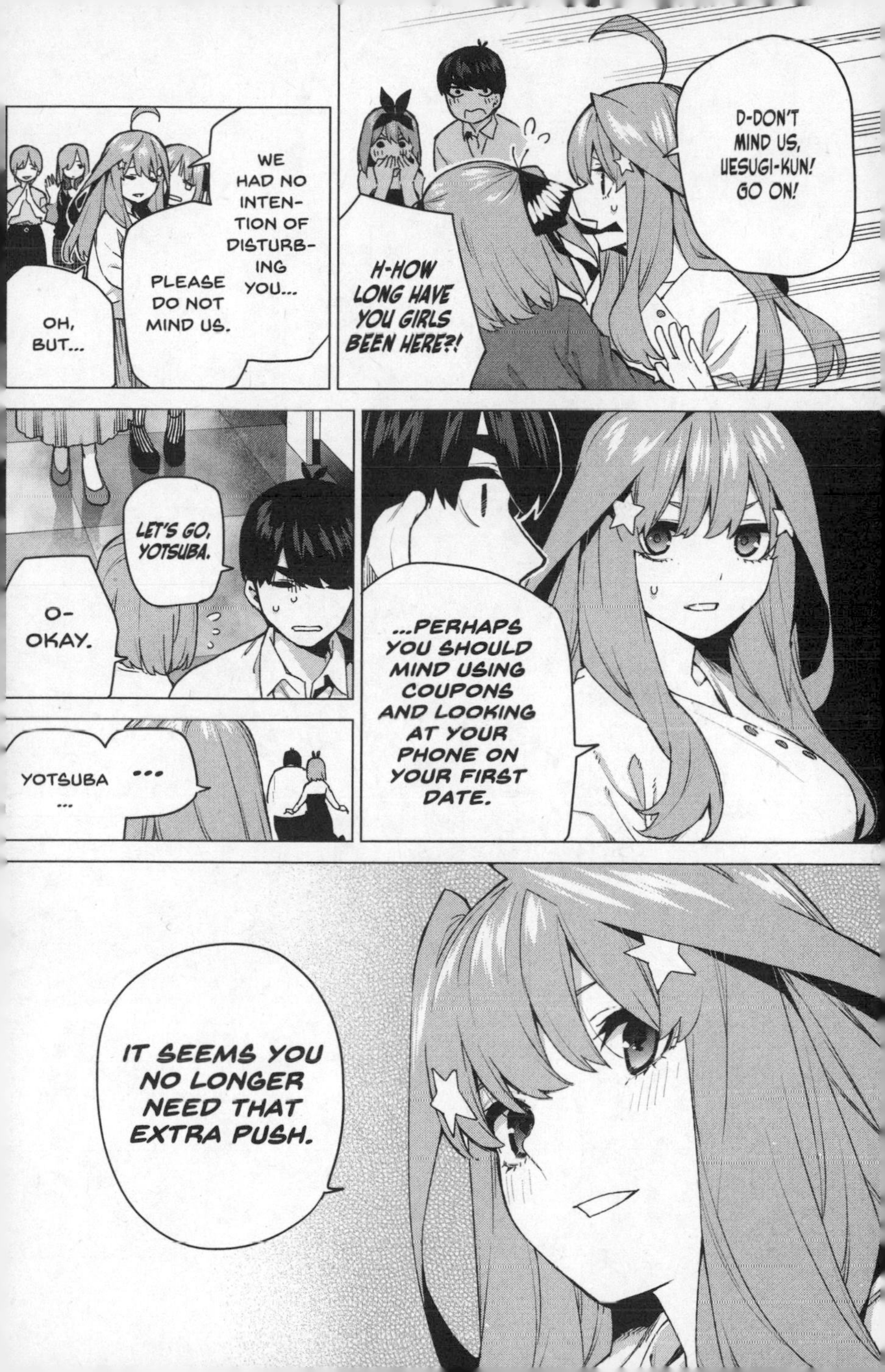
D-DON'T MIND US, UESUGI-KUN! GO ON!
H-HOW LONG HAVE YOU GIRLS BEEN HERE?!
WE HAD NO INTENTION OF DISTURBING YOU...
PLEASE DO NOT MIND US.
OH, BUT...
...PERHAPS YOU SHOULD MIND USING COUPONS AND LOOKING AT YOUR PHONE ON YOUR FIRST DATE.
LET'S GO, YOTSUBA.
O-OKAY.
...
YOTSUBA ...
IT SEEMS YOU NO LONGER NEED THAT EXTRA PUSH.

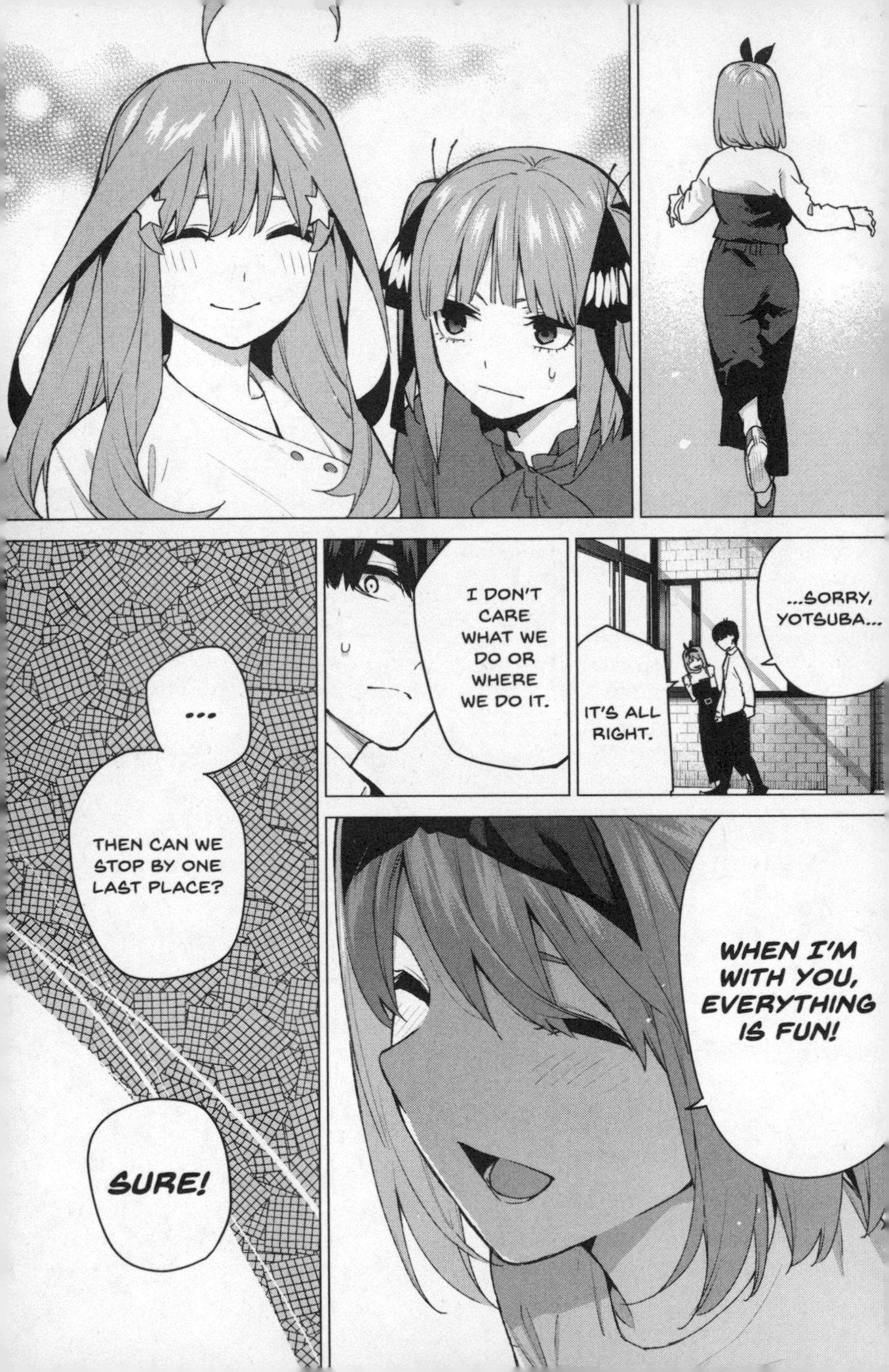

...SORRY, YOTSUBA...
IT'S ALL RIGHT.
I DON'T CARE WHAT WE DO OR WHERE WE DO IT.
WHEN I'M WITH YOU, EVERYTHING IS FUN!
...
THEN CAN WE STOP BY ONE LAST PLACE?
SURE!

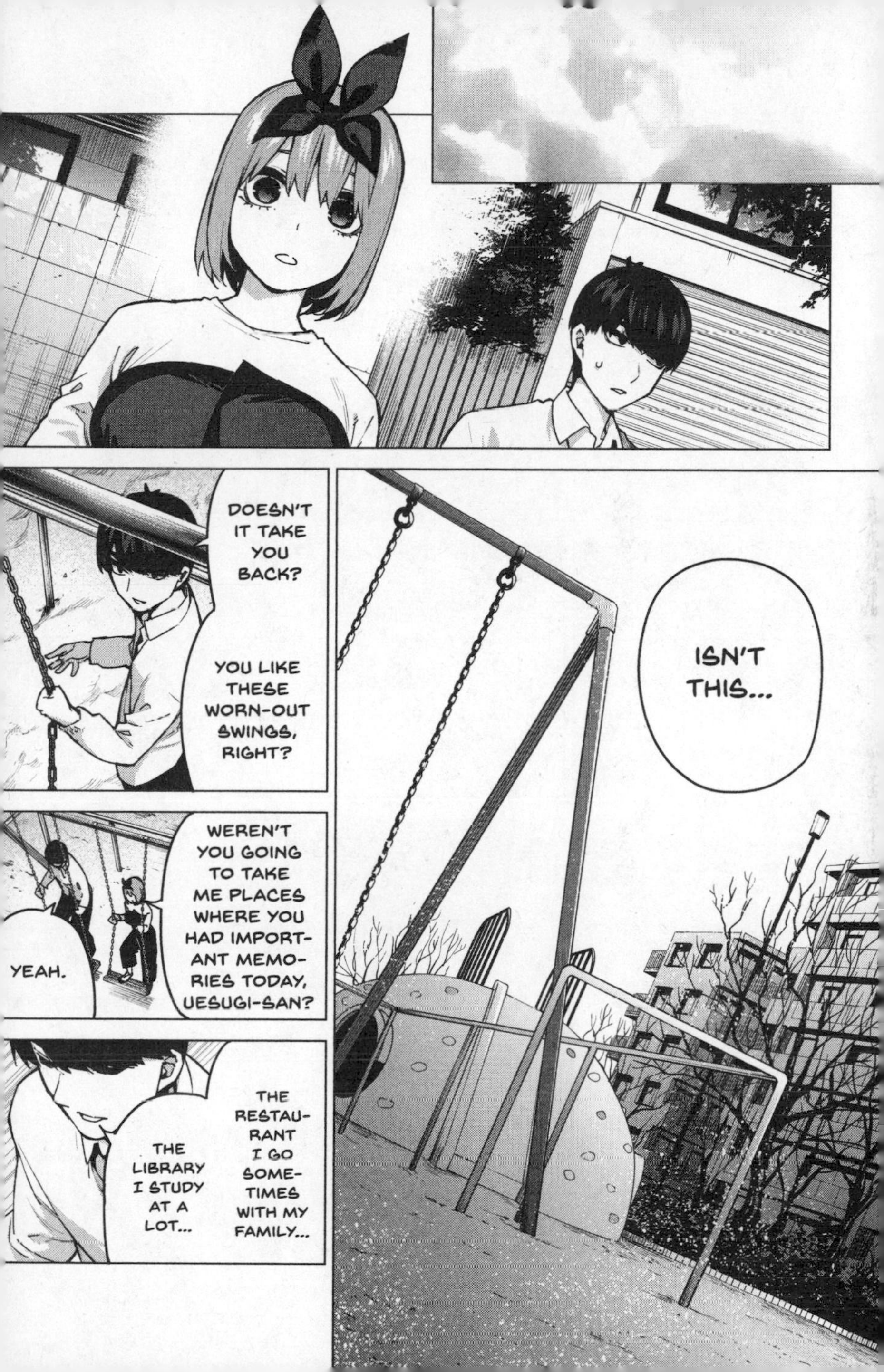
ISN'T THIS...
DOESN'T IT TAKE YOU BACK?
YOU LIKE THESE WORN-OUT SWINGS, RIGHT?
WEREN'T YOU GOING TO TAKE ME PLACES WHERE YOU HAD IMPORTANT MEMORIES TODAY, UESUGI-SAN?
YEAH.
THE RESTAURANT I GO SOMETIMES WITH MY FAMILY...
THE LIBRARY I STUDY AT A LOT...

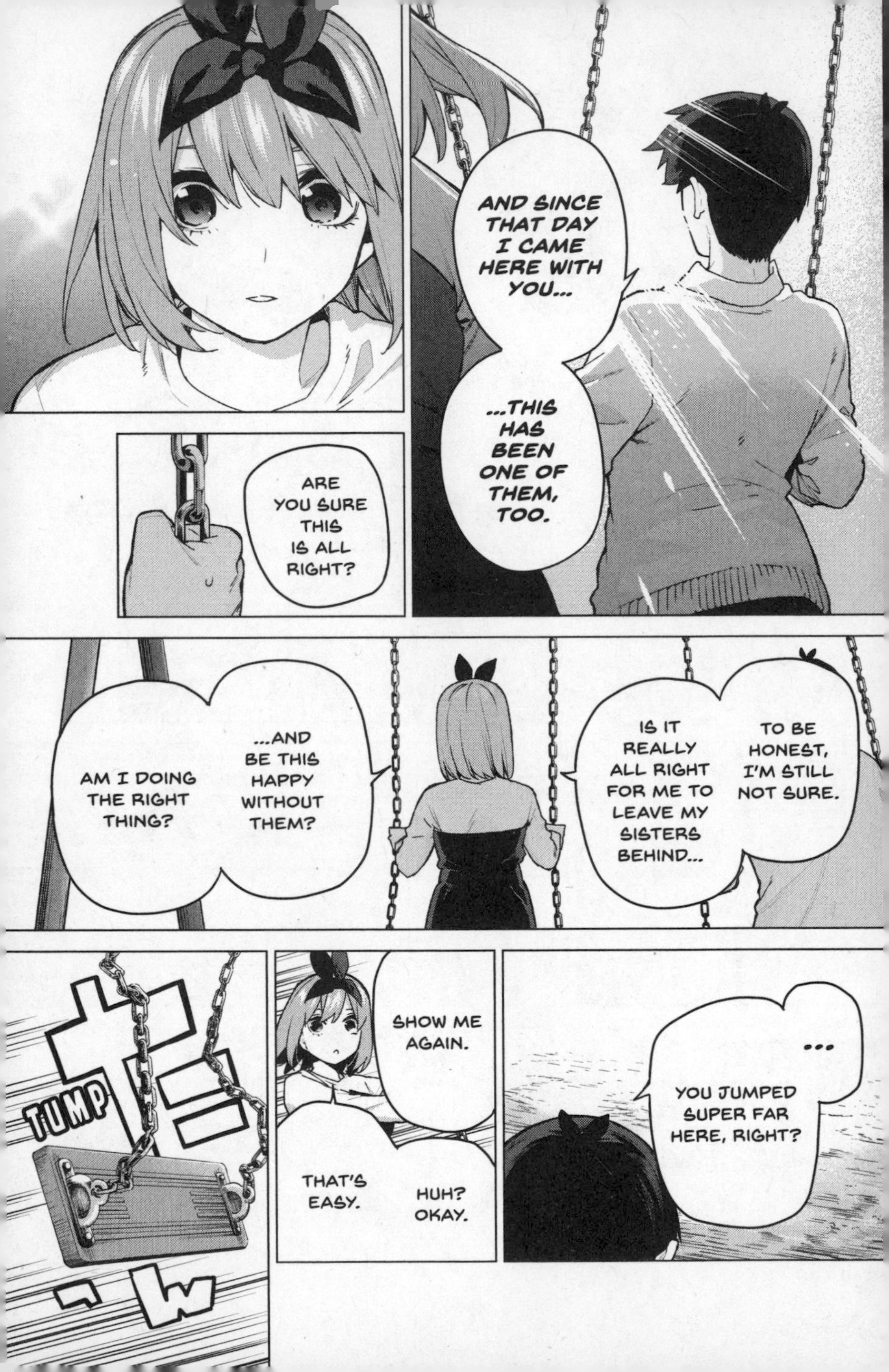
AND SINCE THAT DAY I CAME HERE WITH YOU...
...THIS HAS BEEN ONE OF THEM, TOO.
ARE YOU SURE THIS IS ALL RIGHT?
TO BE HONEST, I'M STILL NOT SURE.
IS IT REALLY ALL RIGHT FOR ME TO LEAVE MY SISTERS BEHIND...
...AND BE THIS HAPPY WITHOUT THEM?
AM I DOING THE RIGHT THING?
...
YOU JUMPED SUPER FAR HERE, RIGHT?
SHOW ME AGAIN.
HUH? OKAY.
THAT'S EASY.
TUMP

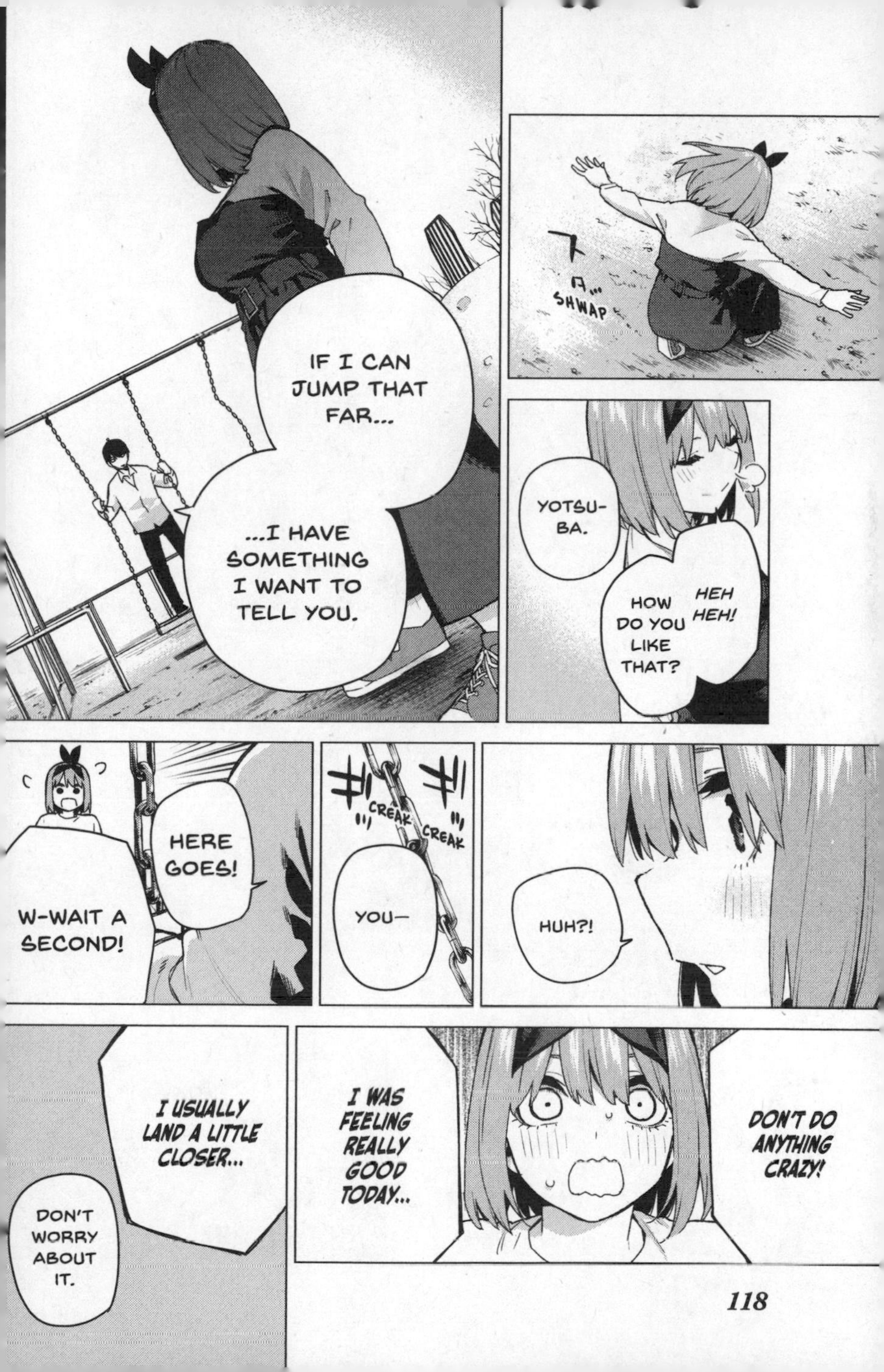
SHWAP
HEH HEH!
HOW DO YOU LIKE THAT?
YOTSU-BA.
IF I CAN JUMP THAT FAR...
...I HAVE SOMETHING I WANT TO TELL YOU.
HUH?!
CREAK CREAK
YOU—
HERE GOES!
W-WAIT A SECOND!
DON'T DO ANYTHING CRAZY!
I WAS FEELING REALLY GOOD TODAY...
I USUALLY LAND A LITTLE CLOSER...
DON'T WORRY ABOUT IT.

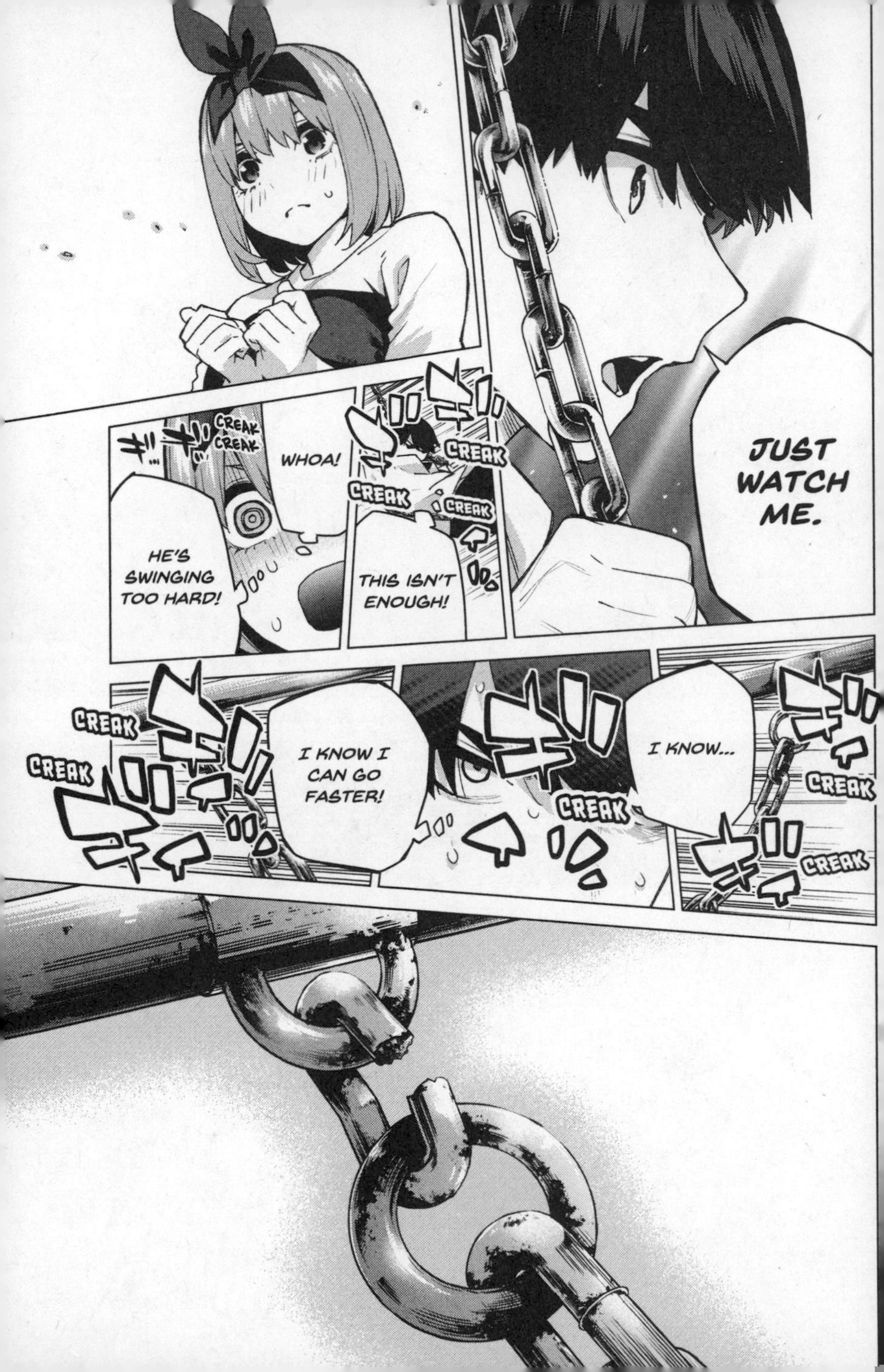
JUST WATCH ME.
CREAK
CREAK
CREAK
THIS ISN'T ENOUGH!
CREAK CREAK
WHOA!
HE'S SWINGING TOO HARD!
CREAK
CREAK
I KNOW...
CREAK
I KNOW I CAN GO FASTER!
CREAK
CREAK

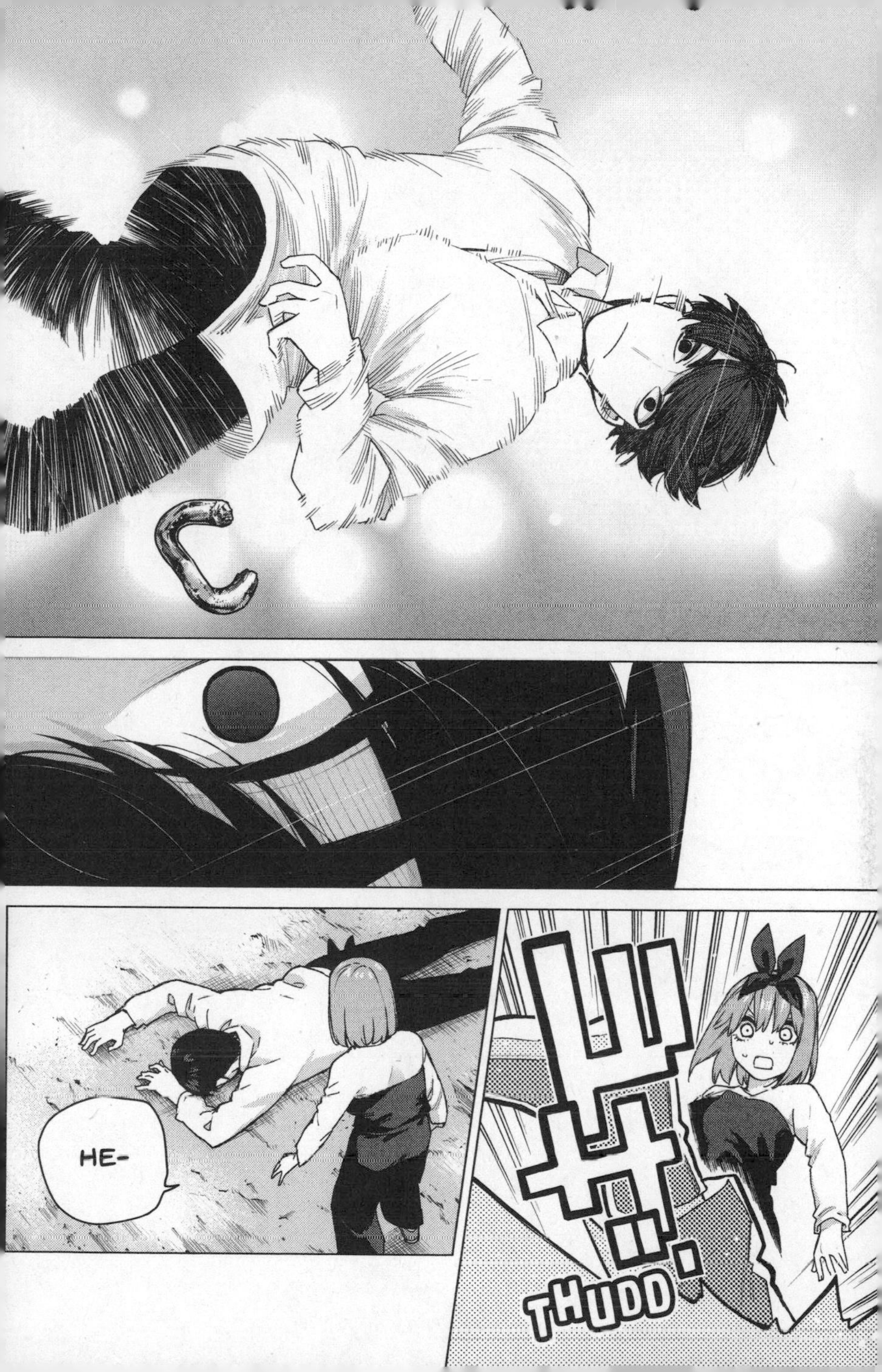
THUDD
HE-

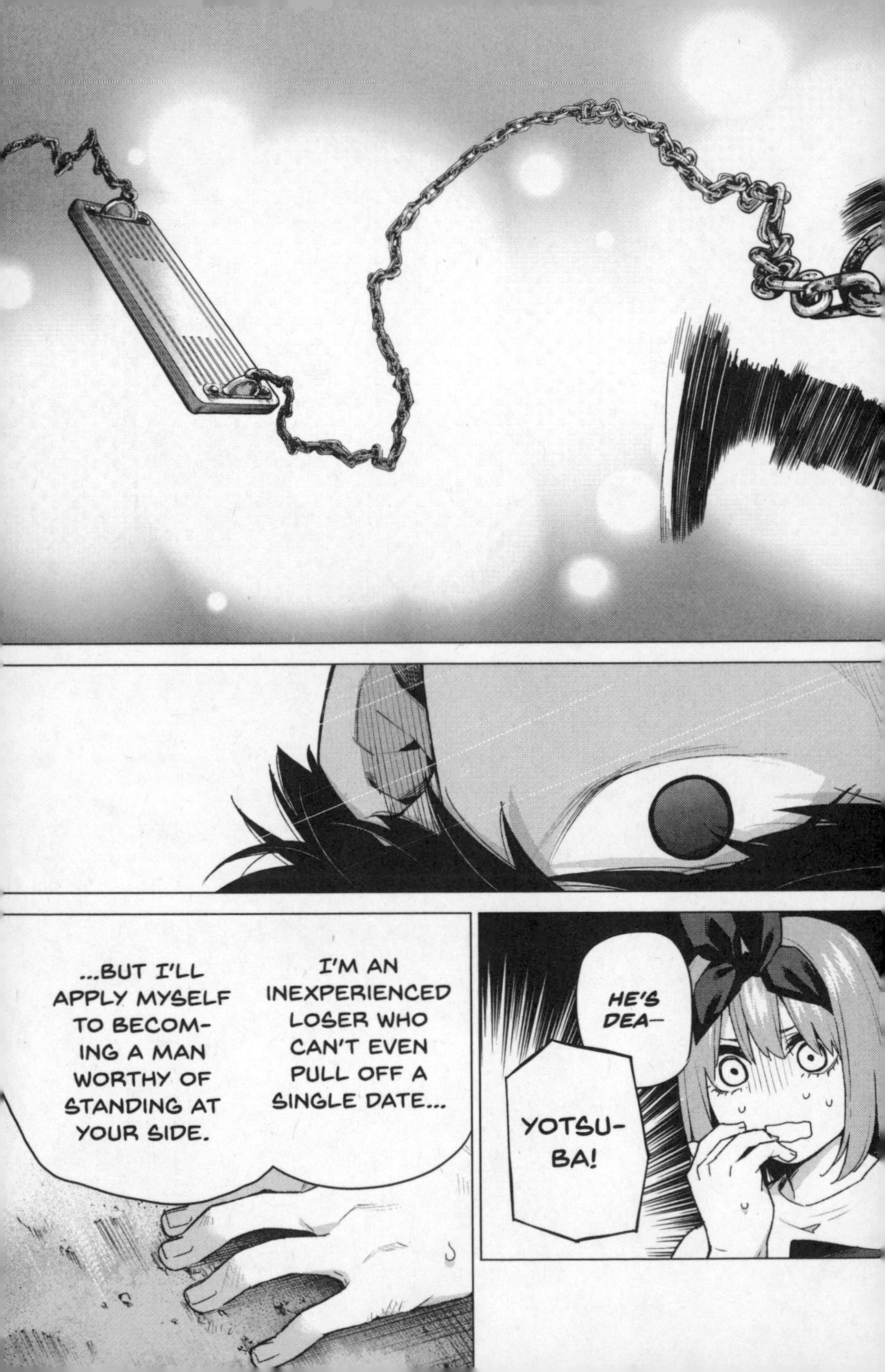
HE'S DEA—
YOTSU-BA!
I'M AN INEXPERIENCED LOSER WHO CAN'T EVEN PULL OFF A SINGLE DATE...
...BUT I'LL APPLY MYSELF TO BECOMING A MAN WORTHY OF STANDING AT YOUR SIDE.

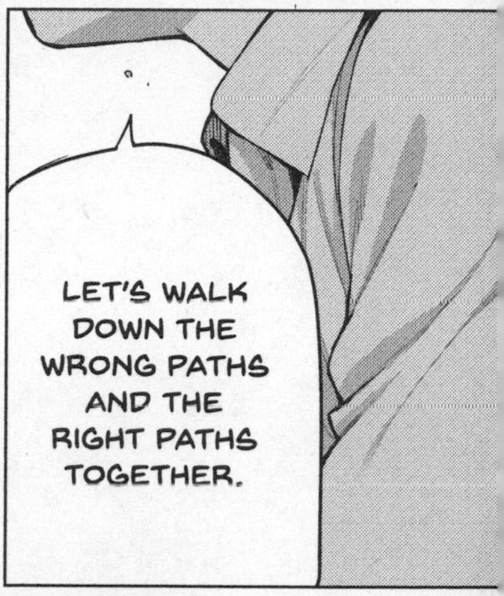
LET'S WALK DOWN THE WRONG PATHS AND THE RIGHT PATHS TOGETHER.
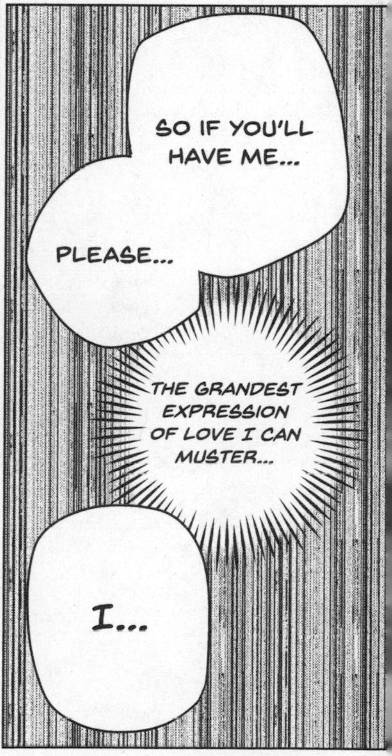
SO IF YOU'LL HAVE ME...
PLEASE...
THE GRANDEST EXPRESSION OF LOVE I CAN MUSTER...
I...
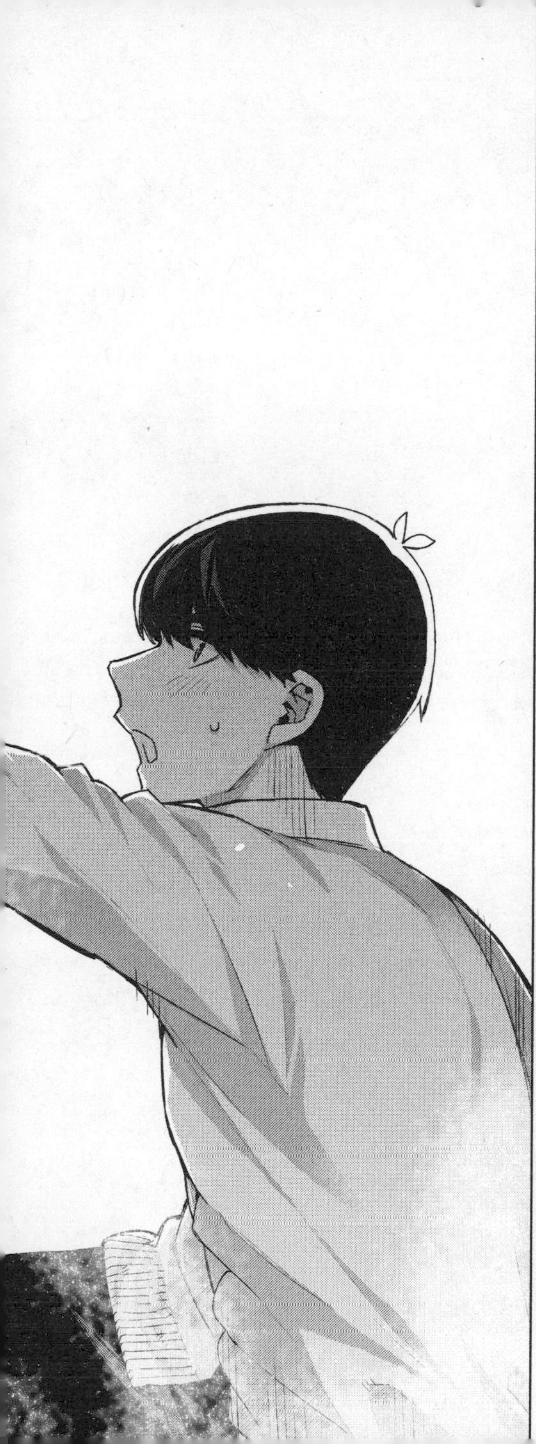

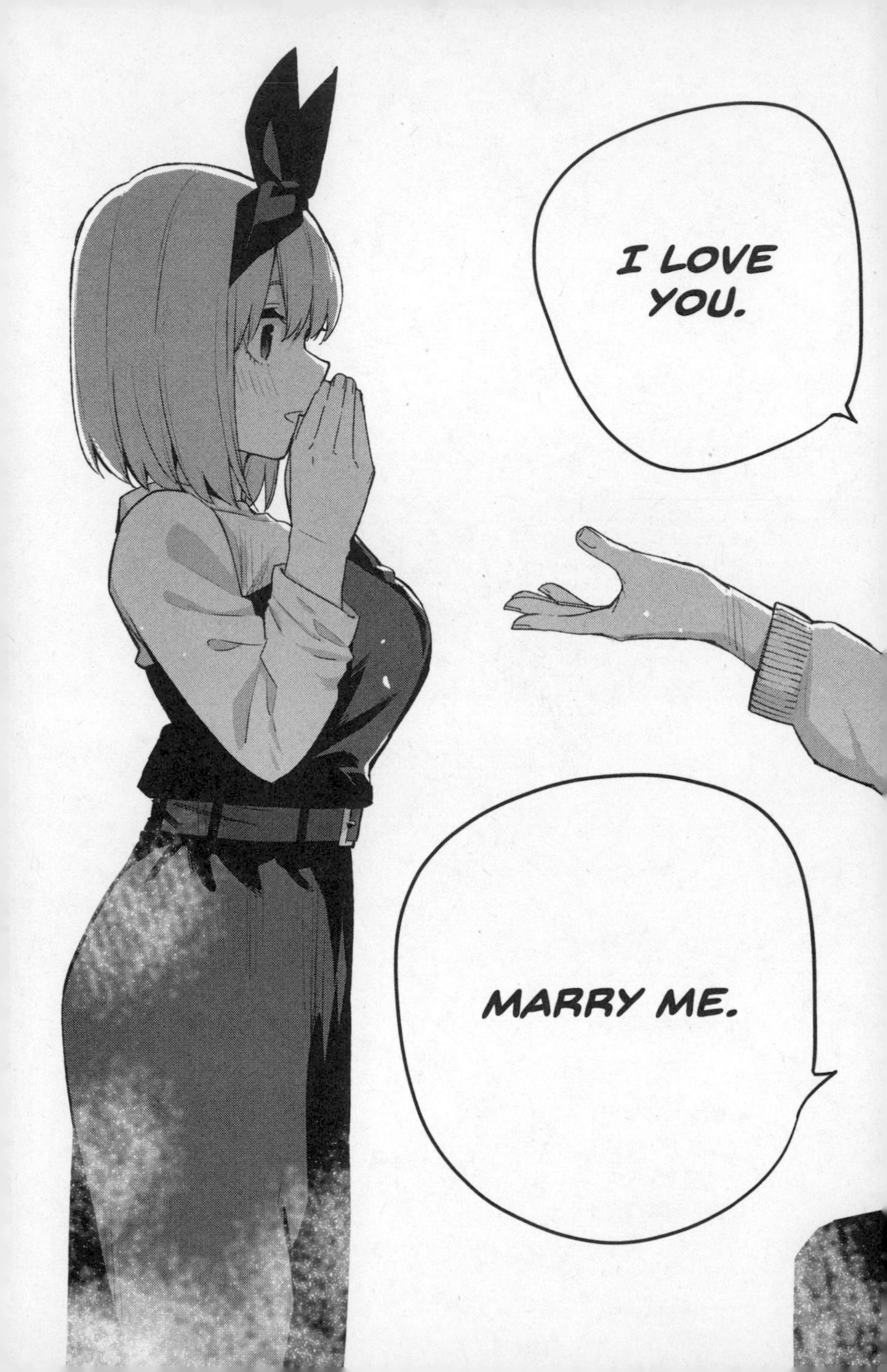
I LOVE YOU.
MARRY ME.

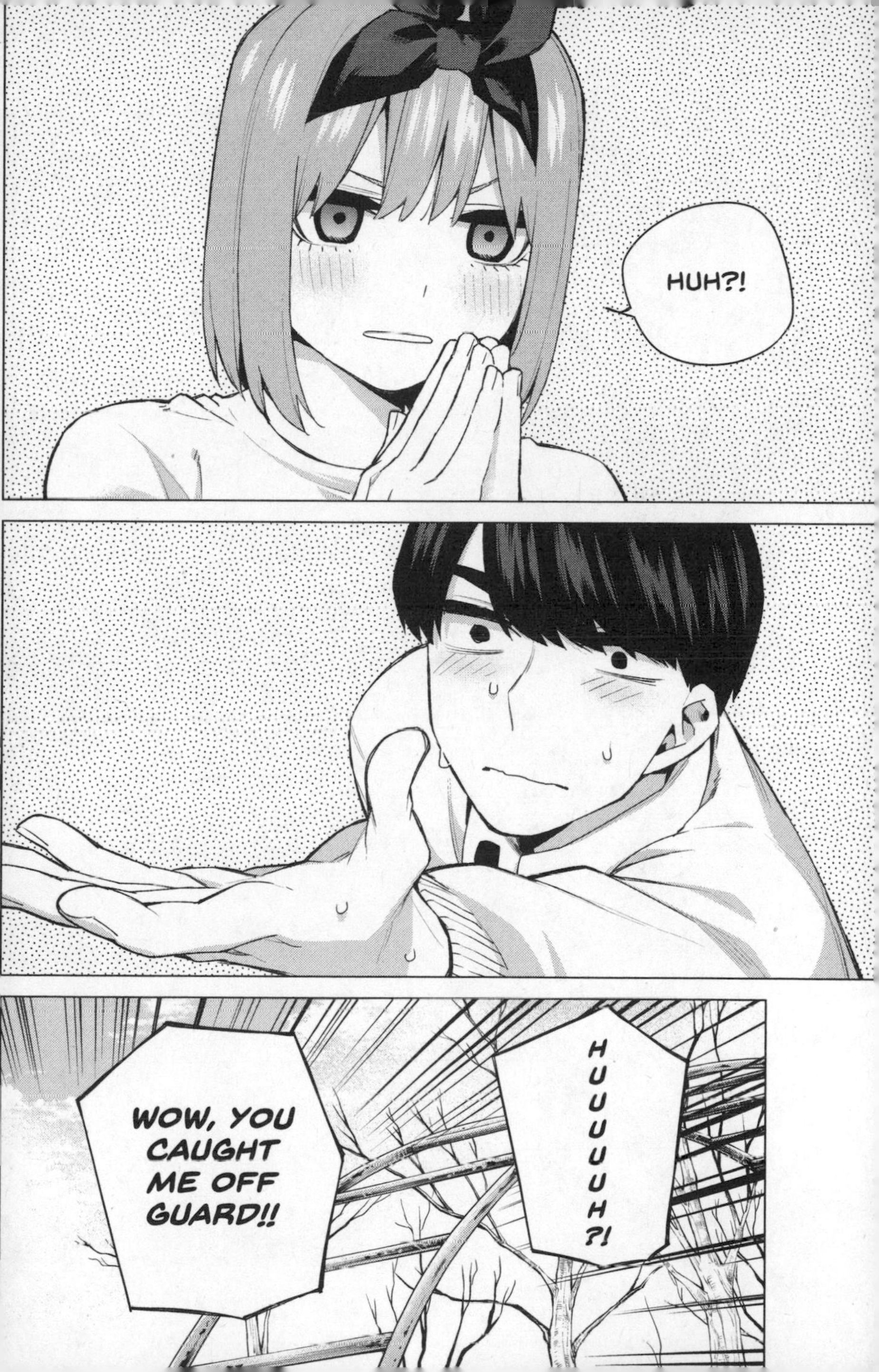
HUH?!
HUUUUUUH?!
WOW, YOU CAUGHT ME OFF GUARD!!

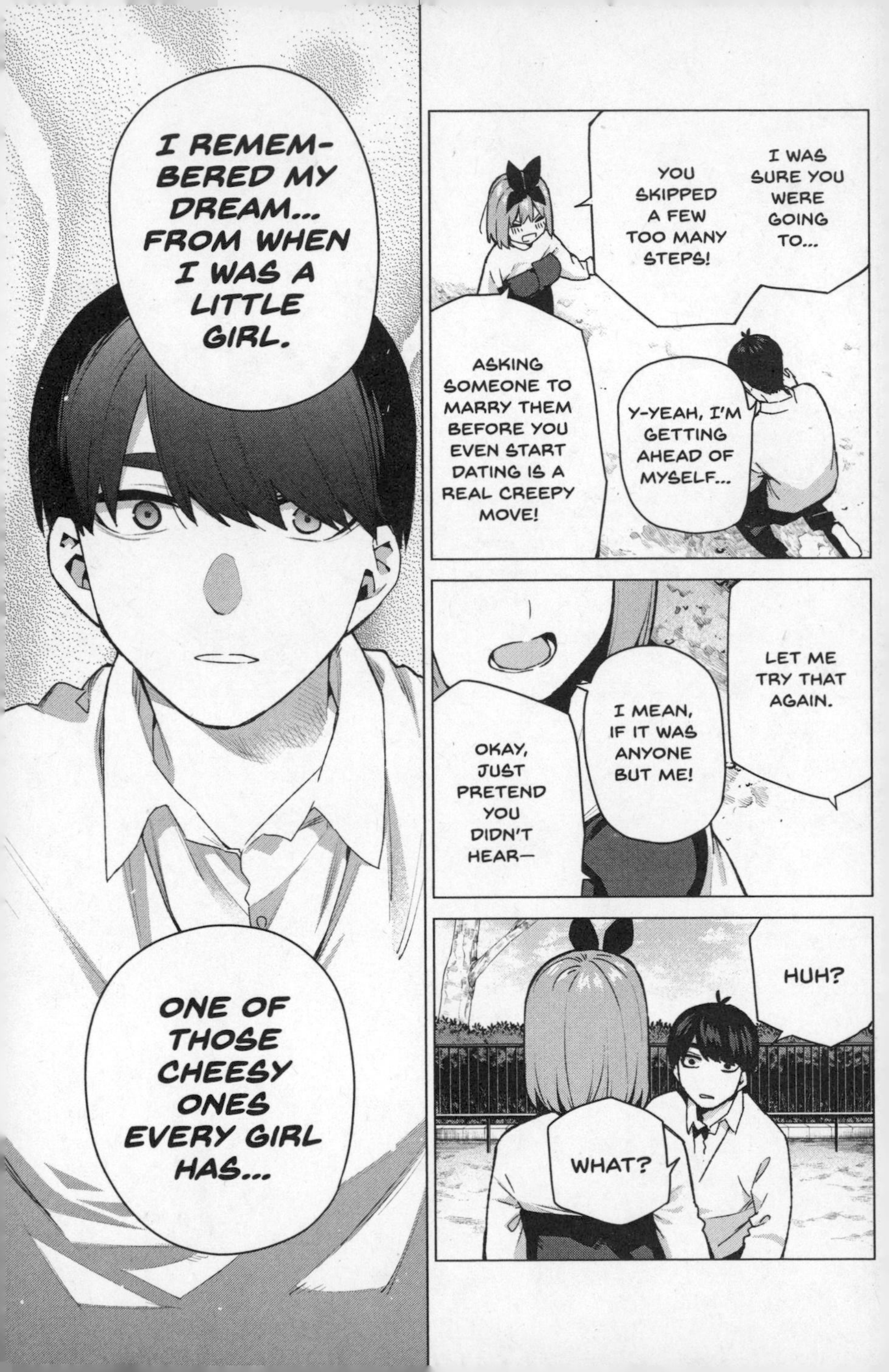
I WAS SURE YOU WERE GOING TO...
YOU SKIPPED A FEW TOO MANY STEPS!
ASKING SOMEONE TO MARRY THEM BEFORE YOU EVEN START DATING IS A REAL CREEPY MOVE!
Y-YEAH, I'M GETTING AHEAD OF MYSELF...
LET ME TRY THAT AGAIN.
I MEAN, IF IT WAS ANYONE BUT ME!
OKAY, JUST PRETEND YOU DIDN'T HEAR—
HUH?
WHAT?
I REMEMBERED MY DREAM... FROM WHEN I WAS A LITTLE GIRL.
ONE OF THOSE CHEESY ONES EVERY GIRL HAS...

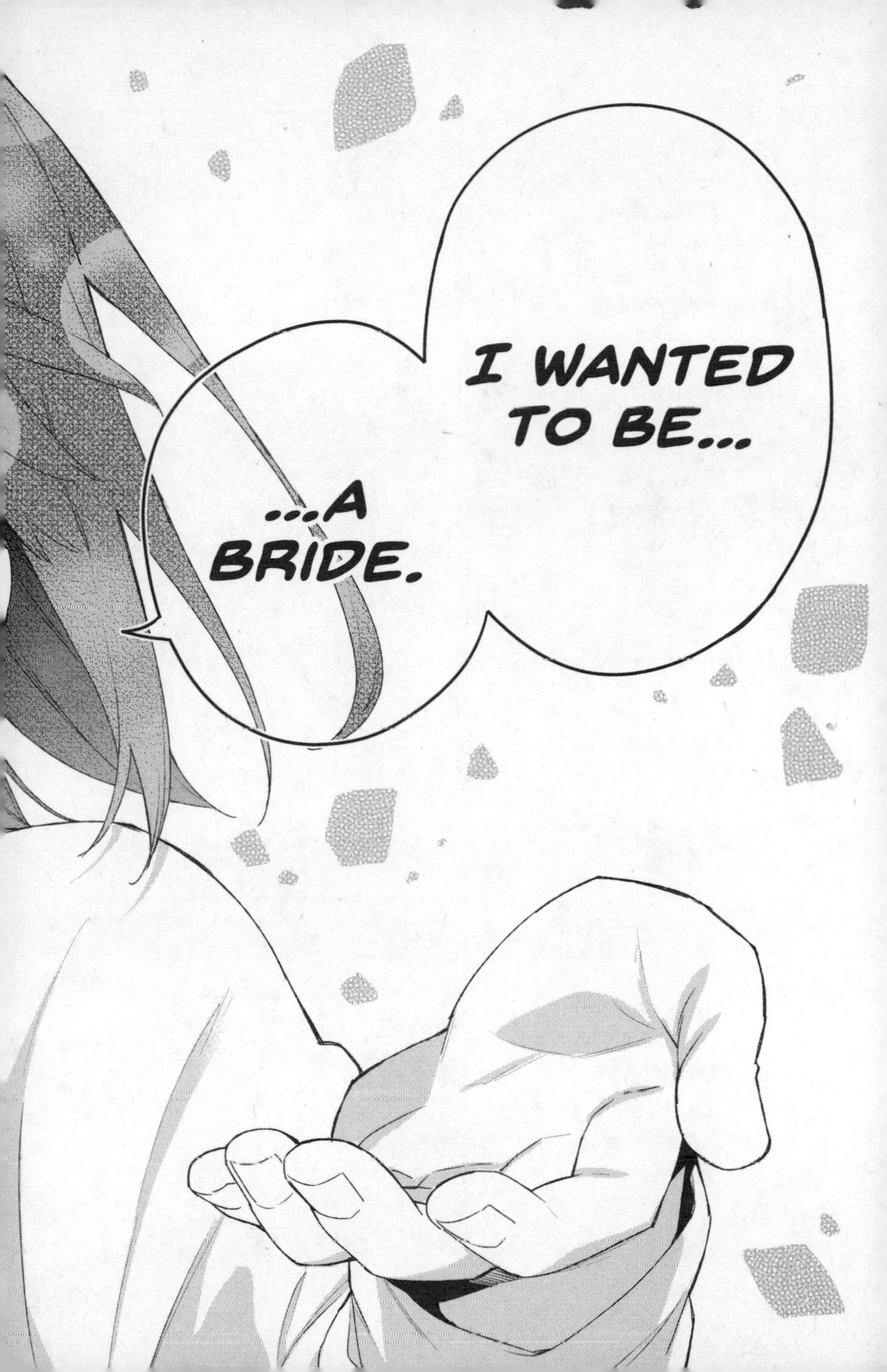
I WANTED TO BE...
...A BRIDE.

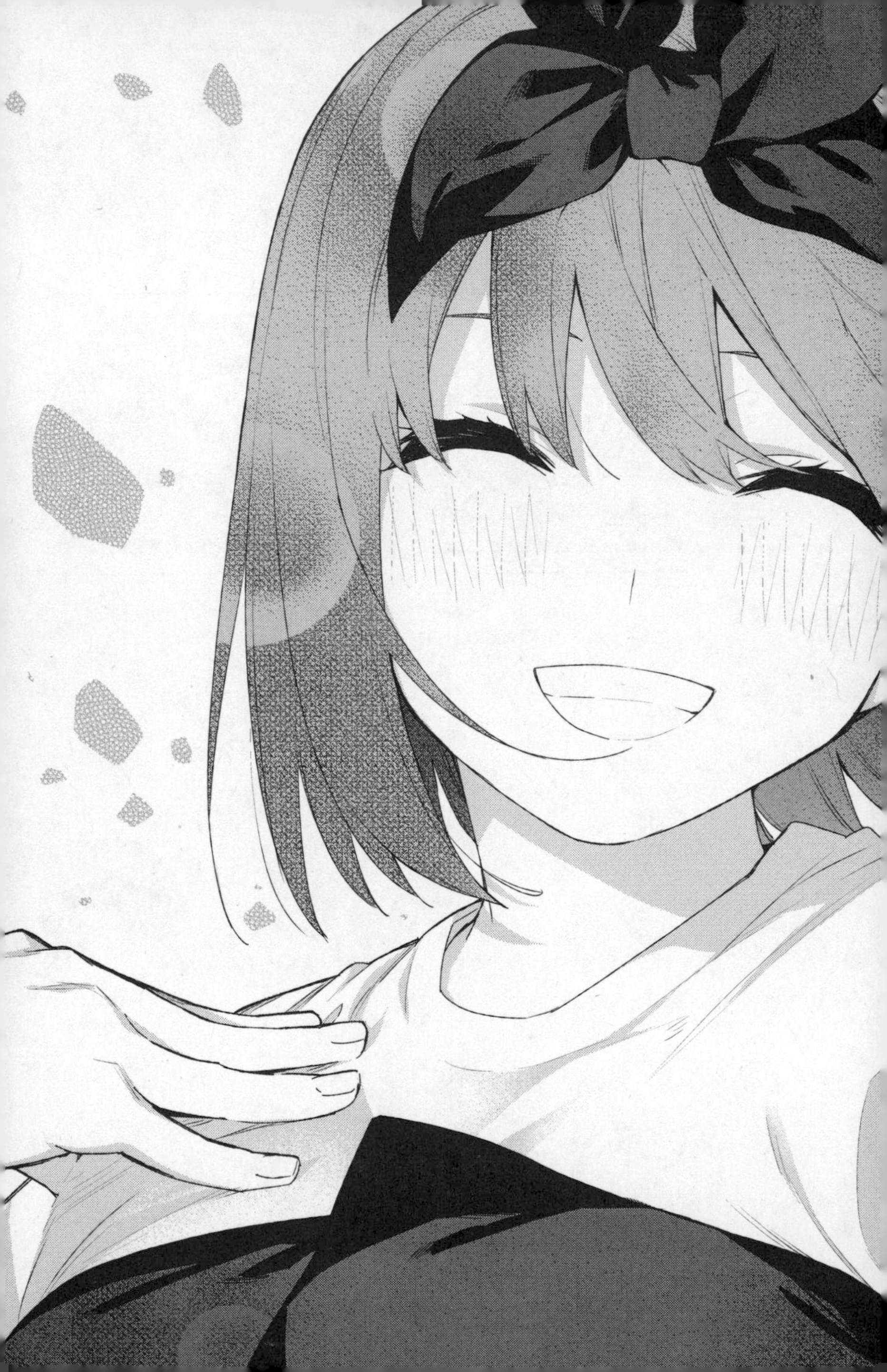

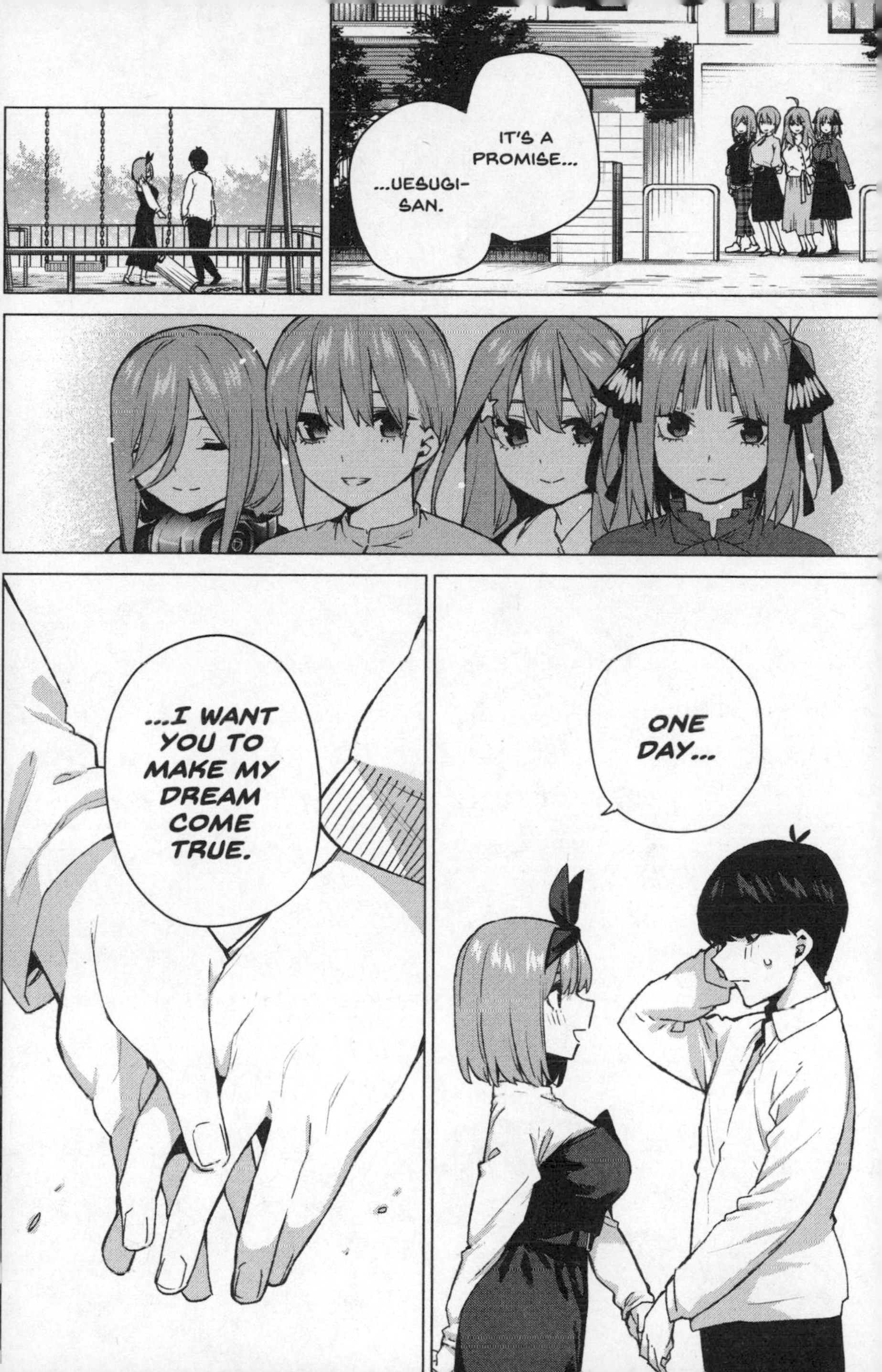
IT'S A PROMISE... ...UESUGI-SAN.
ONE DAY...
...I WANT YOU TO MAKE MY DREAM COME TRUE.

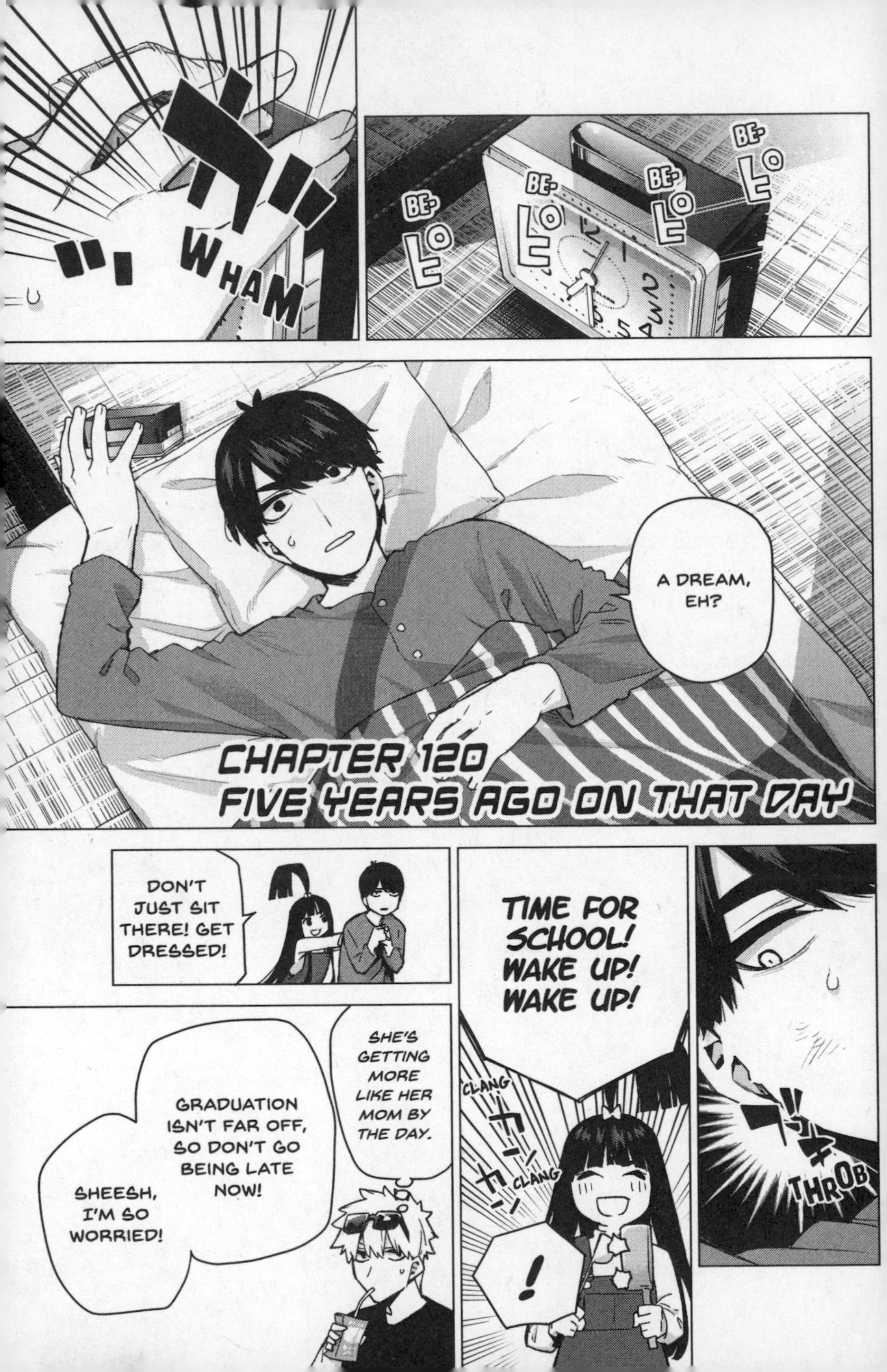
BE-
BE-
BE-
BE-
WHAM
A DREAM, EH?
CHAPTER 120
FIVE YEARS AGO ON THAT DAY
THROB
TIME FOR SCHOOL! WAKE UP! WAKE UP!
CLANG
CLANG
!
DON'T JUST SIT THERE! GET DRESSED!
SHE'S GETTING MORE LIKE HER MOM BY THE DAY.
GRADUATION ISN'T FAR OFF, SO DON'T GO BEING LATE NOW!
SHEESH, I'M SO WORRIED!

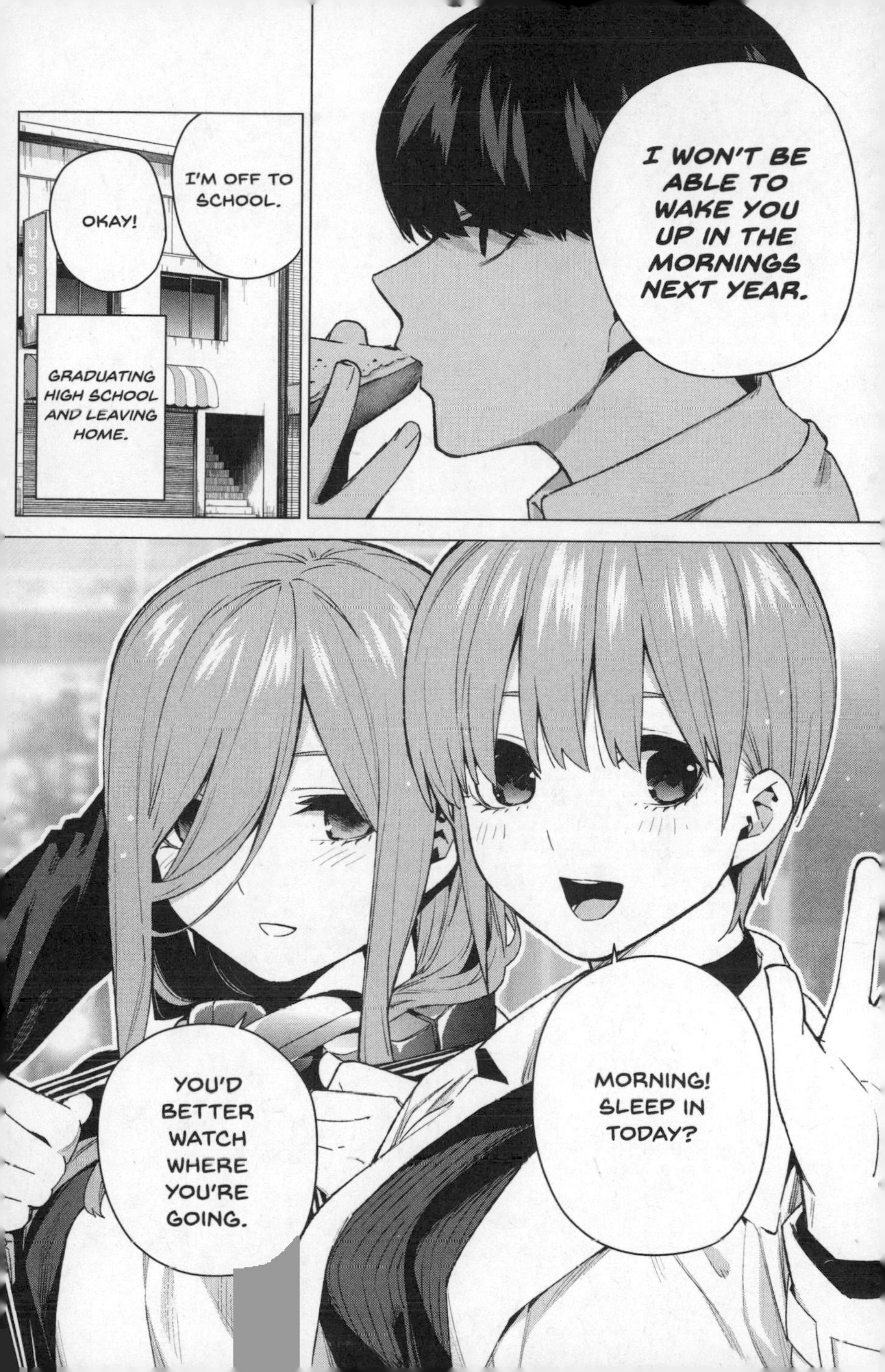
I WON'T BE ABLE TO WAKE YOU UP IN THE MORNINGS NEXT YEAR.
I'M OFF TO SCHOOL.
OKAY!
UESUGI
GRADUATING HIGH SCHOOL AND LEAVING HOME.
MORNING! SLEEP IN TODAY?
YOU'D BETTER WATCH WHERE YOU'RE GOING.

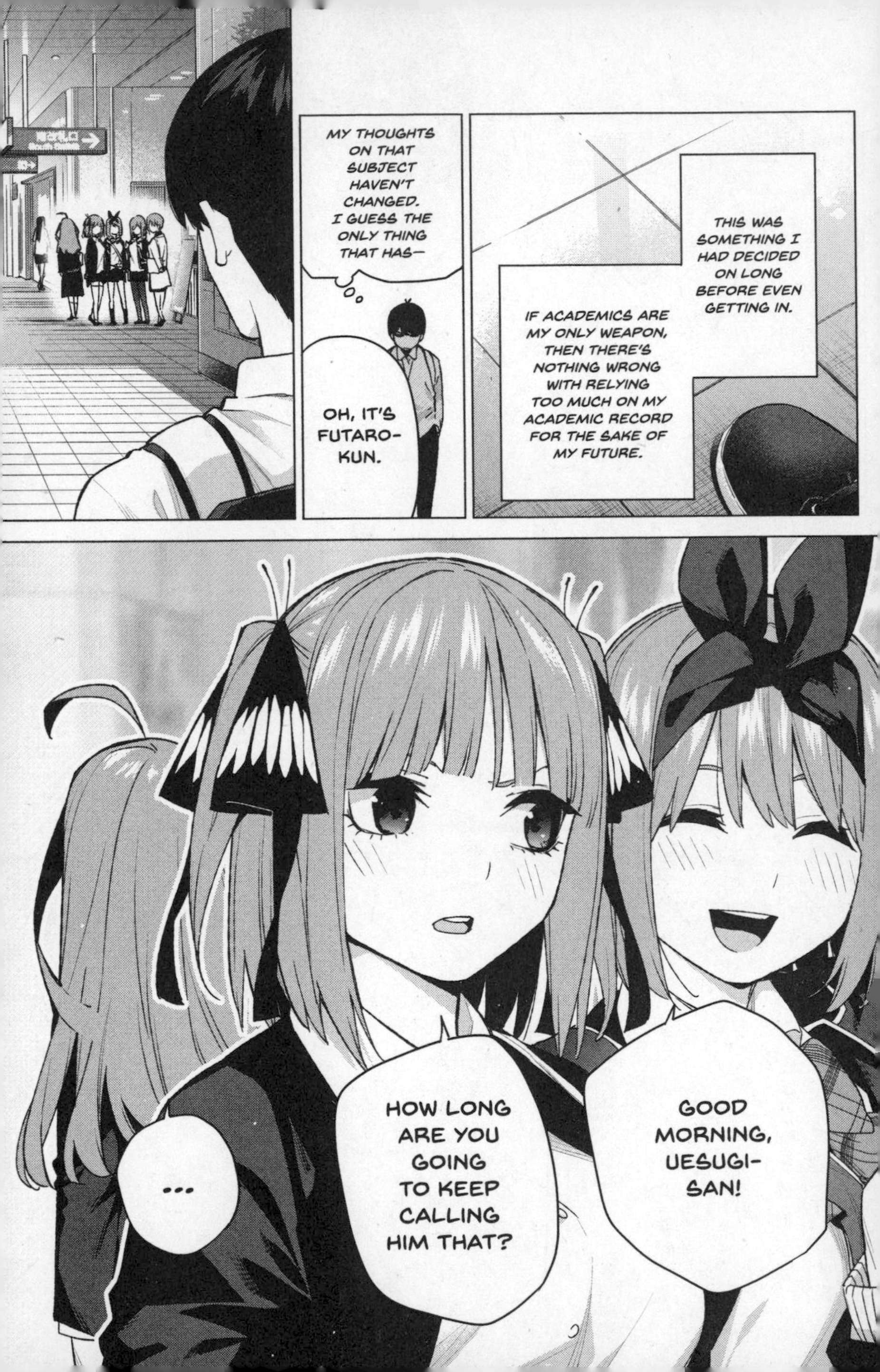
THIS WAS SOMETHING I HAD DECIDED ON LONG BEFORE EVEN GETTING IN.
IF ACADEMICS ARE MY ONLY WEAPON, THEN THERE'S NOTHING WRONG WITH RELYING TOO MUCH ON MY ACADEMIC RECORD FOR THE SAKE OF MY FUTURE.
MY THOUGHTS ON THAT SUBJECT HAVEN'T CHANGED. I GUESS THE ONLY THING THAT HAS—
OH, IT'S FUTARO-KUN.
GOOD MORNING, UESUGI-SAN!
HOW LONG ARE YOU GOING TO KEEP CALLING HIM THAT?
...

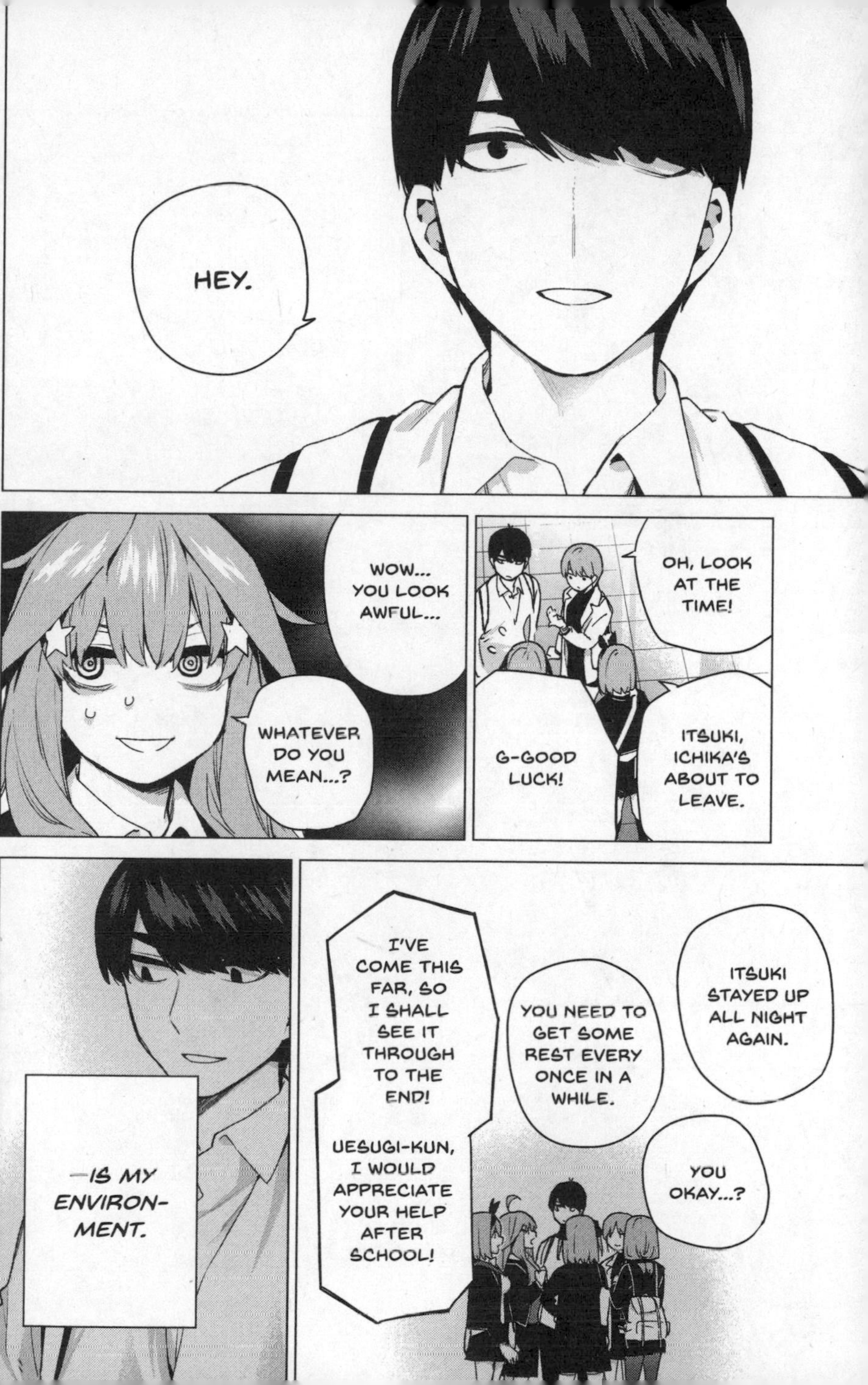
HEY.
OH, LOOK AT THE TIME!
ITSUKI, ICHIKA'S ABOUT TO LEAVE.
G-GOOD LUCK!
WOW... YOU LOOK AWFUL...
WHATEVER DO YOU MEAN...?
ITSUKI STAYED UP ALL NIGHT AGAIN.
YOU NEED TO GET SOME REST EVERY ONCE IN A WHILE.
I'VE COME THIS FAR, SO I SHALL SEE IT THROUGH TO THE END!
YOU OKAY...?
UESUGI-KUN, I WOULD APPRECIATE YOUR HELP AFTER SCHOOL!
—IS MY ENVIRON-MENT.

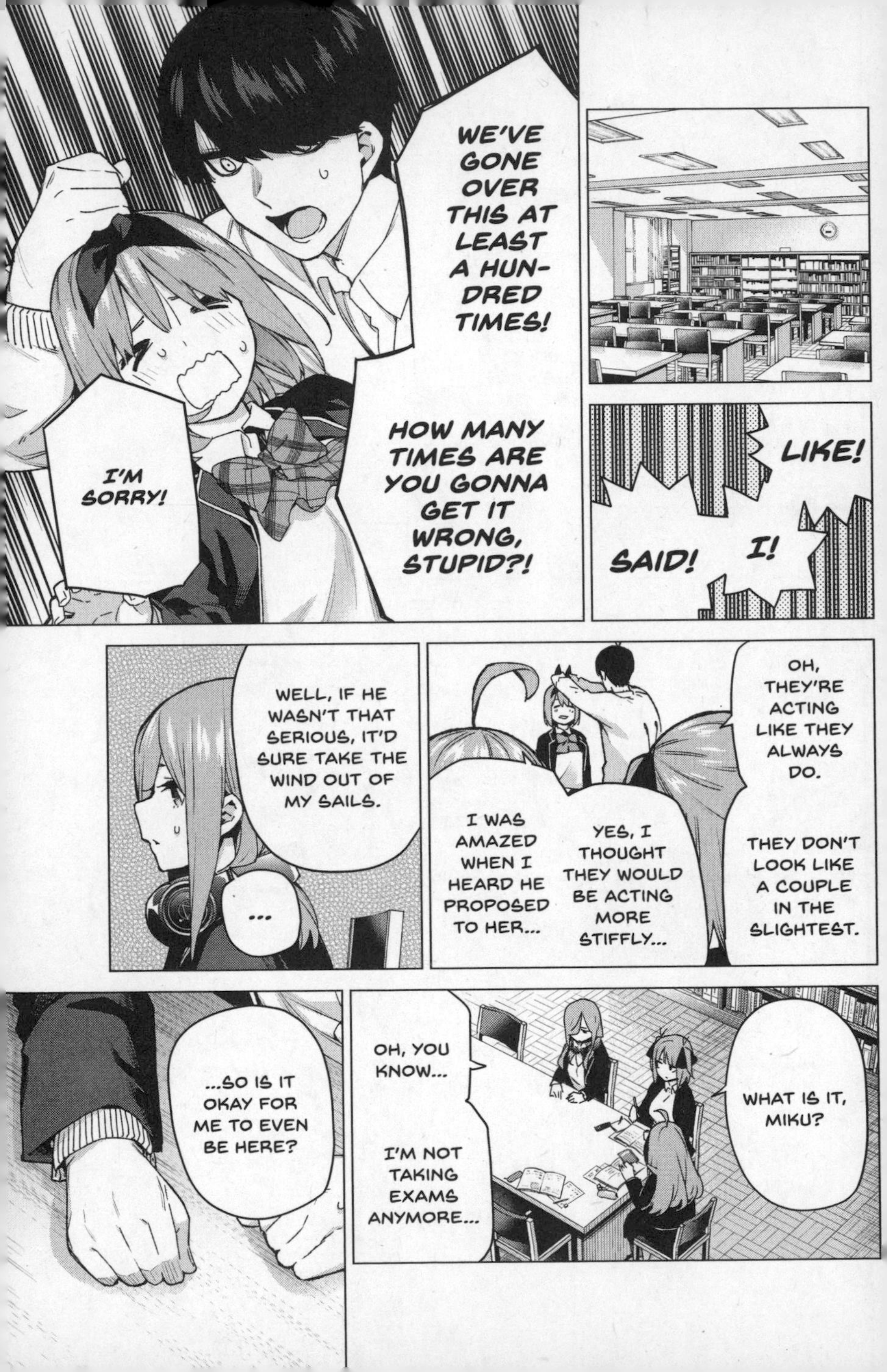
LIKE!
I!
SAID!
WE'VE GONE OVER THIS AT LEAST A HUN-DRED TIMES!
HOW MANY TIMES ARE YOU GONNA GET IT WRONG, STUPID?!
I'M SORRY!
OH, THEY'RE ACTING LIKE THEY ALWAYS DO.
THEY DON'T LOOK LIKE A COUPLE IN THE SLIGHTEST.
YES, I THOUGHT THEY WOULD BE ACTING MORE STIFFLY...
I WAS AMAZED WHEN I HEARD HE PROPOSED TO HER...
WELL, IF HE WASN'T THAT SERIOUS, IT'D SURE TAKE THE WIND OUT OF MY SAILS.
...
WHAT IS IT, MIKU?
OH, YOU KNOW...
I'M NOT TAKING EXAMS ANYMORE...
...SO IS IT OKAY FOR ME TO EVEN BE HERE?

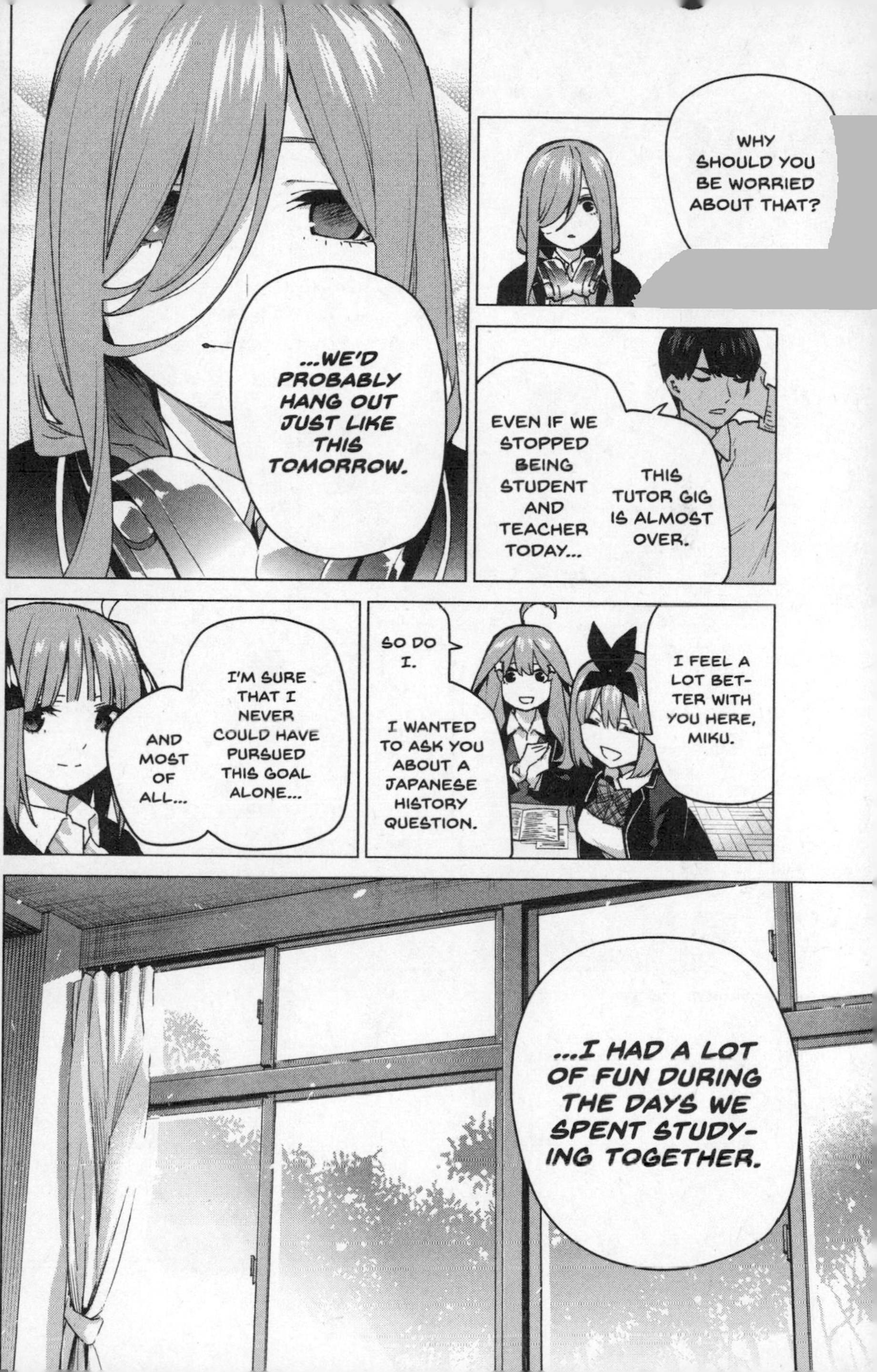
WHY SHOULD YOU BE WORRIED ABOUT THAT?
THIS TUTOR GIG IS ALMOST OVER.
EVEN IF WE STOPPED BEING STUDENT AND TEACHER TODAY...
...WE'D PROBABLY HANG OUT JUST LIKE THIS TOMORROW.
I FEEL A LOT BET-TER WITH YOU HERE, MIKU.
SO DO I.
I WANTED TO ASK YOU ABOUT A JAPANESE HISTORY QUESTION.
I'M SURE THAT I NEVER COULD HAVE PURSUED THIS GOAL ALONE...
AND MOST OF ALL...
...I HAD A LOT OF FUN DURING THE DAYS WE SPENT STUDY-ING TOGETHER.

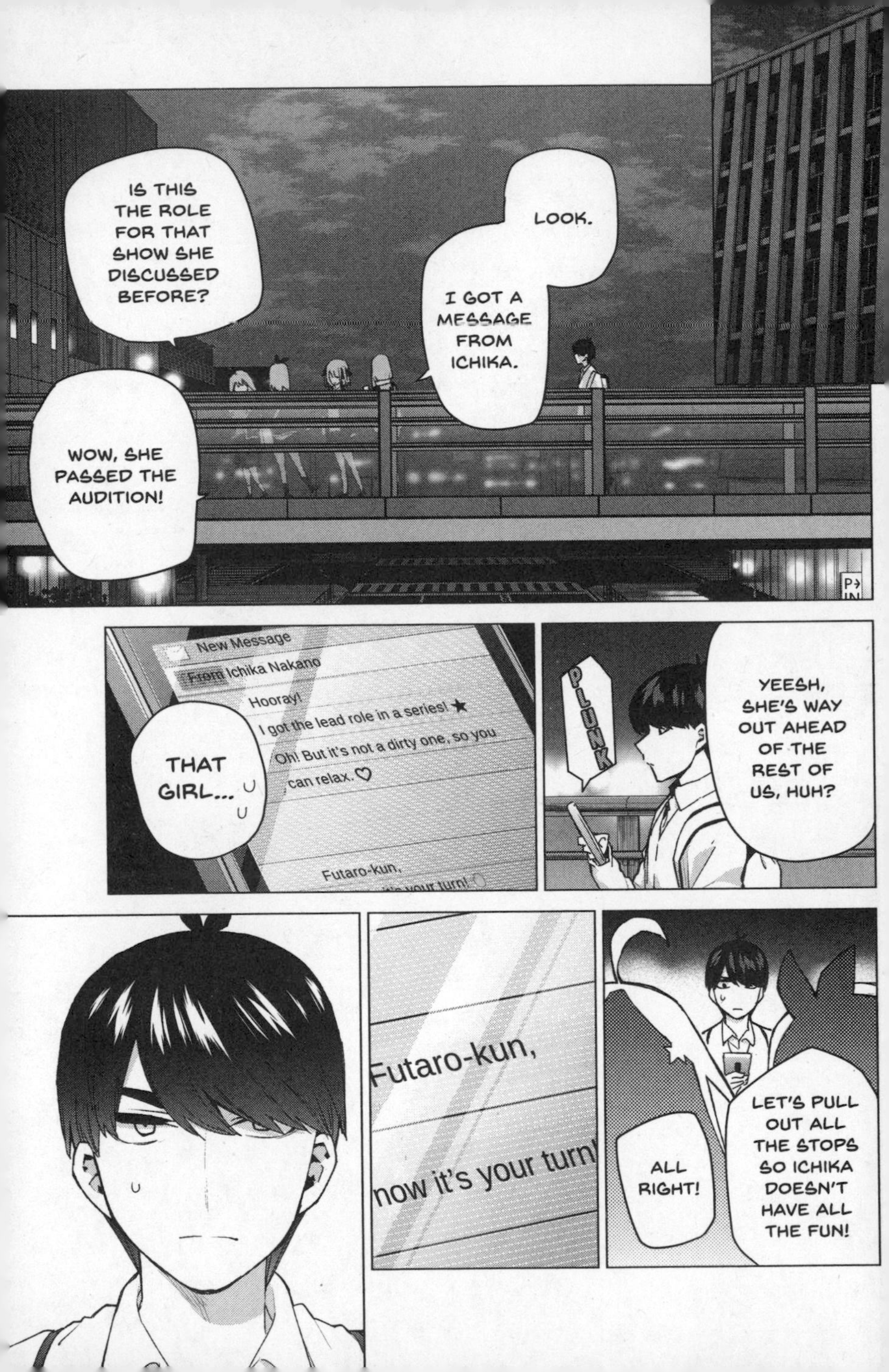
LOOK.
I GOT A MESSAGE FROM ICHIKA.
IS THIS THE ROLE FOR THAT SHOW SHE DISCUSSED BEFORE?
WOW, SHE PASSED THE AUDITION!
PLUNK
YEESH, SHE'S WAY OUT AHEAD OF THE REST OF US, HUH?
New Message
From Ichika Nakano
Hooray!
I got the lead role in a series! ★
Oh! But it's not a dirty one, so you can relax. ♡
Futaro-kun,
THAT GIRL...
LET'S PULL OUT ALL THE STOPS SO ICHIKA DOESN'T HAVE ALL THE FUN!
ALL RIGHT!
Futaro-kun,
now it's your turn!

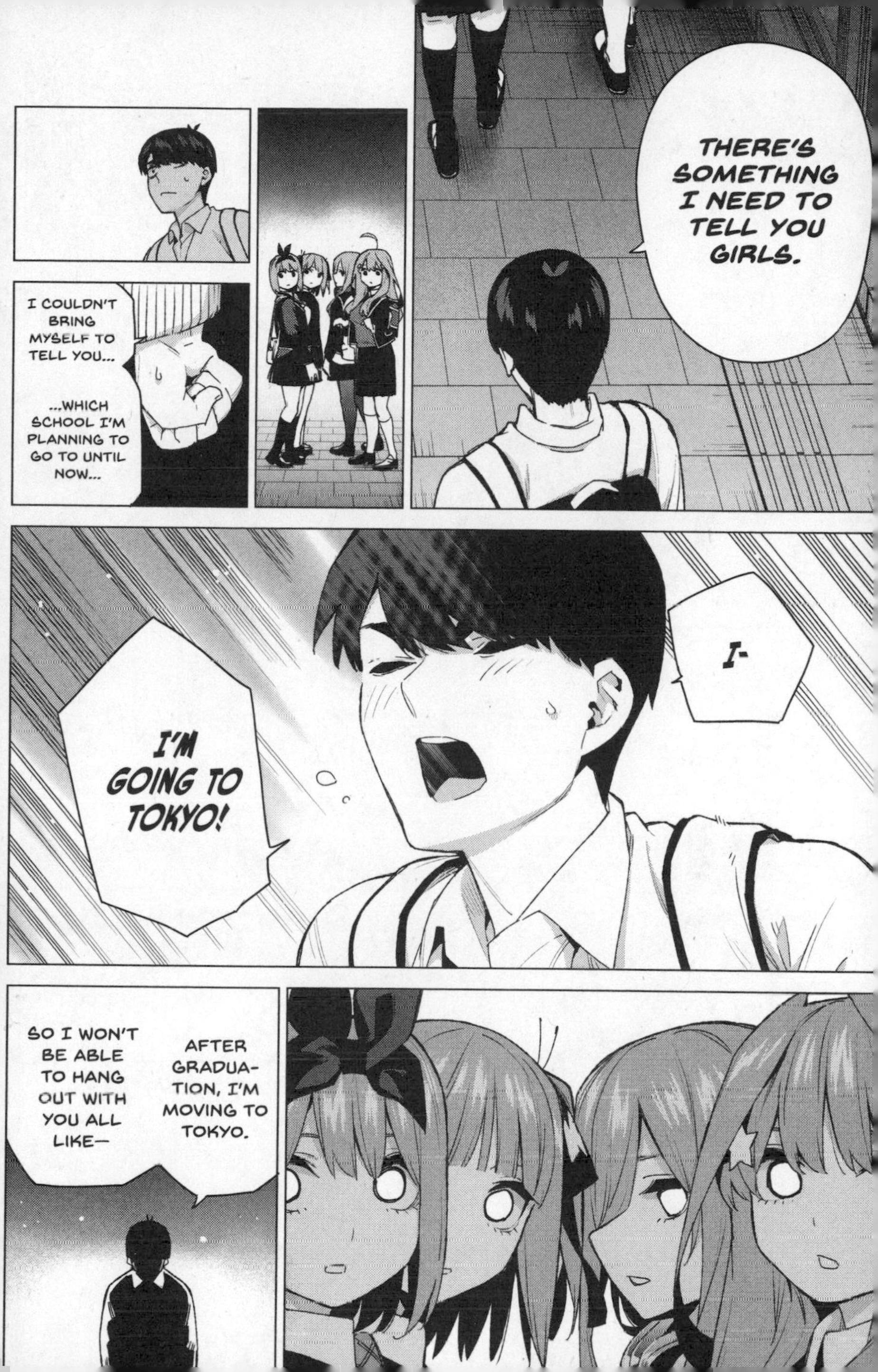
THERE'S SOMETHING I NEED TO TELL YOU GIRLS.
I COULDN'T BRING MYSELF TO TELL YOU...
...WHICH SCHOOL I'M PLANNING TO GO TO UNTIL NOW...
I-
I'M GOING TO TOKYO!
AFTER GRADUATION, I'M MOVING TO TOKYO.
SO I WON'T BE ABLE TO HANG OUT WITH YOU ALL LIKE—

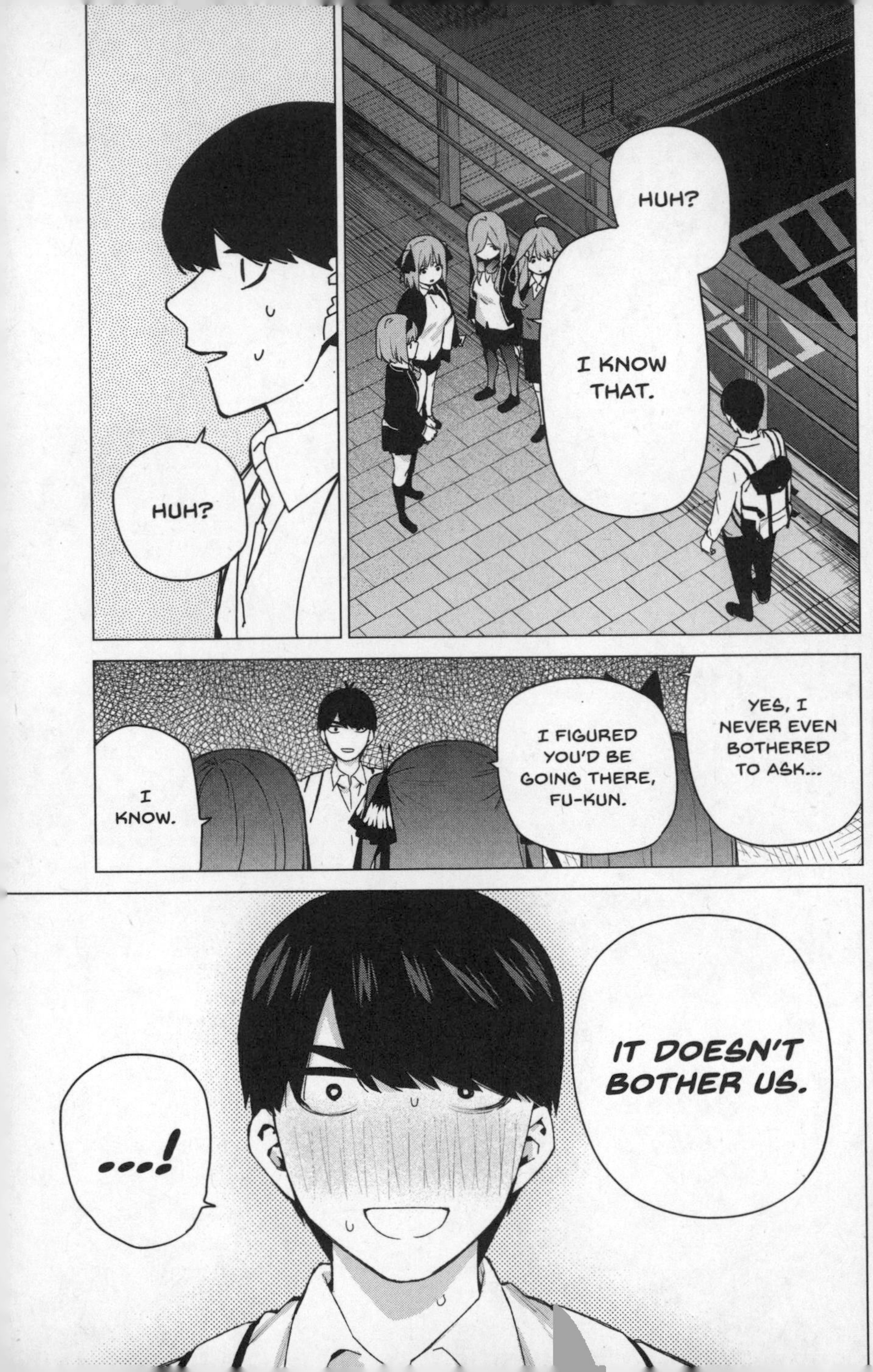
HUH?
I KNOW THAT.
HUH?
YES, I NEVER EVEN BOTHERED TO ASK...
I FIGURED YOU'D BE GOING THERE, FU-KUN.
I KNOW.
IT DOESN'T BOTHER US.
...!

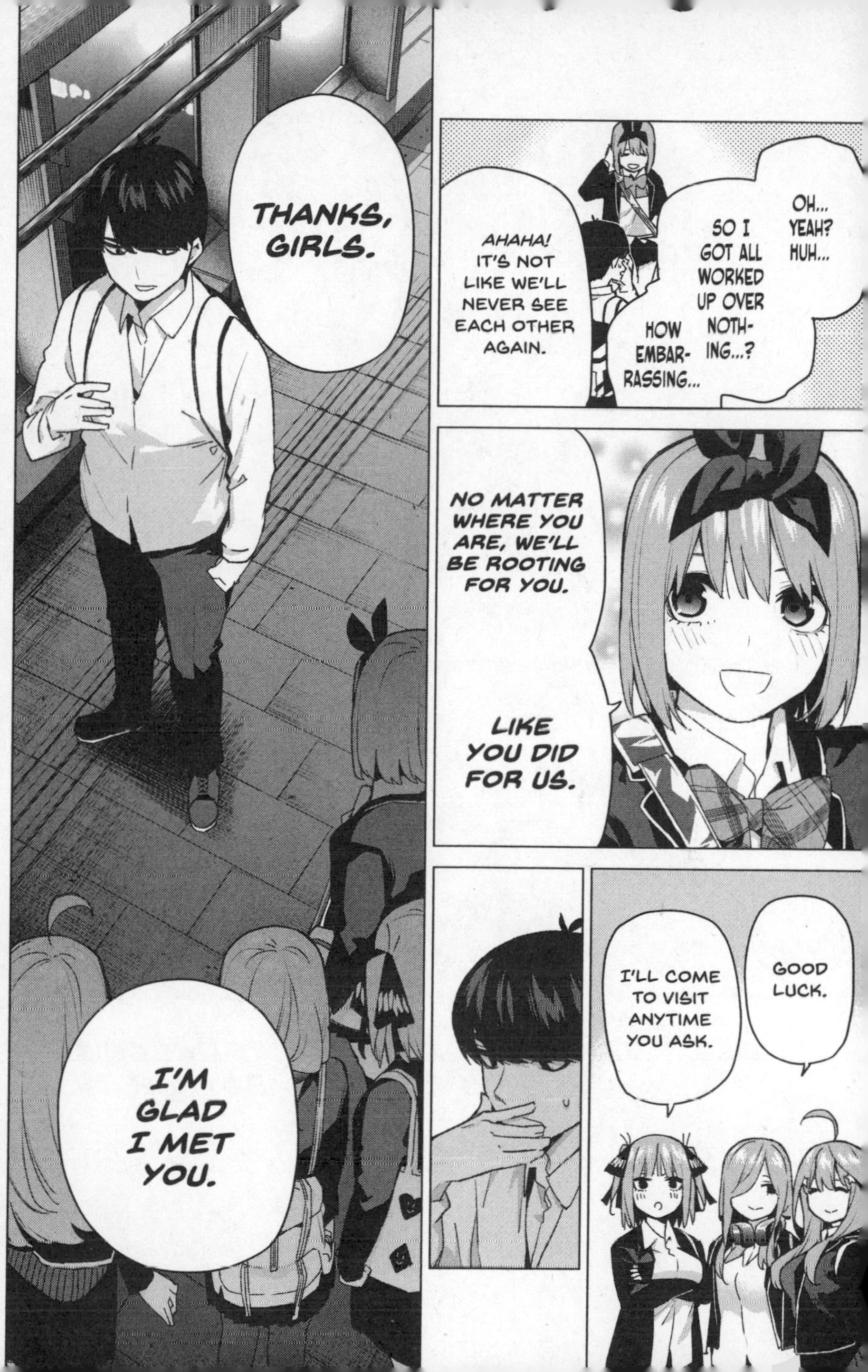
OH... YEAH? HUH...
SO I GOT ALL WORKED UP OVER NOTHING...?
HOW EMBARRASSING...
AHAHA! IT'S NOT LIKE WE'LL NEVER SEE EACH OTHER AGAIN.
NO MATTER WHERE YOU ARE, WE'LL BE ROOTING FOR YOU.
LIKE YOU DID FOR US.
GOOD LUCK.
I'LL COME TO VISIT ANYTIME YOU ASK.
THANKS, GIRLS.
I'M GLAD I MET YOU.

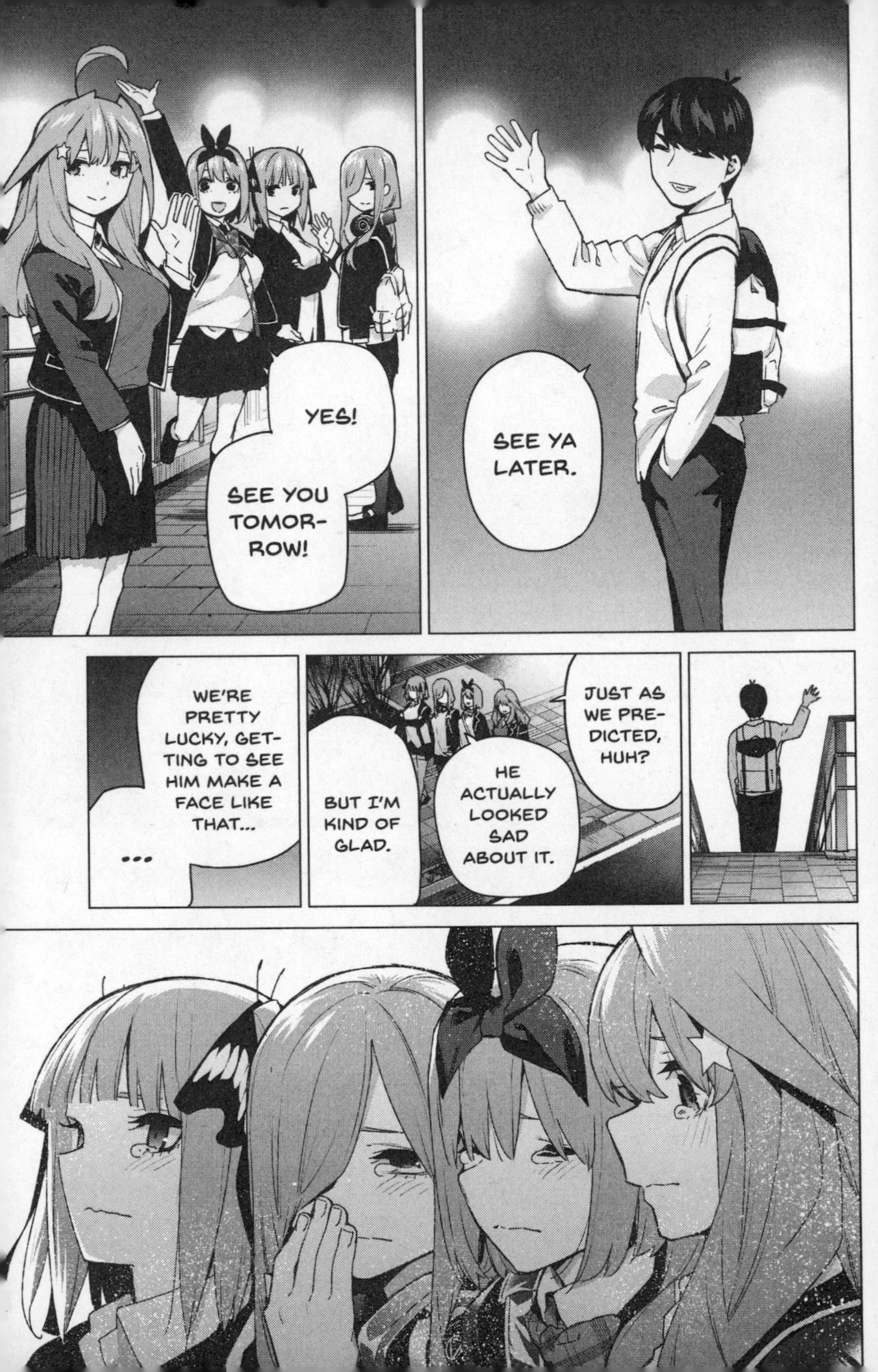
SEE YA LATER.
YES!
SEE YOU TOMORROW!
JUST AS WE PREDICTED, HUH?
HE ACTUALLY LOOKED SAD ABOUT IT.
BUT I'M KIND OF GLAD.
WE'RE PRETTY LUCKY, GETTING TO SEE HIM MAKE A FACE LIKE THAT...
...

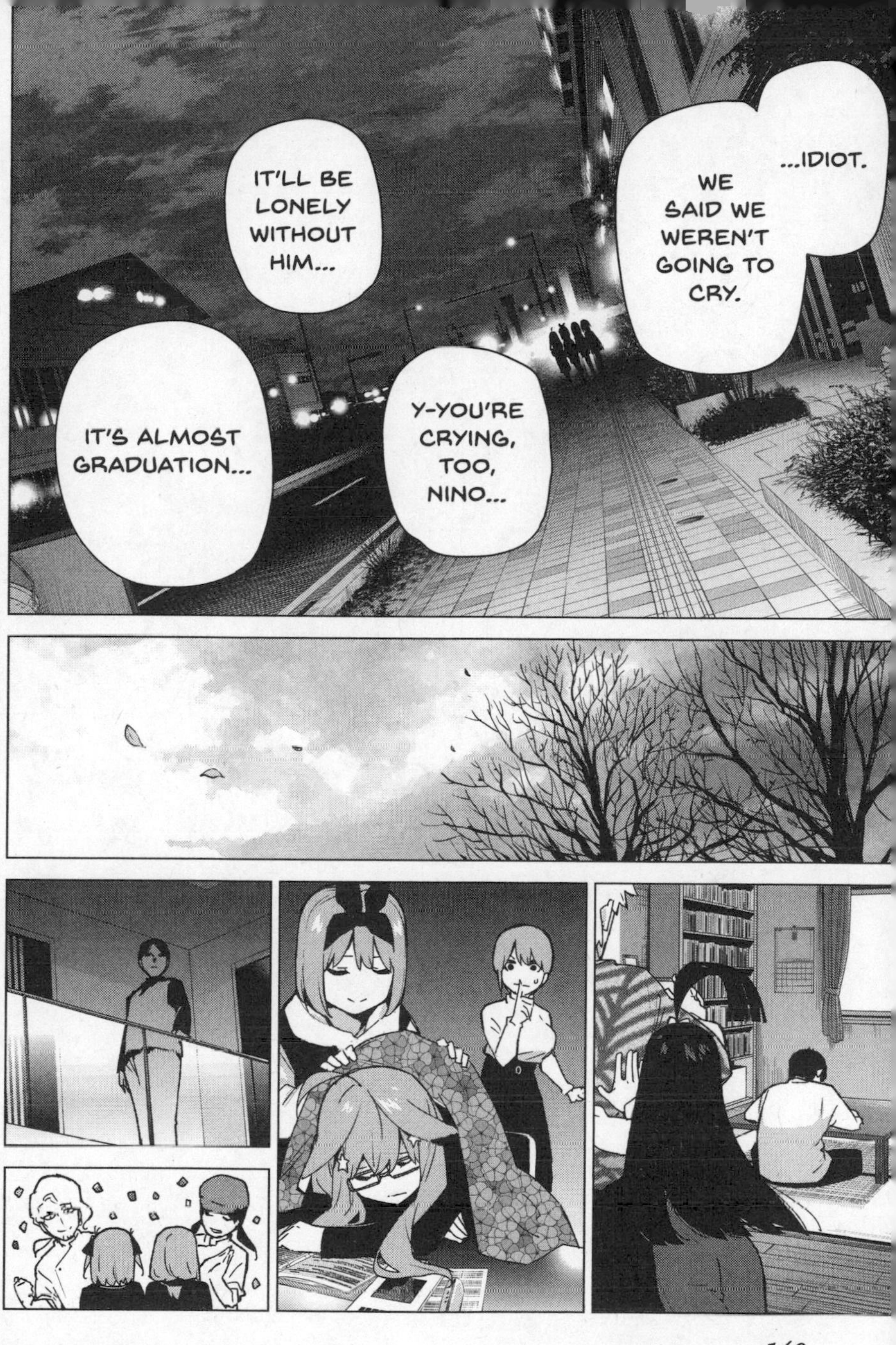
...IDIOT.
WE SAID WE WEREN'T GOING TO CRY.
IT'LL BE LONELY WITHOUT HIM...
Y-YOU'RE CRYING, TOO, NINO...
IT'S ALMOST GRADUATION...

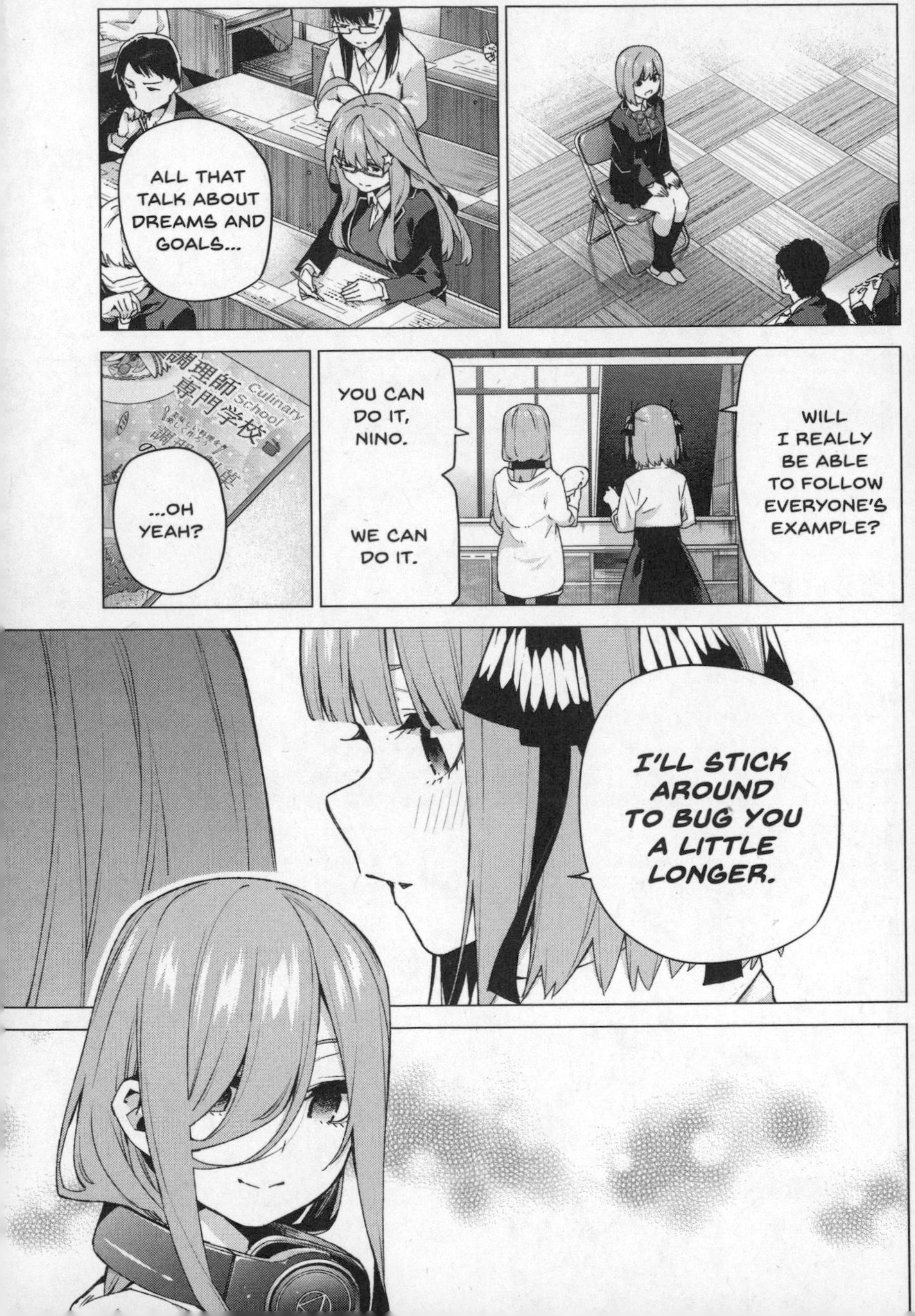
ALL THAT TALK ABOUT DREAMS AND GOALS...
WILL I REALLY BE ABLE TO FOLLOW EVERYONE'S EXAMPLE?
YOU CAN DO IT, NINO.
WE CAN DO IT.
調理師専門学校
Culinary School
...OH YEAH?
I'LL STICK AROUND TO BUG YOU A LITTLE LONGER.

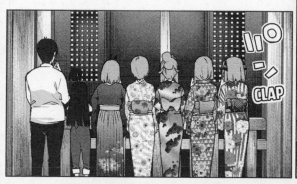

CLAP

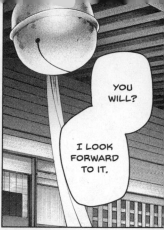

YOU WILL?

I LOOK FORWARD TO IT.

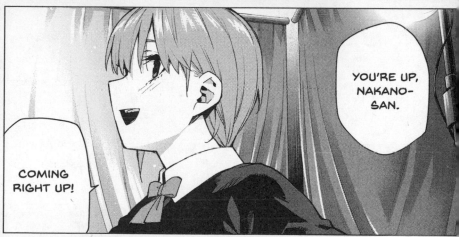

YOU'RE UP, NAKANO-SAN.

COMING RIGHT UP!

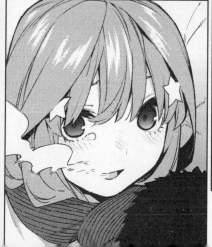

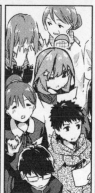

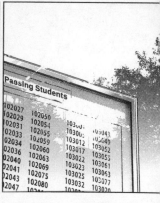

Passing Students

102027	102050	103001	103043
102029	102054	103009	103049
102031	102055	103012	103052
102033	102059	103017	103055
102034	102060	103022	103061
102036	102063	103023	103063
102040	102069	103025	103077
102041	102075	103032	103020
102043	102080	103032	
102047	10201	10302	

142

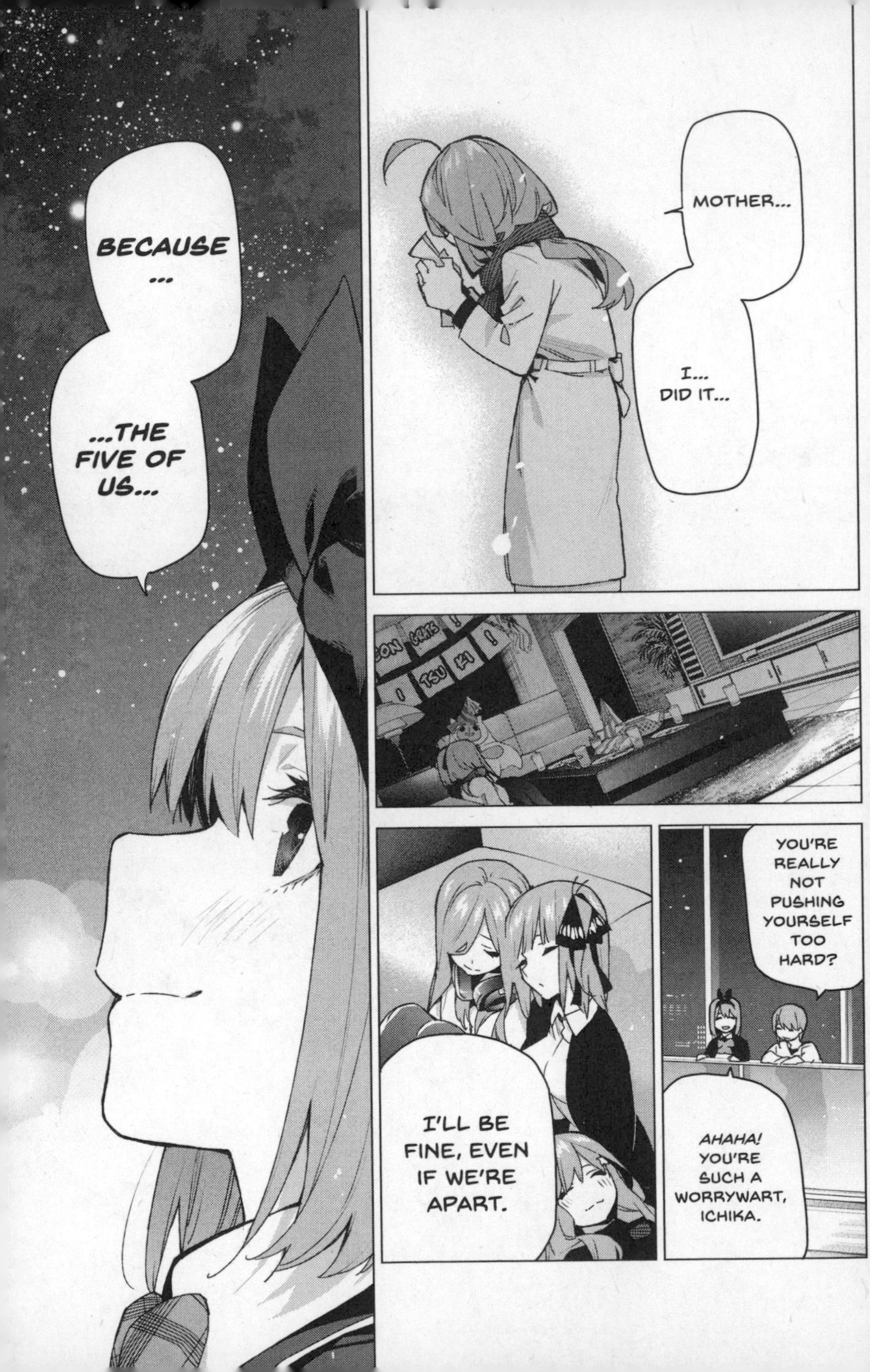
MOTHER...
I... DID IT...
YOU'RE REALLY NOT PUSHING YOURSELF TOO HARD?
AHAHA! YOU'RE SUCH A WORRYWART, ICHIKA.
I'LL BE FINE, EVEN IF WE'RE APART.
BECAUSE ...
...THE FIVE OF US...

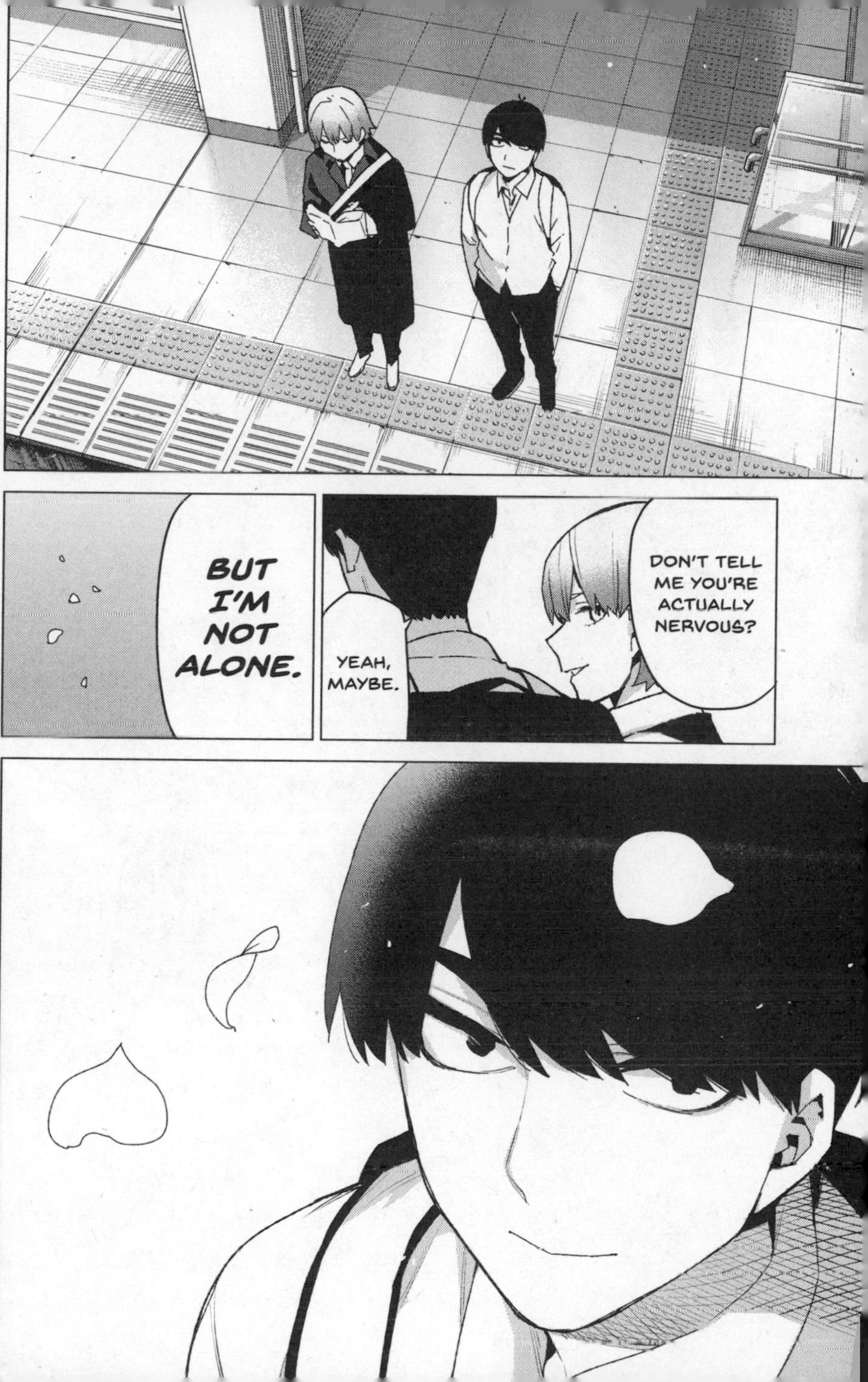
DON'T TELL ME YOU'RE ACTUALLY NERVOUS?
YEAH, MAYBE.
BUT I'M NOT ALONE.

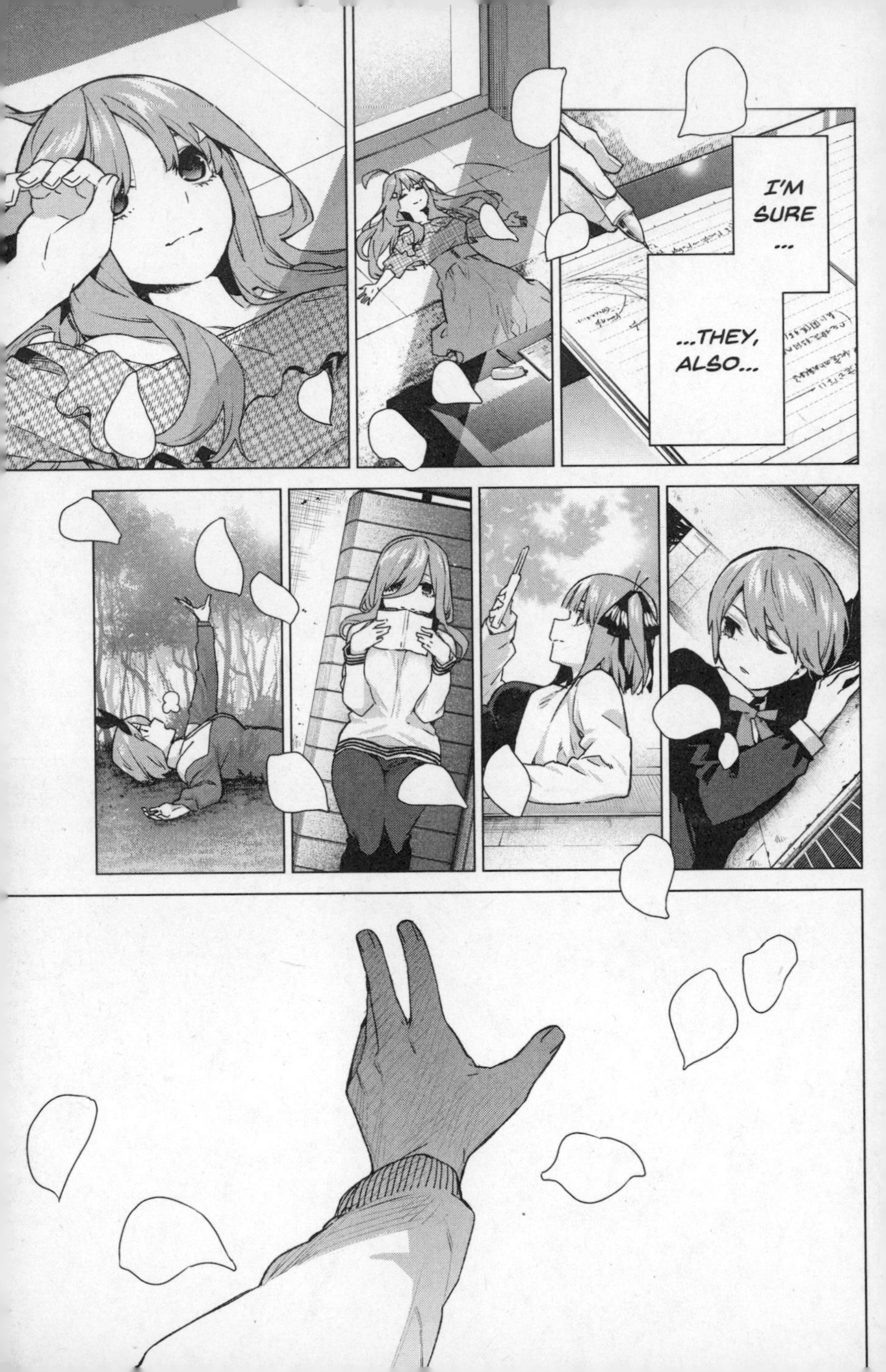
I'M SURE ...
...THEY, ALSO...

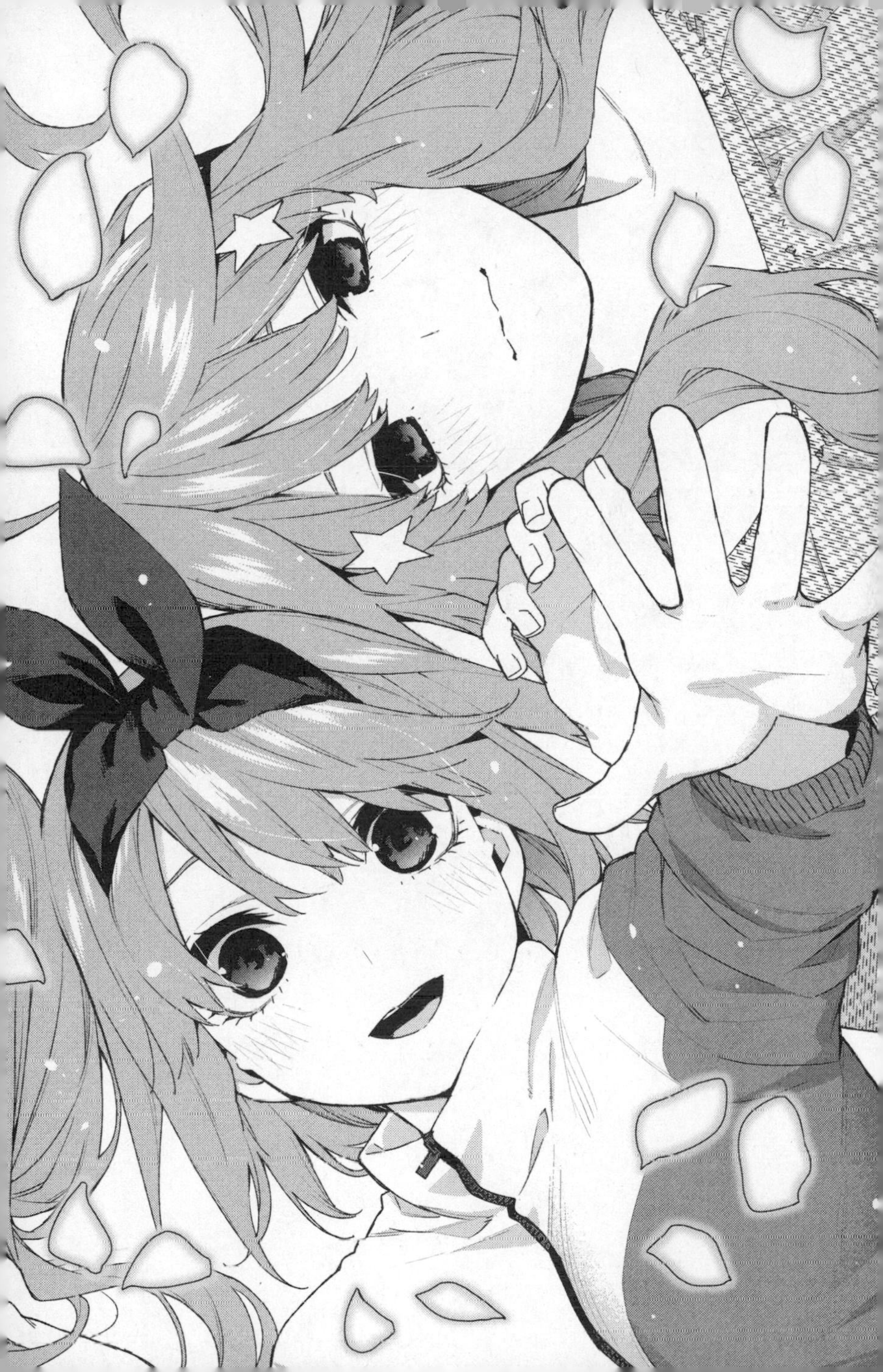

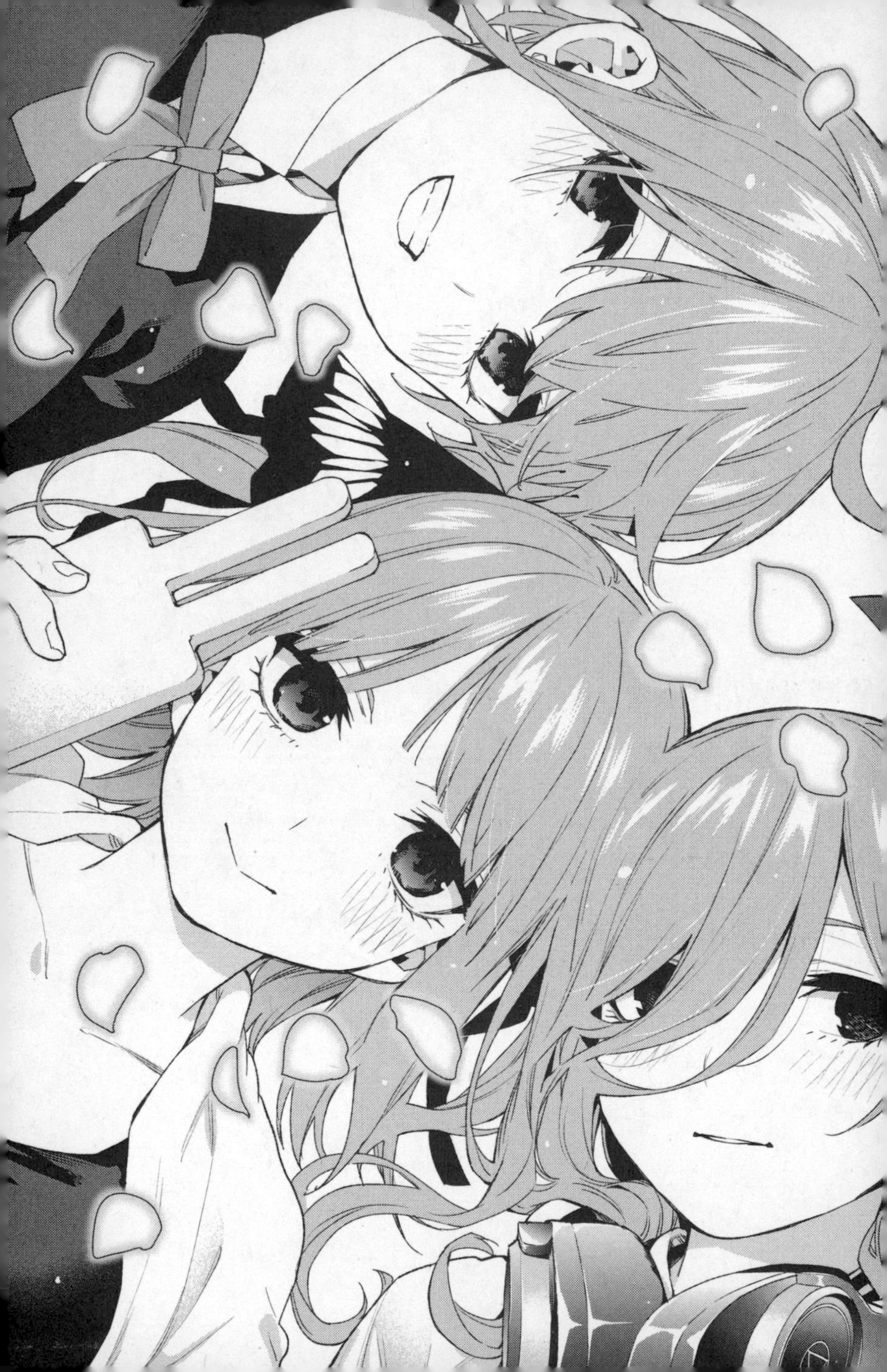

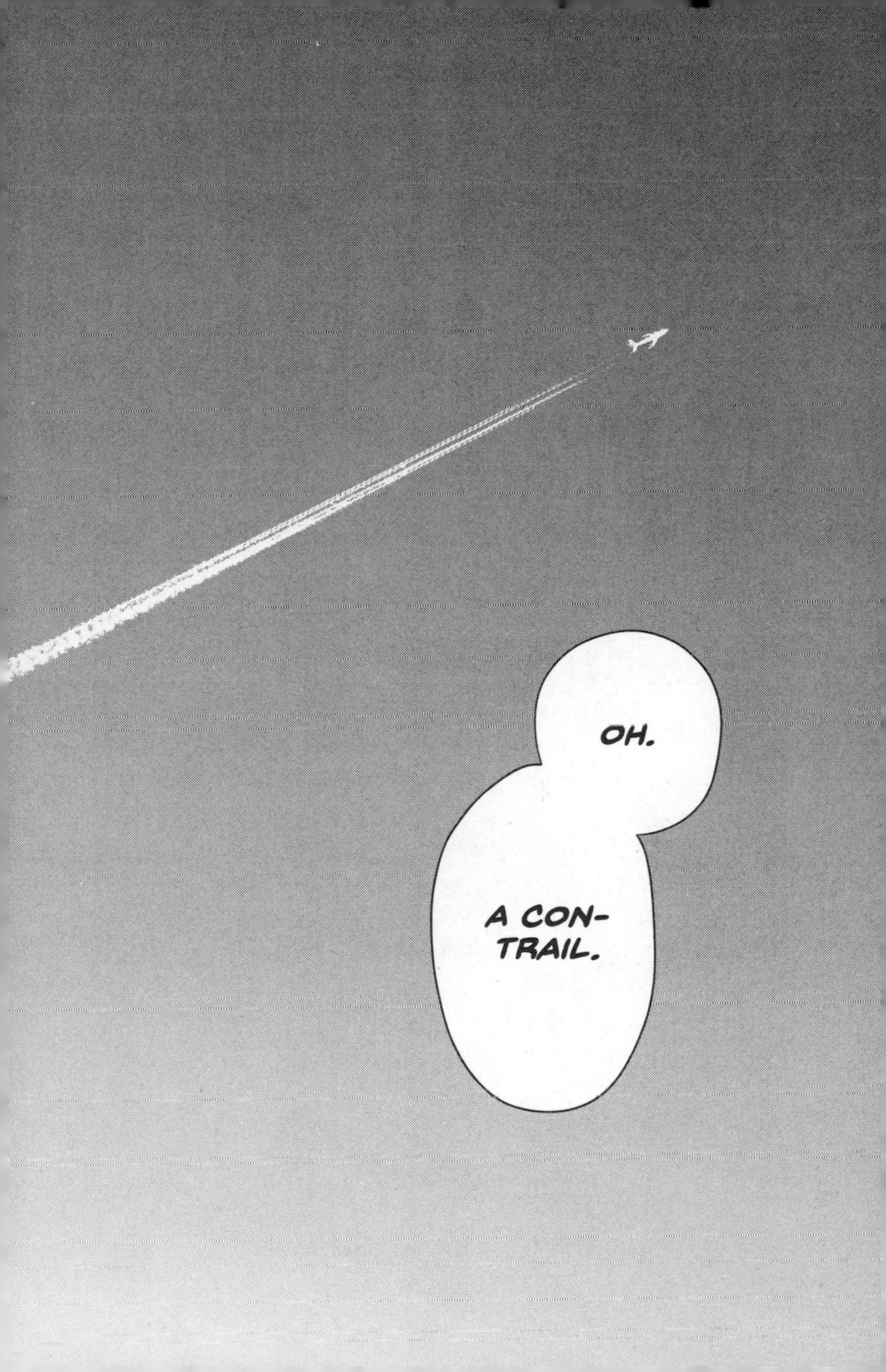
OH.
A CON-
TRAIL.

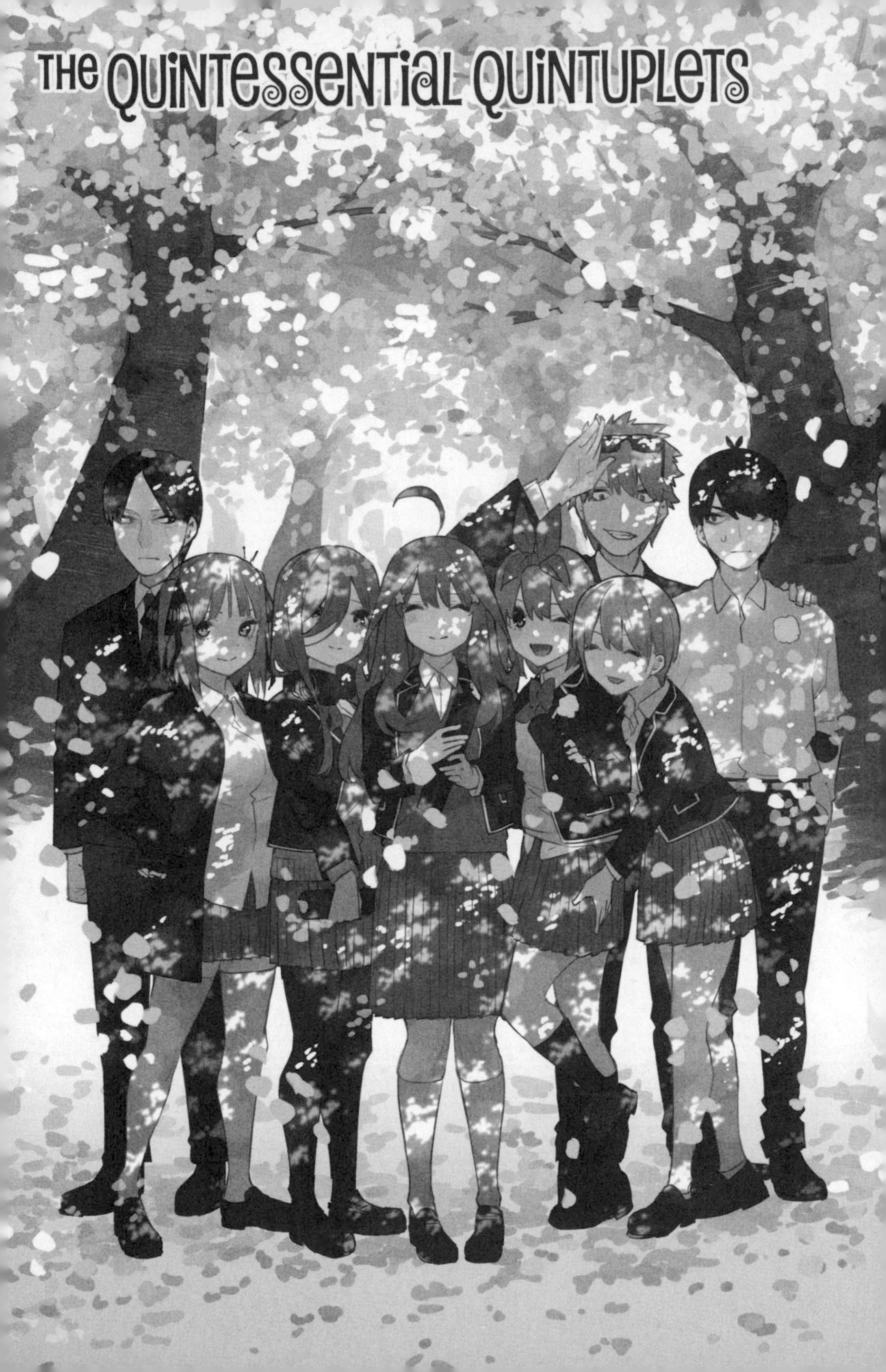
THE QUINTESSENTIAL QUINTUPLETS

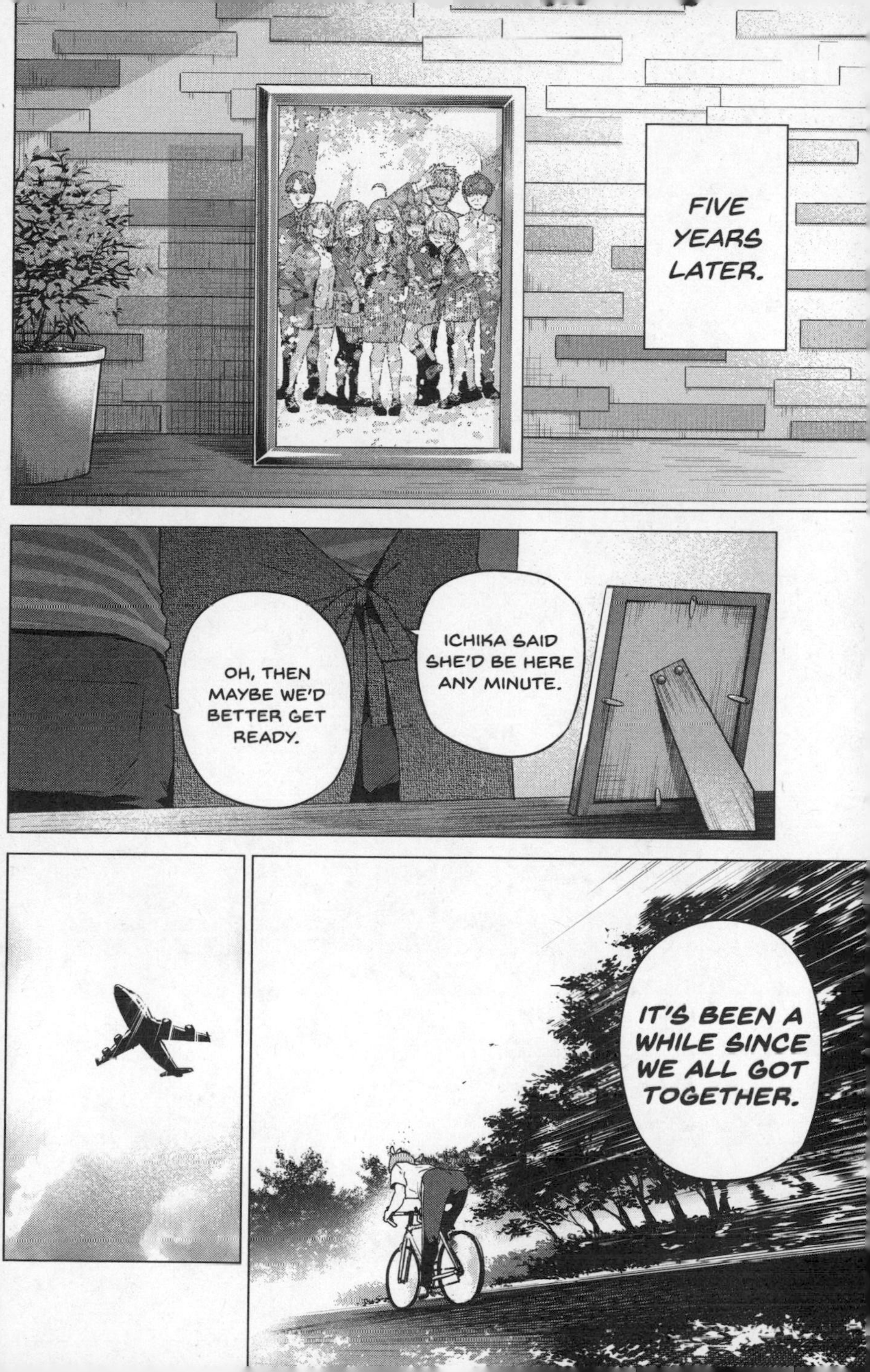

FIVE YEARS LATER.
ICHIKA SAID SHE'D BE HERE ANY MINUTE.
OH, THEN MAYBE WE'D BETTER GET READY.
IT'S BEEN A WHILE SINCE WE ALL GOT TOGETHER.

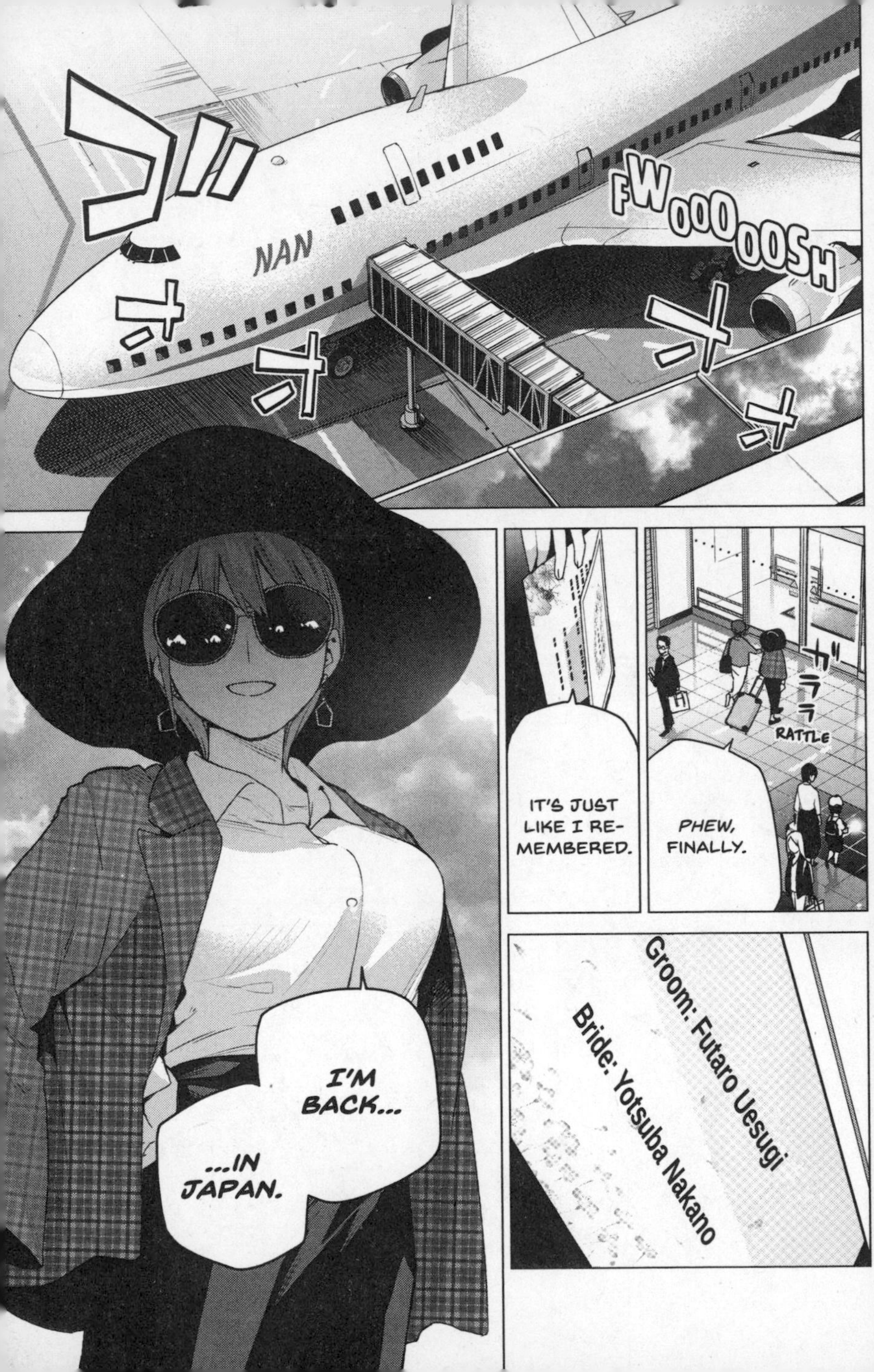

NAN
FWOOOOOSH
RATTLE
PHEW, FINALLY.
IT'S JUST LIKE I RE-MEMBERED.
Groom: Futaro Uesugi
Bride: Yotsuba Nakano
I'M BACK...
...IN JAPAN.

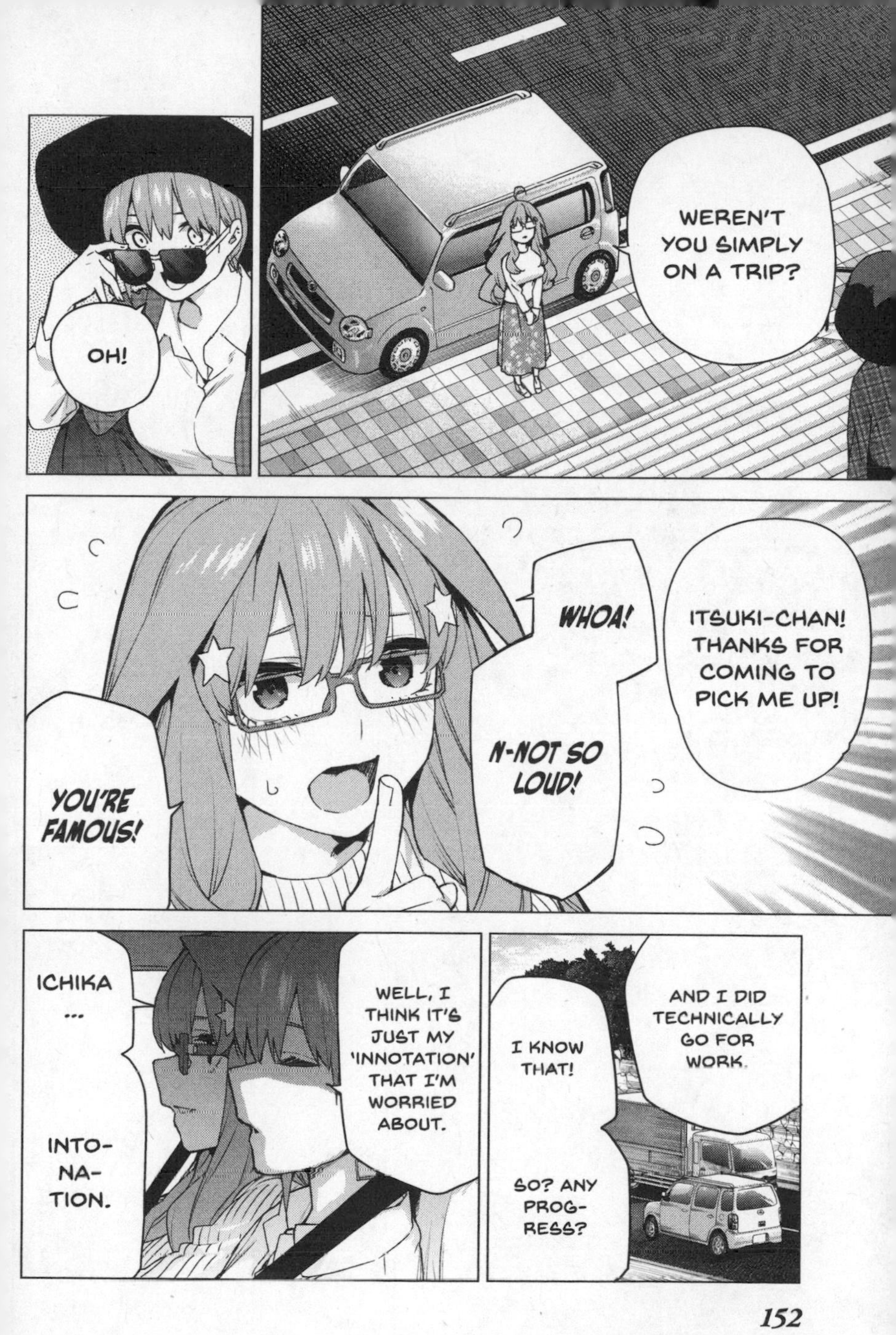
WEREN'T YOU SIMPLY ON A TRIP?
OH!
ITSUKI-CHAN! THANKS FOR COMING TO PICK ME UP!
WHOA!
N-NOT SO LOUD!
YOU'RE FAMOUS!
AND I DID TECHNICALLY GO FOR WORK.
I KNOW THAT!
SO? ANY PROG-RESS?
WELL, I THINK IT'S JUST MY 'INNOTATION' THAT I'M WORRIED ABOUT.
ICHIKA ...
INTO-NA-TION.

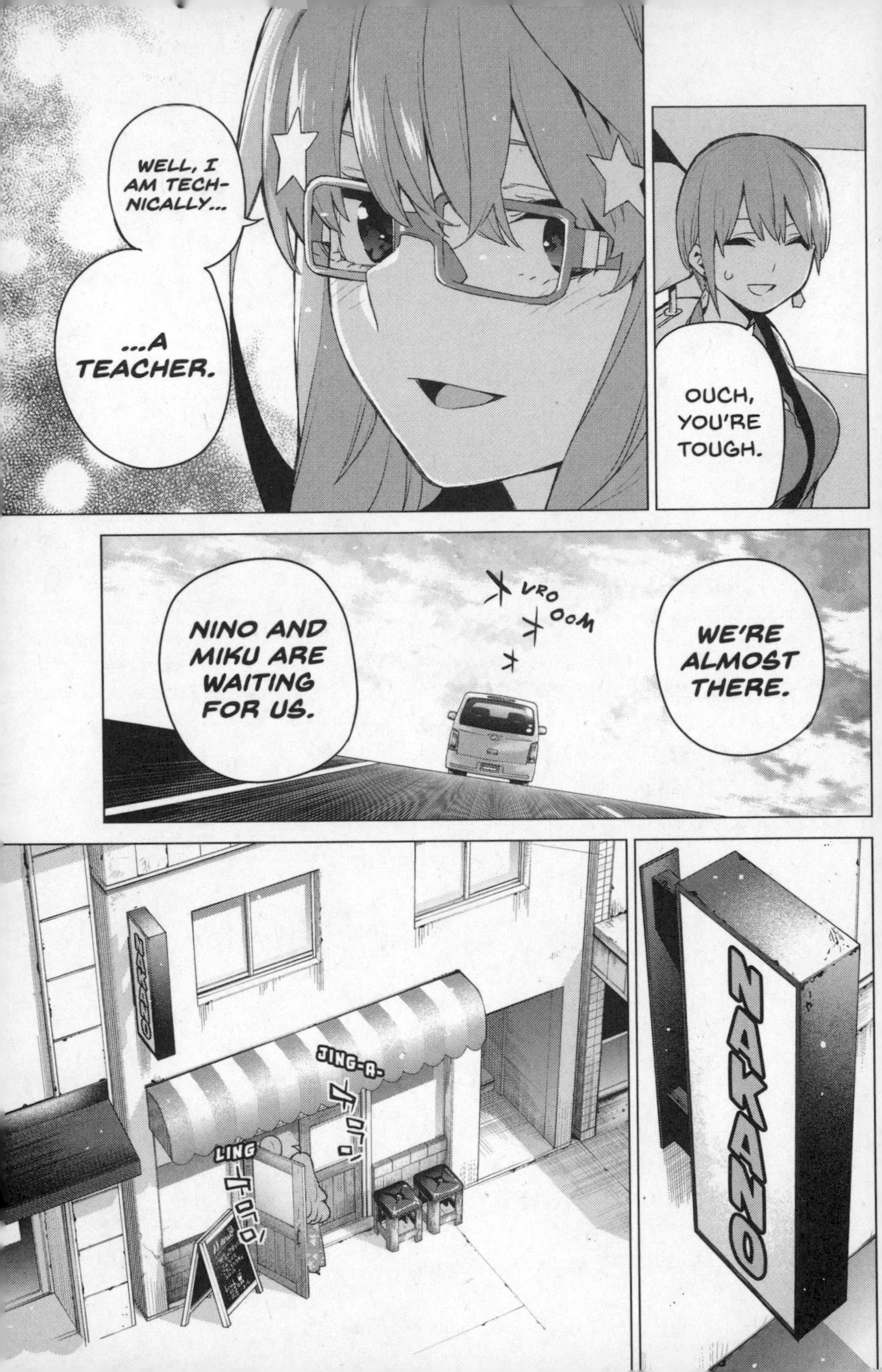
OUCH, YOU'RE TOUGH.
WELL, I AM TECH-NICALLY...
...A TEACHER.
WE'RE ALMOST THERE.
VROOOM
NINO AND MIKU ARE WAITING FOR US.
NAKANO
NAKANO
JING-A-
LING

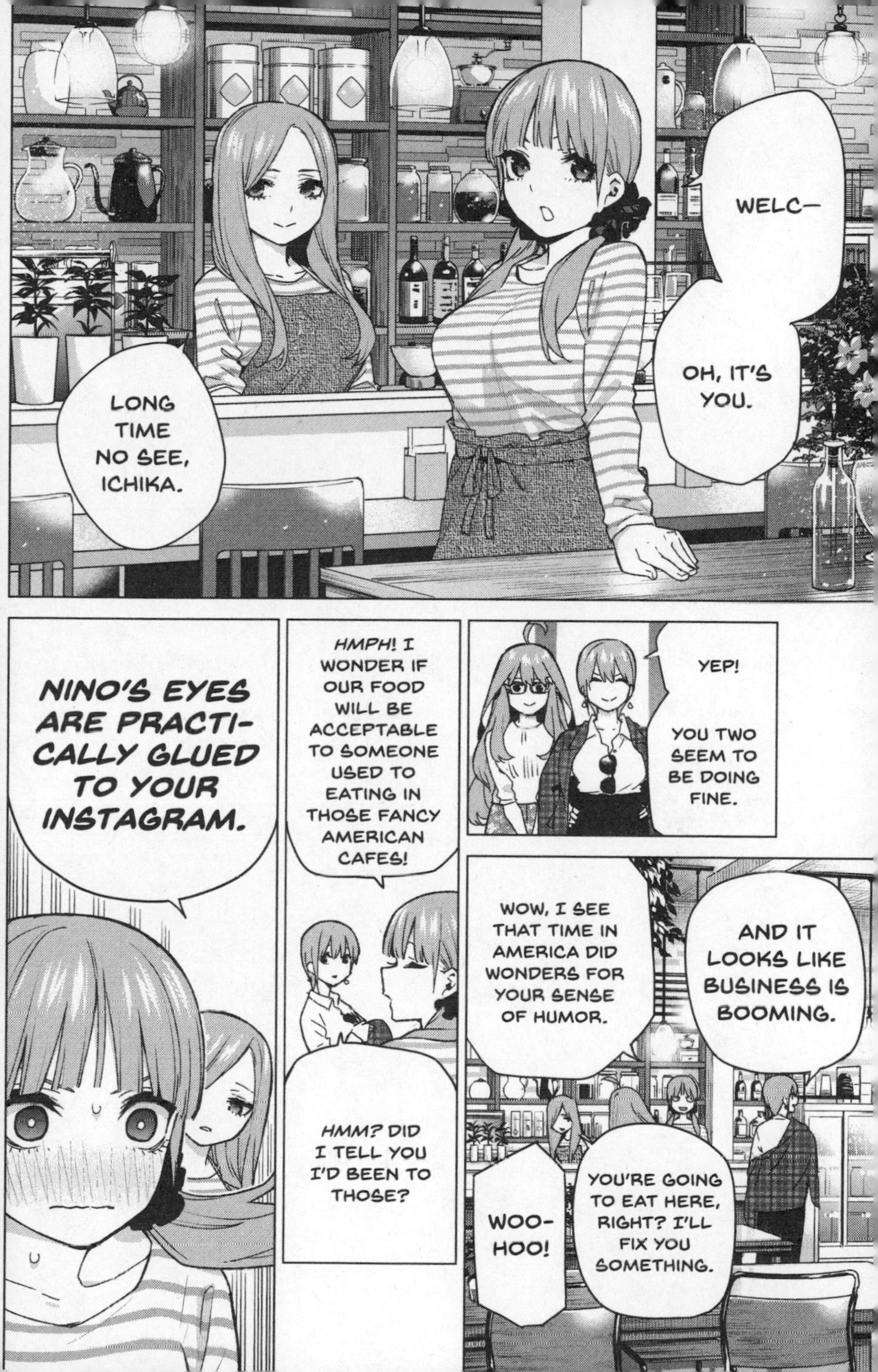

WELC—
OH, IT'S YOU.
LONG TIME NO SEE, ICHIKA.
YEP!
YOU TWO SEEM TO BE DOING FINE.
AND IT LOOKS LIKE BUSINESS IS BOOMING.
WOW, I SEE THAT TIME IN AMERICA DID WONDERS FOR YOUR SENSE OF HUMOR.
YOU'RE GOING TO EAT HERE, RIGHT? I'LL FIX YOU SOMETHING.
WOO-HOO!
HMPH! I WONDER IF OUR FOOD WILL BE ACCEPTABLE TO SOMEONE USED TO EATING IN THOSE FANCY AMERICAN CAFES!
HMM? DID I TELL YOU I'D BEEN TO THOSE?
NINO'S EYES ARE PRACTICALLY GLUED TO YOUR INSTAGRAM.

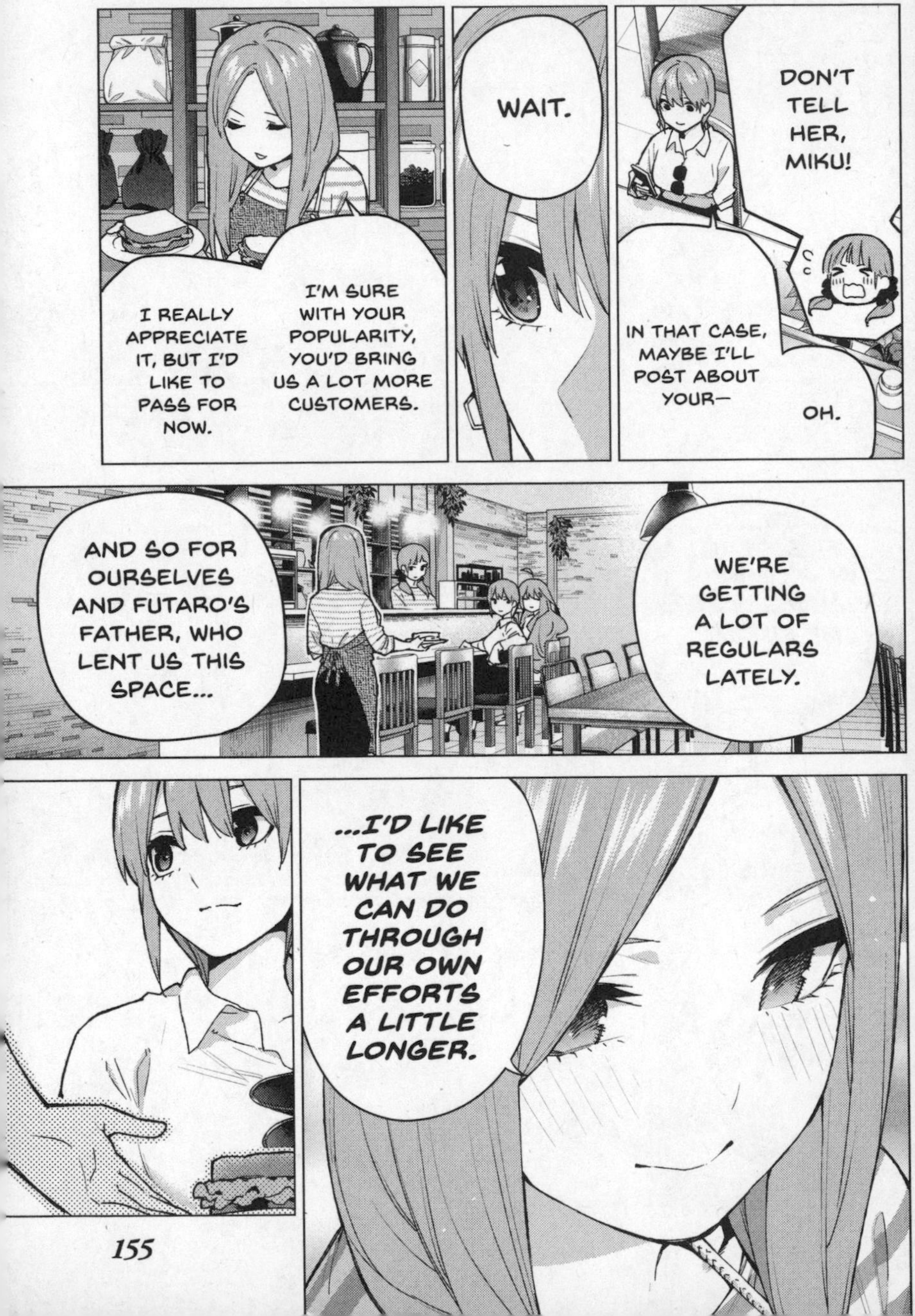
DON'T TELL HER, MIKU!
IN THAT CASE, MAYBE I'LL POST ABOUT YOUR—
OH.
WAIT.
I'M SURE WITH YOUR POPULARITY, YOU'D BRING US A LOT MORE CUSTOMERS.
I REALLY APPRECIATE IT, BUT I'D LIKE TO PASS FOR NOW.
WE'RE GETTING A LOT OF REGULARS LATELY.
AND SO FOR OURSELVES AND FUTARO'S FATHER, WHO LENT US THIS SPACE...
...I'D LIKE TO SEE WHAT WE CAN DO THROUGH OUR OWN EFFORTS A LITTLE LONGER.

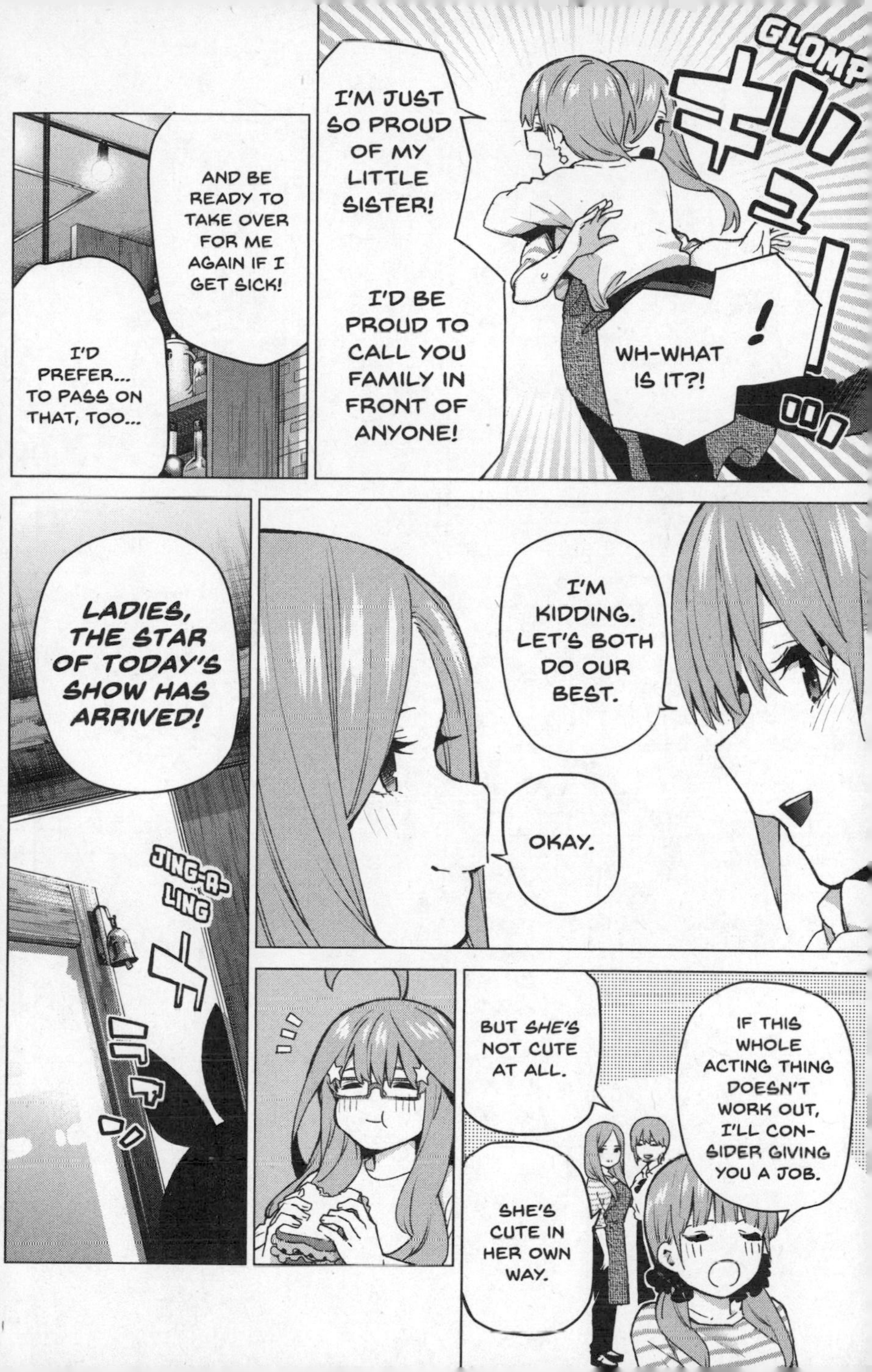
GLOMP
WH-WHAT IS IT?!
I'M JUST SO PROUD OF MY LITTLE SISTER!
I'D BE PROUD TO CALL YOU FAMILY IN FRONT OF ANYONE!
AND BE READY TO TAKE OVER FOR ME AGAIN IF I GET SICK!
I'D PREFER... TO PASS ON THAT, TOO...
I'M KIDDING. LET'S BOTH DO OUR BEST.
OKAY.
IF THIS WHOLE ACTING THING DOESN'T WORK OUT, I'LL CON-SIDER GIVING YOU A JOB.
BUT *SHE'S* NOT CUTE AT ALL.
SHE'S CUTE IN HER OWN WAY.
LADIES, THE STAR OF TODAY'S SHOW HAS ARRIVED!
JING-A-LING

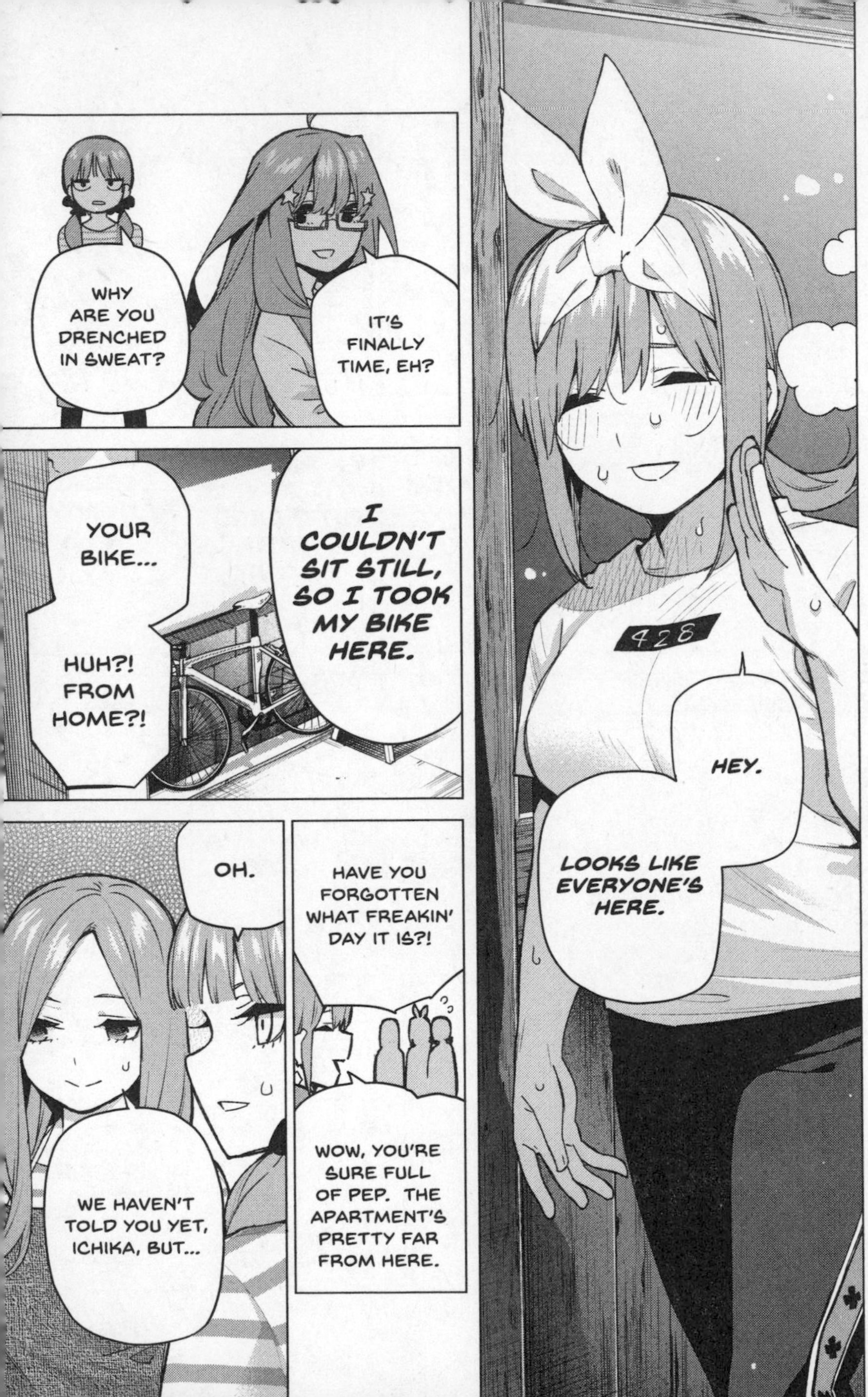
HEY.
LOOKS LIKE EVERYONE'S HERE.
IT'S FINALLY TIME, EH?
WHY ARE YOU DRENCHED IN SWEAT?
I COULDN'T SIT STILL, SO I TOOK MY BIKE HERE.
YOUR BIKE...
HUH?! FROM HOME?!
HAVE YOU FORGOTTEN WHAT FREAKIN' DAY IT IS?!
WOW, YOU'RE SURE FULL OF PEP. THE APARTMENT'S PRETTY FAR FROM HERE.
OH.
WE HAVEN'T TOLD YOU YET, ICHIKA, BUT...

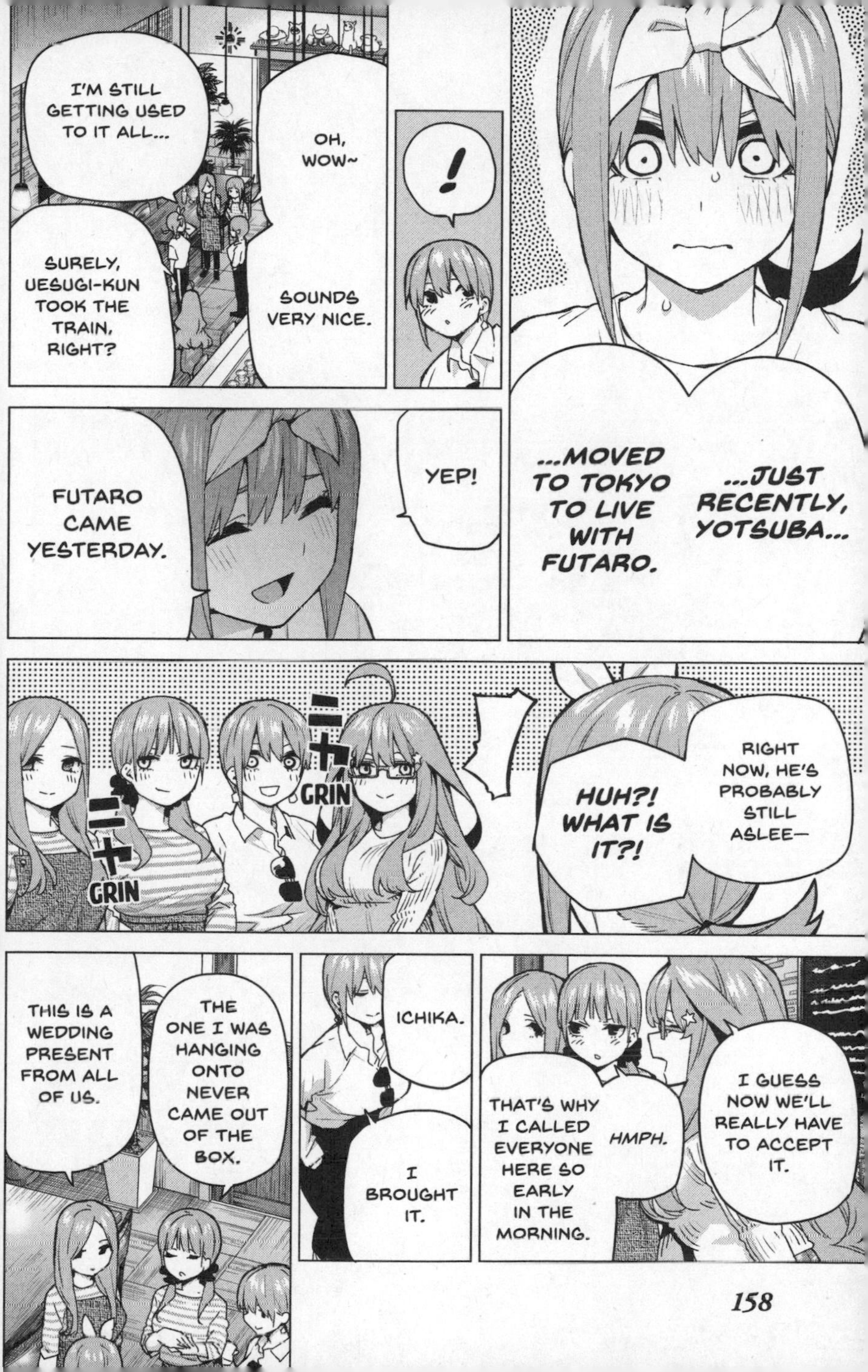
...JUST RECENTLY, YOTSUBA...
...MOVED TO TOKYO TO LIVE WITH FUTARO.
!
OH, WOW~ SOUNDS VERY NICE.
I'M STILL GETTING USED TO IT ALL...
SURELY, UESUGI-KUN TOOK THE TRAIN, RIGHT?
YEP!
FUTARO CAME YESTERDAY.
RIGHT NOW, HE'S PROBABLY STILL ASLEE—
HUH?! WHAT IS IT?!
ニヤ GRIN
ニヤ GRIN
I GUESS NOW WE'LL REALLY HAVE TO ACCEPT IT.
HMPH.
THAT'S WHY I CALLED EVERYONE HERE SO EARLY IN THE MORNING.
ICHIKA.
I BROUGHT IT.
THE ONE I WAS HANGING ONTO NEVER CAME OUT OF THE BOX.
THIS IS A WEDDING PRESENT FROM ALL OF US.

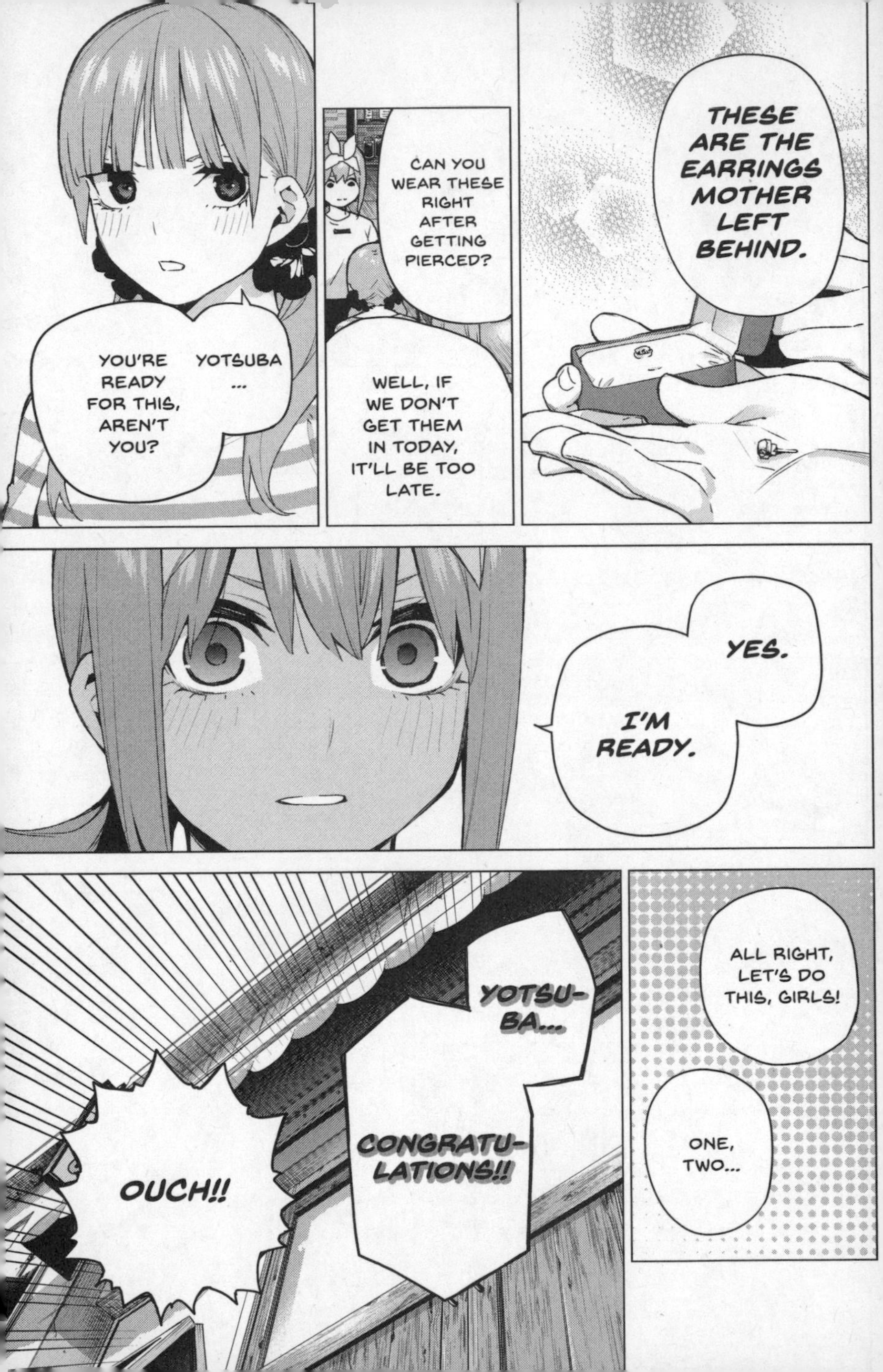
THESE ARE THE EARRINGS MOTHER LEFT BEHIND.
CAN YOU WEAR THESE RIGHT AFTER GETTING PIERCED?
WELL, IF WE DON'T GET THEM IN TODAY, IT'LL BE TOO LATE.
YOTSUBA...
YOU'RE READY FOR THIS, AREN'T YOU?
YES.
I'M READY.
ALL RIGHT, LET'S DO THIS, GIRLS!
ONE, TWO...
YOTSU-BA...
CONGRATU-LATIONS!!
OUCH!!

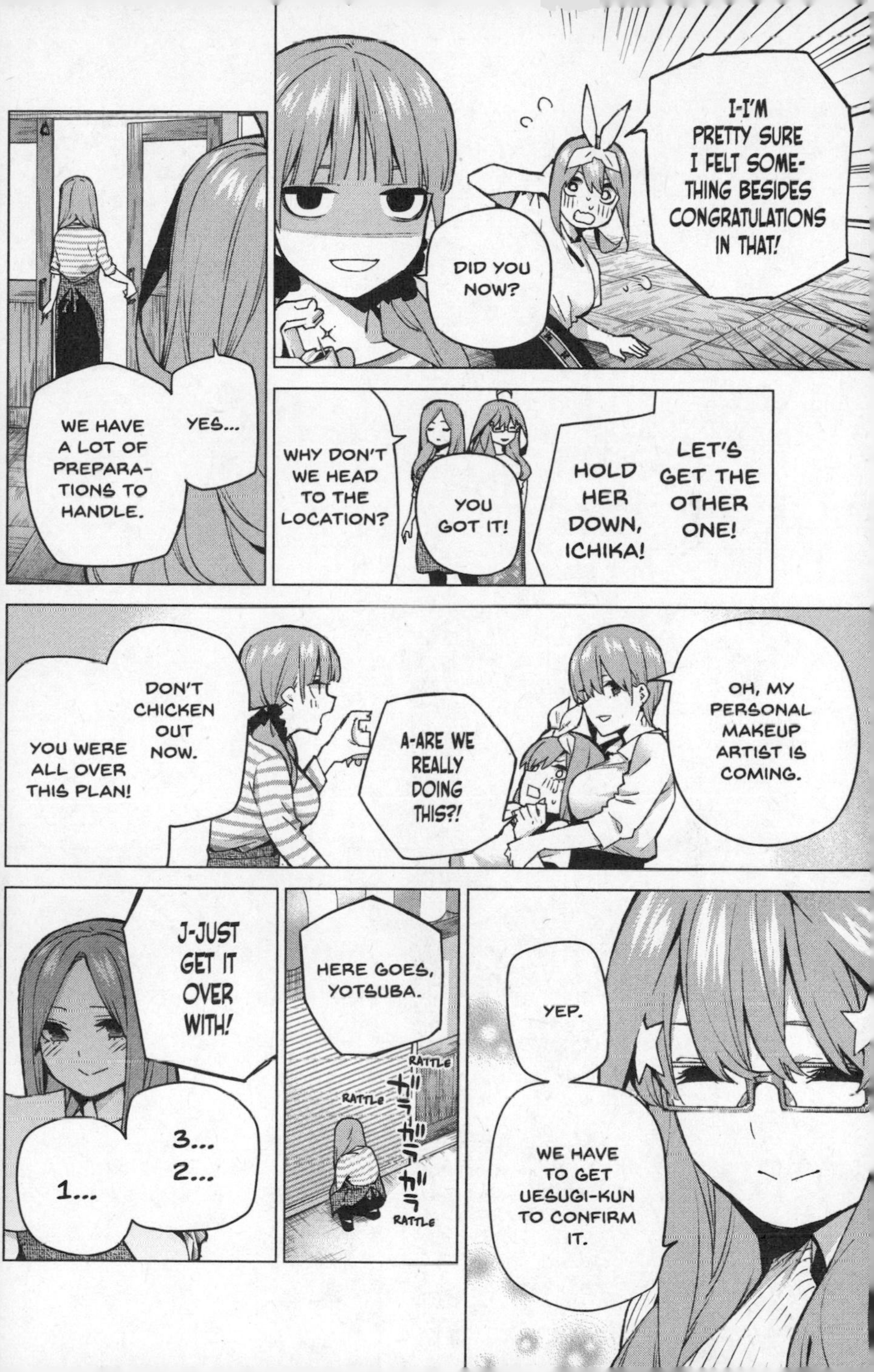
I-I'M PRETTY SURE I FELT SOMETHING BESIDES CONGRATULATIONS IN THAT!
DID YOU NOW?
LET'S GET THE OTHER ONE!
HOLD HER DOWN, ICHIKA!
YOU GOT IT!
WHY DON'T WE HEAD TO THE LOCATION?
YES...
WE HAVE A LOT OF PREPARATIONS TO HANDLE.
OH, MY PERSONAL MAKEUP ARTIST IS COMING.
A-ARE WE REALLY DOING THIS?!
DON'T CHICKEN OUT NOW.
YOU WERE ALL OVER THIS PLAN!
YEP.
WE HAVE TO GET UESUGI-KUN TO CONFIRM IT.
HERE GOES, YOTSUBA.
RATTLE
RATTLE
RATTLE
J-JUST GET IT OVER WITH!
3... 2...
1...

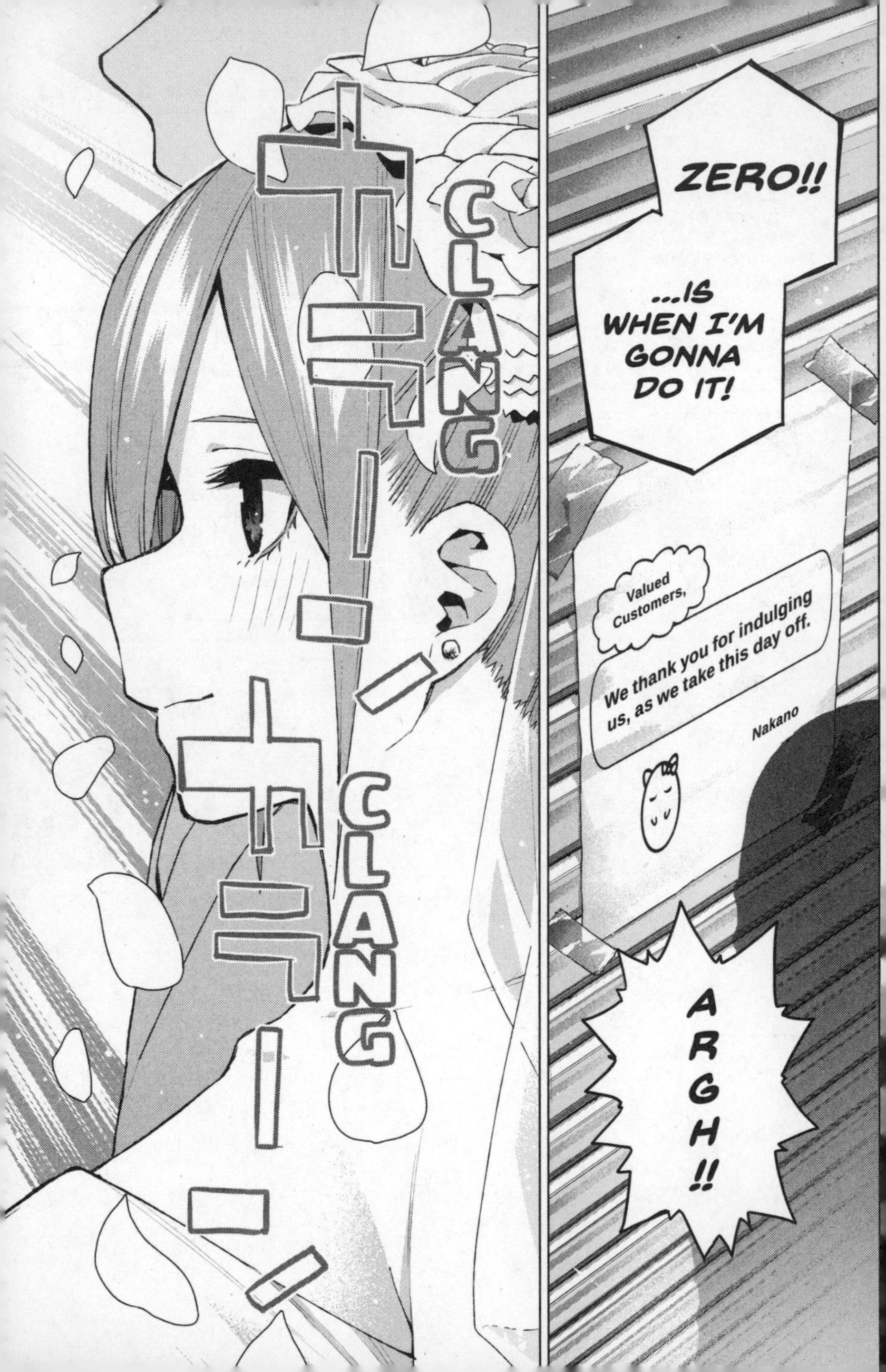
ZERO!!
...IS WHEN I'M GONNA DO IT!
Valued Customers,
We thank you for indulging us, as we take this day off.
Nakano
ARGH!!
CLANG
CLANG

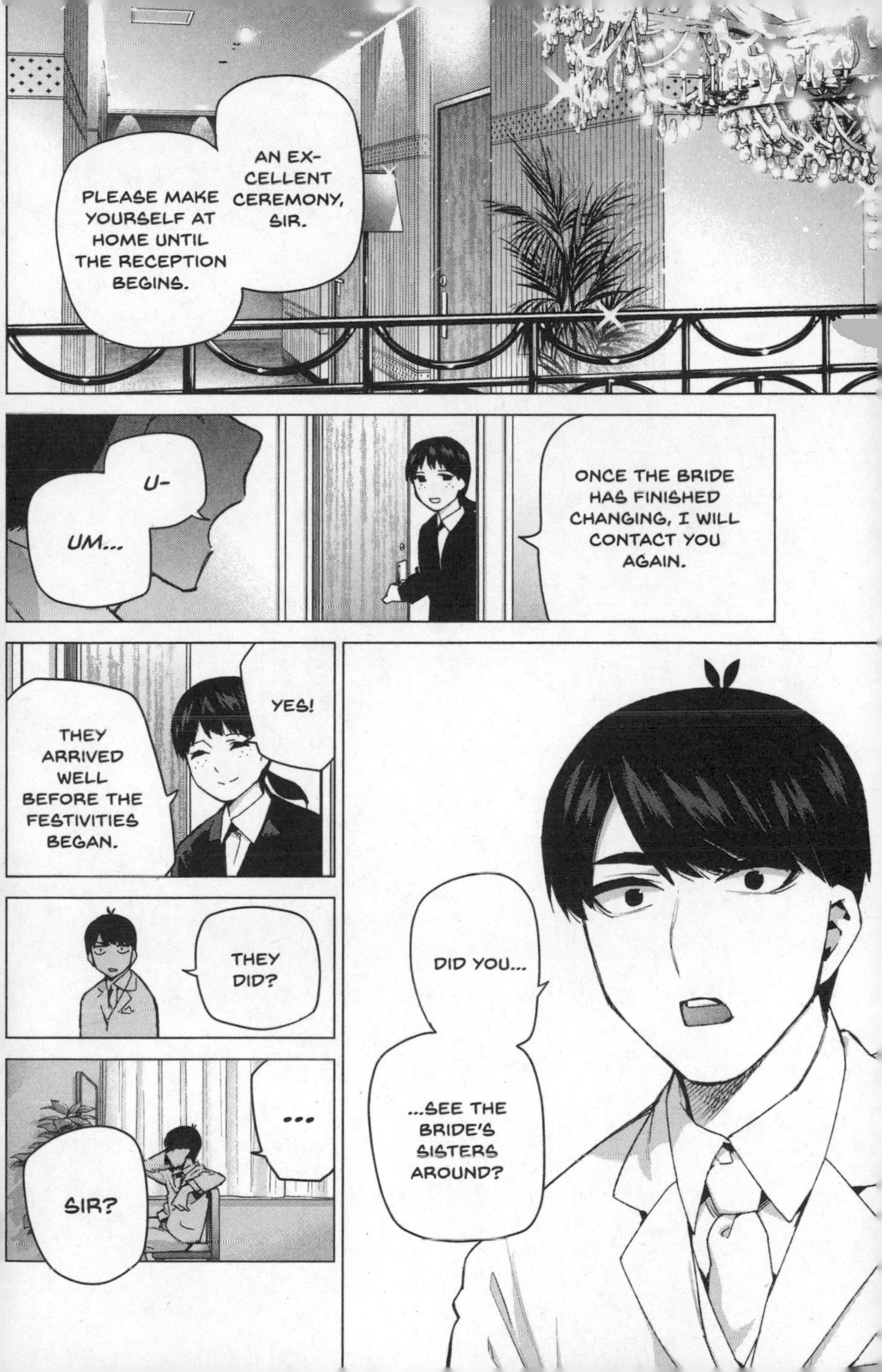
AN EXCELLENT CEREMONY, SIR.
PLEASE MAKE YOURSELF AT HOME UNTIL THE RECEPTION BEGINS.
ONCE THE BRIDE HAS FINISHED CHANGING, I WILL CONTACT YOU AGAIN.
U-
UM...
DID YOU...
...SEE THE BRIDE'S SISTERS AROUND?
YES!
THEY ARRIVED WELL BEFORE THE FESTIVITIES BEGAN.
THEY DID?
...
SIR?

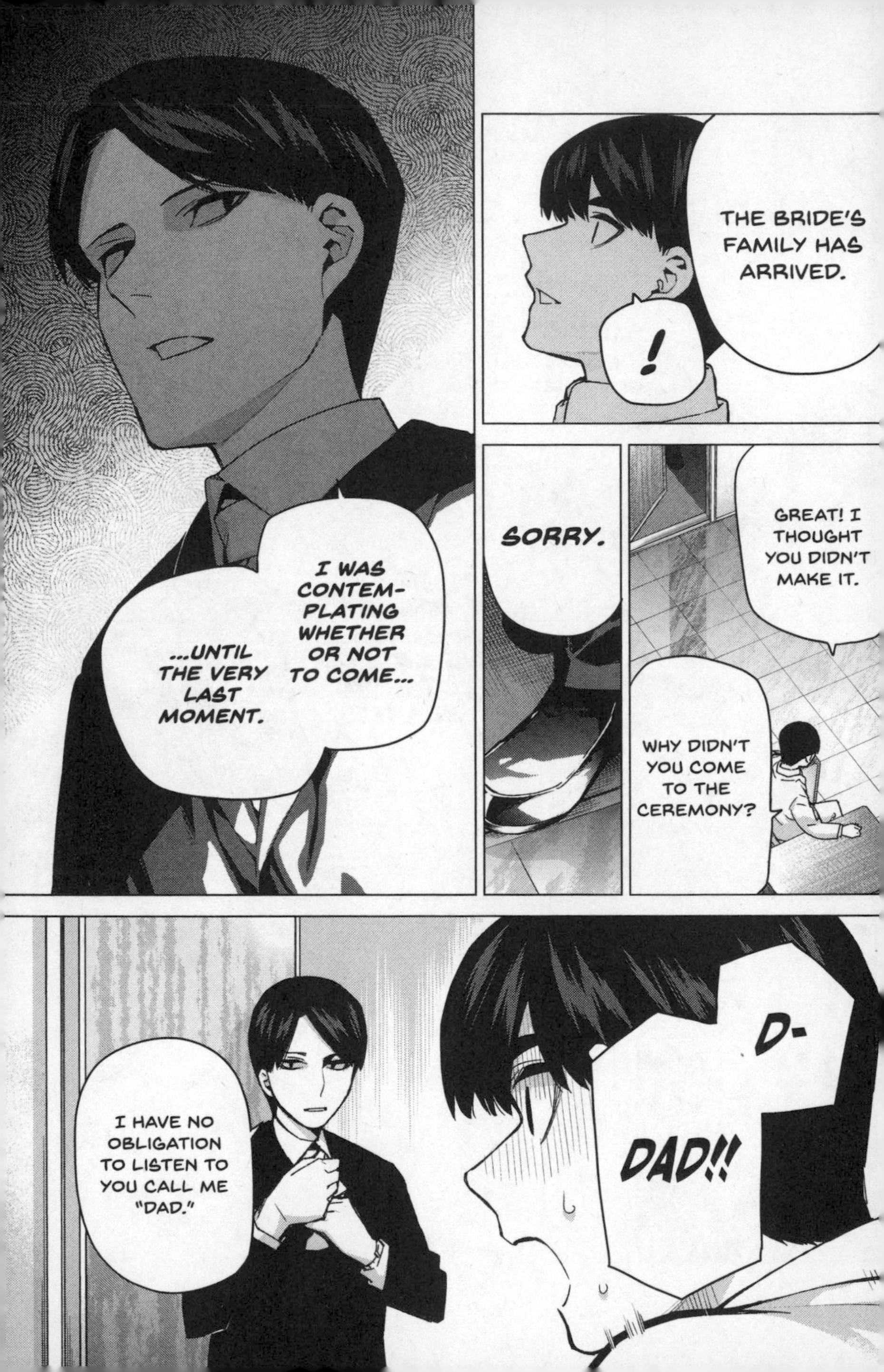
THE BRIDE'S FAMILY HAS ARRIVED.
!
GREAT! I THOUGHT YOU DIDN'T MAKE IT.
WHY DIDN'T YOU COME TO THE CEREMONY?
SORRY.
I WAS CONTEM- PLATING WHETHER OR NOT TO COME...
...UNTIL THE VERY LAST MOMENT.
D-
DAD!!
I HAVE NO OBLIGATION TO LISTEN TO YOU CALL ME "DAD."

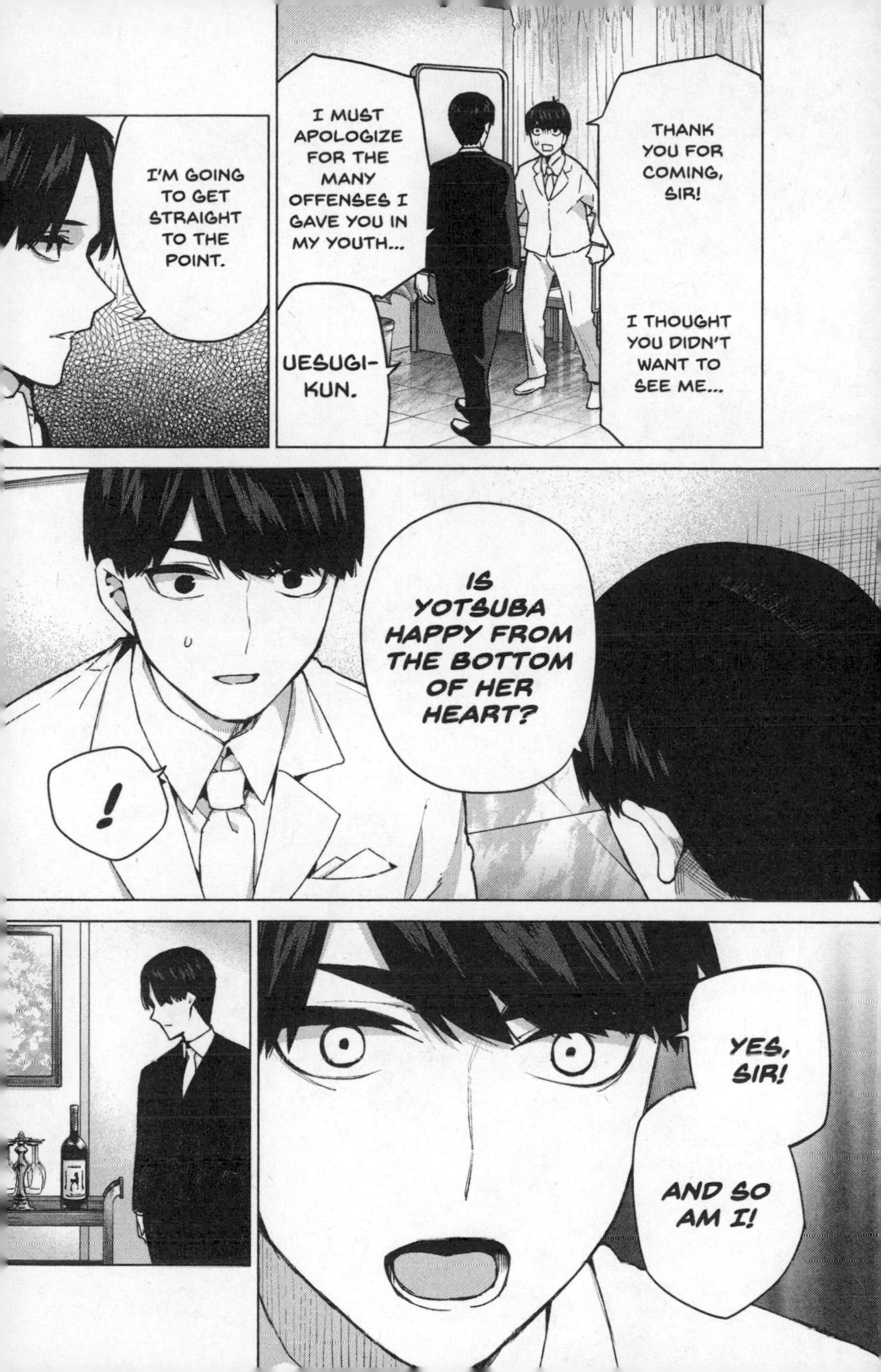
THANK YOU FOR COMING, SIR!
I THOUGHT YOU DIDN'T WANT TO SEE ME...
I MUST APOLOGIZE FOR THE MANY OFFENSES I GAVE YOU IN MY YOUTH...
UESUGI-KUN.
I'M GOING TO GET STRAIGHT TO THE POINT.
IS YOTSUBA HAPPY FROM THE BOTTOM OF HER HEART?
!
YES, SIR!
AND SO AM I!

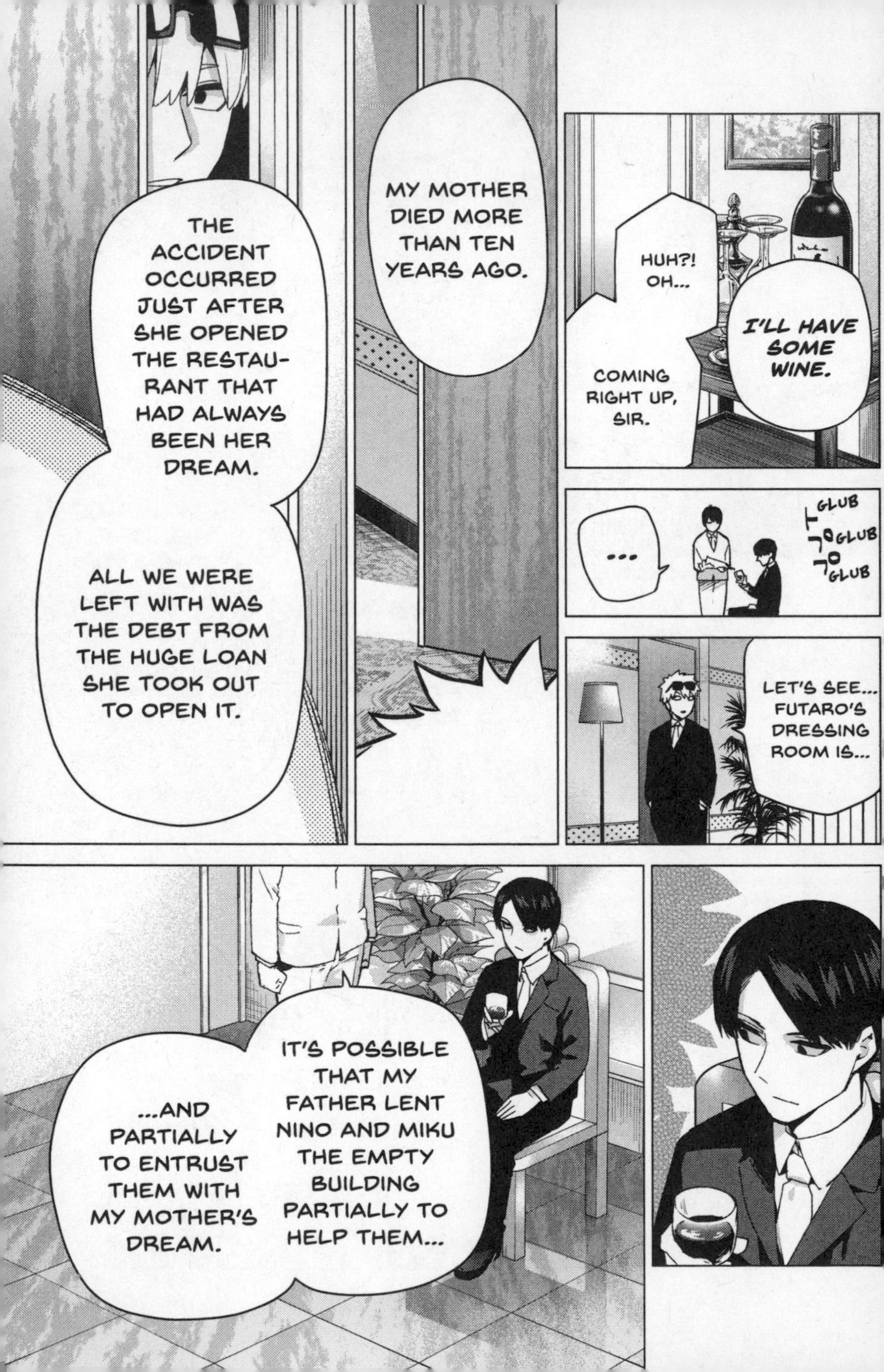
I'LL HAVE SOME WINE.
HUH?! OH...
COMING RIGHT UP, SIR.
GLUB GLUB GLUB
...
LET'S SEE... FUTARO'S DRESSING ROOM IS...
MY MOTHER DIED MORE THAN TEN YEARS AGO.
THE ACCIDENT OCCURRED JUST AFTER SHE OPENED THE RESTAURANT THAT HAD ALWAYS BEEN HER DREAM.
ALL WE WERE LEFT WITH WAS THE DEBT FROM THE HUGE LOAN SHE TOOK OUT TO OPEN IT.
IT'S POSSIBLE THAT MY FATHER LENT NINO AND MIKU THE EMPTY BUILDING PARTIALLY TO HELP THEM...
...AND PARTIALLY TO ENTRUST THEM WITH MY MOTHER'S DREAM.

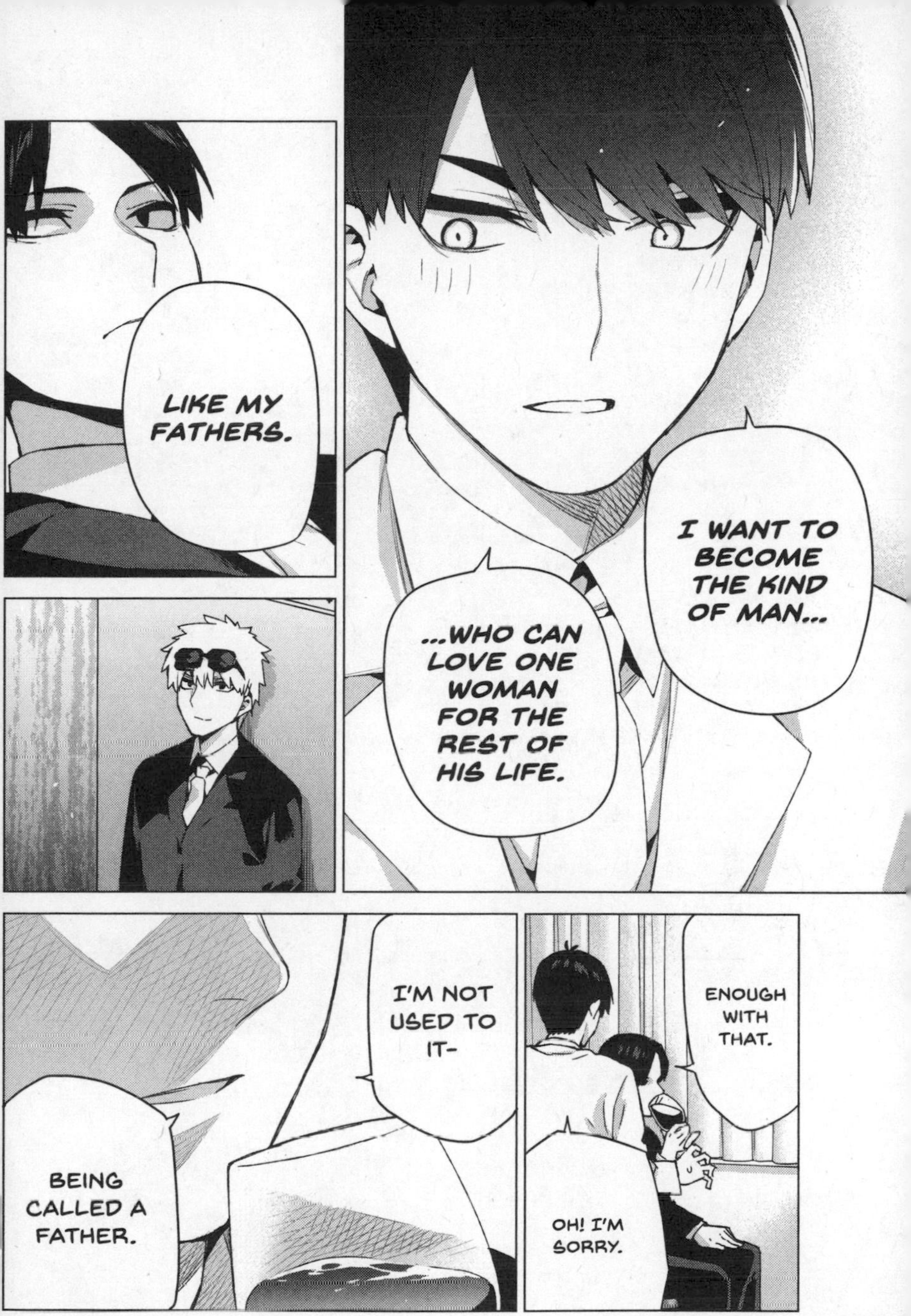
I WANT TO BECOME THE KIND OF MAN...
...WHO CAN LOVE ONE WOMAN FOR THE REST OF HIS LIFE.
LIKE MY FATHERS.
ENOUGH WITH THAT.
OH! I'M SORRY.
I'M NOT USED TO IT-
BEING CALLED A FATHER.

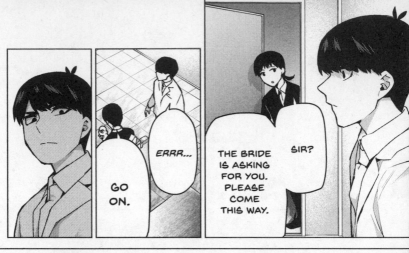

ERRR...

GO ON.

THE BRIDE IS ASKING FOR YOU. PLEASE COME THIS WAY.

SIR?

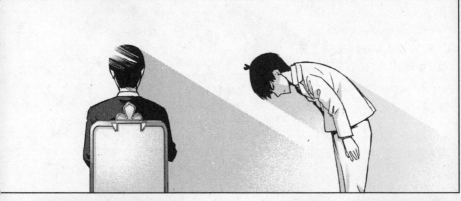

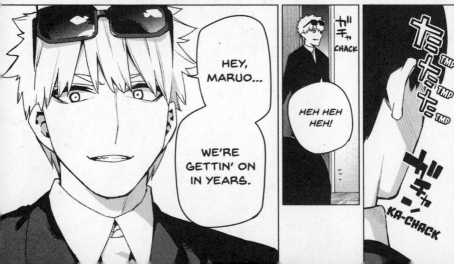

HEY, MARUO...

WE'RE GETTIN' ON IN YEARS.

HEH HEH HEH!

CHACK

TMP

TMP

TMP

KA-CHACK

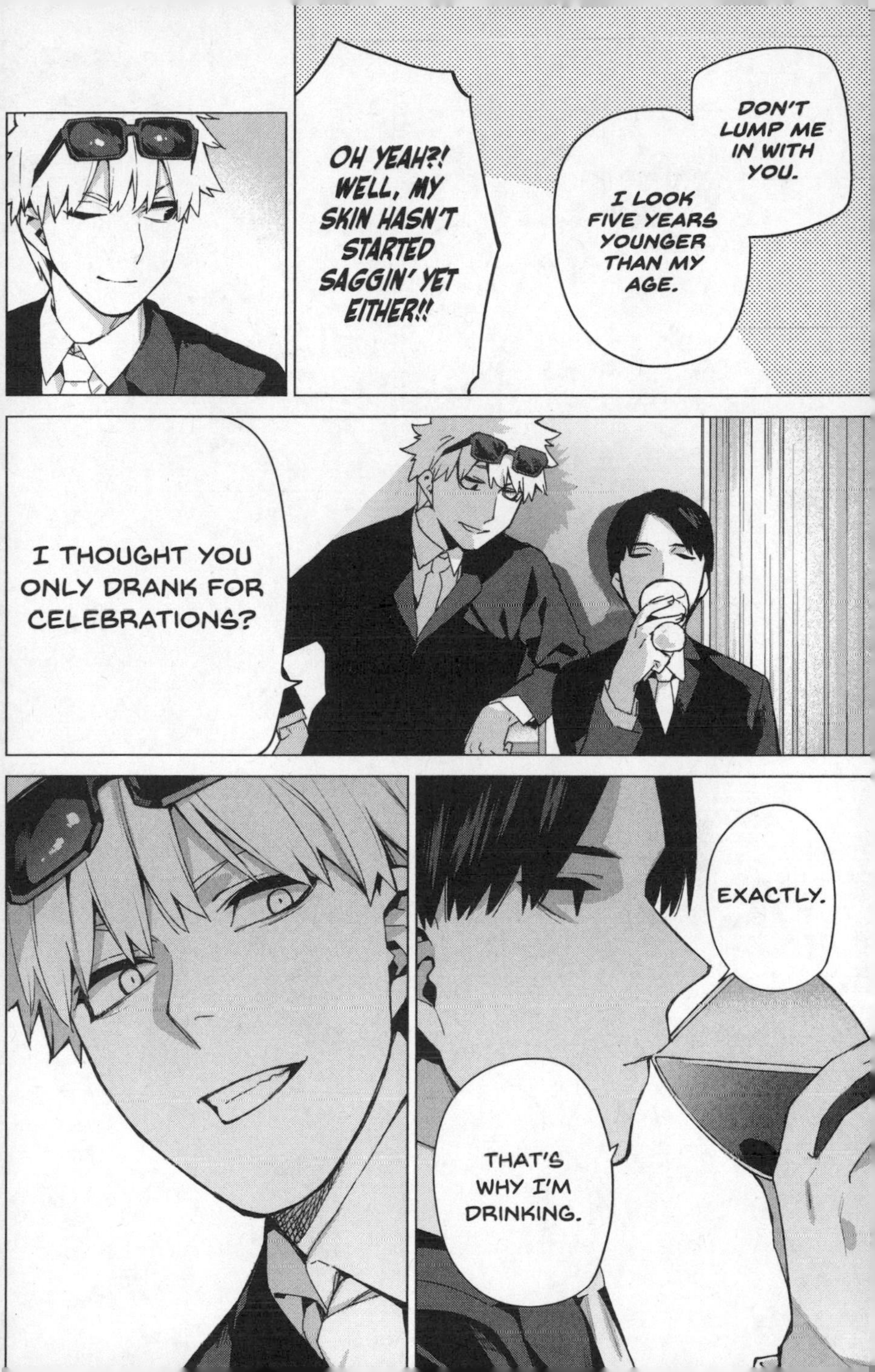
DON'T LUMP ME IN WITH YOU.
I LOOK FIVE YEARS YOUNGER THAN MY AGE.
OH YEAH?! WELL, MY SKIN HASN'T STARTED SAGGIN' YET EITHER!!
I THOUGHT YOU ONLY DRANK FOR CELEBRATIONS?
EXACTLY.
THAT'S WHY I'M DRINKING.

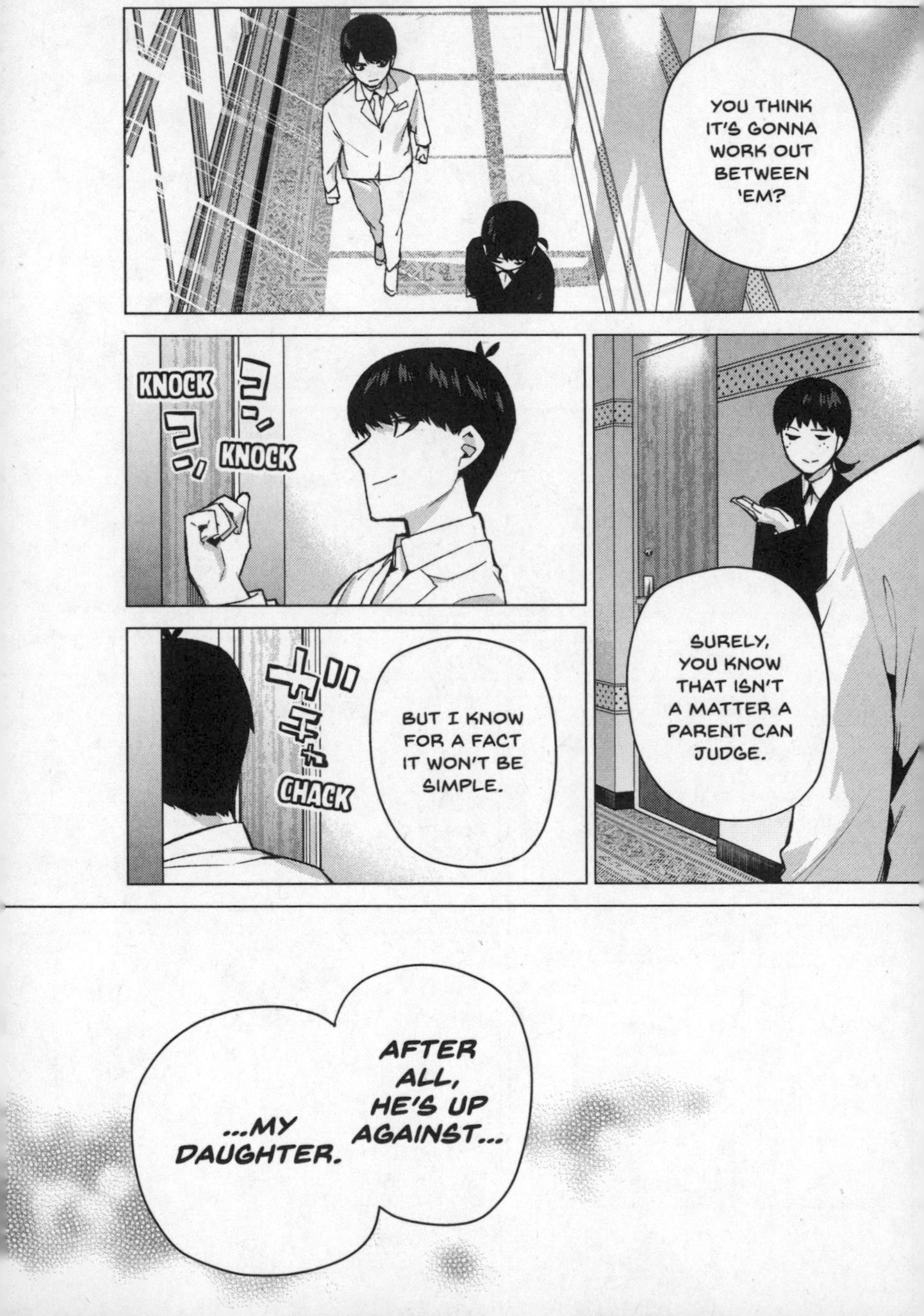
YOU THINK IT'S GONNA WORK OUT BETWEEN 'EM?
SURELY, YOU KNOW THAT ISN'T A MATTER A PARENT CAN JUDGE.
KNOCK
KNOCK
BUT I KNOW FOR A FACT IT WON'T BE SIMPLE.
CHACK
AFTER ALL, HE'S UP AGAINST...
...MY DAUGHTER.

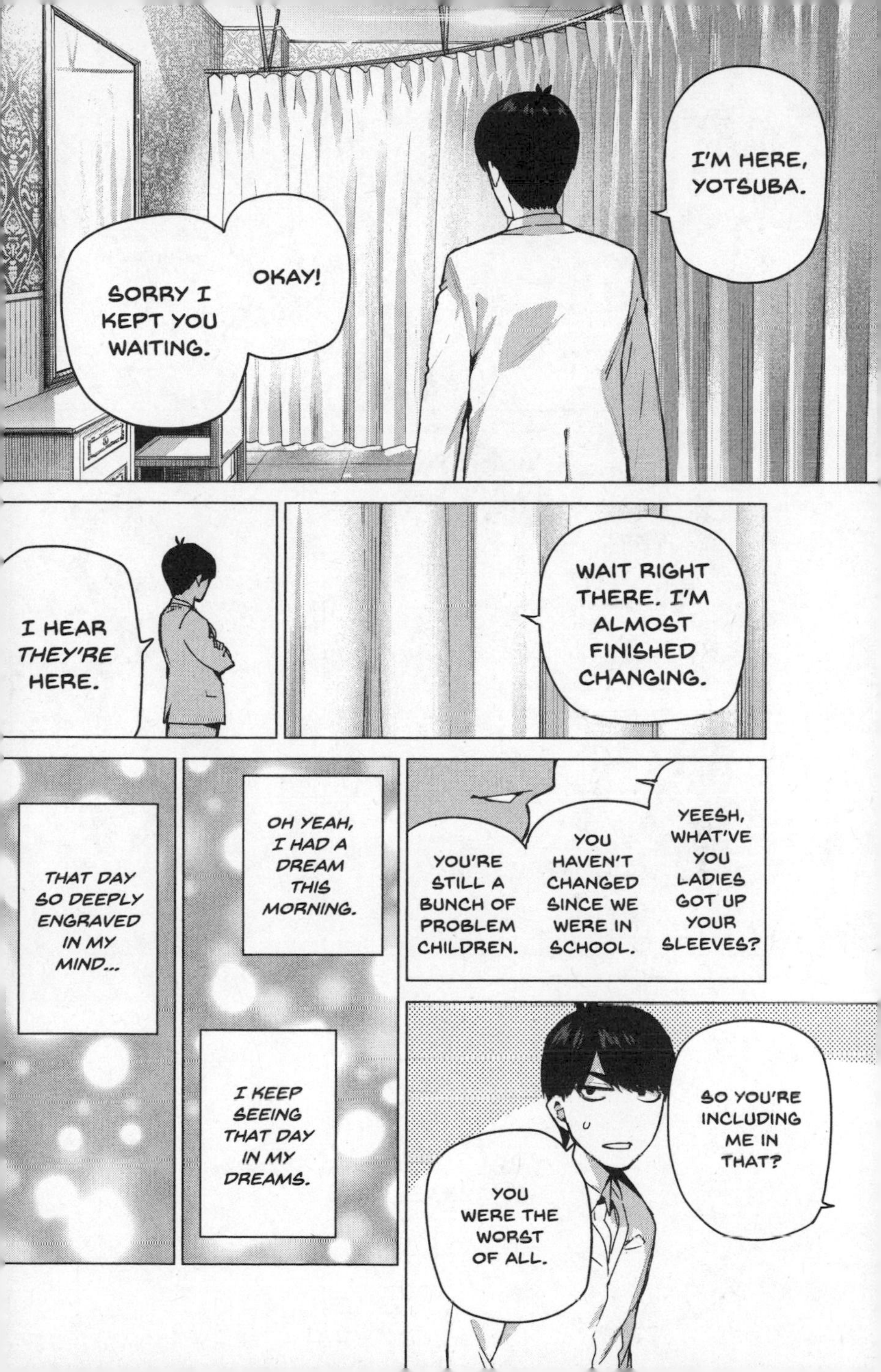
I'M HERE, YOTSUBA.
OKAY!
SORRY I KEPT YOU WAITING.
WAIT RIGHT THERE. I'M ALMOST FINISHED CHANGING.
I HEAR THEY'RE HERE.
YEESH, WHAT'VE YOU LADIES GOT UP YOUR SLEEVES?
YOU HAVEN'T CHANGED SINCE WE WERE IN SCHOOL.
YOU'RE STILL A BUNCH OF PROBLEM CHILDREN.
SO YOU'RE INCLUDING ME IN THAT?
YOU WERE THE WORST OF ALL.
OH YEAH, I HAD A DREAM THIS MORNING.
I KEEP SEEING THAT DAY IN MY DREAMS.
THAT DAY SO DEEPLY ENGRAVED IN MY MIND...

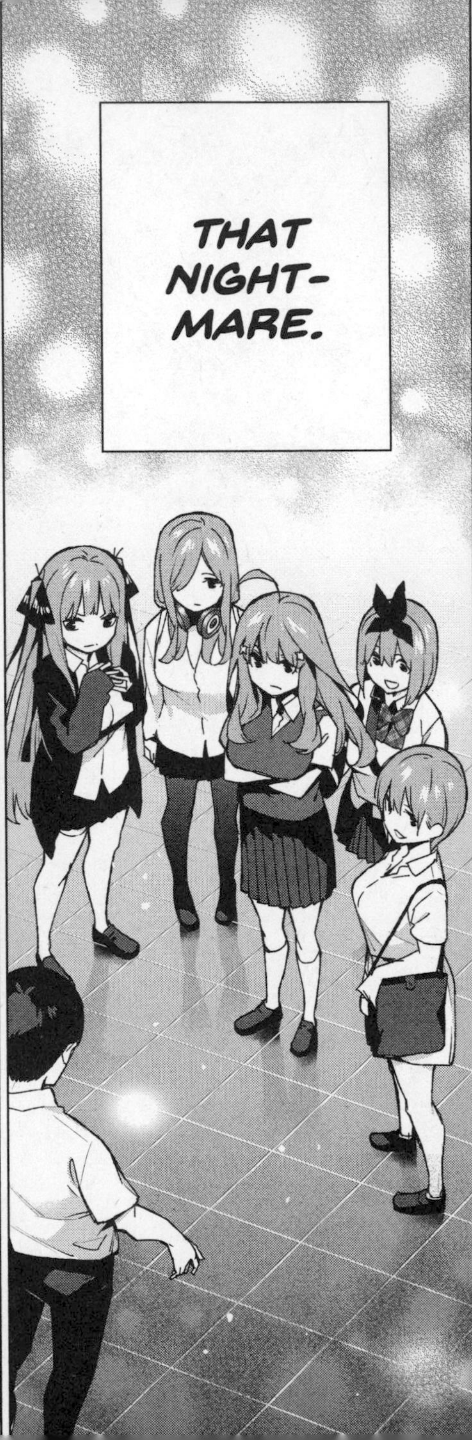
THAT NIGHT-MARE.
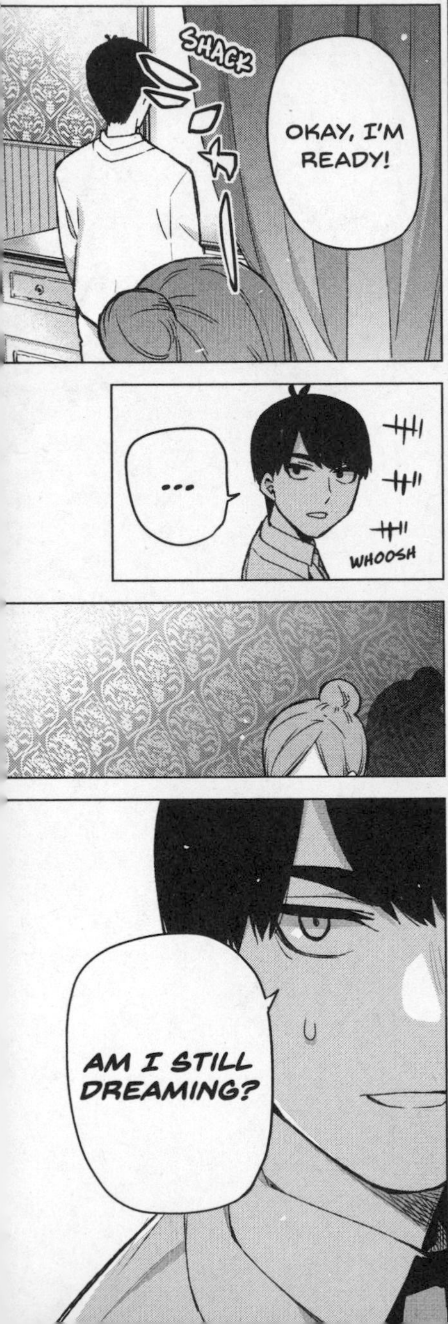
SHACK
OKAY, I'M READY!
...
WHOOSH
AM I STILL DREAMING?

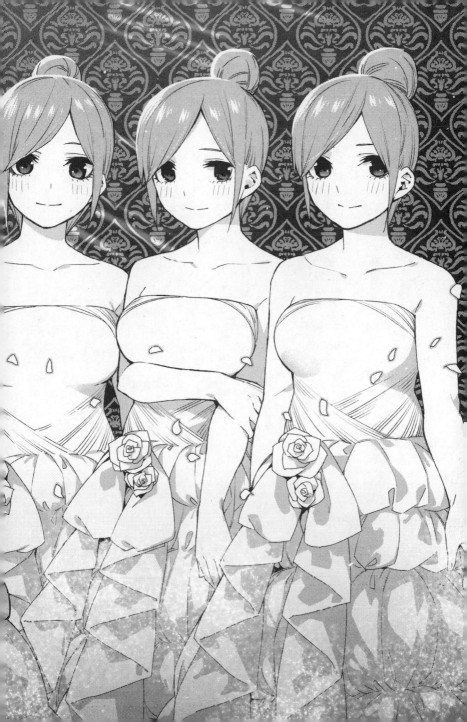

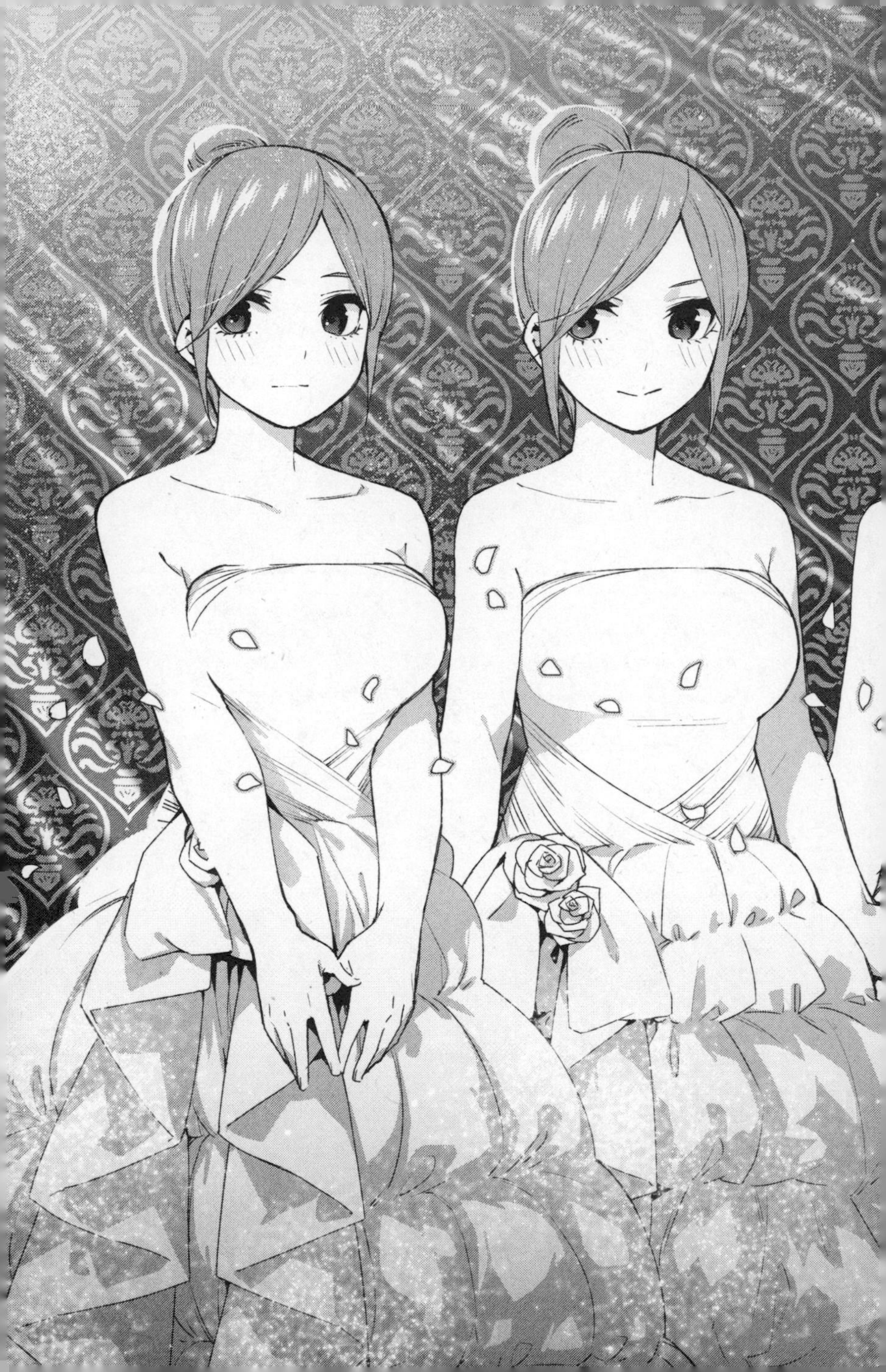

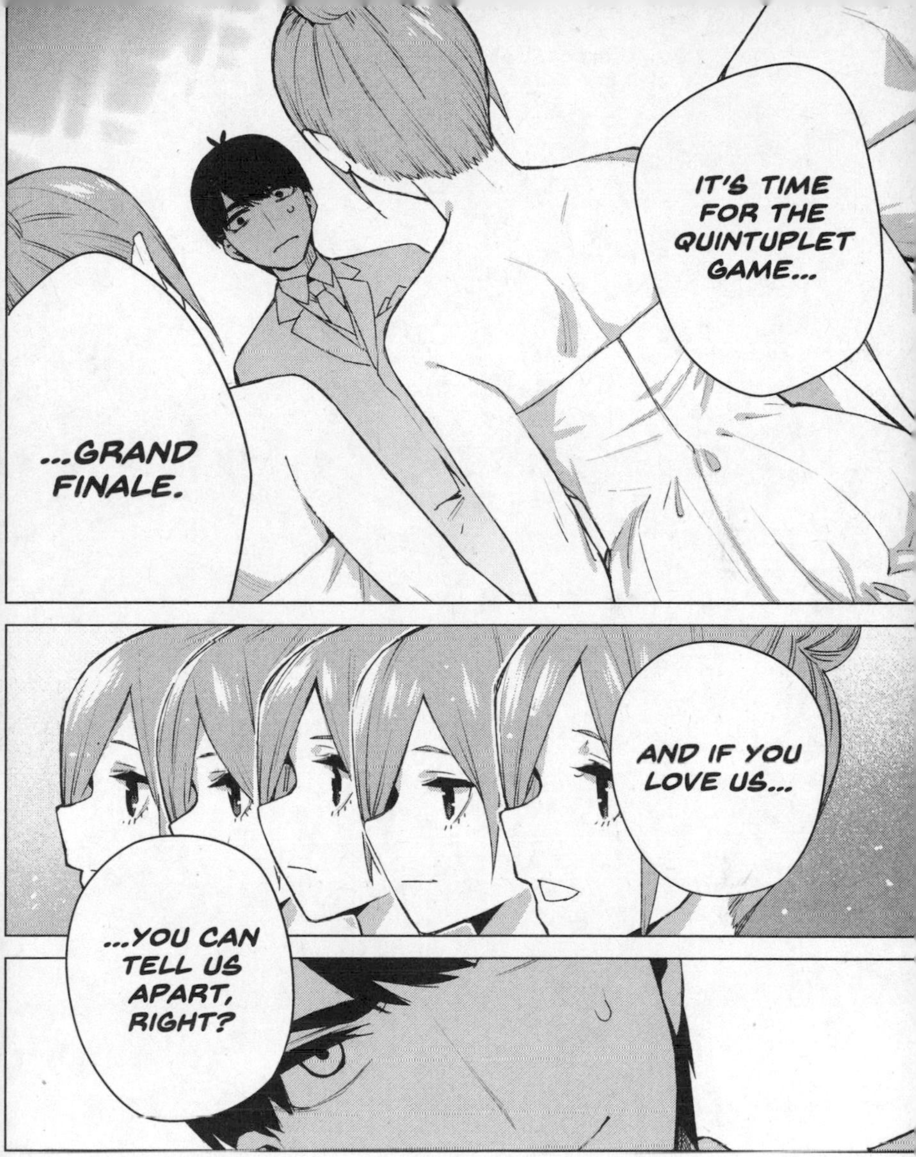
IT'S TIME FOR THE QUINTUPLET GAME...
...GRAND FINALE.
AND IF YOU LOVE US...
...YOU CAN TELL US APART, RIGHT?

CHAPTER 121
ONE IN FIVE CHANCE

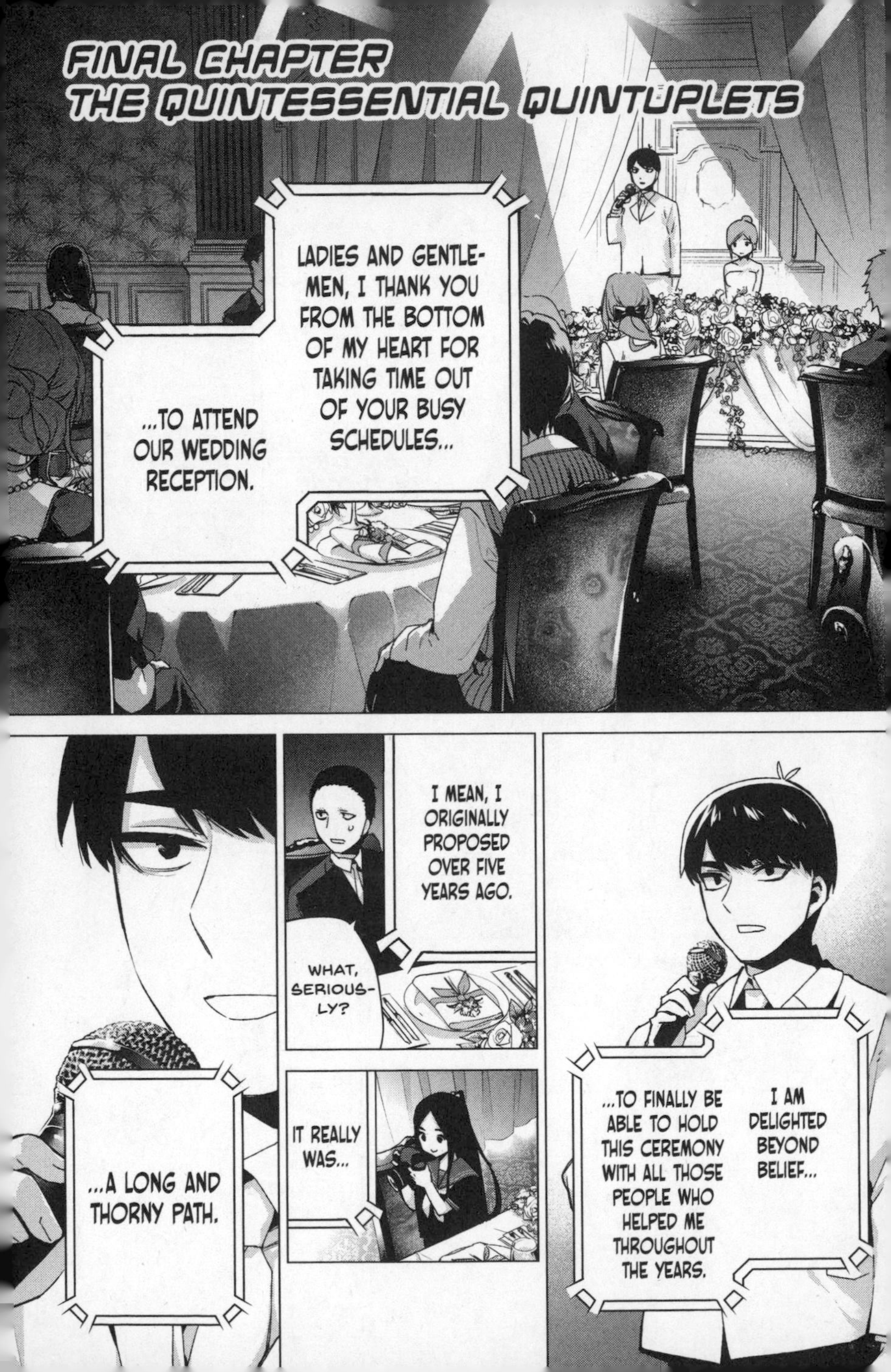
FINAL CHAPTER
THE QUINTESSENTIAL QUINTUPLETS
LADIES AND GENTLE-MEN, I THANK YOU FROM THE BOTTOM OF MY HEART FOR TAKING TIME OUT OF YOUR BUSY SCHEDULES...
...TO ATTEND OUR WEDDING RECEPTION.
I AM DELIGHTED BEYOND BELIEF...
...TO FINALLY BE ABLE TO HOLD THIS CEREMONY WITH ALL THOSE PEOPLE WHO HELPED ME THROUGHOUT THE YEARS.
I MEAN, I ORIGINALLY PROPOSED OVER FIVE YEARS AGO.
WHAT, SERIOUS-LY?
IT REALLY WAS...
...A LONG AND THORNY PATH.

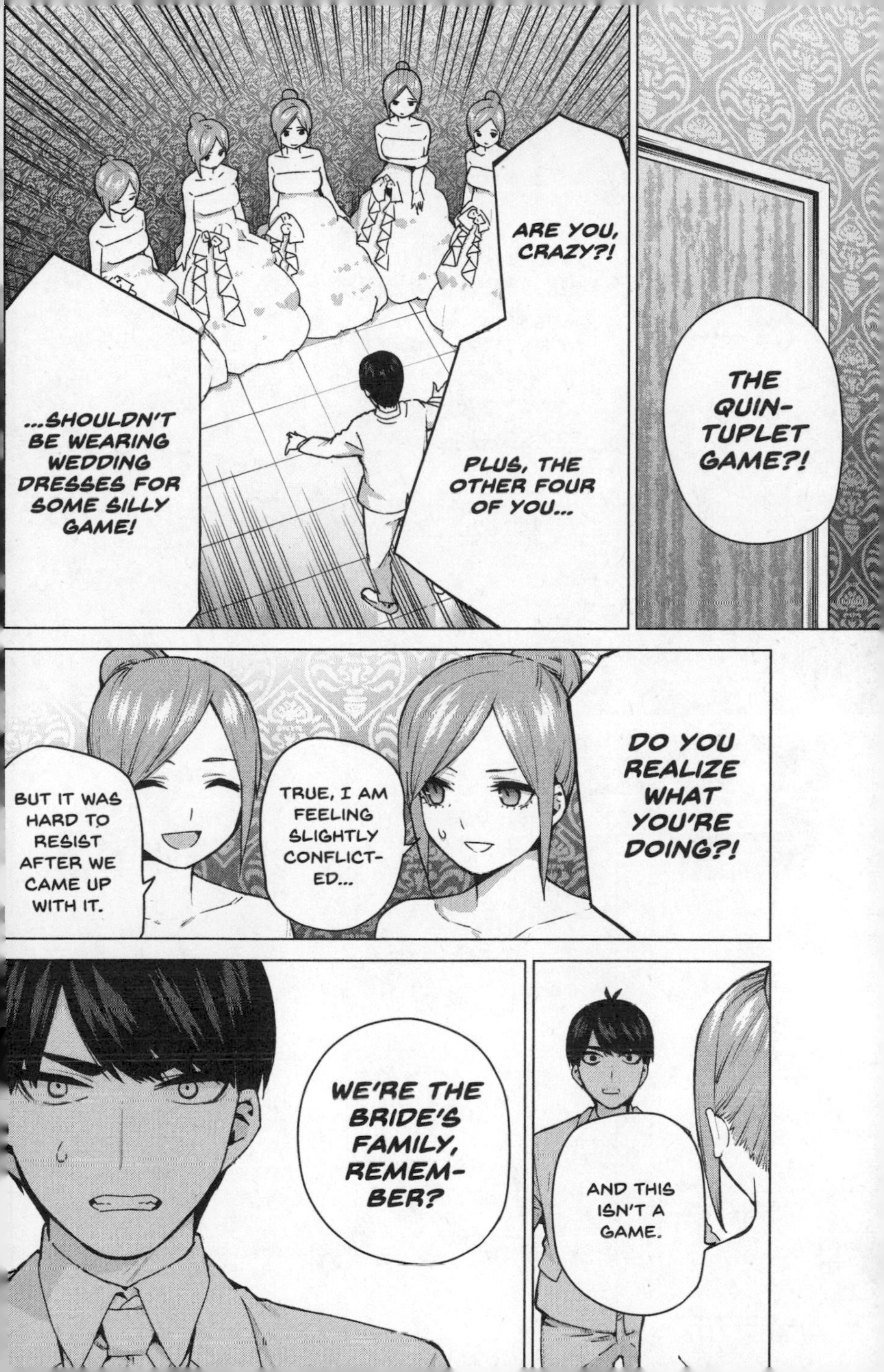
THE QUIN-TUPLET GAME?!
ARE YOU, CRAZY?!
PLUS, THE OTHER FOUR OF YOU...
...SHOULDN'T BE WEARING WEDDING DRESSES FOR SOME SILLY GAME!
DO YOU REALIZE WHAT YOU'RE DOING?!
TRUE, I AM FEELING SLIGHTLY CONFLICT-ED...
BUT IT WAS HARD TO RESIST AFTER WE CAME UP WITH IT.
AND THIS ISN'T A GAME.
WE'RE THE BRIDE'S FAMILY, REMEM-BER?

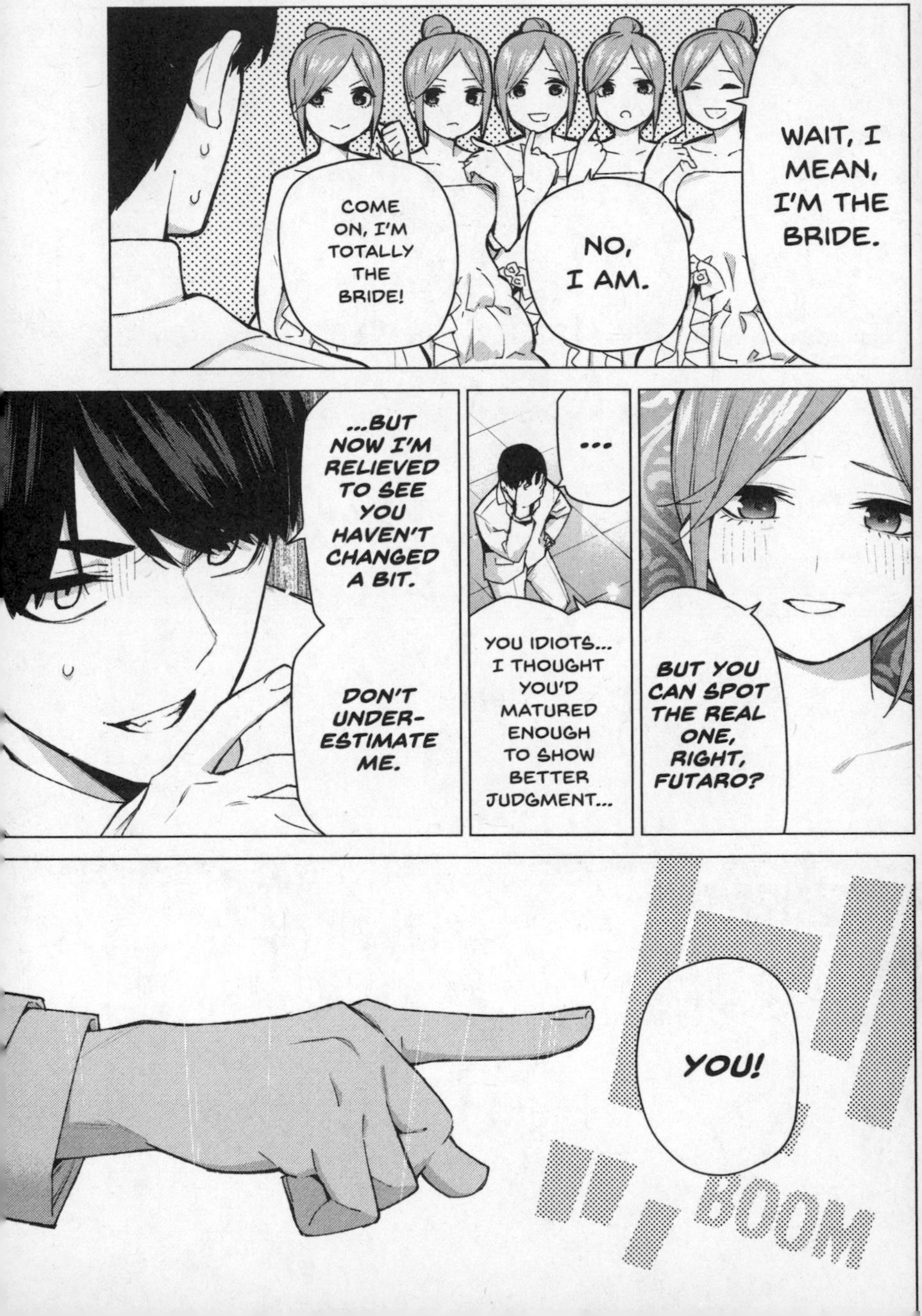
WAIT, I MEAN, I'M THE BRIDE.
NO, I AM.
COME ON, I'M TOTALLY THE BRIDE!
BUT YOU CAN SPOT THE REAL ONE, RIGHT, FUTARO?
...
YOU IDIOTS... I THOUGHT YOU'D MATURED ENOUGH TO SHOW BETTER JUDGMENT...
...BUT NOW I'M RELIEVED TO SEE YOU HAVEN'T CHANGED A BIT.
DON'T UNDER-ESTIMATE ME.
YOU!
BOOM

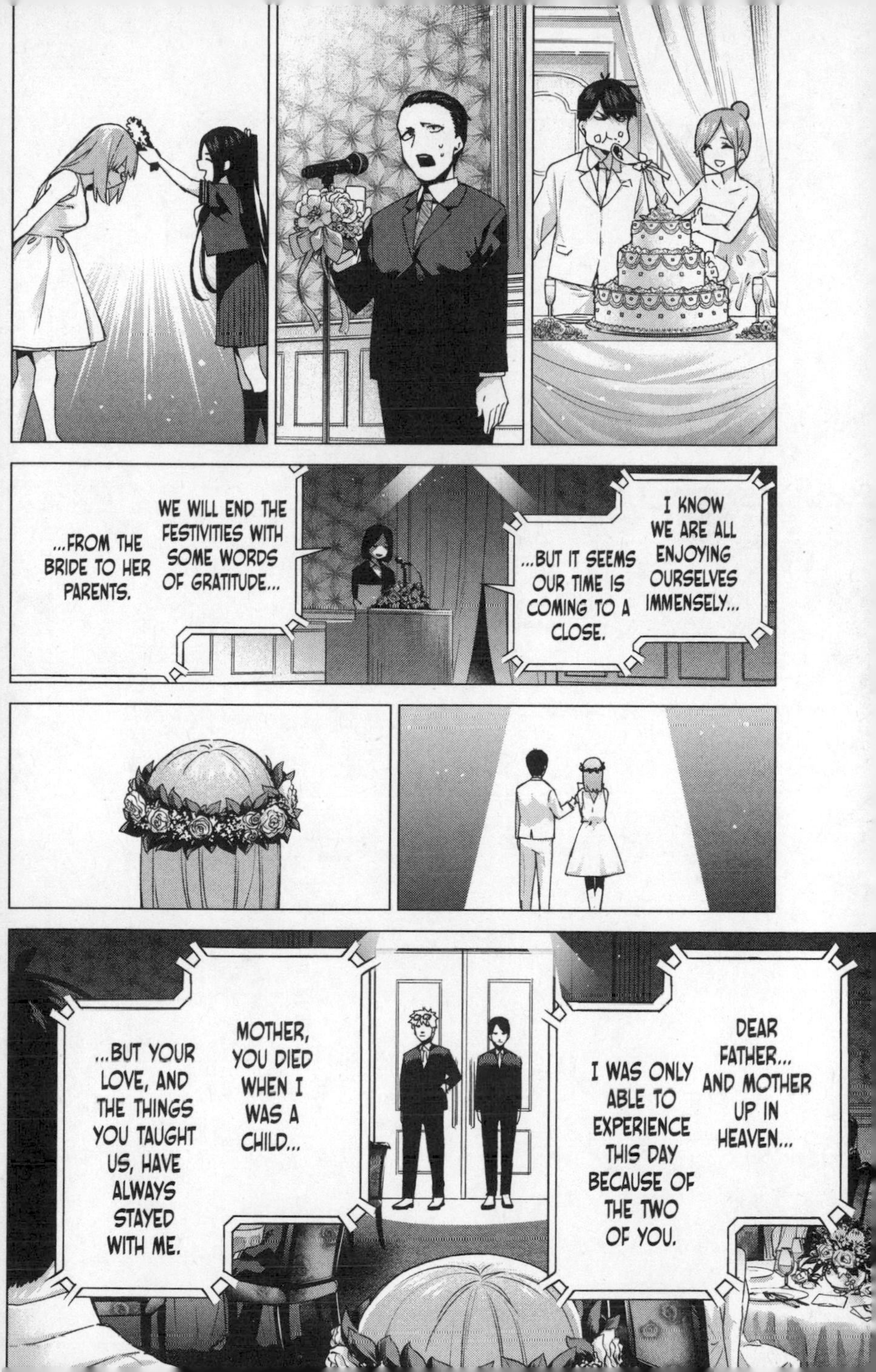
I KNOW WE ARE ALL ENJOYING OURSELVES IMMENSELY...
...BUT IT SEEMS OUR TIME IS COMING TO A CLOSE.
WE WILL END THE FESTIVITIES WITH SOME WORDS OF GRATITUDE...
...FROM THE BRIDE TO HER PARENTS.
DEAR FATHER... AND MOTHER UP IN HEAVEN...
I WAS ONLY ABLE TO EXPERIENCE THIS DAY BECAUSE OF THE TWO OF YOU.
MOTHER, YOU DIED WHEN I WAS A CHILD...
...BUT YOUR LOVE, AND THE THINGS YOU TAUGHT US, HAVE ALWAYS STAYED WITH ME.

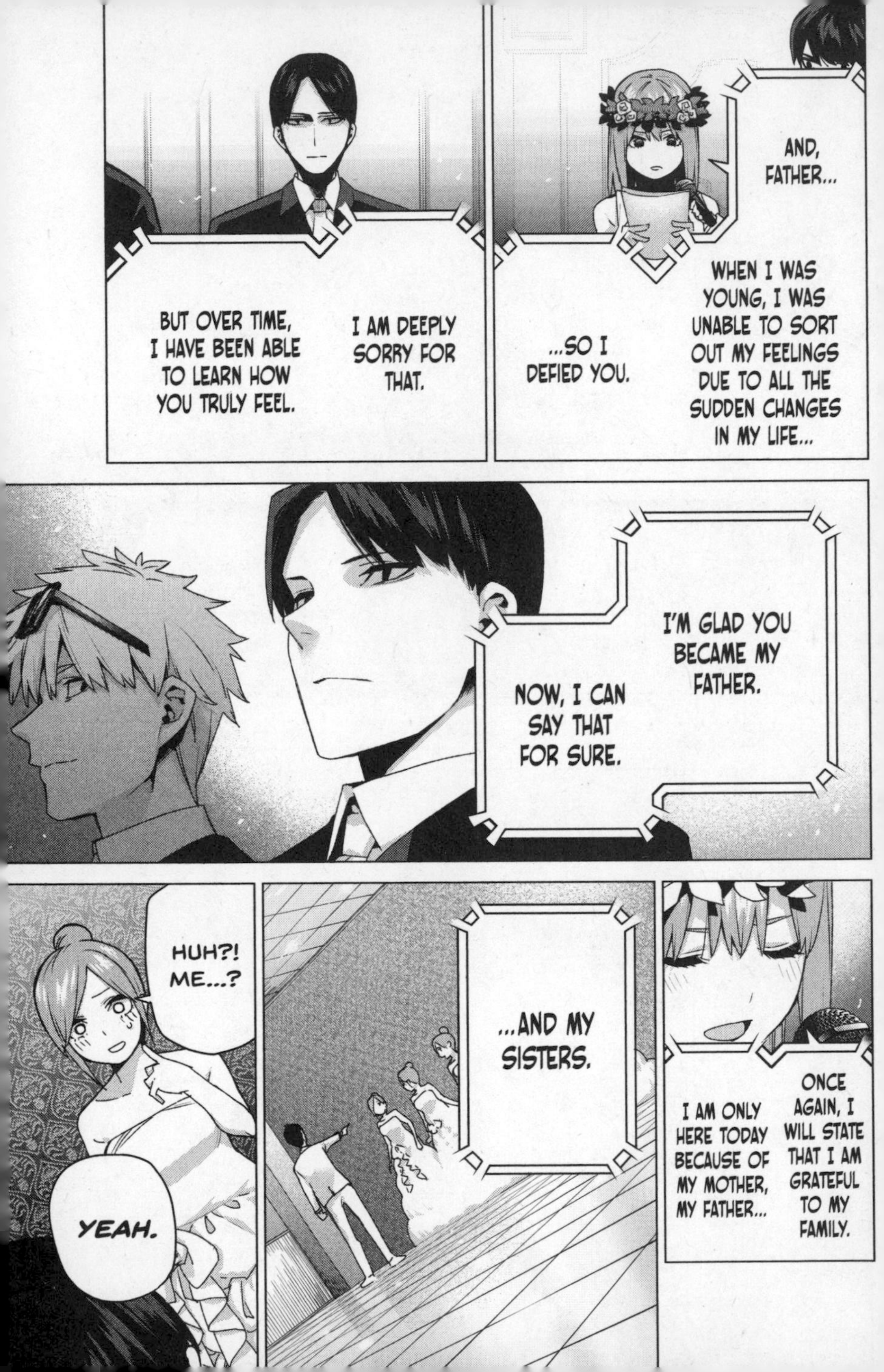
AND, FATHER...
WHEN I WAS YOUNG, I WAS UNABLE TO SORT OUT MY FEELINGS DUE TO ALL THE SUDDEN CHANGES IN MY LIFE...
...SO I DEFIED YOU.
I AM DEEPLY SORRY FOR THAT.
BUT OVER TIME, I HAVE BEEN ABLE TO LEARN HOW YOU TRULY FEEL.
I'M GLAD YOU BECAME MY FATHER.
NOW, I CAN SAY THAT FOR SURE.
ONCE AGAIN, I WILL STATE THAT I AM GRATEFUL TO MY FAMILY.
I AM ONLY HERE TODAY BECAUSE OF MY MOTHER, MY FATHER...
...AND MY SISTERS.
HUH?! ME...?
YEAH.

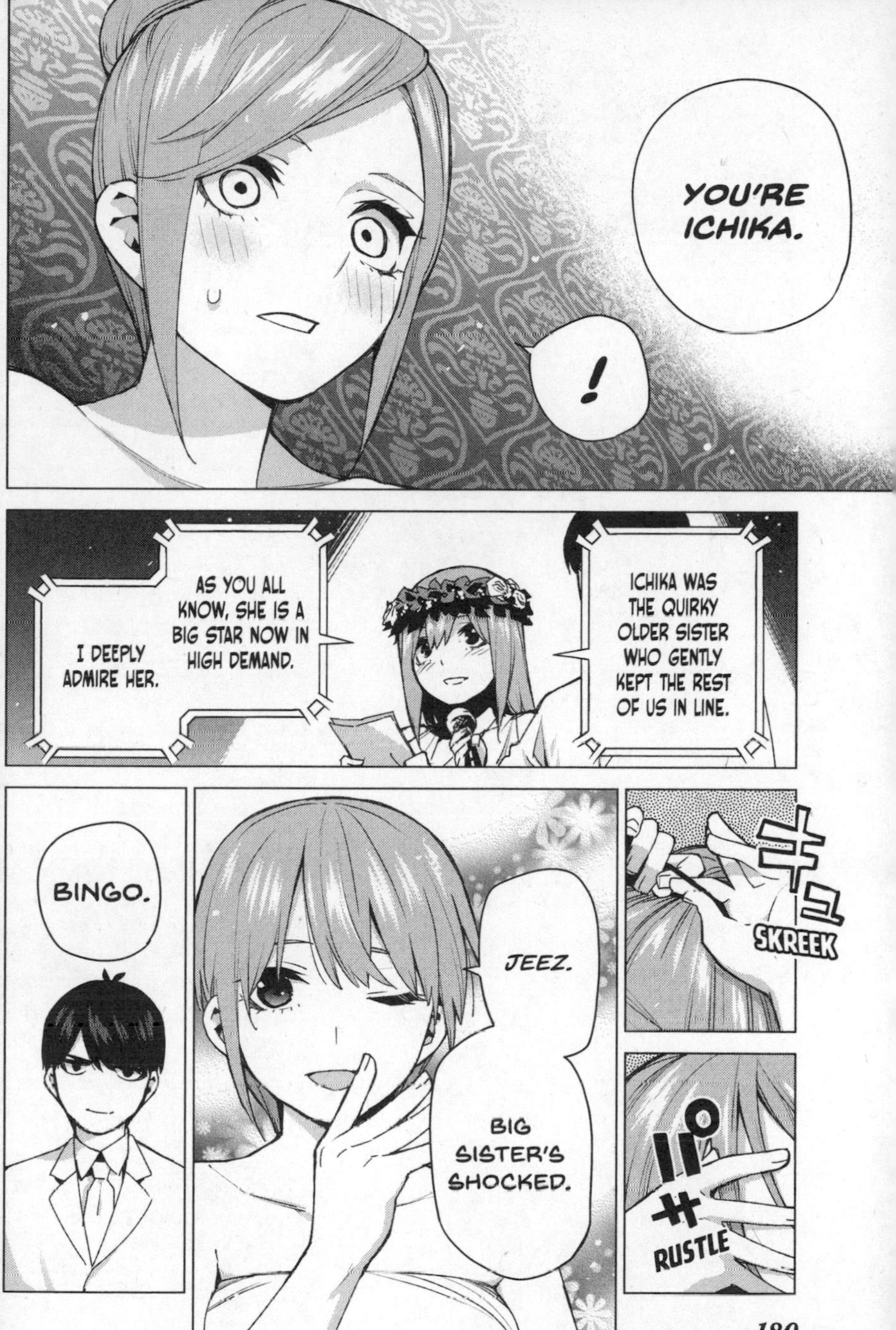
YOU'RE ICHIKA.
!
ICHIKA WAS THE QUIRKY OLDER SISTER WHO GENTLY KEPT THE REST OF US IN LINE.
AS YOU ALL KNOW, SHE IS A BIG STAR NOW IN HIGH DEMAND.
I DEEPLY ADMIRE HER.
キュ
SKREEK
RUSTLE
JEEZ.
BIG SISTER'S SHOCKED.
BINGO.

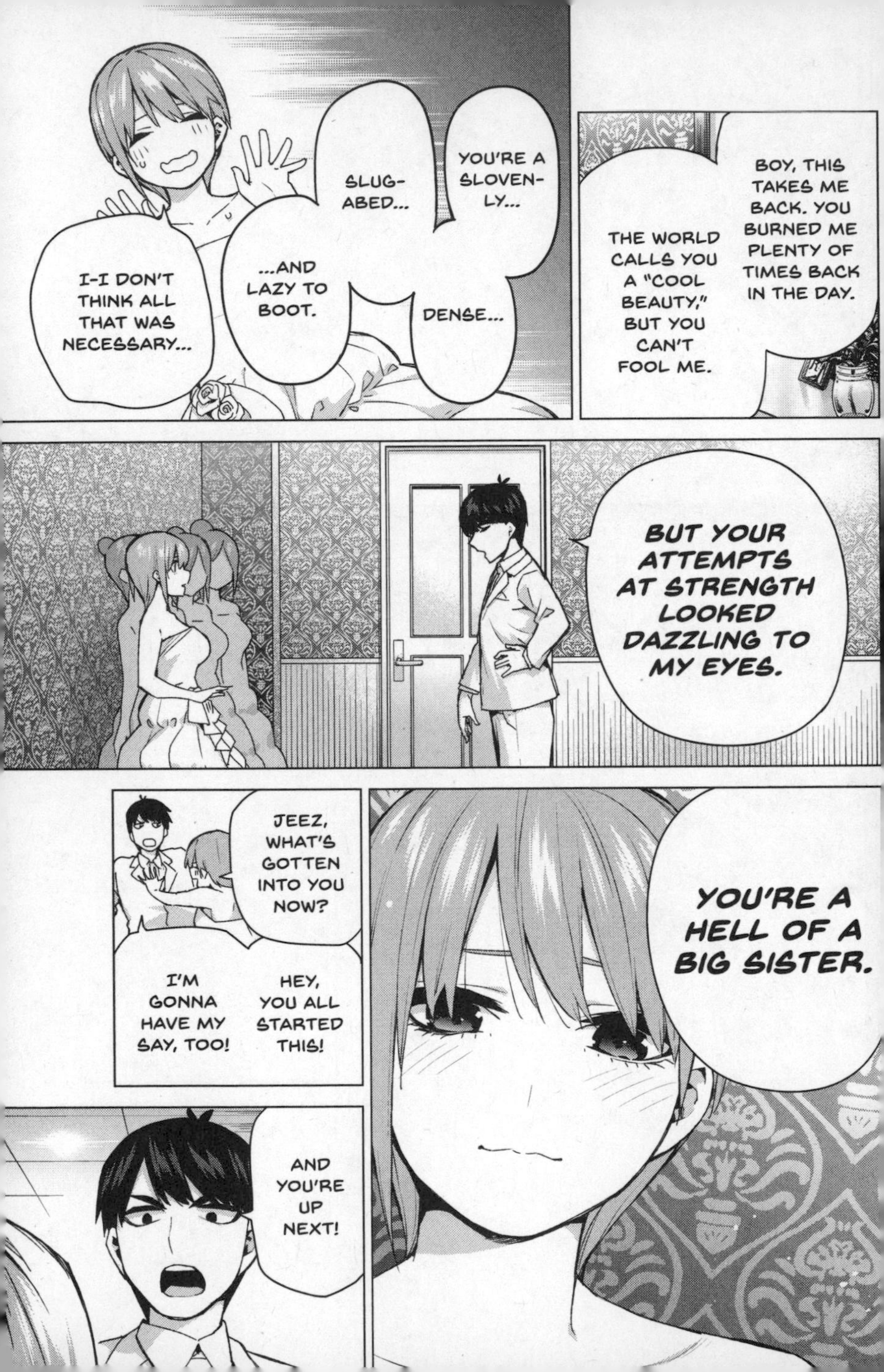

BOY, THIS TAKES ME BACK. YOU BURNED ME PLENTY OF TIMES BACK IN THE DAY.
THE WORLD CALLS YOU A "COOL BEAUTY," BUT YOU CAN'T FOOL ME.
YOU'RE A SLOVEN-LY...
SLUG-ABED...
DENSE...
...AND LAZY TO BOOT.
I-I DON'T THINK ALL THAT WAS NECESSARY...
BUT YOUR ATTEMPTS AT STRENGTH LOOKED DAZZLING TO MY EYES.
YOU'RE A HELL OF A BIG SISTER.
JEEZ, WHAT'S GOTTEN INTO YOU NOW?
HEY, YOU ALL STARTED THIS!
I'M GONNA HAVE MY SAY, TOO!
AND YOU'RE UP NEXT!

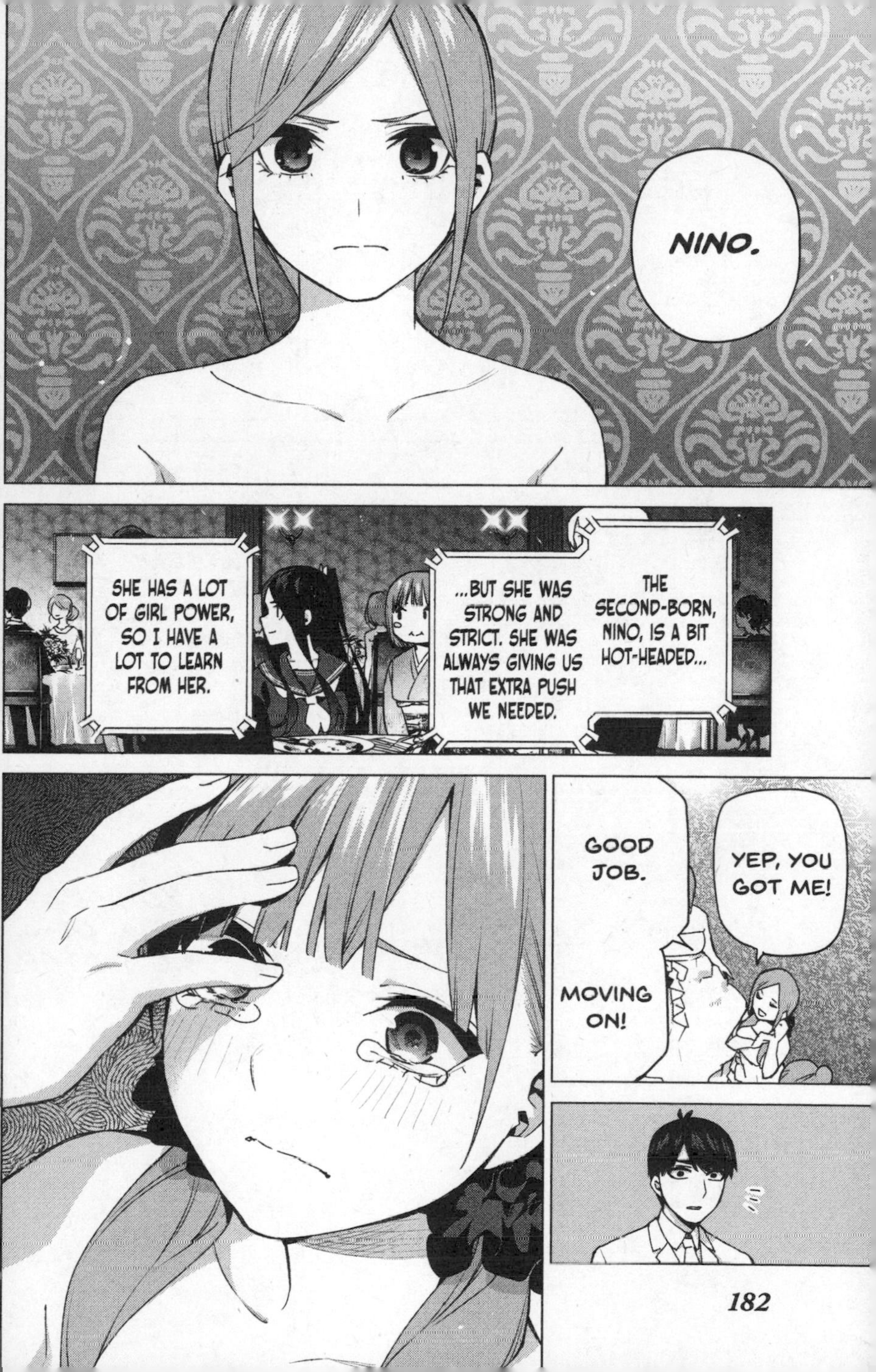
NINO.
THE SECOND-BORN, NINO, IS A BIT HOT-HEADED...
...BUT SHE WAS STRONG AND STRICT. SHE WAS ALWAYS GIVING US THAT EXTRA PUSH WE NEEDED.
SHE HAS A LOT OF GIRL POWER, SO I HAVE A LOT TO LEARN FROM HER.
YEP, YOU GOT ME!
GOOD JOB.
MOVING ON!

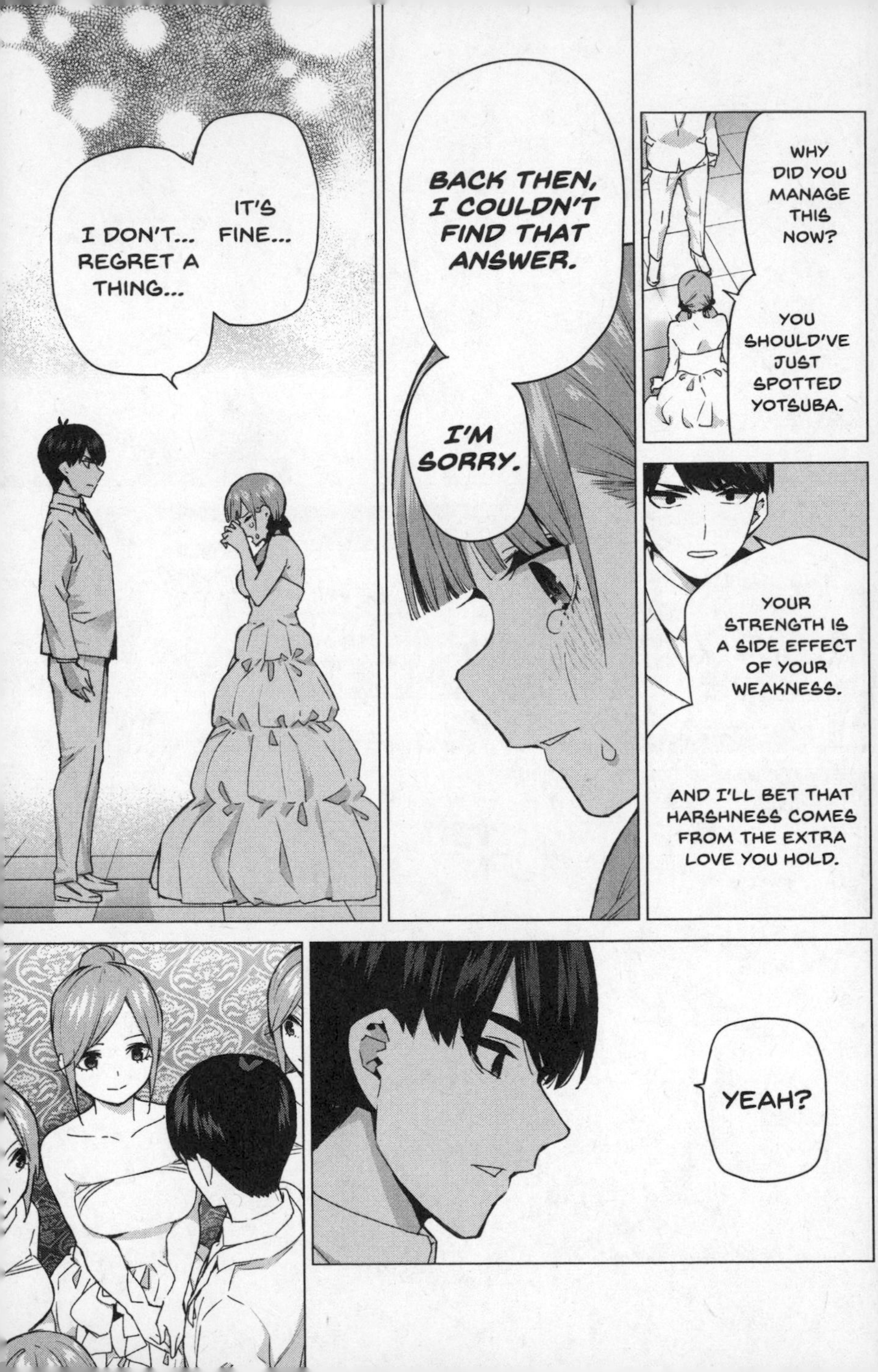
WHY DID YOU MANAGE THIS NOW?
YOU SHOULD'VE JUST SPOTTED YOTSUBA.
YOUR STRENGTH IS A SIDE EFFECT OF YOUR WEAKNESS.
AND I'LL BET THAT HARSHNESS COMES FROM THE EXTRA LOVE YOU HOLD.
BACK THEN, I COULDN'T FIND THAT ANSWER.
I'M SORRY.
IT'S FINE...
I DON'T... REGRET A THING...
YEAH?

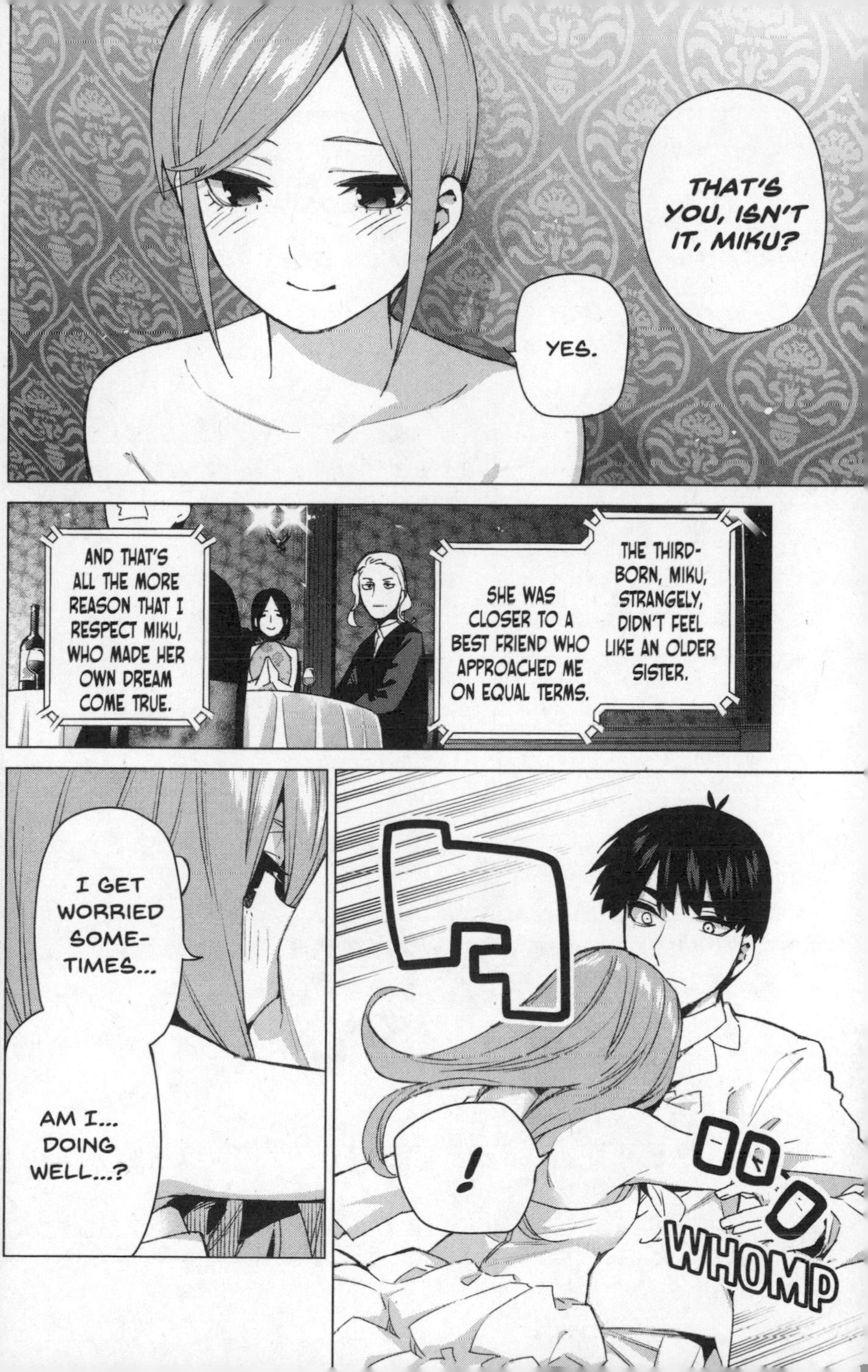
THAT'S YOU, ISN'T IT, MIKU?
YES.
THE THIRD-BORN, MIKU, STRANGELY, DIDN'T FEEL LIKE AN OLDER SISTER.
SHE WAS CLOSER TO A BEST FRIEND WHO APPROACHED ME ON EQUAL TERMS.
AND THAT'S ALL THE MORE REASON THAT I RESPECT MIKU, WHO MADE HER OWN DREAM COME TRUE.
!
WHOMP
I GET WORRIED SOME-TIMES...
AM I... DOING WELL...?

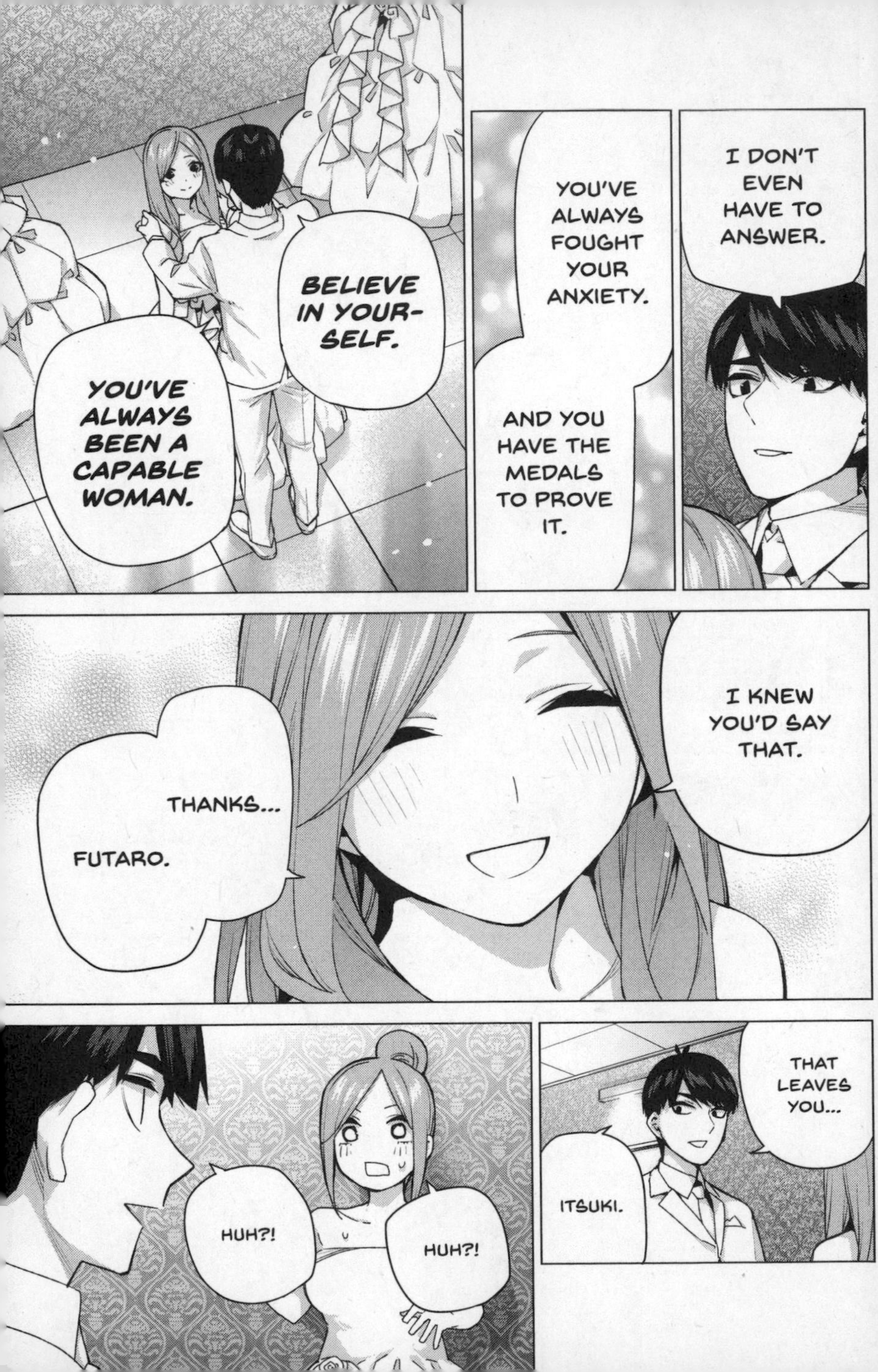
I DON'T EVEN HAVE TO ANSWER.
YOU'VE ALWAYS FOUGHT YOUR ANXIETY.
AND YOU HAVE THE MEDALS TO PROVE IT.
BELIEVE IN YOUR-SELF.
YOU'VE ALWAYS BEEN A CAPABLE WOMAN.
I KNEW YOU'D SAY THAT.
THANKS...
FUTARO.
THAT LEAVES YOU...
ITSUKI.
HUH?!
HUH?!

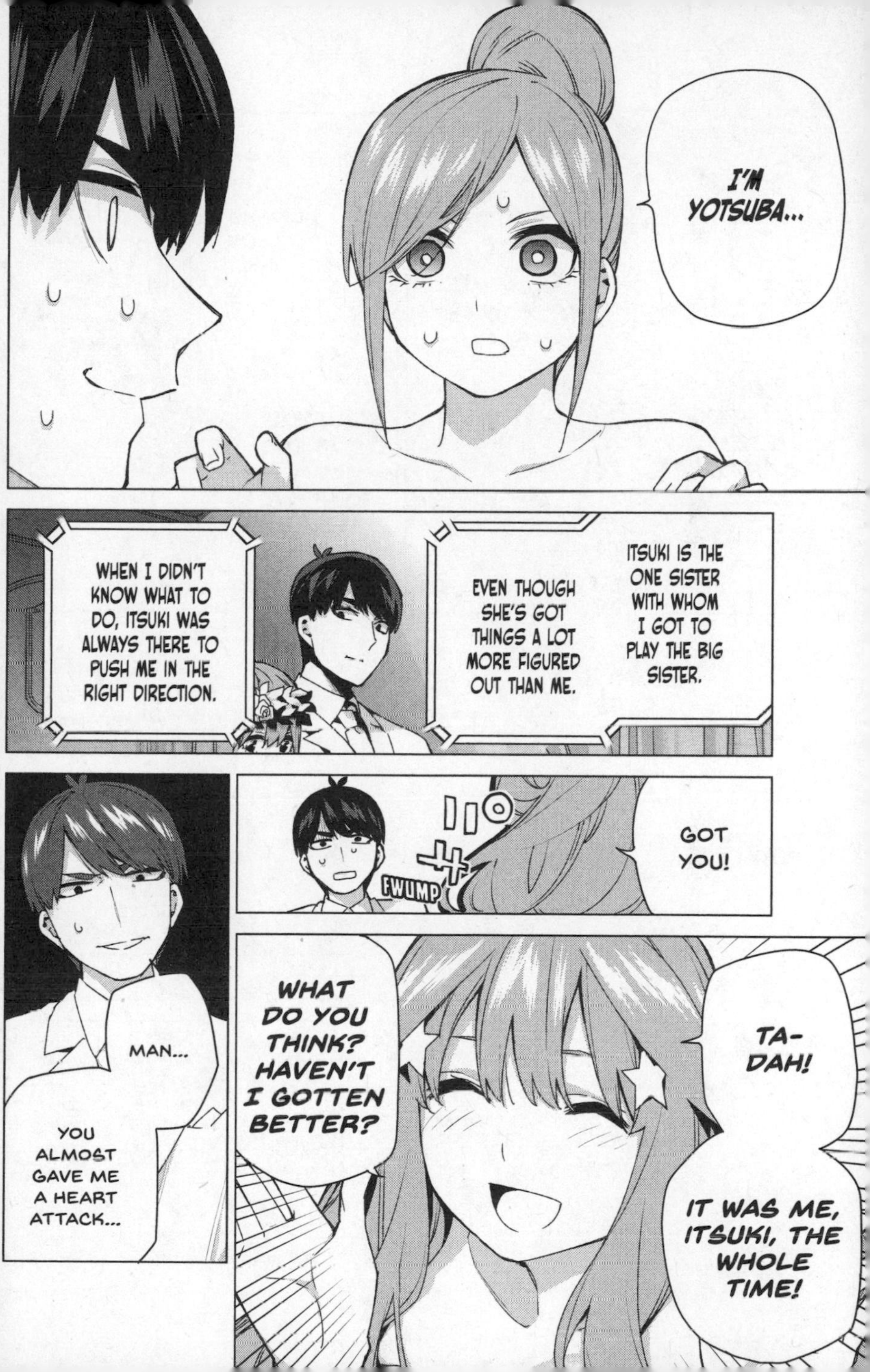
I'M YOTSUBA...
ITSUKI IS THE ONE SISTER WITH WHOM I GOT TO PLAY THE BIG SISTER.
EVEN THOUGH SHE'S GOT THINGS A LOT MORE FIGURED OUT THAN ME.
WHEN I DIDN'T KNOW WHAT TO DO, ITSUKI WAS ALWAYS THERE TO PUSH ME IN THE RIGHT DIRECTION.
GOT YOU!
FWUMP
TA-DAH!
IT WAS ME, ITSUKI, THE WHOLE TIME!
WHAT DO YOU THINK? HAVEN'T I GOTTEN BETTER?
MAN...
YOU ALMOST GAVE ME A HEART ATTACK...

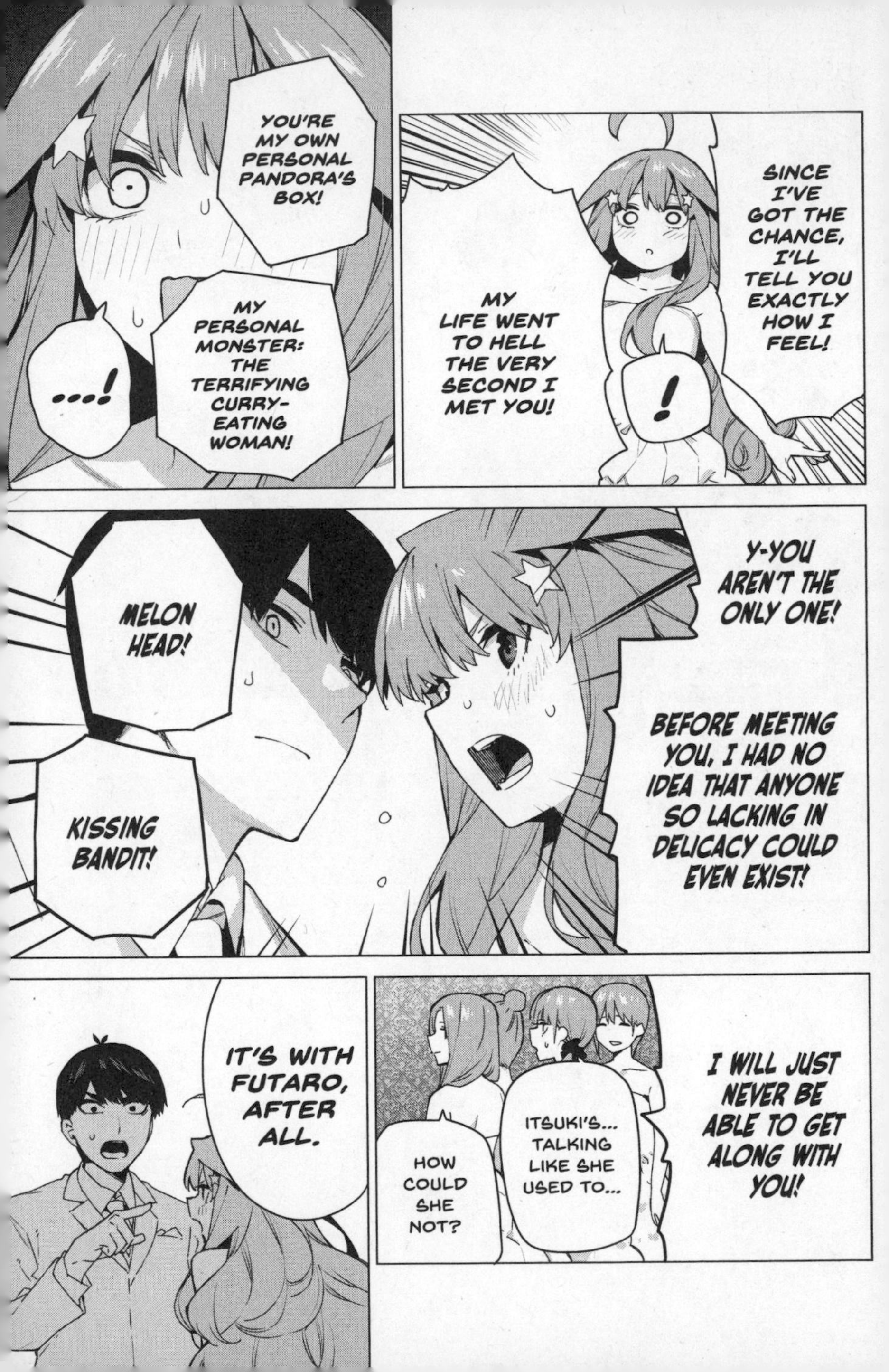
SINCE I'VE GOT THE CHANCE, I'LL TELL YOU EXACTLY HOW I FEEL!
MY LIFE WENT TO HELL THE VERY SECOND I MET YOU!
!
YOU'RE MY OWN PERSONAL PANDORA'S BOX!
MY PERSONAL MONSTER: THE TERRIFYING CURRY-EATING WOMAN!
...!
Y-YOU AREN'T THE ONLY ONE!
BEFORE MEETING YOU, I HAD NO IDEA THAT ANYONE SO LACKING IN DELICACY COULD EVEN EXIST!
MELON HEAD!
KISSING BANDIT!
I WILL JUST NEVER BE ABLE TO GET ALONG WITH YOU!
ITSUKI'S... TALKING LIKE SHE USED TO...
HOW COULD SHE NOT?
IT'S WITH FUTARO, AFTER ALL.

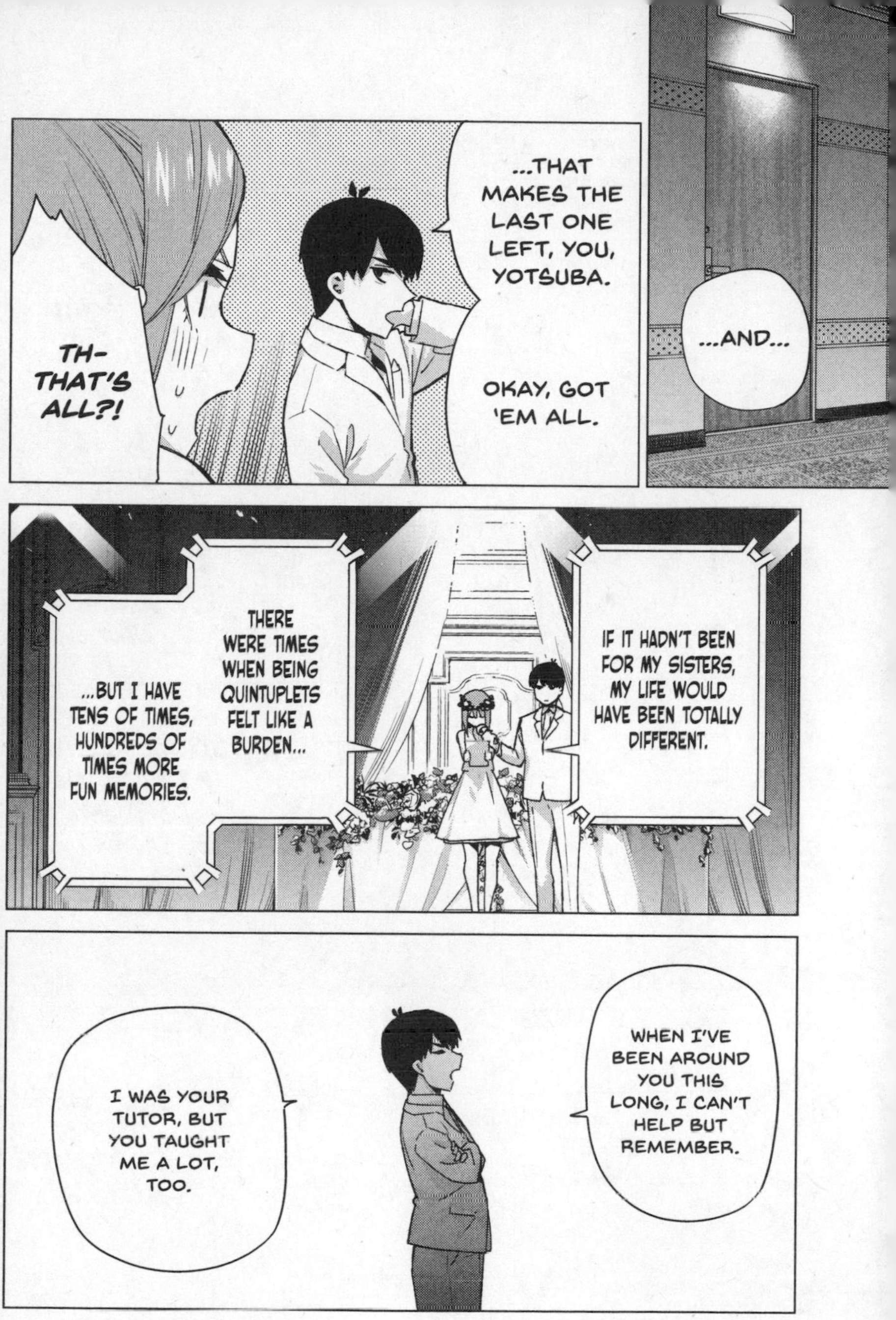
...AND...
...THAT MAKES THE LAST ONE LEFT, YOU, YOTSUBA.
OKAY, GOT 'EM ALL.
TH-THAT'S ALL?!
IF IT HADN'T BEEN FOR MY SISTERS, MY LIFE WOULD HAVE BEEN TOTALLY DIFFERENT.
THERE WERE TIMES WHEN BEING QUINTUPLETS FELT LIKE A BURDEN...
...BUT I HAVE TENS OF TIMES, HUNDREDS OF TIMES MORE FUN MEMORIES.
WHEN I'VE BEEN AROUND YOU THIS LONG, I CAN'T HELP BUT REMEMBER.
I WAS YOUR TUTOR, BUT YOU TAUGHT ME A LOT, TOO.

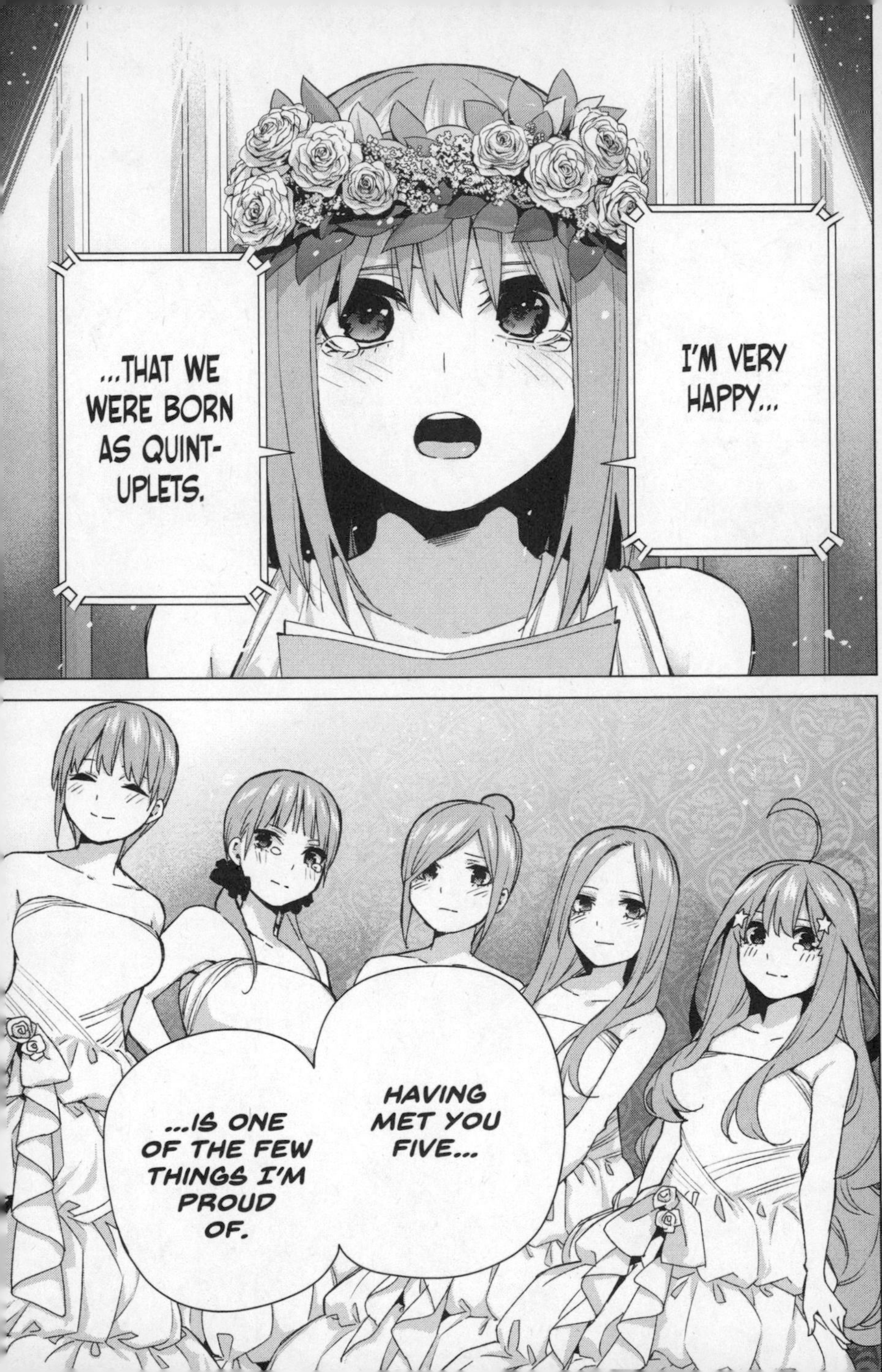
I'M VERY HAPPY...
...THAT WE WERE BORN AS QUINT-UPLETS.
HAVING MET YOU FIVE...
...IS ONE OF THE FEW THINGS I'M PROUD OF.

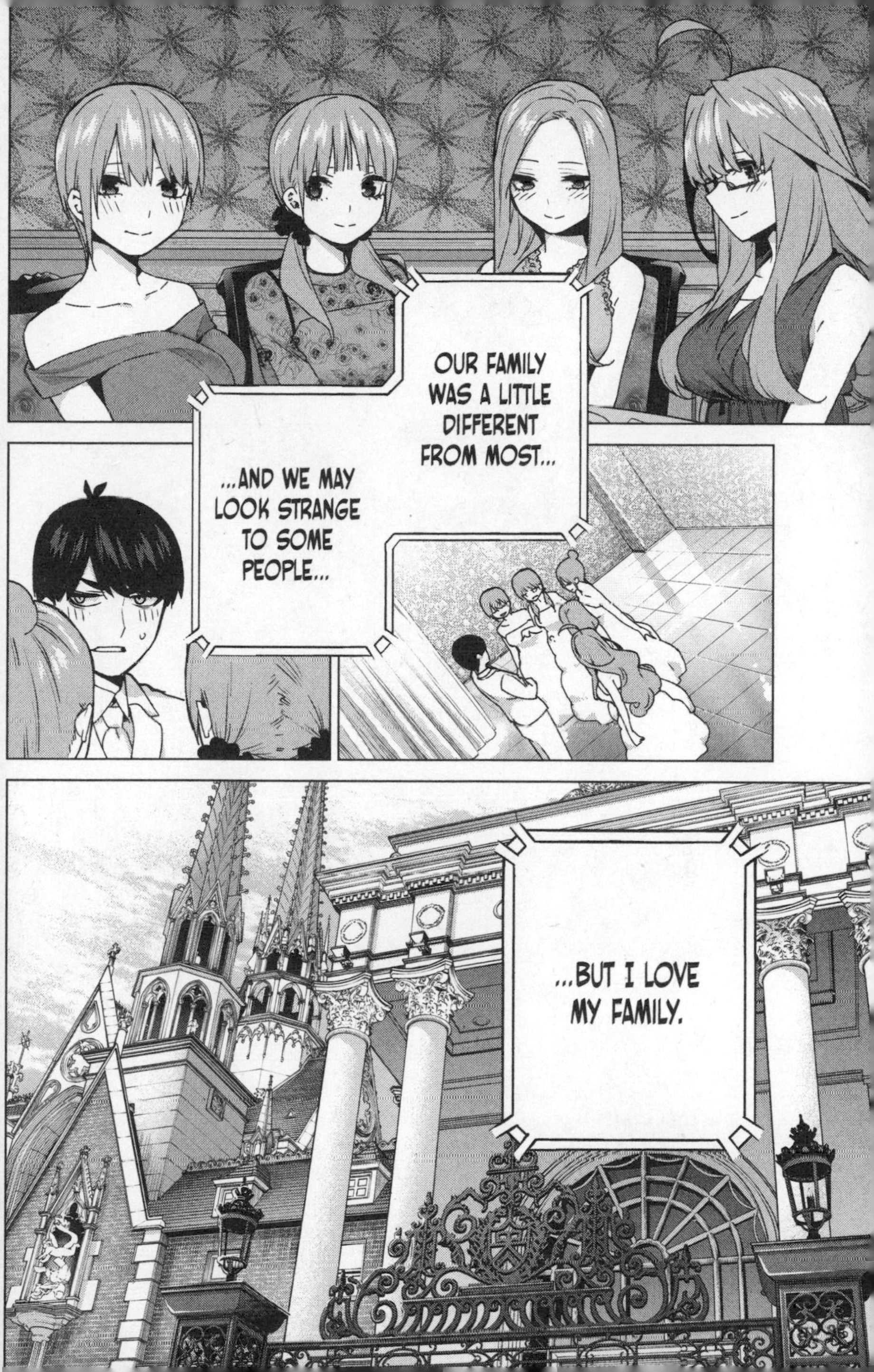
OUR FAMILY WAS A LITTLE DIFFERENT FROM MOST...
...AND WE MAY LOOK STRANGE TO SOME PEOPLE...
...BUT I LOVE MY FAMILY.

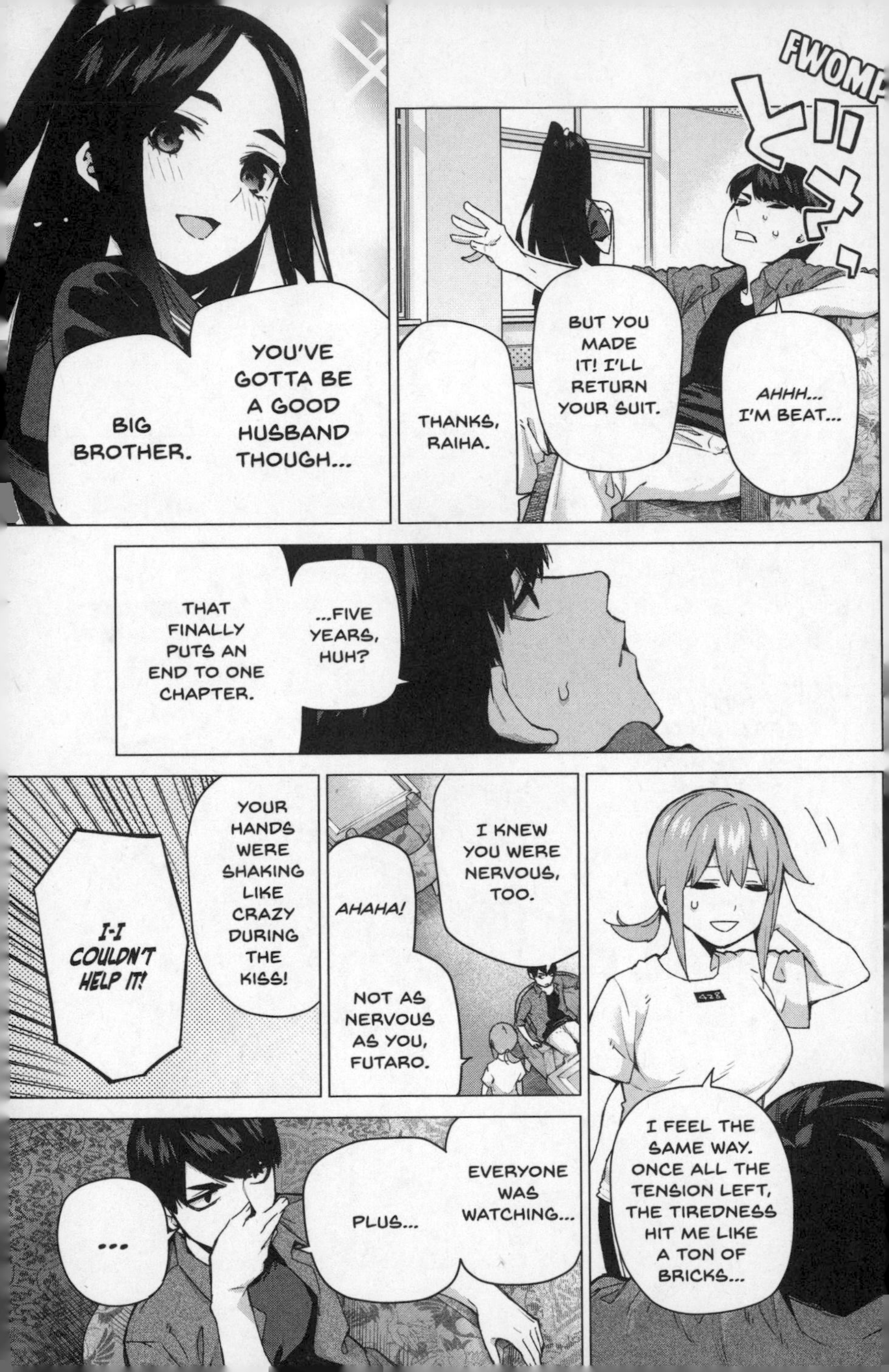
FWOMP
AHHH... I'M BEAT...
BUT YOU MADE IT! I'LL RETURN YOUR SUIT.
THANKS, RAIHA.
YOU'VE GOTTA BE A GOOD HUSBAND THOUGH...
BIG BROTHER.
...FIVE YEARS, HUH?
THAT FINALLY PUTS AN END TO ONE CHAPTER.
I FEEL THE SAME WAY. ONCE ALL THE TENSION LEFT, THE TIREDNESS HIT ME LIKE A TON OF BRICKS...
I KNEW YOU WERE NERVOUS, TOO.
AHAHA!
NOT AS NERVOUS AS YOU, FUTARO.
YOUR HANDS WERE SHAKING LIKE CRAZY DURING THE KISS!
I-I COULDN'T HELP IT!
EVERYONE WAS WATCHING...
PLUS...
...

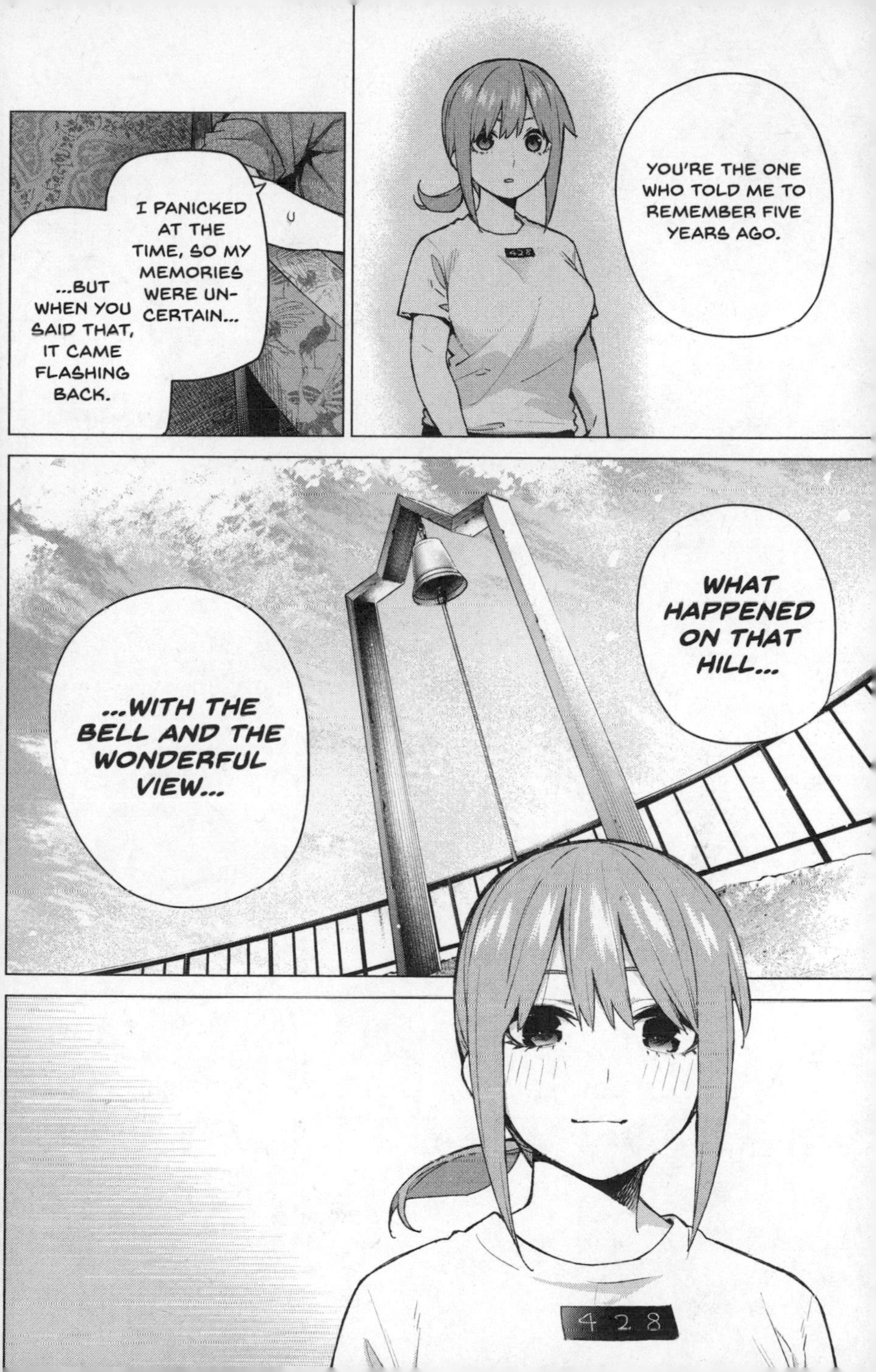
YOU'RE THE ONE WHO TOLD ME TO REMEMBER FIVE YEARS AGO.
I PANICKED AT THE TIME, SO MY MEMORIES WERE UN-CERTAIN...
...BUT WHEN YOU SAID THAT, IT CAME FLASHING BACK.
WHAT HAPPENED ON THAT HILL...
...WITH THE BELL AND THE WONDERFUL VIEW...
428

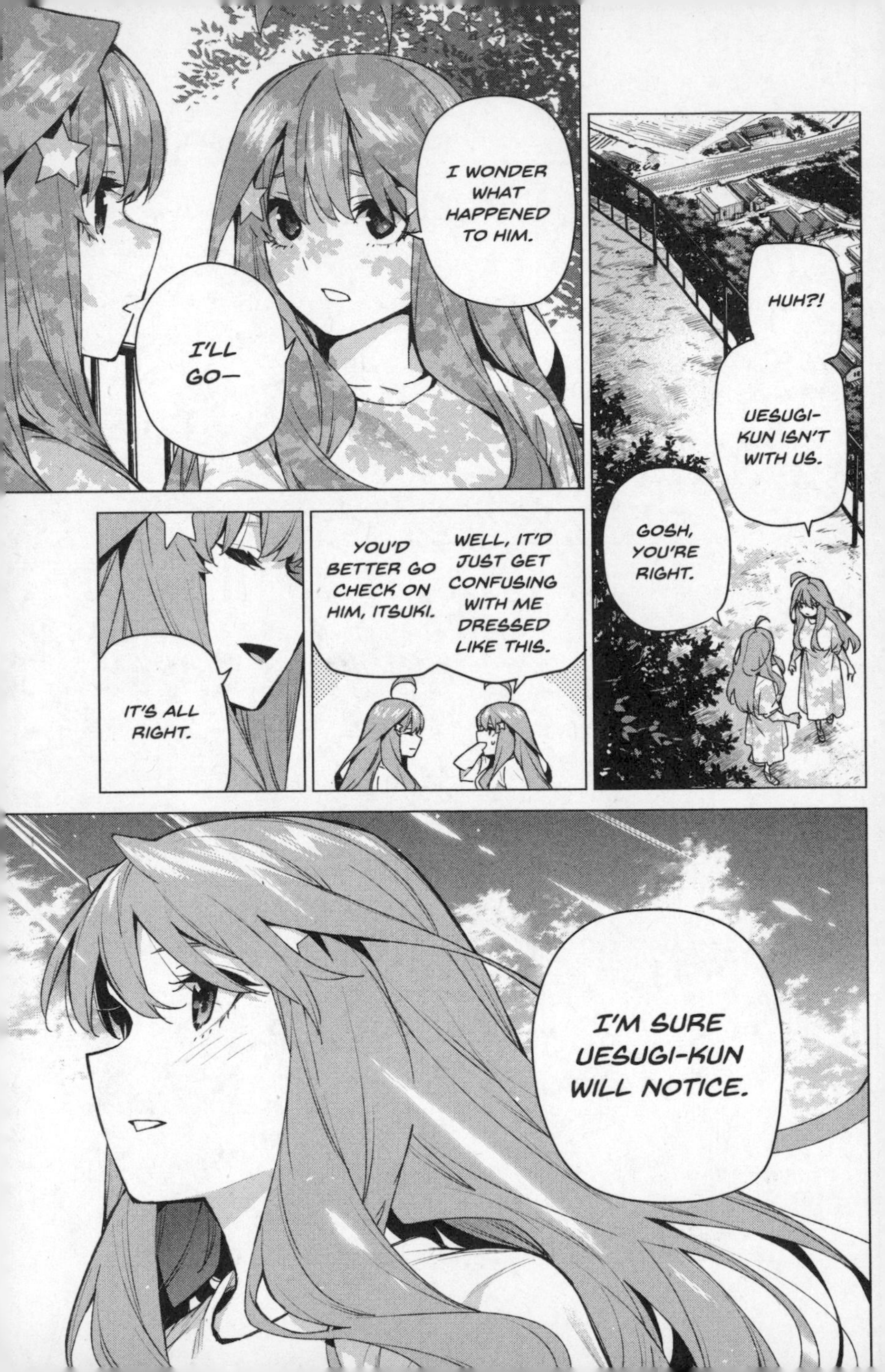
HUH?!
UESUGI-KUN ISN'T WITH US.
GOSH, YOU'RE RIGHT.
I WONDER WHAT HAPPENED TO HIM.
I'LL GO—
WELL, IT'D JUST GET CONFUSING WITH ME DRESSED LIKE THIS.
YOU'D BETTER GO CHECK ON HIM, ITSUKI.
IT'S ALL RIGHT.
I'M SURE UESUGI-KUN WILL NOTICE.

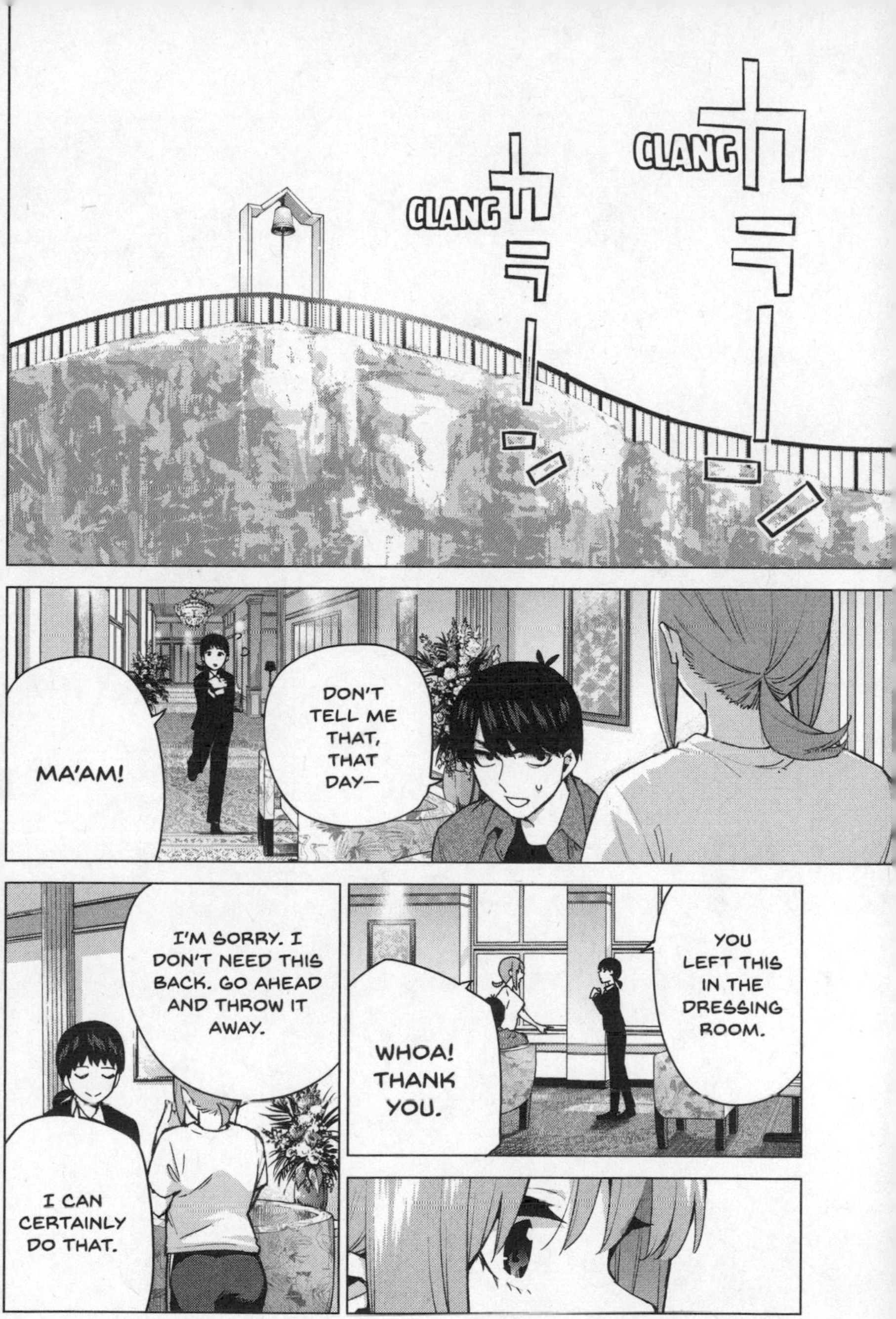
CLANG
カラーン
CLANG
カラーン
DON'T TELL ME THAT, THAT DAY—
MA'AM!
YOU LEFT THIS IN THE DRESSING ROOM.
WHOA! THANK YOU.
I'M SORRY. I DON'T NEED THIS BACK. GO AHEAD AND THROW IT AWAY.
I CAN CERTAINLY DO THAT.

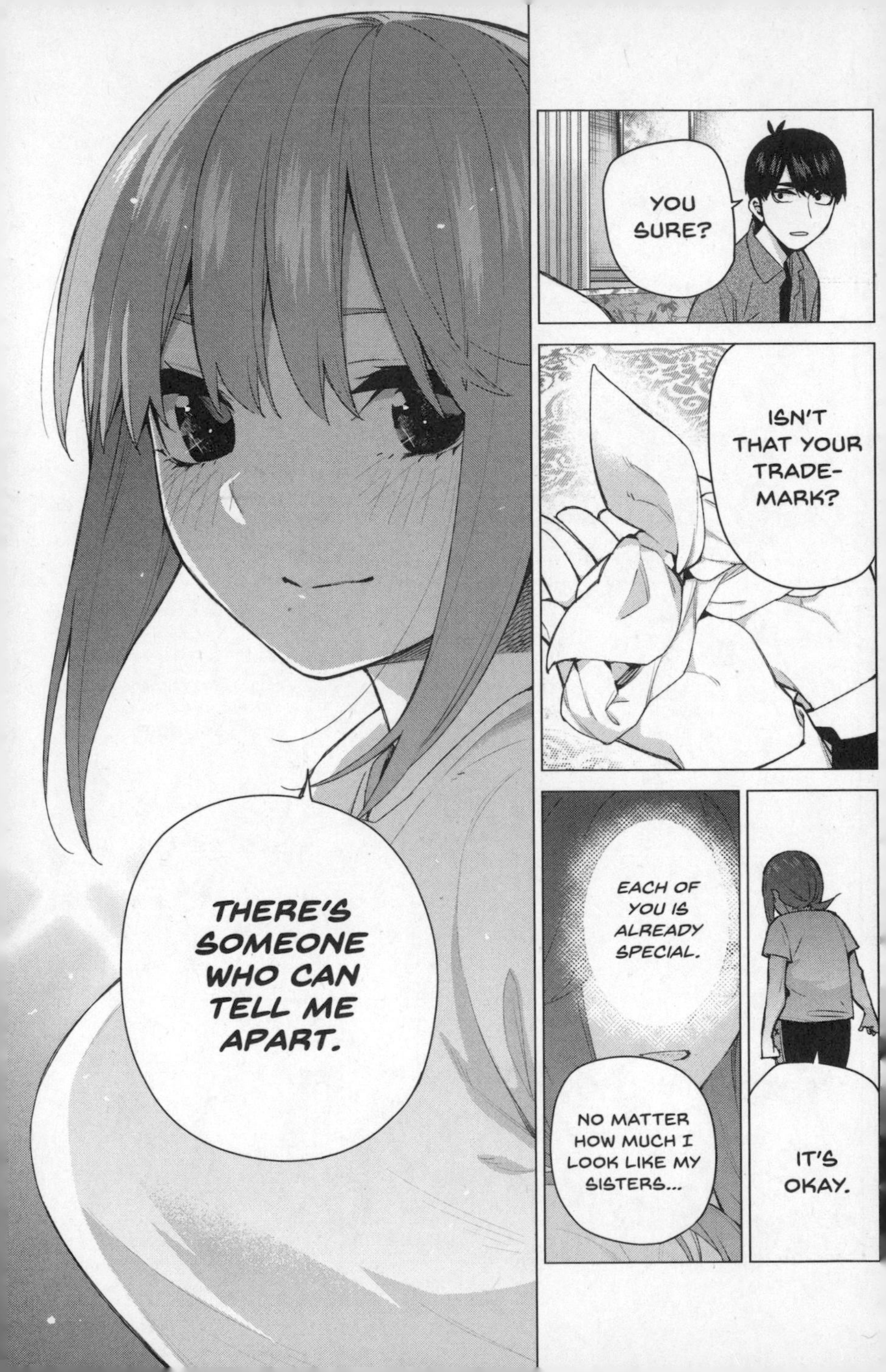
YOU SURE?
ISN'T THAT YOUR TRADE-MARK?
IT'S OKAY.
EACH OF YOU IS ALREADY SPECIAL.
NO MATTER HOW MUCH I LOOK LIKE MY SISTERS...
THERE'S SOMEONE WHO CAN TELL ME APART.

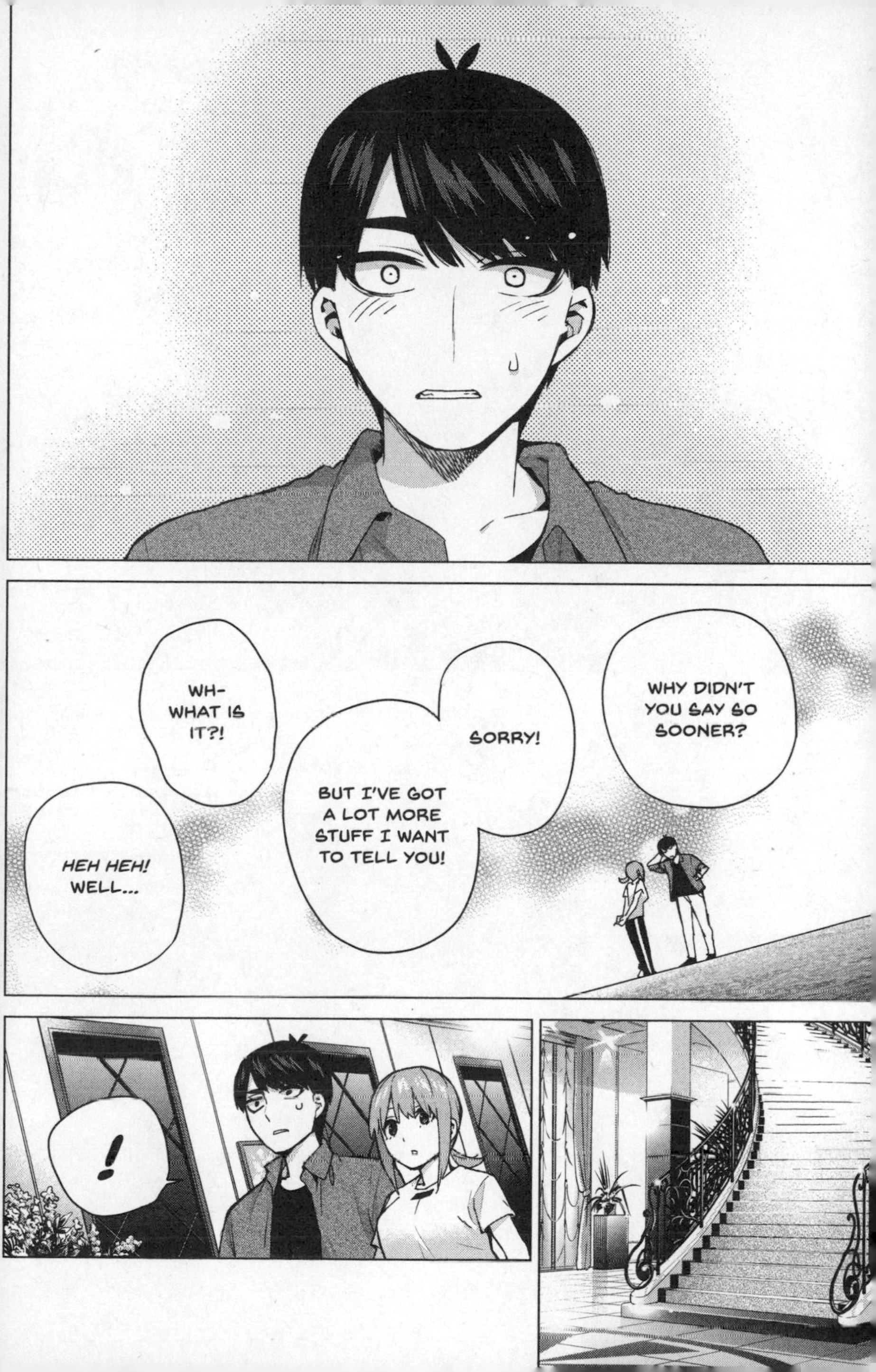
WHY DIDN'T YOU SAY SO SOONER?
SORRY!
BUT I'VE GOT A LOT MORE STUFF I WANT TO TELL YOU!
WH- WHAT IS IT?!
HEH HEH! WELL...
!

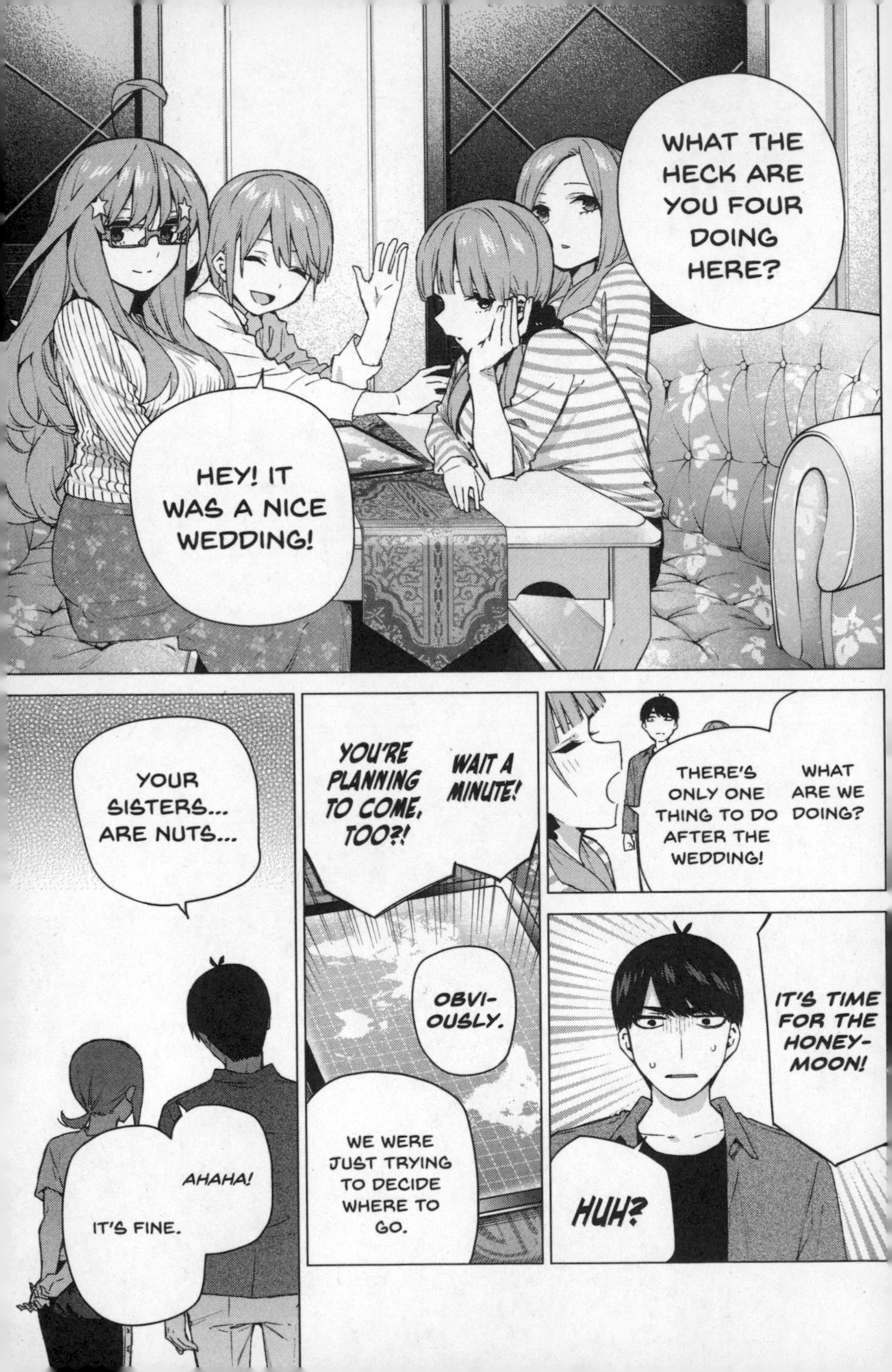

WHAT THE HECK ARE YOU FOUR DOING HERE?
HEY! IT WAS A NICE WEDDING!
WHAT ARE WE DOING?
THERE'S ONLY ONE THING TO DO AFTER THE WEDDING!
IT'S TIME FOR THE HONEY-MOON!
HUH?
WAIT A MINUTE!
YOU'RE PLANNING TO COME, TOO?!
OBVI-OUSLY.
WE WERE JUST TRYING TO DECIDE WHERE TO GO.
YOUR SISTERS... ARE NUTS...
AHAHA!
IT'S FINE.

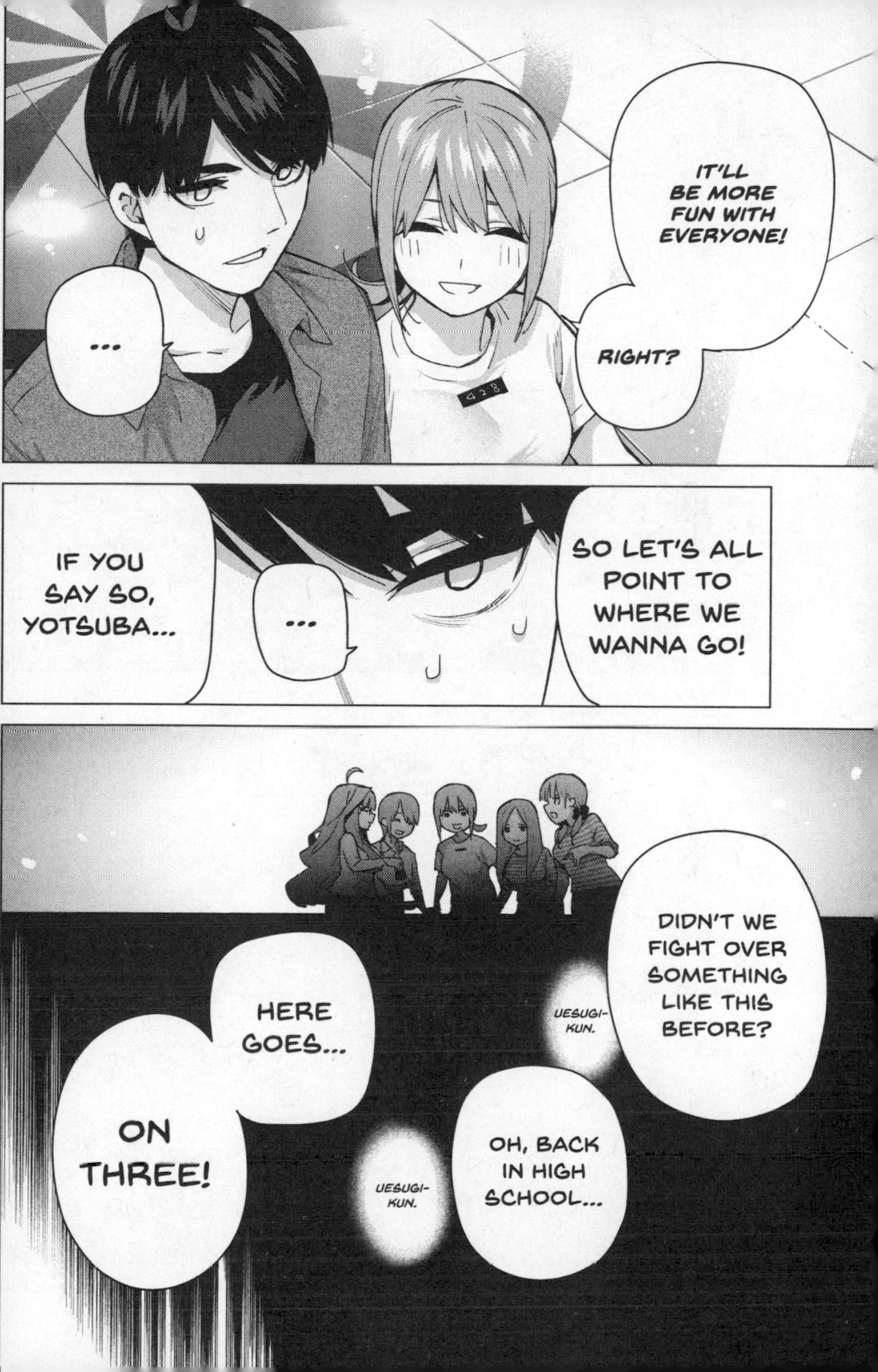
IT'LL BE MORE FUN WITH EVERYONE!
RIGHT?
...
SO LET'S ALL POINT TO WHERE WE WANNA GO!
...
IF YOU SAY SO, YOTSUBA...
DIDN'T WE FIGHT OVER SOMETHING LIKE THIS BEFORE?
UESUGI-KUN.
HERE GOES...
OH, BACK IN HIGH SCHOOL...
UESUGI-KUN.
ON THREE!

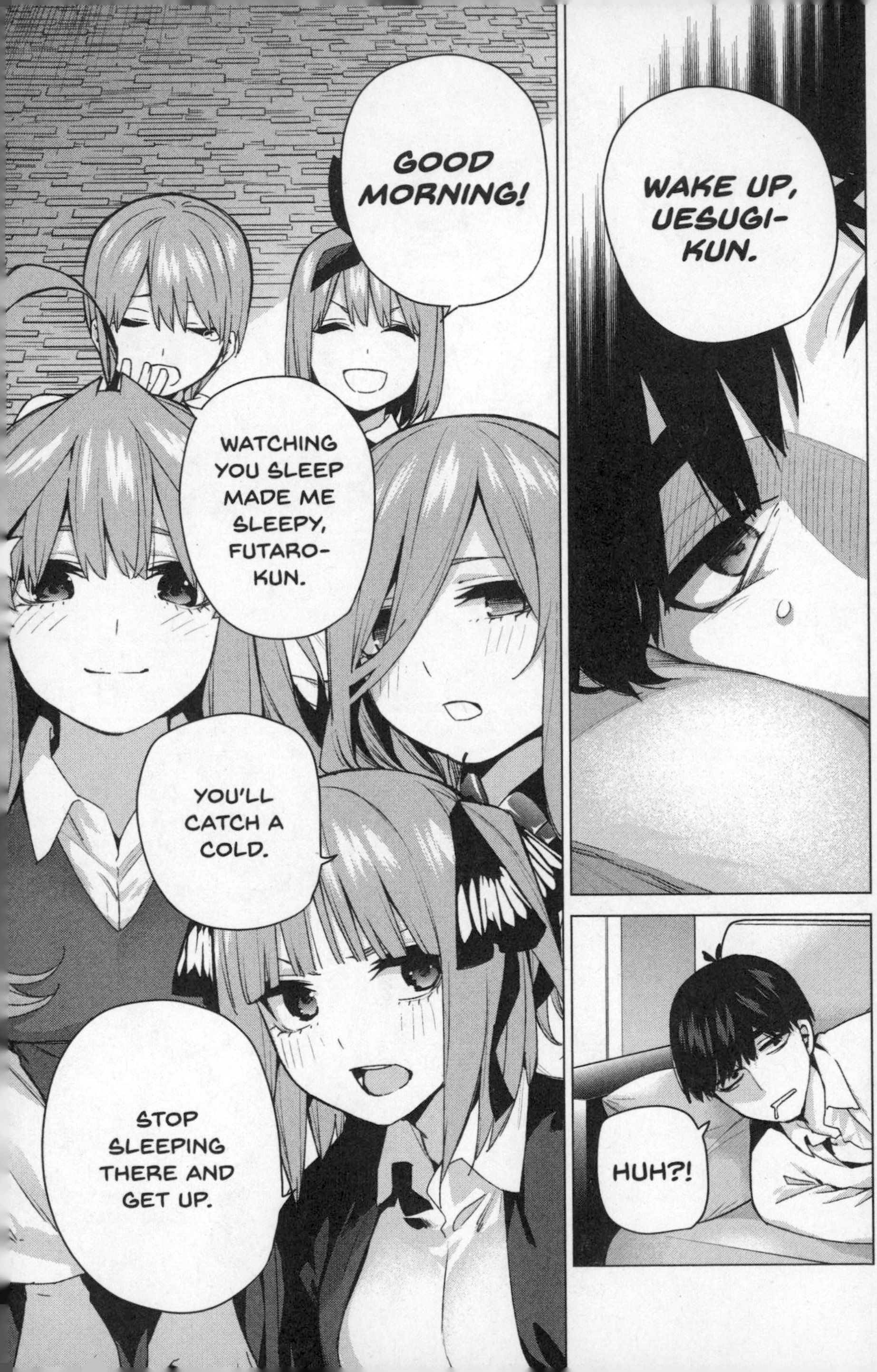
WAKE UP, UESUGI-KUN.
HUH?!
GOOD MORNING!
WATCHING YOU SLEEP MADE ME SLEEPY, FUTARO-KUN.
YOU'LL CATCH A COLD.
STOP SLEEPING THERE AND GET UP.

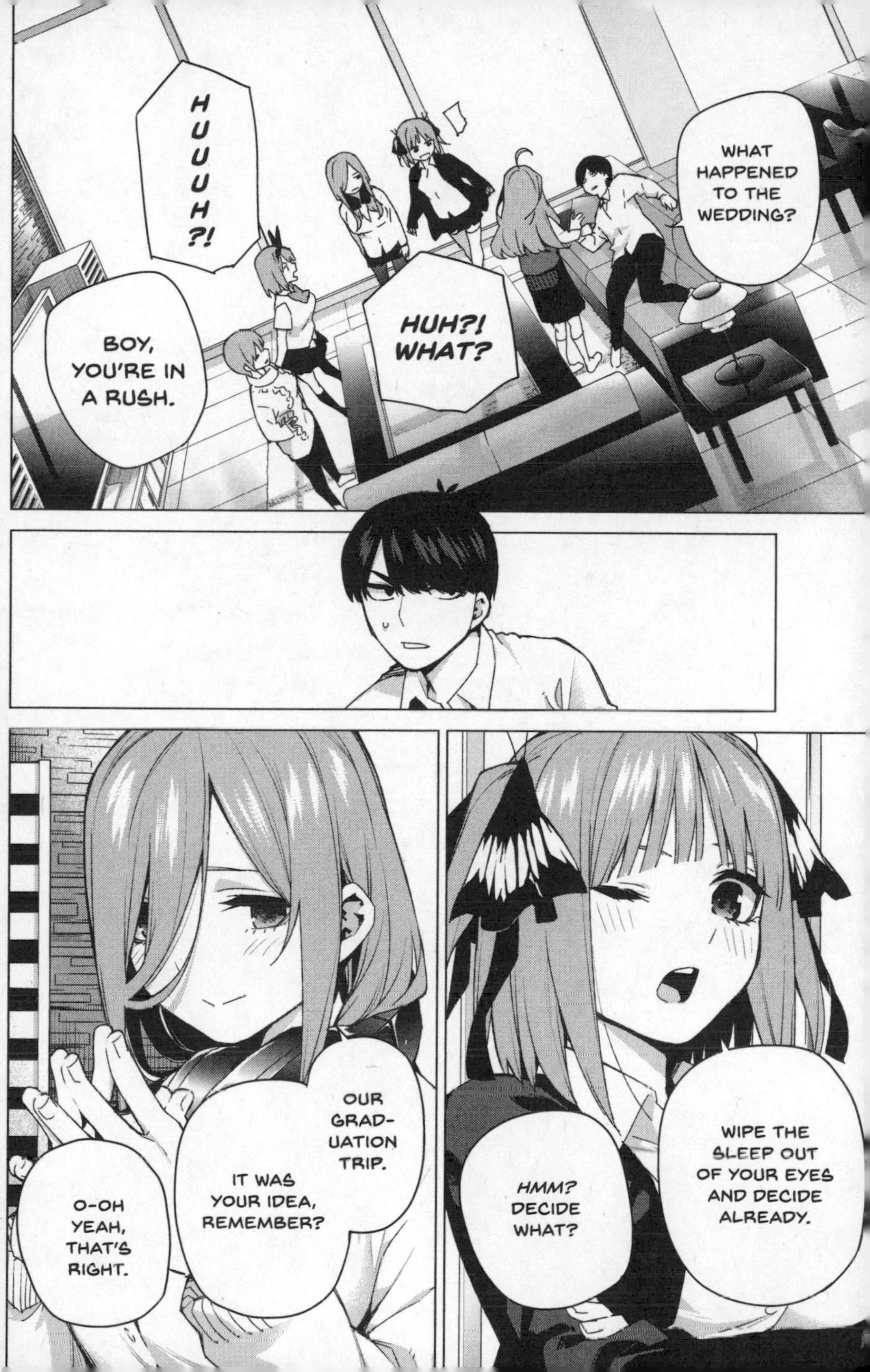
WHAT HAPPENED TO THE WEDDING?
HUUUH?!
HUH?! WHAT?
BOY, YOU'RE IN A RUSH.
WIPE THE SLEEP OUT OF YOUR EYES AND DECIDE ALREADY.
HMM? DECIDE WHAT?
OUR GRAD-UATION TRIP.
IT WAS YOUR IDEA, REMEMBER?
O-OH YEAH, THAT'S RIGHT.

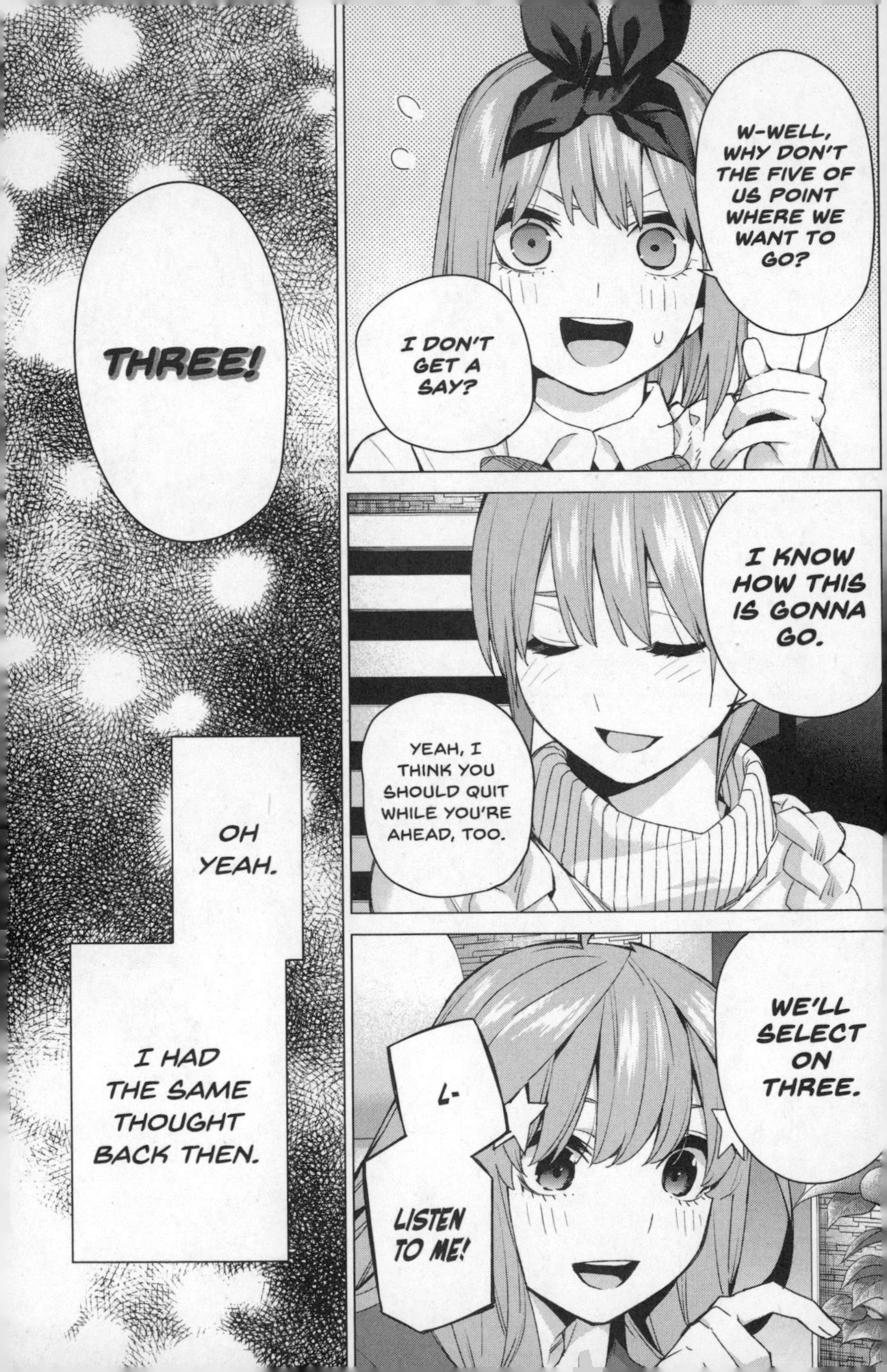
W-WELL, WHY DON'T THE FIVE OF US POINT WHERE WE WANT TO GO?
I DON'T GET A SAY?
I KNOW HOW THIS IS GONNA GO.
YEAH, I THINK YOU SHOULD QUIT WHILE YOU'RE AHEAD, TOO.
WE'LL SELECT ON THREE.
L-
LISTEN TO ME!
THREE!
OH YEAH.
I HAD THE SAME THOUGHT BACK THEN.

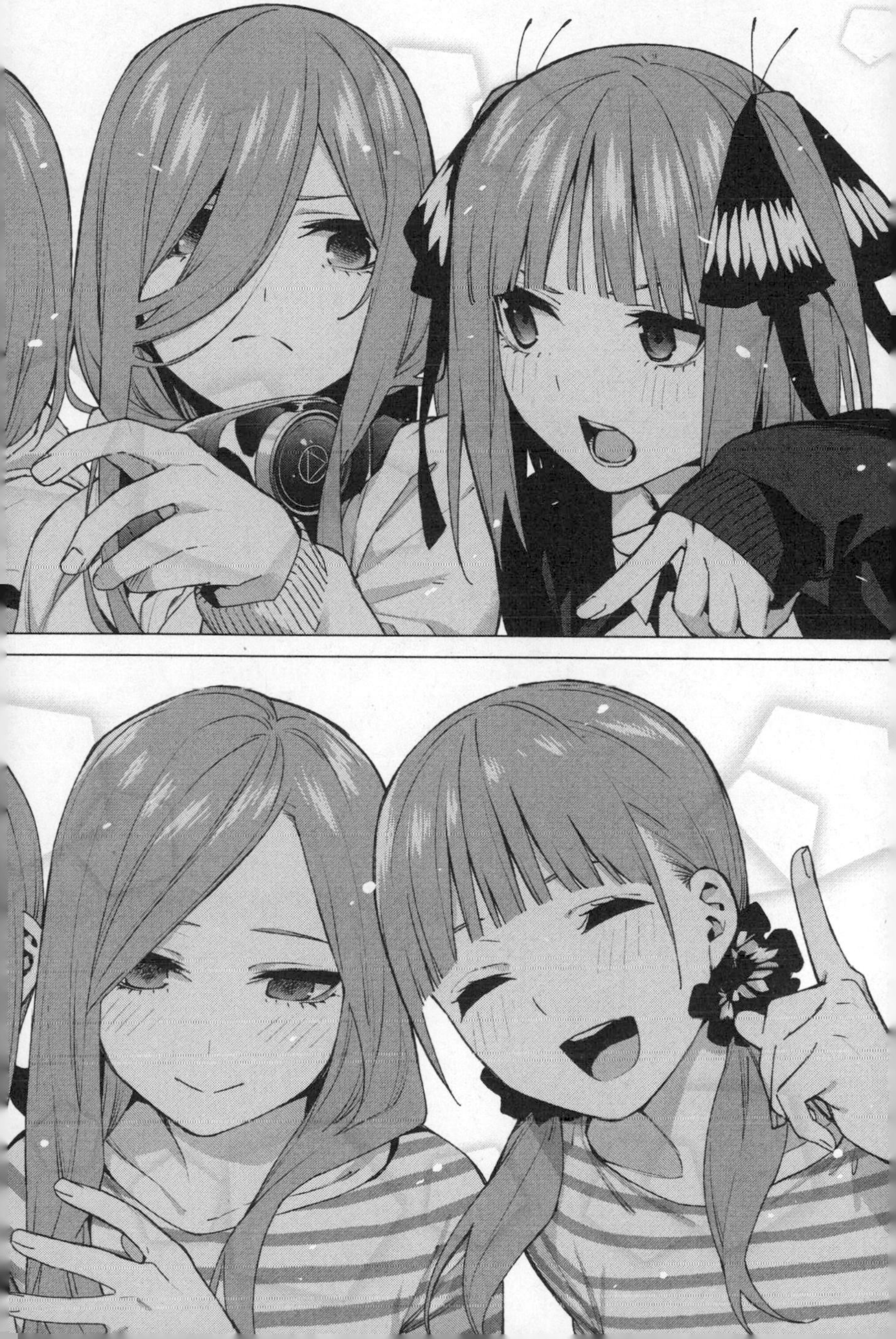

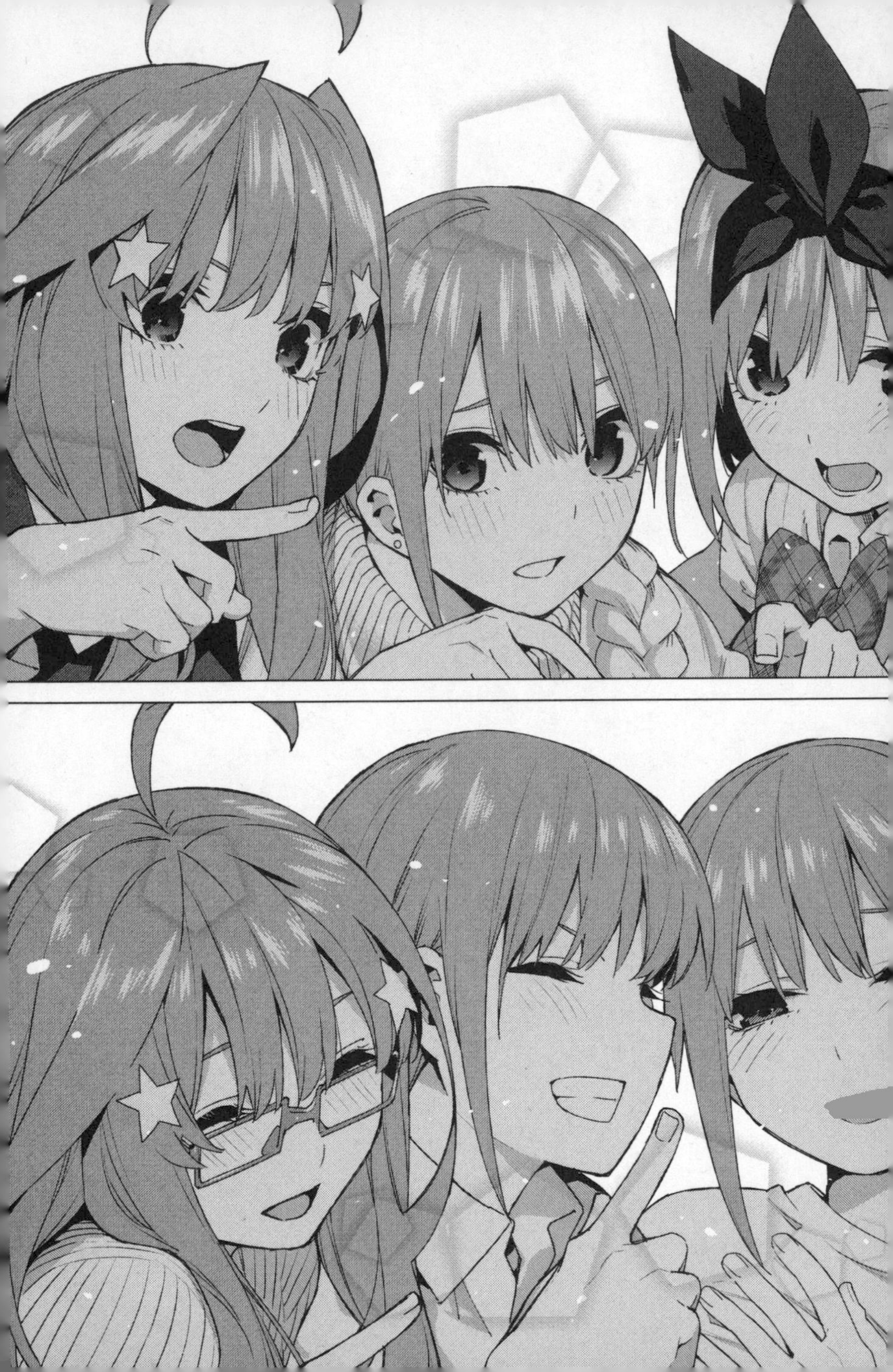

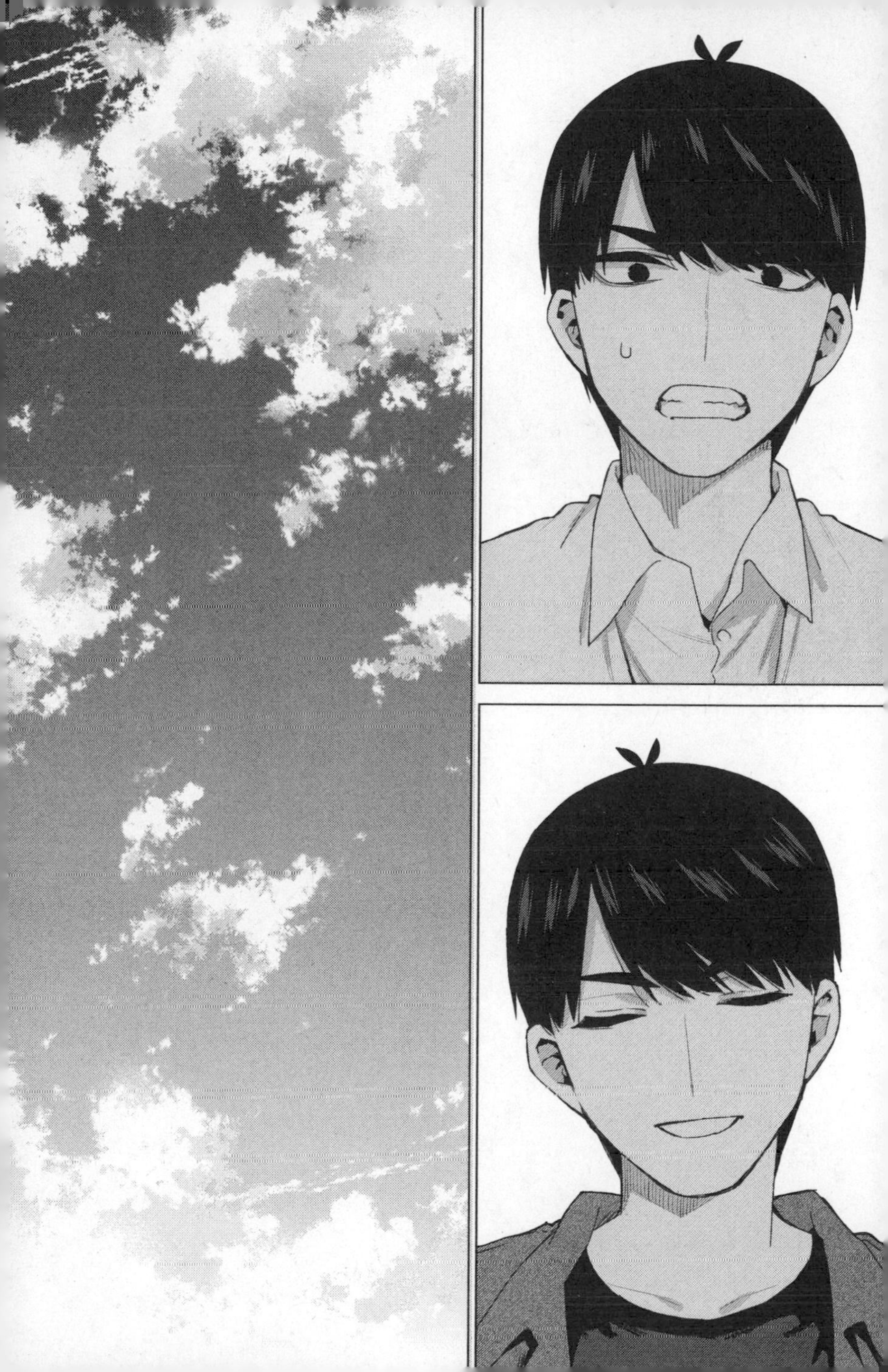

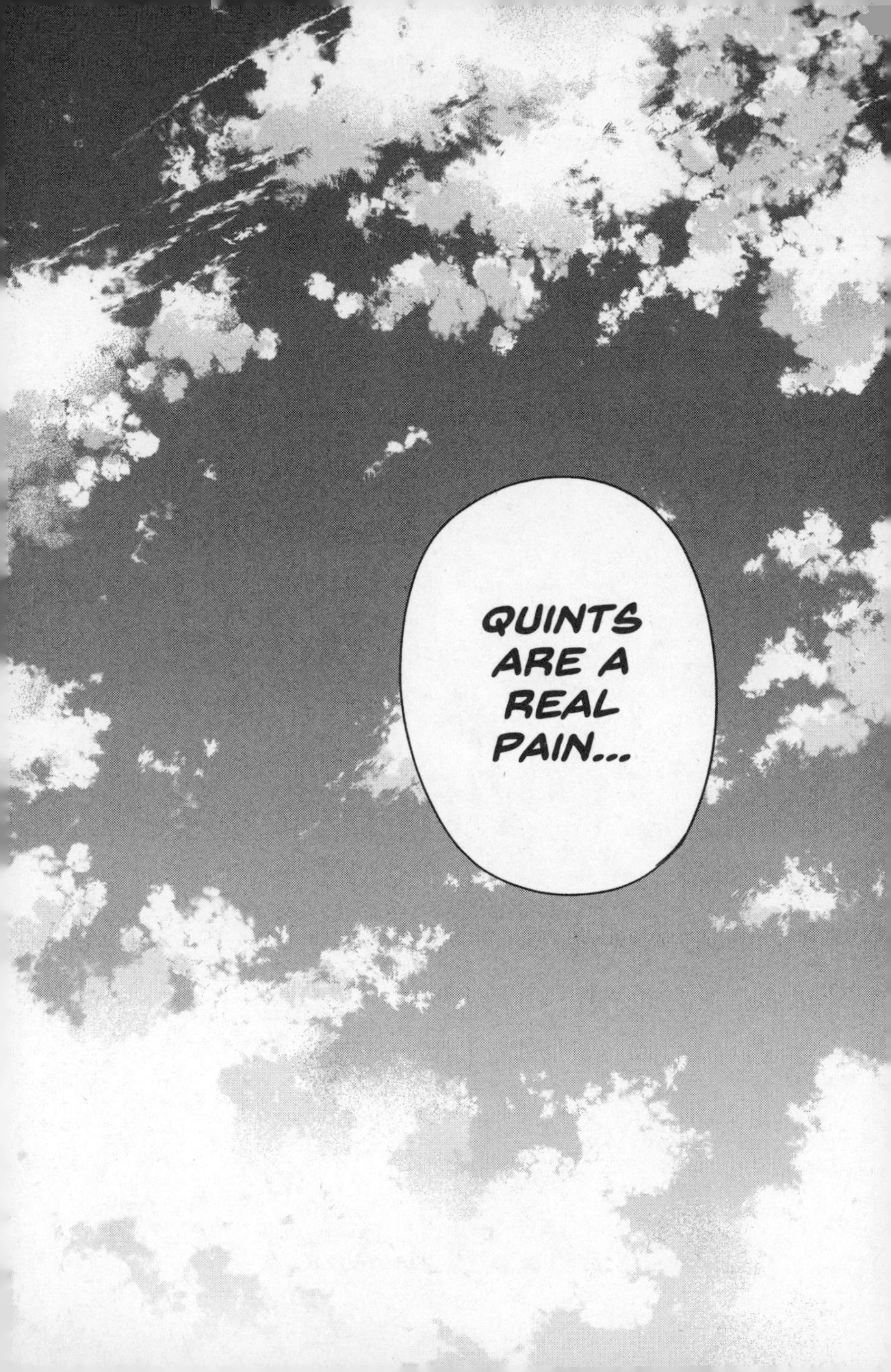
QUINTS ARE A REAL PAIN...

BONUS

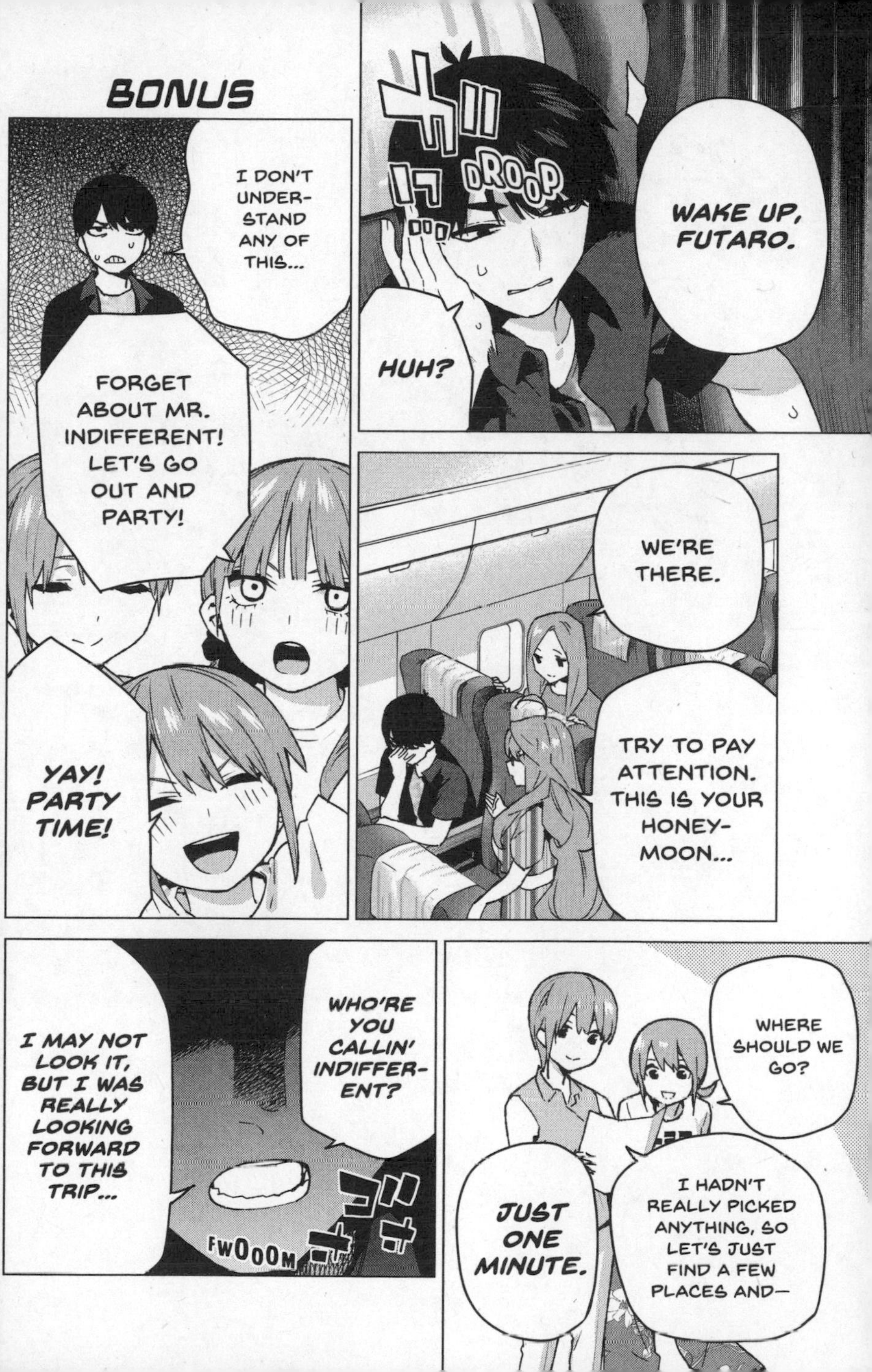
WAKE UP, FUTARO.
DROOP
HUH?
WE'RE THERE.
TRY TO PAY ATTENTION. THIS IS YOUR HONEYMOON...
I DON'T UNDERSTAND ANY OF THIS...
FORGET ABOUT MR. INDIFFERENT! LET'S GO OUT AND PARTY!
YAY! PARTY TIME!
WHERE SHOULD WE GO?
I HADN'T REALLY PICKED ANYTHING, SO LET'S JUST FIND A FEW PLACES AND—
JUST ONE MINUTE.
WHO'RE YOU CALLIN' INDIFFERENT?
I MAY NOT LOOK IT, BUT I WAS REALLY LOOKING FORWARD TO THIS TRIP...
FWOOOM

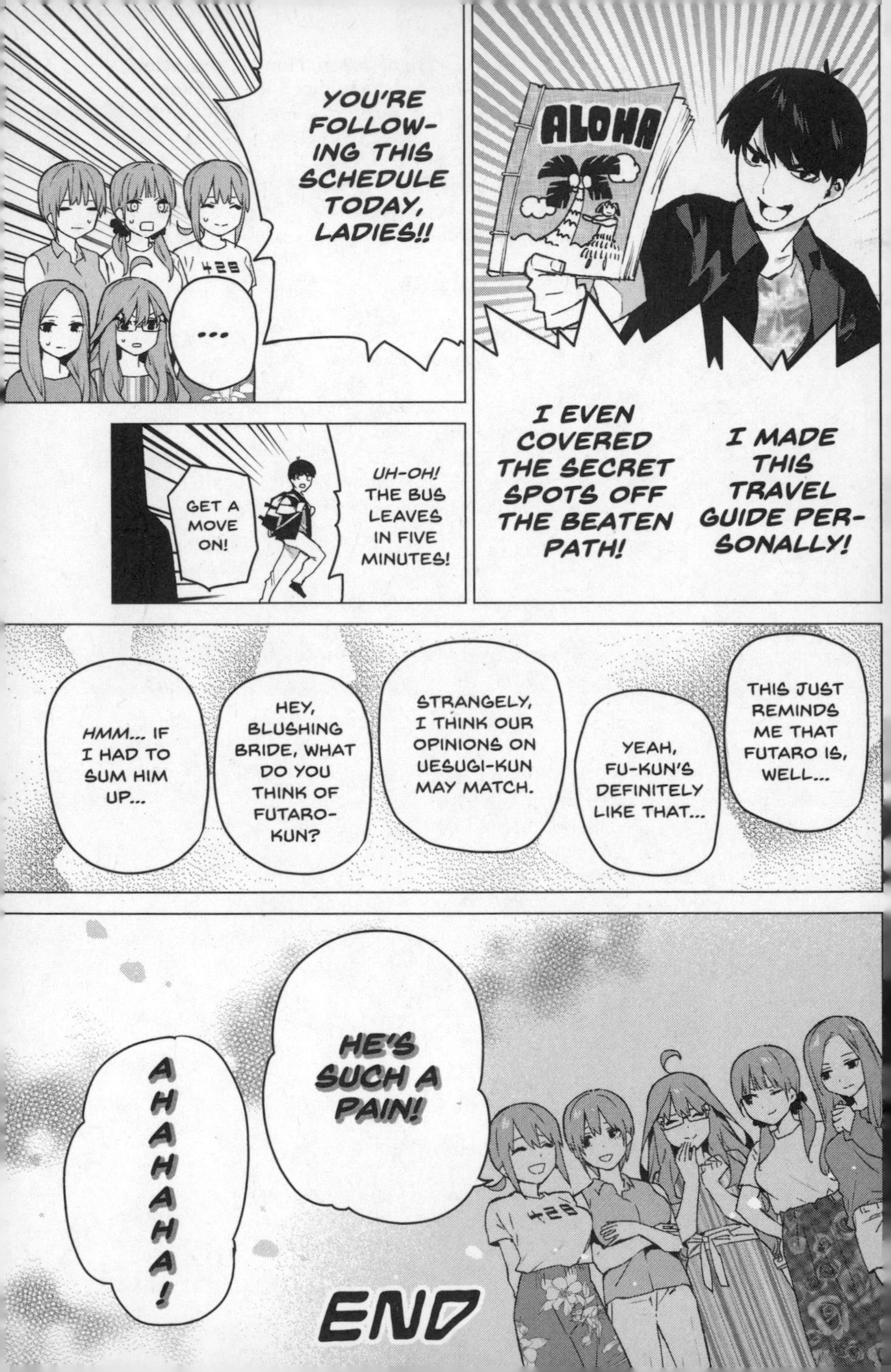
I MADE THIS TRAVEL GUIDE PERSONALLY!
I EVEN COVERED THE SECRET SPOTS OFF THE BEATEN PATH!
ALOHA
YOU'RE FOLLOWING THIS SCHEDULE TODAY, LADIES!!
...
UH-OH! THE BUS LEAVES IN FIVE MINUTES!
GET A MOVE ON!
THIS JUST REMINDS ME THAT FUTARO IS, WELL...
YEAH, FU-KUN'S DEFINITELY LIKE THAT...
STRANGELY, I THINK OUR OPINIONS ON UESUGI-KUN MAY MATCH.
HEY, BLUSHING BRIDE, WHAT DO YOU THINK OF FUTARO-KUN?
HMM... IF I HAD TO SUM HIM UP...
HE'S SUCH A PAIN!
AHAHAHAHA!
END

A Kodansha Comics Trade Paperback Original
The Quintessential Quintuplets 14 copyright © 2020 Negi Haruba
English translation copyright © 2021 Negi Haruba

Published in the United States by Kodansha Comics, an imprint of
Kodansha USA Publishing, LLC, New York.

Publication rights for this English edition arranged through
Kodansha Ltd., Tokyo.

First published in Japan in 2020 by Kodansha Ltd., Tokyo
as *Gotoubun no hanayome*, volume 14.

ISBN 978-1-64651-163-1

Cover Design: Saya Takagi (RedRooster)

Printed in the United States of America.

www.kodansha.us

9 8 7 6 5
Translation: Steven LeCroy
Lettering: Jan Lan Ivan Concepcion
Additional Layout: Belynda Ungurath
Editing: Thalia Sutton, David Yoo
Editorial Assistance: YKS Services LLC/SKY Japan, INC.
Kodansha Comics edition cover design by Phil Balsman

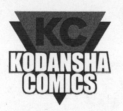

Publisher: Kiichiro Sugawara

Director of publishing services: Ben Applegate
Associate director of operations: Stephen Pakula
Publishing services managing editors: Alanna Ruse, Madison Salters
Production managers: Emi Lotto, Angela Zurlo